DISESTABLISHMENT
IN IRELAND AND WALES

DISESTABLISHMENT IN IRELAND AND WALES

P. M. H. Bell

Published for the Church Historical Society

LONDON

S · P · C · K

1969

No. 90 in the
Church Historical series

First published in 1969
by S.P.C.K.
Holy Trinity Church
Marylebone Road
London N.W.1

Made and printed in Great Britain by
William Clowes and Sons, Limited
London and Beccles

© P. M. H. Bell, 1969

SBN 281 02336 0

CONTENTS

ACKNOWLEDGEMENTS

Thanks are due to the following for permission to use and quote from manuscripts in their possession:

Lord Spencer: the Spencer Papers.

Lord Strachie: the Strachie Mss.

The Archbishop of Canterbury and the Trustees of Lambeth Palace Library: the Tait Papers and Minutes of the Lambeth Conference, 1878.

Mr Mark Bonham-Carter: the Asquith Papers.

The Free Church Federal Council and the Greater London Record Office: Liberation Society Papers.

The Keeper of State Papers, State Paper Office, Dublin: Chief Secretary's Office, Registered Papers; the Burke Papers.

The National Trust: the Hughenden Papers.

Thanks are also due to the following for permission to quote from copyright sources:

The Editor of the *Church of Ireland Gazette*.

The Editor of *The Times*.

J. D. Lewis & Sons Ltd (Gomerian Press, Llandyssul): *The Later Life of Bishop Owen*, by Eluned Owen.

John Murray (Publishers) Ltd: *Life of Disraeli*, by W. F. Monypenny and G. E. Buckle.

S.C.M. Press Ltd: *F. D. Maurice and Company*, by A. R. Vidler.

PREFACE

The idea of an established Church has a long history in these islands, and the idea of disestablishment can still arouse interest and controversy. Within the last hundred years, two Anglican Churches within the British Isles—those in Ireland and Wales—have been disestablished by Act of Parliament. This book attempts to describe how this came about; what the political circumstances were; what arguments were advanced for and against disestablishment; what was involved in the process of disestablishment; and how the two Churches met their new situations. It requires some temerity for an Englishman to venture into the histories of Ireland and Wales; I can only hope that readers from those countries will bear with an outsider whose interest has been caught by their affairs.

I am very happy to have this opportunity to thank those who have helped in the writing of this book. Professor David Quinn, Professor Alec Myers, the Reverend Michael Hennell, and the Reverend Canon Hugh Rees have kindly read all or part of the work in manuscript; I am most grateful to them for their comments and criticism. At an earlier stage in the writing, my wife and my father read, shortened, and improved some very long drafts. My wife has also shared in the work in many different ways. I am grateful to Miss Kathleen Doyle, Mrs Beryl Hart, Mrs Sylvia Hughes, and Miss Lesley Roberts for their work in typing the manuscript. I am glad to thank the University of Liverpool for a number of research grants, and the Church Historical Society for a grant in aid of publication.

Finally, and in a wider context than the writing of this book, I owe much to Mr A. F. Thompson, who taught me a great deal about history when I was an undergraduate at Oxford, and who has continued his help and friendship ever since.

School of History, University of Liverpool　　　　　　　　P. M. H. BELL
May 1969

ABBREVIATIONS

Archbishops' Commission on Church and State, *Report*, and *Evidence of Witnesses*	Church Assembly, *Church and State: Report of the Archbishops' Commission on the relations between Church and State, 1935* (London 1936), vol. I, *Report*, vol. II, *Evidence of Witnesses*
Lib. Soc.	Liberation Society
I.C. Commission, Report	*Report of Her Majesty's Commissioners on the revenue and condition of the Established Church in Ireland*, H.C. 1867–8, xxiv
Parl. Deb.	*Parliamentary Debates*
I.E.G.	*Irish Ecclesiastical Gazette*
First or *Second Report of CCTW*	*First* or *Second Report of the Commissioners of Church Temporalities in Wales*

1

"BY LAW ESTABLISHED"

The history of the relations of Church and State, of which the disestablishment of the Churches in Ireland and Wales forms a small part, has been bedevilled by the different meanings which may be attached to each word. Church is the more troublesome of the two. Every Sunday Christians declare in the words of the Nicene Creed that they "believe one Catholic and Apostolic Church"; or in the words of the Apostles' Creed, that they "believe in the Holy Ghost; the holy Catholic Church; the Communion of Saints;...". Belief in the Church is thus put among the great tenets of Christian faith, to be mentioned in the same breath as the Holy Ghost—and no more susceptible of precise description. St Paul was on the same plane of understanding when he referred to "the Church, which is his [Christ's] body" (Eph. 1.22–3). The nineteenth of the Thirty-nine Articles of Religion of the Church of England has an appearance of greater clarity:

> The visible Church of Christ is a congregation of faithful men, in the which the pure Word of God is preached, and the Sacraments be duly ministered according to Christ's ordinance in all those things that of necessity are requisite to the same.

Reflection, especially on the last phrase, shows the appearance to be misleading.

The terms used by St Paul and the nineteenth Article are imprecise, but they are authentic. If the claims of Christians are to be fully reckoned with, some such wording must be used to describe the Christian Church. But the Church is not only a mystical body of Christ made up of faithful people, it is also a series of earthly bodies, possessing property, bound by rules, and in which particular persons hold particular offices. Such bodies can be examined and described by lawyers, so let us next take a definition by an English lawyer in 1935. "A Church may be regarded in the eyes of the law as an association possessing a visible and external order and composed of persons who profess a common body of religious doctrine and use a common form of worship."[1] This definition no longer talks of "the Church", but of "a Church", which is an important distinction. Yet it is very like the nineteenth Article in speaking of an association of persons identified by common doctrine and worship. There is no mention of clergy or laity, whereas there are other definitions of Church which do make this distinction, and narrow the terms of the association sharply. The *Concise Oxford Dictionary*, for example, among several definitions, has this: "organization, clergy and other officers, of a religious society or corporation". Or again, this dictionary acknowledges as a definition of the word "Church"—"clerical profession", as in the phrase "go into the Church", meaning to become a clergyman.

This has taken us all the way from the solemn words of the Creeds to a slack expression of everyday speech. All the definitions have some validity, according to the context and the way in which the word Church is being used. All are likely to be met in discussions of relations between Church and State. The second term, State, presents a less extensive variety of meanings in its normal usage, but there are still two distinct definitions which are important here. One is the use of the word to mean an organized, sovereign community, within defined boundaries; under this definition, every member of the community is a member of the State. The other uses the word State to mean the organs of government and administration—the executive, legislature, civil service, armed forces. In this sense, it is permissible to speak, for example, of the rights of the individual over against the rights of the State. The word is frequently used in both senses when the relations of Church and State are being dealt with. For instance, when one theorist, Hooker, asserted that in England, Church and State were coextensive, he was plainly using the word State to mean all the people in England. Another theorist, Warburton, when he wrote of an alliance between Church and State, appears to have been thinking of State in terms of government.

The words Church and State are not only used by theologians, political theorists, and the compilers of dictionaries. In the events to be considered in this book, they were used by politicians who knew that they wielded the powers of the State to change the position of Churches which they could recognize clearly enough to draft a Bill about them. They were used too by those who called themselves Churchmen, clerical and lay, who knew that they belonged to bodies which would be affected by these Bills. Empiricism triumphed over problems of language. In practice, the word Church was normally used in these episodes in the sense of an association of persons with common forms of doctrine and worship, with a strong admixture of the usage which treated a Church as a body of clergy and other officials. State was used primarily as meaning the organs of government and administration. However, the problems of language were still there, and arguments about the desirability and consequences of disestablishment were often clouded by variations in the usage of the two words.

Assuming that for practical Parliamentary purposes one could recognize Church and State, without the need for strict definition, it still remains to be seen what is meant by disestablishment, or the separation of Church from State by severing the connections which existed between the two under the state of affairs known as establishment. A study of disestablishment can only make sense if one starts by trying to say what is meant by an established Church. Here the problems of definition return with a vengeance, for a great variety of meanings may be attached to this phrase—and, as is often the case, the vaguer the usage, the more powerful is the emotion attached to it. But to take an example which involves not emotional association but the state of the law, the established Church of Scotland has, at the present time, a wholly different legal position from that of the established Church of England. The Church of Scotland Act of 1921 confirmed that Church in its right to legislate and adjudicate for itself in all matters of doctrine, worship, government, and discipline. This position is said to combine the principle of establishment with complete spiritual freedom.[2] This is a wholly different state of affairs from that in the Church of England, with its system of Crown appointments to important posts and the remaining supremacy of Parliament in many of the Church's affairs. Yet both Churches are described as established.

For the purposes of this study, the best way to approach an answer to the question of the meaning of establishment is to take a stand in the middle of the nineteenth century and examine the position of the then established United Church of England and Ireland. At that time, the two Churches of England and Ireland were legally united by the Act of Union of 1800; while what was later to be the disestablished Church in Wales was four dioceses within the Church of England. This position had various aspects: the state of the law; the theory used to justify the law; and the web of interests and sentiment which had grown up with the establishment and become part of it.

The legal position of the established Church was the product not of a single act or contract but of long growth and accretion of statute and precedent.[3] It may be summed up under the headings of the control exercised by the State over the Church, and the legal privileges enjoyed by the Church. State control over the Church was most obviously seen and regularly used in the right of the Crown to appoint all bishops and deans. This right was exercised in practice by the Prime Minister of the day, though Queen Victoria was certainly no cipher in the process of deciding on names. The Crown also regulated the existence and working of Convocation, the representative body of the clergy, which could not meet without royal writ, nor make canons without the royal licence. Parliament possessed the right to define the doctrines and forms of worship of the Church, as it had done in successive Acts of Uniformity; the Book of Common Prayer was itself a schedule to the Act of Uniformity of 1662. In all legal cases arising in ecclesiastical affairs, including issues of doctrine and ritual, the final court of appeal was the Judicial Committee of the Privy Council, a lay tribunal, though bishops attended as assessors without votes when it was considering ecclesiastical cases. Parliament also had the right to regulate the property and revenues of the Church, as it did in England, for example, in the 1830s by setting up the Ecclesiastical Commission to administer and redistribute Church property. In Ireland, the Church Temporalities Act of 1833 suppressed two archbishoprics and eight bishoprics, amalgamating them with other dioceses with effect from the next vacancy, and putting their revenues at the disposal of the Irish Ecclesiastical Commissioners, also created by the Act. The State had other extensive powers over the administration of the Church. Only an Act of Parliament could create a new diocese, change the circumstances in which a clergyman could be dismissed from his office, or prevent pluralism. An Order in Council was necessary to create or unite parishes, or to change their boundaries. Thus the authority of the State (meaning in this context the Crown, Parliament, and lay courts) extended over the appointment of the Church's highest dignitaries, over its doctrines and forms of worship, over the administration of its property, and over much of its internal organization. These powers in the mid-nineteenth century were no dead letter. During the 1830s the Church was transformed—very much to its own benefit—by the reforming hand of the State, mainly through the activities of the Ecclesiastical Commissioners and the statutes which followed their recommendations. In the 1850s and 1860s, a series of crucial cases on doctrine and ritual were decided by the Judicial Committee of the Privy Council. The authority of the State did not merely exist, but was exercised.

The legal privileges of the established Church were also considerable. The Sovereign was bound by law to be a member of the Church, a legal provision which carried with it political and social advantages for the Church. The archbishops and bishops of the Church of England (except the most junior, after the creation of the see of Manchester in 1847), and certain Irish prelates, were entitled to sit in the House of Lords—though against this clergy of the established Church were debarred from election to the House of Commons. The payment of tithe by all owners of land subject to it was enforced by law, and statutes of the 1830s had provided for the old payments in kind to be commuted into money payments. The Church rate, for the maintenance of the parish church, was enforceable by law on all occupiers of property in a parish (except in Ireland, where it was abolished in 1833). There were a number of other privileges of a different kind. Marriages performed in a church by a clergyman of the established Church did not require the presence of a registrar to receive legal recognition—others did. The rites of the Church had to be used at burials in churchyards, whatever the faith of the person being buried. Degrees at the universities of Oxford and Cambridge were available, before 1854, only to members of the Church of England; fellowships of colleges remained confined to Anglicans until 1870.

This was the legal aspect of establishment in the middle of the nineteenth century. It derived to some extent from statutes of the sixteenth century, from the breach with Rome in the reign of Henry VIII, and from the Elizabethan settlement of 1559. In that century, and for some long time afterwards, royal authority in ecclesiastical affairs, and uniformity in the religious observances of subjects, was a matter of political necessity, in nearly all other European countries as well as in England. But it was possible to plead in support of these arrangements in the sixteenth century not only political necessity, but also plausible politico-religious theory. Richard Hooker, in his *Ecclesiastical Polity*, written during the 1590s, maintained that Church and State were simply two aspects of the same thing. "There is not any man of the Church of England, but the same man is also a member of the Commonwealth, nor any man a member of the Commonwealth which is not also of the Church of England."[4] Since the two entities were in this way really identical, the regulation of the affairs of the Church by the authorities of the State, and the then exclusive position of the Church within the State, were right as well as expedient.

Hooker's statement was not literally true even in his own day. There were English Roman Catholics, and there were those like the Brownists who asserted the idea of a "gathered Church", a group of believers who consciously bonded themselves together to form a worshipping community—a very different conception from that of a national Church into which one was simply born. In the next century it became steadily less and less true that membership of the State and of the established Church was identical. The Toleration Act of 1689 allowed Protestant Nonconformists freedom of worship, but they were still excluded from public life by the Corporation and Test Acts. To this extent, a form of Hooker's assertion could be maintained: membership of the established Church and of the political nation, that part of the nation which could take a full part in politics and local government, was still the same. In practice the system worked smoothly. Dissenters found it expedient to remain quiet, and in the Church there was a "confident optimism concerning the correspondence between the establishment of England and the eternal order of the universe".[5] But eventually the gap between theory and fact grew too wide to be wholly ignored.

The crucial development was the repeal of the Test and Corporation Acts in 1828. It was long since they had been strictly enforced, but with their repeal and the passage of the Catholic Emancipation Act in the following year, Protestant Dissenters and Roman Catholics were legally allowed to take a full part in public life and to hold any public office, with a very few exceptions.

With these steps the basis of the ecclesiastical settlement established in the sixteenth century disappeared. It had originated in political necessity and been justified by Hooker's theory. It had become politically inexpedient (indeed impossible to maintain), and the theory had ceased to have even a vestigial correspondence to reality. The established Church, however, remained. It was possible to seek for some way of alleviating this anomaly, as did Thomas Arnold, who advocated restoring as far as possible the identity of Church and people. In his *Principles of Church Reform* he argued that the established Church should be retained, but its bounds should be widened to include all Protestant Dissenters who would acknowledge the Trinity—he would exclude Roman Catholics, Quakers, and Unitarians. But this was a pipe-dream— no such alleviation was possible. The anomaly remained. Other theories and justifications were produced, and will be considered later.

There was more to the position of the established Church in the middle of the nineteenth century than its legal standing and outdated political theory. Because it was so deeply rooted in history, there had grown up round the establishment both feelings and interests, closely interlinked. These can be no more than sketched in here; something more of their significance will appear later in the narrative. One powerful sentiment was the association of the fact of establishment with the Reformation and Protestantism. Careful and subtle historians of the relations of Church and State before the sixteenth century would certainly see this as an over-simplification. But none the less it was the case that important statutes setting out the position of the established Church dated from the reigns of Henry VIII and Elizabeth, and were directly connected with the breach with Rome, and later the great struggle against Catholic Spain. Equally, readers of Macaulay on the reign of James II had a clear picture of the Church of England as a bulwark against a Catholic plot. The same view of history, incidentally, bound the establishment up not only with anti-Catholicism, but also with English patriotism. Moreover, since to right-thinking people in most of Britain in the middle of the nineteenth century Protestantism was the true religion, the establishment tended to be linked with the security of religion itself.

This view of the importance of establishment to religion was not necessarily associated with either a crude view of history or violent anti-Catholicism, but could come from quite a different view of the purpose of establishment. F. D. Maurice, one of the most influential theologians of the century, of wide sympathies and elevated views, held a conception of the importance of establishment to religion which was far removed from Protestant drumbanging. He held that Church and State were united by more than law or the accident of history.

> We hold the State and the Church do live to promote the same end; that both alike are religious societies instituted and ordained by God, that both alike are to accomplish His will towards His creature man, that both alike are to preserve that creature from the mischiefs to which an evil nature exposes him.[6]

He thought that ending the connection between Church and State in England would mean telling "the State that it has the most solemn functions to perform for the lives and properties of men: but that it is not based in righteousness; that it has no responsibility to God".[7] Again:

> A National Church should mean a Church which exists to purify and elevate the mind of a nation; to give to those who make and administer and obey its laws a sense of the grandeur of law and of the source whence it proceeds, to tell the rulers of the nation, and all the members of the nation, that all false ways are ruinous ways, that truth is the only stability of our time or of any time. . . . This should be the meaning of a National Church; a nation wants a Church for these purposes mainly; a Church is abusing its trust if it aims at any other or lower purposes.[8]

It followed from such a view of establishment that to end it would damage both the State and true religion. The mind of the nation would no longer be purified and elevated—if the initiative for the breach came from the State, then presumably it would no longer *wish* its mind to be purified and elevated. If a man of Maurice's calibre could write in such a fashion, it is not surprising to find many expressions during debates on disestablishment of the view that establishment meant the State's acknowledgment of the importance of religion, or of the authority of God in human affairs, and that conversely disestablishment would mean the repudiation of religion and divine authority. It is interesting that even a century after the period we are considering, Cyril Garbett, Archbishop of York, wrote: "There is little doubt that if the Church of England were disestablished at the present time, the world would interpret this as the national repudiation of Christianity."[9]

The establishment, then, had grown to represent the cause of the Christian religion itself in many minds. Interests of a more solid and material kind had also grown up around it. Over many centuries a substantial number of laymen had secured the right to appoint clergymen to particular churches and parishes—the right of presentation to livings. This right was treated as a piece of property, which could be passed on to one's heirs or sold in the market. It was of considerable value in providing for one's family or friends, and a useful means of increasing one's influence and prestige. This right of presentation by laymen was not formally a part of the relationship between Church and State, but because it was treated as a matter of property it was under the control of the civil courts, and it was generally regarded as a part of what was meant by establishment. It was certainly taken for granted that disestablishment would bring it to an end, as in Ireland and Wales it did.

The case of another, and far more important, material interest was similar. The endowments of the established Church were widely taken to be connected with the fact of establishment. Whether this should be so or not was a matter of argument, which will recur in these pages. On the one hand, it was held that endowments, with few exceptions, came not from the State but from the generosity of private individuals, and that there was no logical connection between the endowments and establishment. On the other hand, it was asserted that tithes in particular were the product of public law, and that most endowments were given to the Church when it was the only religious body in the country, and that it forfeited its right to them when it became only one such body among many.[10] At any rate, as with lay presentation to livings, it was generally assumed that disestablishment would involve disendowment; and again in Ireland and Wales it did, though in differing degrees.

Finally, the establishment had great social significance. Through its connection with the monarchy, through the prestige of its bishops as peers of the realm, through its long monopoly of education at Oxford and Cambridge, and through its recognition

by law in a law-respecting society, the established Church had a
higher social standing than any other religious body.[11] More than
this, the established Church was seen by the conservatively
minded as a vital cement of social order. This was most clearly
seen during the period after 1815, when fear of revolution produced the only two occasions when Parliament voted money for
the building of churches: a million pounds in 1818, and another
half million in 1824. Part of these sums went to the established
Church of Scotland, but most to the Church of England to build
churches in the new industrial cities, where many of them still
stand. These measures had no successors—Peel refused to make a
similar grant when pressed to do so in the 1840s. But the assumption behind them was constantly made and repeatedly expressed,
as in a letter from Bickersteth, Archdeacon of Buckingham, to
Disraeli in 1862 (he was passing on a letter from Wordsworth* on
the need to increase the number of bishops):

> He [Wordsworth] says, and I think truly, that even on Political
> grounds the Conservatives do not seem to understand that the best
> way to strengthen the Church party in the country is to set the
> Clergy vigorously to work in the parishes, especially in preparing
> their young people for Confirmation, & training them up regularly
> to be communicants; and that if this were effectively done then Radi-
> calism & Dissent would be gradually undermined; and that this
> never can be done without a considerable increase of the Episcopate.
> There is great truth in this. I can see on every side the proof that
> where the Church system is adequately administered the people un-
> consciously become Conservative.[12]

So stood the ancient building of the established Church in the
middle of the nineteenth century, with the shell of its legal position
almost intact, though its buttresses of justificatory theory were in
ruins, and with thick growths of interest and sentiment covering it
on all sides and sometimes obscuring its true outlines from view. It
was a situation which caused considerable embarrassment and
difficulty for all those involved: the State, the Church, and those
outside the Church.

For the State, the lingering idea that Parliament should be, if
no longer an Anglican, at least a Christian body, brought prob-

---

* Christopher Wordsworth, then a canon of Westminster, appointed to the
see of Lincoln by Disraeli in 1868.

lems. Jews were excluded until 1858. Atheists presented greater difficulties still, amply demonstrated in the long struggle of Bradlaugh to take his seat in the 1880s. The law of marriage and divorce was another area where long-existing assumptions arising out of the fact of establishment were breaking down; but no clear new assumptions had arisen to take their place. Civil marriage valid in law was introduced in 1836. But Parliament steadily refused to allow marriage with a deceased's wife's sister. Until 1857, no divorce was possible at all except by special Act of Parliament. When it came, the discussion on the subject was mainly in terms of the correct interpretation of texts in the New Testament on adultery. Even with divorce only on grounds of adultery there was raised the possibility of a clash between the law of the State and the law of the established Church on the remarriage of divorced persons. Parliament had to legislate in such matters, and its position was complicated by the legal standing of the established Church and by the still current assumption that the State itself was a Christian body.

Government and Parliament also had to face the recurrent strain of conflicts and crises arising out of their relationship with the established Church. These could take up a great deal of parliamentary time, in debates on the Irish Church for example, on Church rates (especially in the 1860s, when a motion to abolish them was an annual affair), or on education. Even Peel's powerful government met overwhelming opposition to the education clauses of the Factory Bill of 1843 because of the advantages they would have given to the established Church. The clauses were dropped. Prime Ministers could also run into great waves of ecclesiastical obloquy over appointments within the Church, as Russell did when he appointed Hampden to the see of Hereford in 1847, and Gladstone when he appointed Temple to Exeter in 1869. Even in normal circumstances the constant stream of Church appointments was as much of a trial for Prime Ministers as it was a source of political advantage.

For the Church too there were serious disadvantages in the situation. These arose to some extent out of this same matter of appointments. This was not because of the political element in them, which was generally accepted, but on the occasions when a question of orthodoxy was felt to be at stake. In 1836 the

Convocation of Oxford University had formally voted that it had no confidence in the theological position of Dr Hampden, just appointed by Melbourne to the Regius professorship of Divinity. When Russell made Hampden Bishop of Hereford in 1847, this condemnation still stood. There was a great outcry in the Church against the appointment of a bishop whose orthodoxy was in question. Thirteen bishops protested publicly, and the Dean of Hereford cast his vote against Hampden at his formal election by the Dean and Chapter. The position of Frederick Temple, whom Gladstone made Bishop of Exeter in 1869, was similar. He had been a contributor to *Essays and Reviews* (1860), a book condemned by the great majority of the clergy of the Church of England. His appointment to a bishopric, like that of Hampden, was widely held to be an abuse of the royal supremacy, and caused the supremacy itself to be called in question.

The *Essays and Reviews* affair was one of three important cases involving doctrine which brought out the problems involved for the Church in its establishment. The first in point of time was the Gorham case. In 1848 the then Bishop of Exeter, Phillpotts, refused to institute George Gorham to a living in his diocese on the ground that Gorham did not hold the true doctrine of baptismal regeneration as required by the Church of England. In 1849 the Court of Arches upheld the bishop, to the dismay of Evangelicals. Then, on appeal, the Judicial Committee of the Privy Council in 1850 reversed this verdict and decided in favour of Gorham, this time to the dismay of the Tractarians and of others who regretted that a decision of this kind was made by a lay tribunal.

The judgements in the case of *Essays and Reviews* varied similarly. First the Court of Arches found two of the contributors, Williams and Wilson, guilty of heresy, and then on appeal the Judicial Committee in 1864 acquitted them. On that occasion the main issues were the doctrine of eternal punishment and the inspiration of Scripture. The verdict of the court has in retrospect been generally held to have been wise, but at the time the most obvious fact was that the highest court of appeal had ruled that it was possible for clergymen of the established Church to hold views which the great majority of their fellows thought to be at best objectionable and at worst heretical. And there was nothing that could be done about it, because of the legal structure to which the Church was subject by the fact of its establishment.

The third case involving a doctrinal issue, again arising out of the problem of biblical criticism, was that of Colenso, Bishop of Natal, who in 1862 published a book on the Pentateuch and the book of Joshua, denying the historical accuracy of many statements in these books. Colenso was deprived of his see by the Bishop of Cape Town. On appeal, the Judicial Committee of the Privy Council ruled that the Bishop of Cape Town had no valid jurisdiction, though he was in name Colenso's metropolitan, and therefore his sentence was null and void. This judgement involved no pronouncement on the question of Colenso's heresy or otherwise, but its practical effect was to keep him in his bishopric when the previous year forty-one bishops had held that his opinions were inconsistent with his office. When it was taken in conjunction with the decision in the case of *Essays and Reviews*, it appeared that "there was now a settled policy on the part of the courts to prevent the enforcement upon the clergy of any standards of belief".[13] (Colenso was further confirmed in the possession of his bishopric by English civil courts in 1866, when it was ruled that the Colonial Bishoprics Fund must continue to pay him his salary.) But in this affair the verdict of the Judicial Committee was not meekly accepted. The Judicial Committee in its judgement had denied the right of the Crown to create a bishopric in South Africa at all, thus casting a fog of legal uncertainty over the whole position. Taking advantage of this, Gray, the Bishop of Cape Town, in January 1869 consecrated a new bishop, called the Bishop of Maritzburg, to replace Colenso. This was tacitly accepted by the English bishops, though it amounted to a defiance of the Judicial Committee and struck at the basis of Church order as generally accepted in the home country. The *Record*, the chief Evangelical organ, commented on proposals to consecrate a rival to Colenso that in them "we only hear the knell of departing Church establishments". If Colenso were legally convicted of heresy and the Queen were advised to remove his patent, then the *Record* would rejoice. But as long as he was legally Bishop of Natal, then to consecrate a rival bishop was "an act of violence to law, and an affront to the Church of England as by law established".[14] The *Record* had put its finger on the crucial point.

The same period of the 1850s and 1860s also saw the first of the cases on matters of ritual which arose as the Tractarian movement spread and began to express its theology and devotion to antiquity in forms of ceremonial and vestments. In 1854 a case was brought against Robert Liddell, the vicar of St Paul's, Knightsbridge, by one of his churchwardens. It went ultimately to the Judicial Committee of the Privy Council, which ruled that crosses (but not crucifixes) were lawful decorations, though they should not be placed on the holy table; stone altars were ruled illegal. The court also declared that eucharistic vestments were legal, which pacified the ritualists. In 1865, however, the Church Association was formed to suppress ritualism by legal action, and the first action they brought, against Mackonochie, the vicar of St Alban's, Holborn, had more serious consequences. The Court of Arches in 1867 ruled that it was legal to place two lighted candles on the communion table, and to kneel or prostrate oneself before the consecrated elements. The Judicial Committee, on appeal, reversed both these rulings: standing was the only admissible posture during the prayer of consecration, and candles were permissible only if they were needed to give light. There were those in the High Church party, including Mackonochie himself and Pusey, who advocated disestablishment after this decision; others talked of secession by the Catholic wing in the established Church. The *Church Times* denounced the decision as that of a bare majority in "a packed tribunal", and declared that it had no moral force, but advocated acceptance, on the grounds that true doctrine could not be affected and that secession would be inexpedient. If Catholics formed a free Church, it would have two million souls within twenty years; but if they could remain within it, the whole Church of England would be theirs.[15] In 1869, not long after the final judgement against Mackonochie, a case was brought against Purchas, perpetual curate of St James's, Brighton, and in this case the Judicial Committee, in 1871, declared illegal the chasuble (when worn in a parish church), the eastward position for celebrating Holy Communion, the mixed chalice, and wafer bread. This was an even more swingeing blow, delivered by a lay tribunal, against the practices and beliefs of the High Church party. But the difficulty for the Church did not end with resentment against such pronouncements on matters of deeply held beliefs. In the event, the rulings of the Judicial Committee were widely disregarded. Prosecutions could not keep up with breaches of the law. The Public Worship Regulation Act of 1874 failed in fact to regulate public worship, and prosecutions under it resulted only in the martyrdom by imprisonment of a small number of dedicated parish priests. The final result was the complete breakdown of the public law of the established Church.

There were other matters, of lesser importance than these for the Church, but irritating none the less. In the 1860s the long-standing question of securing more bishops for the Church arose once more. There was a very strong case, in the increasing amount of work to be done by bishops, and the increasing conscientiousness with which they were doing it. But in 1865 the government refused a request for more bishops. In 1867 a Bill to increase the episcopate received no support even from a Conservative government, and had to be dropped.[16] In 1869 the Archbishop of Canterbury, Tait, tried again, this time approaching Gladstone privately. But the Prime Minister wished to avoid controversy in Parliament, and thought it would be inexpedient to apply for authority to create the three new sees Tait wanted. Instead, a statute of Henry VIII's reign which provided for the consecration of suffragan bishops was used as a device to get round the difficulty. Bishop Baring of Durham felt strongly that this was an unsatisfactory solution, and that Gladstone had shrunk from a measure which would have been unpopular with his radical allies. He thought it was a step towards disestablishment, and speculated on the possibility of anticipating events by removing bishops from the House of Lords, reducing their incomes to £2,000, doing away with deans, and having at least one bishop to every county—drastic suggestions for a Palmerstonian, Evangelical bishop.[17]

This array of problems arising out of the establishment in the 1860s intensified a movement of opinion already present within the Church in favour of disestablishment. This came almost entirely from the Tractarian wing of the Church. The Oxford Movement had had as its starting-point Keble's sermon of 14 July 1833 against the suppression of Irish bishoprics by Act of Parliament— against, that is, intervention by the State in a vital matter of Church order. This stand was implicit in the movement's whole view of the Church of England as part of the Church universal, one, Catholic, and Apostolic. Newman asked in the second *Tract for the Times* the explosive question: "Did the State make us? Can it unmake us?" To which his answer was obviously "No". Hurrell Froude wanted to restore the ancient right of the Church to appoint its own bishops, and was willing to accept the consequences in the shape of disestablishment. The three moving spirits of the Oxford Movement thus took up similar positions in the 1830s on the question of the establishment, and the party which they founded inherited their views. Pusey, who came to be accepted as the leader of the movement when Newman joined the Roman Church, was willing to advocate disestablishment, and sometimes, in face of unfavourable decisions by the Judicial Committee of the Privy Council, actually did so. By the beginning of 1868 the movement against the establishment in the High Church party had grown to such an extent that Dean Stanley could seriously speak of it as perhaps the most formidable of the attacks upon the establishment. He rightly traced it back to the Non-jurors of the late seventeenth century, as well as the early *Tracts for the Times*, and thought it had "reached its highest flights in our own day".[18] Certainly the English Church Union, founded in 1860 to advocate and advance High Church doctrines and interests, was from the start strongly opposed to the imposition of lay authority on the Church.

The position of the Church under establishment was thus one of considerable difficulty, and produced a reaction against it even within the Church. For those outside the Church, the difficulties and grievances were yet more obvious and more material. They were implicit in the account already given of the legal position of the established Church. Church rates in England and Wales, tithe in England, Wales, and Ireland, were paid by some Protestant Dissenters and Roman Catholics as well as by Anglicans. In most cases such people were doubtless also contributing to the upkeep of their own religious organizations, and this represented a grievance which was at once material and conscientious. Those outside the established Church also suffered from a number of educational disabilities and difficulties, and from the position of social inferiority implicit in the establishment. Roman Catholics also laboured under the irritant of the Ecclesiastical Titles Act of 1851, which (in so far as it may be said to have been designed to do anything) was intended to protect the position of the established Church against "Papal aggression" by making the use by Roman Catholic prelates of territorial titles illegal. The Act was not enforced, but its very existence (until repealed in 1871) was an irritating sign of inferiority.

In England and Wales, Protestant Dissenters were very numerous. They became conscious of their own numbers and strength when the religious census of 1851 attributed to them over four and a half million attendances at services on census Sunday, compared with over five and a quarter million attendances at Church of England services.* This knowledge gave an extra impetus to the demands of Protestant Dissenters to be relieved from their disabilities. A movement to organize the Nonconformist Churches for political action after their long quiescence had made some progress in the 1830s and 1840s.[19] In the 1840s the most prominent figure in this movement was Edward Miall, who was a Congregationalist minister in Leicester until in 1840 he gave up his charge there to become the editor of a new and militant weekly paper, the *Nonconformist*, which began publication in 1841.[20] The main concern of this paper in its early years was a campaign against Church rates, but it also attacked the established Church as such. In other matters it was strongly radical, supporting both the Chartists and the Anti-Corn Law League, pronouncing in favour of manhood suffrage, and forgeing for the first time an effective alliance between political Dissent and democracy.

In 1844 this propaganda and political activity resulted in the foundation of the Anti-State Church Association, which in 1847 put up thirty candidates in the general election. Miall himself entered Parliament in 1852 as a Liberal, being recommended to the Liberal selection committee in Rochdale by John Bright. In 1853 the Association changed its name to the Society for the Liberation of Religion from State Patronage and Control. It was usually referred to as the Liberation Society, but its full stately title has some significance, because its leaders always argued that their

* These figures must be treated with caution. They were for attendances, which means that they certainly included many individuals who attended church or chapel twice or even three times in the day. The returns on which they were based were not wholly above suspicion; and the final figures included estimates for those places of worship for which no returns were received. See Owen Chadwick, *The Victorian Church*, Part I (London 1966), pp. 363-9.

wish was not to damage any Church, but only to free all Churches from the trammels of state control to enable them to do their proper work. In the next few years, the Liberation Society made its presence felt both in Parliament and in the country as the mainspring of an attack on the position of the established Church. It became, indeed, something of a King Charles's head to defenders of the establishment, who tended to attribute to it rather more, and more sinister, influence than in fact it possessed.

Miall claimed in 1865 that the Society had not pursued a systematic plan, but had been opportunist, following the lead provided by events. There was doubtless some truth in this, but it was not the whole truth, for a great deal of effort was put into making parliamentary activity on behalf of the Society a regular and organized business. The Society had its own parliamentary group, which met frequently and had its own whip on certain issues. Its greatest successes were in the annual motions against Church rates in the House of Commons. The majority in favour of these motions rose from twenty-eight in 1855 to sixty-nine in 1859, though after that it encountered a reaction—the votes moved the other way, and in 1862 there was a majority of one in favour of Church rates. The Society had to take stock of this new position. Miall himself and H. S. Skeats, a prominent member of the Society and one of its most skilful pamphleteers, reviewed the situation for the Executive Committee in September 1861. They noted the new strength of opposition to their activities:

> The sentiment in sympathy with the State Church, previously latent, has been excited and become visible, but it is, for the most part, a sentiment based upon Education, habit, association, taste and prejudice, and not upon intelligent conviction. It is partly religious, still more largely political, but predominantly social. It roots itself mainly in the pride of supremacy, and in the apprehension that the Church of England should be brought down to the level of the sects.

They argued that there was nothing to be done with the then Parliament, and that the Liberation Society should transfer its efforts to influencing public opinion and the next elections. A special electoral effort should be made in Wales, where there were many Nonconformists not yet mobilized for election purposes. After a period of discussion, it was resolved in October 1861 to move along these lines, by appointing a body of lecturers, by issuing pamphlets and working on the press, and by instructing the Parliamentary committee to act also as an electoral committee.[21]

These decisions were put to the Council of the Liberation Society in February 1862, and defended with the argument that "the Conservative party, when acting *as* a party, can now successfully oppose almost any measure based on the principle of religious equality".[22] This was true, even though the Conservatives did not in any strict sense possess a majority in the House of Commons. The Society then proceeded to its new plan of campaign. It had very considerable financial resources for its task. Its income in the year 1866–7 was £8,281; in 1868–9 it was £8,913—very large sums for the time.[23] These funds were used, as resolved, on propaganda and electoral organization.

The Society's own journal was the monthly *Liberator*, whose circulation in 1863 was about 6,000, and which in 1865 was subsidized by the Society to the extent of between five and six hundred pounds. It was a shrewdly edited and well-presented paper, which made the most of the extensive target presented by the anomalies of the established Church. It contrasted the large incomes of bishops in England and Ireland with the exiguous revenues of those in Scotland and the colonies. It made the most of *Essays and Reviews* and the Colenso case, remarking that the established Church, though pledged to uniformity, was in fact split on questions of belief, and clergymen could publish with impunity works subversive of all Christian belief. It kept before its readers, as a contrast, a highly favourable view of the state of religion in the United States, a country where the establishment of any religion was forbidden by the constitution. Subscribers to the *Liberator* were presumably converted already, but they had ample ammunition for controversy with the unregenerate. Copies were sometimes distributed free where they would be useful: it was proposed to give away at least a thousand copies during 1865, an election year.[24]

More important, the Society put much of the material from the *Liberator* into other publications, both pamphlets and substantial books. For this purpose they sought to study the market and adapt themselves to it. They believed in 1865 that the controversy about establishment was entering a new stage, engaging the attention of, as they put it, a higher class of mind than before. They therefore produced a plan for a series of works suitable for men of education—they invited Bryce, already a well-known figure, to write a book on the rise and effects of State Churches in Europe. (He declined, after a very long delay.) At the same time it was proposed to produce a new series of controversial tracts, and to put out a sixpenny edition of Skeats's book on the Irish Church. In April 1866 the publishing sub-committee reported a demand for a brief work on the Irish Church; and in December suggested a work on sects and parties within the Church of England, to show how far away it was from its professions of uniformity. In 1867 the sub-committee proposed to reprint Miall's *Title Deeds of the Church of England to her parochial endowments*, which they had not thought it worth while to do two years earlier. In January 1868 the publishing sub-committee reported an increased demand for their publications, and estimated that a total of half a million copies (of all types of works) had been circulated during the previous two years.[25] This effort reached its peak during the general election of 1868.

The second half of the strategy decided on in 1861–2 was electoral. The Liberation Society decided to bring direct pressure to bear on the Liberal party in the constituencies. In each constituency they would make demands on the Liberal candidate in proportion to their strength, and if these demands were not met, the Society would refuse its support. They believed that the Liberal party managers would come round to the view that "they need us quite as much as we need them". They calculated that there were thirty-three boroughs where the Society could effectively intervene in this manner. The demands they were prepared to make varied with their voting strength, from the right of nomination in some constituencies to a pledge to vote for the unconditional abolition of Church rates in others.[26] This strategy was put into action in the election of 1865. An electoral agent was appointed by the Society in December 1864, and after Parliament was dissolved the election committee sat daily to watch over the particular constituencies which the Society was trying to influence. They claimed a number of successes, in the withdrawal of Liberal candidates who were unsound on the Church rates question, and even the return of some Tories instead of unsatisfactory Liberals. Two members of the Society's Executive Committee and fifteen other subscribing members secured seats in the Commons.[27]

The Liberation Society, then, was a significant, well-organized and persistent pressure-group, which publicly affirmed that its ultimate object was the end of all establishments in the United Kingdom. The campaign against Church rates was only one step towards this end. In September 1862 a sub-committee on policy advised that the best means to attain general disestablishment were to be found in Ireland, Wales, or Scotland, either separately or together.[28] By October 1863 they had decided that the established Church in Ireland was showing hopeful signs of being the best place for an attack. The question had been raised by two Liberal members (Dillwyn and Bernal Osborne—not members of the Society), and it would probably continue to engage Parliamentary attention. At that time they still did not believe that the general political circumstances were favourable to their activities —the "Upper Ten Thousand" had the game in their hands.[29] But, by September 1865, the situation appeared to have changed. The Society's Secretary (Carvell Williams) reported that antagonisms within the Church were working against a united defence of its endowments and privileges, and this defence, recently so effective on the question of Church rates, seemed to be losing some of its vigour. Even within the Church there was an increasing disposition to consider the possibility of ending State interference with religion. The position both of the establishment and of public opinion had become "eminently favourable" to the propagation of the Liberation Society's views.[30]

The connection between Church and State was thus causing serious difficulties even within the established Church itself, and there was a movement inside the Church in favour of disestablishment. Outside the Church, militant Dissent in the shape of the Liberation Society was working systematically for the same end. One consequence of all this was a widespread impression in the 1860s that disestablishment was in fact approaching. This impression grew stronger as the attack on the established Church in Ireland reached its climax in 1868 and 1869. Indeed, it was because disestablishment, even in England, was widely felt to be inevitable that Irish disestablishment was genuinely seen by many people as merely the first step in this process.

Within the Church a number of distinguished men expressed the view that disestablishment was bound to come. Pusey wrote in *The Times* of 22 August 1868 on the subject of Coleridge's Bill about the Universities of Oxford and Cambridge, that "in all human appearance the days of establishments are numbered"; he also expressed his willingness to co-operate in the process of ending them. C. J. Vaughan, then the vicar of Doncaster and later Master of the Temple and Dean of Llandaff, preached a sermon in September 1868 on the occasion of the first offertory to be made in his church. He told his congregation that the younger of them would see the Church of England solely dependent on voluntary giving; the connection between Church and State would be severed, and the Church disendowed.[31] Henry Alford, Dean of Canterbury, wrote in the *Contemporary Review* of October 1868 a long and closely reasoned article on "The Church of the Future". He argued that first toleration of different Churches, and then the removal of disabilities from non-Anglicans, had started a process which was not yet complete. The next stage in it would be the severance of Church and State, which would be accomplished however long it took. (He did not estimate how long this would be, though he did remark that there was hardly a thinking man in the country who looked for the existence of an established Church a century later.) He also claimed that it would be calamitous for the Church to fight the inevitable inch by inch: instead its members should prepare for the change and cheerfully acquiesce in it.

These three gentlemen viewed the prospect of coming disestablishment without anxiety, and in Pusey's case with eagerness. Alexander Ewing, Bishop of Argyll and the Isles, who knew from the inside the problems of the unestablished, unendowed Episcopal Church of Scotland, did not wish to see disestablishment in England.[32] But he too thought it was coming. He wrote to his friend Tait, then Bishop of London, in March 1868, sending him an article he wished to publish "to inflict a blow on what grows an impending danger, the separation of Church and State".[33] And he wrote again a little later: "I don't suppose you *can* long retain the Establishment in England—the clergy kick against it, and the *people* are indifferent."[34] In public he argued the case for establishments, but admitted that their position was becoming untenable.

He wrote that previously it had been possible to have an established Church by a majority compelling a minority to accept and support it, or through the absence of any strong hostile feeling. These conditions no longer prevailed; indeed, many now thought it improper to compel a minority in this way. The tide was setting so strongly from different quarters against the principle of state establishment of religion that it could not be resisted.[35] The Bishop of Ely in 1868 also saw a movement in society towards disestablishment. A large proportion of the population was alienated from the established Church, and those same people were gaining more political power; these facts were bound to have their effect.[36]

Among Church papers, the *Church Times* was strongly of the opinion that disestablishment was coming, and was not unduly perturbed. In a leading article of 20 July 1867, for example, it wrote of a marked tendency of the age against established Churches and endowments. It thought the great bar to its success was the system of lay patronage—so many M.P.s and peers were patrons of livings that the then Parliament was as unlikely to disestablish the Church as to abolish primogeniture. But when a class other than landowners came to power, then "Disestablishment will certainly come, and soon". By 21 March 1868 it thought that the new temper of the House of Commons was conclusive—"the days of the Established Church are numbered, not only in Ireland, but in England". The *Church Times* felt bound from time to time to protest that High Churchmen and ritualists were not advocating the separation of Church and State on principle. But they could read the signs of the times—by the march of democracy establishments were doomed.[37] But some of its language showed a positive wish for disestablishment. Even though the results of disendowment would be very damaging, it argued once, separation from the State would get rid of "all the host of those who believe in money, in the Royal Supremacy, in Antinomianism, in respectability, in everything but the Holy Catholic Church".[38] The *Guardian*, less fiercely High Church than the *Church Times*, was less sure of the certainty of disestablishment. It commented, for example, on Vaughan's sermon and predictions of inevitable disestablishment that at the utmost it only loomed in the distance. But a year later the *Guardian* too was writing that the English establishment would fall in ten or twelve years at the latest.[39]

It is worth adding that the *Globe*, a vigorous Conservative paper, normally argued that disestablishment must be fought and could be staved off—Churchmen should not only pray for their Church, they should vote for it. It denounced Dean Alford as an enemy of the Church within the gates.[40] But even the *Globe*, looking gloomily back over the past year on 31 December 1868, wrote that "the unmistakable tendency of events is, in Great Britain, towards what is called religious equality". The abolition of Church rates that year was one sign of this. There was also the demand within the established Church for freedom from the State. This was not likely to be granted in that generation, but it would increase, and if greater liberty were refused even moderate Churchmen would lose interest in the establishment.

Outside the Church, and among those unsympathetic to establishment, there were repeated expressions of the same view. These varied a good deal in the way they were put. The *Freeman's Journal* of Dublin was exultant, indeed rash, when on 20 March 1868 it wrote:

> The issue [of the Irish Church] will involve not only the fate of the Ministry, but the fate sooner or later of the dominant State Church, not only in Ireland but in England. The great Liberal Party are determined to deal a death blow to all State endowments, and the new constituencies which the Reform Bill has called into requisition will fully endorse that policy.

The Liberal *Daily Telegraph* thought that the Church of England presented "an example of almost absolute anarchy", which put the establishment in peril to a degree which was underrated by the Church's own bishops.[41] The *Westminster Review* declared in an article of July 1868 that the established Church must be subjected to the same tests as everything else: "We place every institution and every theory upon trial. If they commend themselves to reason, they must be good, and we shall retain them; if not—why, let them go, though they be sanctified with the dust of centuries."[42] Needless to say, the established Church failed to pass the *Westminster's* test. The *Saturday Review* thought that Pusey's letter to *The Times* about disestablishment might be seen in five or ten years' time as a turning-point in the history of the Church of England.[43] The *Pall Mall Gazette* commented on Vaughan's sermon that the odds were in favour of his prophecy of disestablishment coming true, though not so soon as he thought. It diagnosed a loss of confidence in the Church, ascribing it to the separation of the laity, who remained instinctively Protestant, from large numbers of the clergy, who had accepted High Church principles.[44]

Those who predicted inevitable disestablishment did not have things all their own way. The *Daily News*, a Liberal paper, was sceptical about Vaughan's sermon, though its mode of disputing his argument was double-edged: every moderately informed Englishman, it wrote, knew that the Church was safe as long as it had the people.[45] Dean Alford's article in the *Contemporary* drew a fierce reply in *Blackwood's Magazine* for November 1868. Disestablishment had a strange charm for some members of the Church of England—"the minds of the clergy are giving way"—but it was not inevitable. The writer denied that there was any wide movement against the establishment; and in any case "our duty is to sustain what we know to deserve sustaining".[46] The *Pall Mall Gazette*, though it believed that there was a real crisis in the Church, thought the most likely result for some long time would be the maintenance of the *status quo* with palliatives. The compromise which had stood for 300 years would last longer yet.[47]

In England at any rate the *status quo* with palliatives has persisted to the present day. But in 1868, despite the dissentient voices, the general trend of opinion was that the day of Church establishments was over. Disestablishment was coming. The *Liberator* advanced the crowning piece of evidence for this in January 1869. Anxiety over the position of the Church was actually affecting the prices of livings put up for sale. At a recent auction one living in the gift of the Duke of Norfolk, worth according to the auctioneer eight or nine thousand guineas, had got no bid and had been withdrawn.[48] It was a sign of the times.

2

THE IRISH CHURCH ON
THE EVE OF DISESTABLISHMENT

The Established Church in Ireland

After the Act of Union of 1800, the legal status of the established Church of Ireland was that of a part of the united Church of England and Ireland. Article V of the Act of Union laid down:

> that the Churches of England and Ireland, as now by law established, be united into one Protestant Episcopal Church, to be called "The United Church of England and Ireland"; and that the doctrine, worship, discipline and government of the said United Church shall be, and shall remain in full force for ever, as the same are now by law established for the Church of England; and that the continuance and preservation of the said United Church as the Established Church of England and Ireland shall be deemed and taken to be an essential and fundamental part of the Union.

In other ways, however, the positions of the two Churches were very different. The Church of Ireland had had a different role in history, in politics, and in society, from that of the Church of England. The Reformation, which had come in large part from within England and had taken firm hold on that country, was imposed on Ireland from without. In Ireland there had never been even the appearance that Hooker's theory that Church and people were identical held good. The established Church in Ireland was in origin an instrument for making the Irish people Protestant, and thereby making England more secure in the international situation of the sixteenth century. In this it failed. However, in various ways, substantial Protestant communities were created in Ireland during the sixteenth and seventeenth centuries. English security was maintained by concentrating all authority and social advantage in the hands of these communities —the Protestant ascendancy. The functions of the established Church in this situation became in part to act as an organ of

CHURCH OF IRELAND

Diocesan Divisions at the date of Disestablishment

government and political influence, and in part to be a prominent symbol of Protestant ascendancy. In both functions it was necessarily in opposition to a large majority of the population, which remained Catholic.

In playing such a role in politics and society, the established Church of Ireland was not unique. Throughout much of Christian Europe in the sixteenth and seventeenth centuries, and to a large degree in the eighteenth century too, religious policy was a part of state policy, and Churches were used as instruments of government. Penal laws against Catholics in Britain and Ireland were deemed essential for the security of the realm, just as, at certain times, were penal laws against Protestants in France. It was in accordance with the normal practice of the time that bishops, whatever their Church or country, should take part in the administration of these laws. Also, the performance of these political and social functions did not preclude the assumption by the Irish Church of a genuine religious mission, mainly towards its own members, but fitfully also towards the Catholic majority in Ireland. In particular it was the mission of the Irish Church to uphold, and if possible to advance, the cause of Protestant truth.

The role of the Church of Ireland had thus been both to symbolize and maintain Protestant ascendancy, and to be an advocate of Protestant faith and practice. Many people after the middle of the sixteenth century would have seen these as being proper functions of the Church of England also, so in that way the union of the two Churches was natural. But in England the performance of these functions had meant going with the tide of national development and popular wishes, in Ireland it meant going against the tide. The result by the nineteenth century was that the two Churches, though legally united, held different positions in their different countries.

These matters will recur later in this chapter, when the arguments about the Irish establishment are discussed. Certain facts about the material condition of the Irish Church must next be set out, if these arguments and the process of disestablishment are to be understood.

First, there is the question of the annual revenue of the Church of Ireland on the eve of its disestablishment and disendowment. A Royal Commission was set up in 1867 to inquire into the property of the Irish Church, and whether any improvements in its administration and distribution might be made. It reported in 1868. It found the net annual revenue of the Church (after deducting poor rates, expenses of collection, and quit rents) to be:

From lands let to tenants	£204,932	19s	7d
From tithe rent-charge	£364,224	16s	11d
From other sources	£15,530	6s	1d
	£584,688	2s	7d
Annual value of houses and lands occupied by the clergy (glebe-houses and lands)	£32,152	0s	0d
	£616,840	2s	7d[1]

There were other assessments besides this one. Maziere Brady, rector of Donaghpatrick in the diocese of Meath and one of the few Irish clergy to support disestablishment, argued that the Commission's figures were too low, on the ground that the poor-law valuation used to estimate the value of the glebe-houses and lands was notoriously below the actual letting value of the property.[2] Gladstone too thought the Commission's total too low, and preferred an estimate of about £700,000 per annum.[3] On the other hand, some Irish clergymen argued for considerably lower figures than those of the Commission. Alfred Lee, rector of Ahoghill and a vigorous pamphleteer in the cause of the establishment, argued in 1866 that the net revenue, after making all allowances for taxes, poor rate, and for money which merely went in a circle from the clergy to the Irish Ecclesiastical Commissioners and back again, was only just over £540,000.[4] It is not hard to account for discrepancies between different assessments. Something depended on what were considered proper deductions from gross revenue to arrive at net revenue. The tithe rent-charge varied according to the price of cereals. It was generally assumed that much Church land was let at rents well below its true value, so that with different management the revenue of the Church could be increased.[5] In fact, when the Church's property came, after disestablishment, into the hands of the Church Temporalities Commissioners appointed by the government, they secured approximately £66,000 per annum more from lands and tithe rent-charge than the figures given by the Royal Commission.[6] This would have meant a figure of £683,000 as the net annual revenue of the Church.

In view of the variables involved, and of the difficulties of computing the value of property in terms of annual revenue, it is pointless to seek further precision in this matter. It is equally pointless to seek to arrive at a useful estimate of the total capital value of the Church's property. This depended in effect on what the Church's lands and buildings, and the tithe rent-charge, would fetch if sold. Gladstone did in fact make such an estimate when presenting his Irish Church Bill in the House of Commons, giving a round figure of £16,000,000.[7] This proved in the event to be misleading, because the property could not be sold at the values he was assuming. If Gladstone could go astray thus, it is best for the mere historian not to speculate.

Of the different sources from which the Irish Church derived its revenue, tithe rent-charge requires special mention. The nature of the payment, its amount, and the mode of its collection had all been changed during the first half of the nineteenth century. In 1832 an Act of Parliament made the composition of tithes compulsory, that is, they were to be paid in money and not in kind. In 1838, to put an end to a "tithe war" in which the payment of tithes had been violently resisted for some seven years, a further Act was passed, by which the tithe was replaced by a rent-charge, amounting to £75 for every £100 of tithe, to be paid by land-owners and certain long lease-holders. This meant that the clergy no longer had to collect tithe from a large number of individual small tithe-payers, but from a few substantial land-holders. But it meant too that they lost a quarter of the revenue from tithe to which they had been previously entitled. This quarter was suppressed in order to lighten the burden on the landlords, or (looked at another way) to compensate them for their work in collecting the tithe in the new way. It was a notable act of disendowment, though the precedent of simply suppressing a portion of the tithe was not to be followed in 1869.

The position of the tithe rent-charge in Ireland on the eve of disestablishment was thus that its amount was variable, moving with the price of cereals, and its incidence was somewhat arbitrary. It was a charge on arable land, paid by landlords most of whom were Protestants, but still affecting the mainly Catholic tenants through the rents they paid for their land. Town-dwellers, who included in the middle classes a good proportion of the members of the established Church, did not pay tithe rent-charge.

This property and income supported a Church which in 1868 was divided into two provinces and twelve dioceses. With one exception these were united dioceses—unions of varying numbers of previously separate dioceses. The most recent and far-reaching of these unions had come about by the Church Temporalities Act of 1833, which had reduced the previous four archbishoprics and eighteen bishoprics to two archbishoprics (Armagh and Dublin) and ten bishoprics.

The twelve dioceses in 1868 were:

PROVINCE OF ARMAGH

Armagh and Clogher
Meath
Down, Connor, and Dromore
Derry and Raphoe
Kilmore, Elphin, and Ardagh
Tuam, Killala, and Achonry

PROVINCE OF DUBLIN

Dublin and Kildare
Ossory, Ferns, and Leighlin
Cashel, Emly, Waterford, and Lismore
Killaloe, Kilfenora, Clonfert, and Kilmacduagh
Limerick, Ardfert, and Aghadoe
Cork, Cloyne, and Ross

The net revenues of the bishops of these dioceses, including the value of their residences, as given by the Irish Church Commission, were:[8]

Armagh and Clogher	£9,798
Meath	£3,782
Tuam, Killala, and Achonry	£4,767
Down, Connor, and Dromore	£3,763
Derry and Raphoe	£6,171
Kilmore, Elphin, and Ardagh	£5,255
Dublin and Kildare	£7,387
Ossory, Ferns, and Leighlin	£3,579
Cashel, Emly, Waterford, and Lismore	£4,347

Limerick, Ardfert, and Aghadoe   £3,874
Killaloe, Kilfenora, Clonfert, and Kilmacduagh   £3,130
Cork, Cloyne, and Ross   £2,174

The existence of cathedrals and their dignitaries was not inter-
fered with by the Church Temporalities Act of 1833. In consequence, thirty corporations of Deans and Chapters still existed in
1868, though very few of these dignitaries retained their revenues,
which had for the most part been transferred to the Ecclesiastical
Commissioners. There thus existed numbers of deans, archdeacons, canons, and prebendaries, often without official income
or duty, and on occasion without a cathedral either.[9] The usual
arrangement was for a cathedral office to be attached to a benefice.

The total number of benefices with incumbents was 1,518, of
which 1,484 had parishes or districts attached.[10] The incomes of
these benefices varied a great deal, as was shown by a table compiled by the Irish Church Commission (net revenues):[11]

£1,000 to £1,100	7
£900 to £1,000	3
£800 to £900	9
£700 to £800	17
£600 to £700	23
£500 to £600	53
£400 to £500	107
£300 to £400	225
£200 to £300	356
£100 to £200	421
Under £100	297

The numbers and distribution of lay members of the established
Church in Ireland were known in detail because the census of
1861 included (in Ireland only) a question on religious affiliation.
The membership of the Irish Church according to the census returns was 693,357, out of a total population of 5,798,967. The
distribution of these members among the united dioceses was as
follows:[12]

	NO. OF BENEFICES	NO. OF CHURCH MEMBERS
Armagh and Clogher	170	150,778
Meath	105	16,289
Tuam, Killala, and Achonry	77	17,157
Down, Connor, and Dromore	150	146,136

	NO. OF BENEFICES	NO. OF CHURCH MEMBERS
Derry and Raphoe	112	69,951
Kilmore, Elphin, and Ardagh	118	53,196
Dublin and Kildare	154	112,766
Ossory, Ferns, and Leighlin	171	35,663
Cashel, Emly, Waterford, and Lismore	104	13,853
Limerick, Ardfert, and Aghadoe	95	15,103
Killaloe, Kilfenora, Clonfert, and Kilmacduagh	89	15,906
Cork, Cloyne, and Ross	170	43,228

The members of the established Church were thus concentrated in the north and down the east coast, especially round Dublin. Elsewhere, in the west and south of Ireland, they were thinly scattered over large areas.

The distribution of members among benefices was set out by the Irish Church Commission thus:[13]

Over 5,000	4
2,000 to 5,000	63
1,000 to 2,000	115
750 to 1,000	100
500 to 750	122
200 to 500	336
100 to 200	254
40 to 100	287
30 to 40	59
20 to 30	48
Under 20	92

There were thus 486 benefices with 100 or less Church members.

There were other aspects of the Irish Church, which could not be reduced to figures, but which require mention before discussion of the arguments on disestablishment. The general standard of conscientiousness and application among the clergy had improved markedly since the beginning of the nineteenth century. Notably, non-residence, which had been frequent in Ireland, as in England, had very largely disappeared. The Evangelical movement did its work in Ireland in producing a mood of earnestness and a new theological temper among the Irish clergy. The earnestness showed itself too in fresh attempts to convert Irish Catholics to the established Church. Five national societies were set up before 1830, mostly to distribute bibles and tracts—one of them to provide literature in Irish.[14] Power le Poer Trench, Archbishop of Tuam from 1819 to 1839, promoted the appointment of Irish-speaking clergy in his diocese, and encouraged missionary work among Catholics, including that of Edward Nangle on Achill Island. In 1849 the Society of Irish Church Missions to the Roman Catholics was set up, and sponsored efforts in the west of Ireland during the next twenty years. These activities provoked active resentment and opposition among Catholics in those areas.[15]

These missionary societies to the Catholics were sustained by voluntary work and gifts of money, and they lay outside the parochial system of the Irish Church. Another example of activity outside this system was the creation, notably in Dublin, of a number of proprietary churches, built, maintained, and staffed by their congregations. In Dublin in the 1860s such churches were well attended by solid Evangelical citizens who were prepared to pay substantial pew-rents to get the sort of sermons and services they liked, and to confirm their social distinction at the same time. The parish churches of Dublin suffered from this competition; but it showed the resources of both money and earnestness which were available among the middle-class adherents of the Irish Church.[16]

The Evangelical movement was common to both the established Church and the Presbyterian Churches in Ireland. There was indeed a good deal of sympathy between different Protestant bodies in Ireland, based on their natural political alliance as well as on similarity of religious outlook. Presbyterians had a stake in Protestant ascendancy in Ireland, and the appreciation of British governments of their political value had long been expressed in the *Regium Donum*, an annual government grant for the payment of the Presbyterian clergy. This political connection was a source of strength to the Irish Church, but the theological sympathy between Churchmen and Presbyterians and other Protestant Dissenters could cause uneasiness among those who valued and emphasized the distinctive features and teachings of the Church. William Fitzgerald, Bishop of Killaloe, for example, in 1860 reproved those who were impatient of "any peculiar institution which distinguishes us from other denominations of Protestants". He saw this as the fault of his own Church: "I believe there is hardly any communion in which less pains are taken, generally and methodically, to make the people acquainted with the distinctive character of its institutions than our own."[17]

There was thus life and energy in the Irish Church, which tended to overflow the Church's existing structure. However, the connection between Church and State had for so long been the chief support of the Irish Church, and in a sense its *raison d'être*, that it still appeared to most members of that Church to be a necessary condition of its existence. The relationship between Church and State in Ireland was in its legal aspects, in terms of control by the State and privileges conferred by the State, very similar to that in England. The Crown made appointments to bishoprics and deaneries, and also held the patronage of 146 benefices, with a hand in that of fifty-three others.[18] In the eighteenth century this right of appointment had been used openly and almost entirely for political purposes. In the nineteenth century, as in England, this practice diminished, though it was still taken for granted that a man's politics were important and might be decisive. Henry Newland dated the change in policy to the time of the Union, since when he claimed that bishops had been chosen at least in part for their piety and character as well as for political reasons.[19] By 1862 this process had gone so far that Palmerston's government was under fire from its supporters in Ireland for not looking after its political friends in the Church and appointing Conservatives to Cork and Armagh. The same appointments were naturally welcomed by Conservative newspapers as the choice of the best man for the post, irrespective of party.[20]

It was for long a complaint in Ireland that the right of Crown appointment was used to promote English rather than Irish clerics to important and lucrative positions in the Irish Church. This was certainly true in the eighteenth century. Before the Church Temporalities Act of 1833, the revenues of Irish sees were extremely high, and proportionately attractive to those who wished to found or sustain a landed family.[21] This indeed was probably a more important element in the system than the promotion of Englishmen as such. There was a close connection between the episcopate of the Irish Church and the English and Anglo-Irish ruling classes. (Godkin compiled a list of 127 bishops of the Irish Church, out of 326 between 1558 and 1867, who, he claimed, had founded landed families whose representatives were still in existence.[22]) This was not so much an abuse of the system of appointments as the inevitable result of the position of the Church in the political and social structure of Ireland. (It was not, of course, a position peculiar to Ireland—high office in the Church has been for long periods in most European countries a recognized road to wealth and social advancement.) After 1833 the greatest extremes of wealth combined with small duties were ended. English clergymen appointed to the Irish bench after then were men of merit, and sometimes of real distinction, like the two successive Archbishops of Dublin, Whately and Trench.*

State control over the organization, finances, and administration of the Irish Church was felt most powerfully in the 1830s, as it was in England. In that decade, as has already been mentioned, Acts of Parliament suppressed two archbishoprics and eight bishoprics; changed the nature and mode of collection of tithe, and diminished its amount by a quarter; and set up the Irish Ecclesiastical Commissioners. This body received and used for Church purposes the revenues of the suppressed sees, and of a number of suspended cathedral dignities, and also the proceeds of a tax on clerical incomes of over £300 per annum, introduced by the Church Temporalities Act of 1833.

A number of administrative tasks within the Church were performed by the Irish Privy Council. These included decisions on the union of parishes and the redistribution of revenues, and the supervising of the regulations on the use of burial grounds. The Privy Council also had to promulgate special forms of prayer, as in the Order in Council of 30 June 1868 for thanksgiving for the preservation of the Duke of Edinburgh from the hand of an assassin, and for the success vouchsafed to Her Majesty's forces in Abyssinia.[23] The two Archbishops and the Bishop of Meath were *ex officio* members of the Privy Council, and so were able to take part in these functions, but the Council itself was an arm of government, not of the Church.

The Irish Church also felt the weight of the control of the State in the question of reviving the Irish Convocation. In 1853 the

---

* It is true that Richard Chenevix Trench was born in Ireland, a member of an influential and widespread Irish family, but by upbringing, education, and inclination he was an Englishman, and he had made his career in England, being Dean of Westminster at the time of his appointment to Dublin.

Convocation of Canterbury had begun to meet again after a long period of merely formal existence; in 1861 that of York was similarly revived. Unless the Irish branch of the United Church also revived its Convocation (which had not met since 1713), or devised some new type of representative body, there was an anomaly here which would emphasize the separateness of the Irish Church and reveal an unreality in its legal union with the Church of England. In 1861 the Irish prelates pointed out to the Home Secretary that the Convocation of Canterbury had repealed the twenty-ninth English canon of 1603, and were preparing new forms of service for various occasions. If such changes were brought about in the Province of Canterbury, or those of Canterbury and York, to the exclusion of the Irish provinces, it would disturb the uniformity of the United Church and be against the spirit of the Act of Union. They therefore asked that a General Synod of the United Church should meet and its advice be obtained before any changes were made in doctrine, worship, discipline, or government. No reply was received, so in 1862 they tried again, only to have their request refused. As a second best, the Irish prelates then asked that the Queen should give the necessary authorization to convene the Irish Convocation, on the obvious ground that the Irish branch of the Church should have equal privileges with the provinces of Canterbury and York. They tried again in 1864 and 1865, but the government refused, saying that there was no sufficient reason to call the body into existence again after 150 years. By 1867 even a Conservative Home Secretary, Gathorne Hardy, could simply mark an address from the Convocation Society on the subject "Usual answer".[24] To allow the creation of a General Synod of the United Church, or even the lesser step of reviving the Irish Convocation, would have been a political act, strengthening the position of the established Church in Ireland. No government found this expedient, because no one at the time wished to grapple with the problem of the ecclesiastical situation in Ireland. None the less, Convocation was revived in England for sound ecclesiastical reasons, which could also have been valid for Ireland. There was no impediment in law to the summoning of the Irish Convocation,[25] and what stood in the way of the wish of the Irish bishops was simply the refusal of governments to issue the necessary writ.

The privileges conferred on the Irish Church by its relationship with the State were in one way very limited. Four seats in the House of Lords were allotted to Irish prelates on a rotation system. In Ireland, the two Archbishops and the Bishop of Meath served on the Privy Council, and it was possible for one of the Archbishops to be titular head of the Irish government in the absence of the Lord Lieutenant. The prelates of the established Church took precedence on social and ceremonial occasions over Catholic prelates. The verdicts of Irish ecclesiastical courts had the force of law. However, it was not in such limited privileges that the real advantage of establishment to the Irish Church lay. It lay in social precedence and prestige, in government protection for the wealth of the Church, and in government recognition of Protestantism as the religion of the State in Ireland.

The fact of establishment, and of the very wide measure of government control over the Irish Church which has been described, did not prevent serious conflicts between Church and government. The most serious of such conflicts in the mid-nineteenth century was over the Irish Education Act of 1831. This inaugurated what came to be called the national system of education, under the supervision of the Board of Commissioners of National Education, which included both the Archbishops of Dublin (Anglican and Catholic) as well as two Presbyterian ministers. The board attempted to proceed on the principle of joint nonsectarian education in all secular subjects, with separate religious instruction for the different denominations; it also sought to devise, by means of an anthology of passages of Scripture, some religious instruction which could be given to all children together. Each of the three main denominations in Ireland was divided on this scheme. But most of the Catholic bishops supported it, and turned it to their advantage in large parts of the country where Catholics formed the vast majority of the population. The Presbyterians were divided, and for some years a majority in the Synod of Ulster opposed the scheme, but in 1839, in return for certain concessions, they accepted it. The great majority of both the bishops and clergy of the Irish Church, on the other hand, long continued to oppose the national system. They made great efforts to maintain their own schools, staffed by members of the Church, where the Authorized Version of the Bible was used by all children. The opponents of the national system argued that for practical purposes it handed the major share in the control of education over to the Catholic Church; and also that the whole of Scripture should form part of the general educational syllabus. "The principle of this new Board is the exclusion of the Sacred Scriptures from the public and general course of the National Education; a principle familiar to the Church of Rome, but alien and abhorrent from the profession of Protestants."[26] In 1839 the Church Education Society was set up to raise funds, to supervise the Church schools, and to provide new ones. This opposition to the national system of education was kept up with determination, fading only in the late 1850s and the 1860s. This was in spite of the fact that the patronage of at any rate Whig administrations was normally extended to supporters of the system—something only partly offset by the opposing bishops' patronage being used in the contrary sense.

The national system of education was a symbol of a change in the whole climate of the government of Ireland, which in the first half of the nineteenth century marked the end of the old position of the established Church. The national system was a genuine attempt to provide education in a form suited to the whole Irish people, giving all denominations some share in its control while maintaining a measure of government supervision. Ireland was no longer governed for the benefit of Protestants alone. As long ago as the reign of William III and the grant of the *Regium Donum* to the Presbyterians there had been no exclusive alliance between the government and the established Church. When the grant to Maynooth College for the training of priests was given in 1793, government endowment was used to buy the loyalty of Catholics, and the membership of the alliance was extended.* Emancipation greatly strengthened the position of the Catholics, and made their support important to British governments. The co-operation between the Whigs and O'Connell in the 1830s showed this clearly, and Peel's Conservative government of 1841–6 maintained its predecessors' educational policy and increased the Maynooth grant.

There were two elements in this situation. One was that after 1829 and the creation of a substantial Irish Catholic vote, some

---

* The *Regium Donum* was the annual government grant to Presbyterian ministers; the Maynooth grant was the sum paid annually to the Catholic seminary at Maynooth.

understanding with Catholic Ireland was valuable to any government, and virtually indispensable to a Whig government. The
other was that British governments, of both parties, had in the
nineteenth century a different conception of the government of
Ireland from that of the eighteenth century. They differed in
method and in emphasis, and under one party one section of the
Irish population would be more favoured than under another, but
in general all governments sought an honest administration for the
benefit of the whole country. Accordingly Protestant ascendancy
ceased to be a useful instrument of government, and became in
some circumstances an obstacle to good government and the
maintenance of public peace. When this happened, the established Church in Ireland had outlived its political usefulness. This
was something which was rarely said during the debates on
whether the Church should remain established or not, but it was
the fact which lay behind all the discussion.

The Debate on the Irish Church Question in the 1860s

After the tithe war of the 1830s had been settled by the Act of
1838, the established Church in Ireland enjoyed about a quarter-
century of comparative peace. It was a cause for complaint among
Irish Catholics that the privileges of establishment and great
wealth from endowments should be in the hands of the Church of
a minority. Someone could usually be found saying that the established Church was a badge of conquest. But little was heard of the
matter in the 1840s, when attention was concentrated on O'Connell's movement for repeal of the Union, and later on the great
famine and its consequences. The Independent Irish Party of the
1850s included disestablishment and disendowment among its objectives, but in the event came to concentrate on the land question and tenant right. Only twice did its members put forward
motions on the Church, Moore in 1853 and Shee in 1854.[27]

The position changed in the 1860s through a combination of
circumstances. One element was the Irish religious census of 1861,
which showed the following position:

Population of Ireland	5,798,967
Members of established Church	693,357
Roman Catholics	4,505,265

Presbyterians	523,291
Methodists	45,399
Other Protestant Dissenters	31,655[28]

Members of the established Church thus formed just over 11·9 per cent of the population, against just over 77·6 per cent for the Roman Catholics, and just over 9 per cent for the Presbyterians. Statistics always provide good ammunition for controversy, and these census returns helped to revive attacks on the established Church of Ireland.

An event which did much to give weight to discussion of the Irish Church question, and new impetus to the attack on the establishment, was the foundation in December 1864 of the National Association of Ireland.[29] The intention of the National Association was to launch a constitutional movement for the redress of three specific Irish grievances. A resolution stated its objects thus:

> 1st. To secure by law to occupiers of land in Ireland compensation for all valuable improvements effected by them. 2nd. The disendowment of the Irish Protestant Church, and the application of its revenues to purposes of national utility, saving all vested rights. 3rd. Freedom and equality of education for the several denominations and classes in Ireland.[30]

Though the Irish Church question was only one of three objectives, and placed second in the list, it was of great importance that a new and powerful movement had taken it up. The National Association had the support of the Irish hierarchy. Seven prelates were on the platform at its first meeting, including Cullen, Apostolic Delegate in Ireland, who was to receive his cardinal's hat in 1866. It also attracted widespread lay support, and set out from the beginning to gain also the support of Liberal opinion in Britain. In this the Irish Church question was of particular value, for disestablishment and disendowment was a cause which would attract Liberal Dissenters in Britain. Education, on the other hand, where the Irish hierarchy wanted to revert to a denominational schools system and to get a charter for a Catholic university, was a subject on which they were likely to clash with British Liberals, especially Dissenters. Land was a subject which successive tenant right bills had shown to be bristling with technical

4

difficulties. Thus the Irish Church question was tactically the best of the three objectives to push forward.

It was the more so because it held out the prospect of an alliance with the Liberation Society. O'Neill Daunt, one of the principal movers behind the National Association, had been in correspondence with the leaders of the Liberation Society since 1856. He had worked to make an alliance feasible by persuading the Liberation Society to drop its agitation against the Maynooth grant, and by insisting that the National Association adopt a policy of voluntaryism—that is, that it should press for the disendowment of the Irish Church without asking that any of the endowments should pass to the Catholic Church.[31] From 1865 the co-operation between the two bodies was close, and in 1867 Carvell Williams, the secretary of the Liberation Society, visited Ireland to see Daunt and six Catholic bishops.

This arrangement, of course, suited the Liberation Society as well as the National Association. The Society saw the established Church in Ireland as the weakest point in the whole system of establishment in the British Isles, and welcomed an active movement in Ireland against it. The *Liberator*, indeed, had often chided the Irish for their apathy, and exhorted them to organize and agitate.[32] Carvell Williams, on his return from Ireland, was confident that the Catholics would refuse any endowment, and that Irish co-operation would be valuable to the Society. He saw too, however, the limits of what could be expected from the National Association, and insisted that the Liberation Society must chiefly count on its influence on the Liberal party to achieve the abolition of the Irish establishment.[33] With this note of caution in private, the Society decided in 1867 to launch a campaign on the Irish Church question. A special committee was set up in July, which reported at the end of October on the propaganda measures to be taken over the next six months.[34] A new series of tracts was launched. A parliamentary breakfast was held for sympathetic Liberals, including ten M.P.s, on 10 March 1868.[35]

The agitation of the Irish Church question on both sides of the Irish Sea was accompanied by increased parliamentary attention to the question. In March 1865 Dillwyn, a Liberal Dissenter, introduced a motion in the Commons on the state of the Irish Church. Then, in April 1866 and again in May 1867, Sir John

Gray, an Irish Liberal M.P. and owner of the Dublin *Freeman's Journal*, a leading Liberal newspaper which generally reflected the views of the Irish hierarchy (though Gray himself was a Protestant), put down motions that Parliament consider the state of the Irish Church.[36] The second of these, in 1867, was lost by only twelve votes. The *Liberator* took some pleasure in tabulating the progress made since Edward Miall had moved a similar motion in 1856. The number of M.P.s in favour of the motion (including tellers) had risen from 95 to 185; the majority against it had gone down from 70 to 12; and the number of Liberals voting against it had gone down from 36 to 9.[37] This was indeed progress.

The alliance between the Liberation Society and the National Association, and the general support given by many members of the Liberal party to the movement for disestablishment, ensured a vigorous discussion of the Irish Church question between 1865 and 1868. In this debate, the same arguments were repeatedly used by both sides, and, when in 1868 Gladstone carried his resolutions on disestablishment in the House of Commons, the ground was gone over again. The general election of 1868, fought primarily on the issue of the Irish Church, saw the same arguments renewed in the press and from platforms all over the country. Neither controversialists nor the public seem to have wearied in the fight, but the modern reader may, and it will be best to attempt a summary of the arguments rather than to follow them in detail.

The arguments for disestablishing and disendowing the Irish Church may be summed up under four heads: the argument from numbers; the argument from wealth; the argument from history, nationality, and religion; and the argument from politics.

The argument from numbers was very simple: that it was wrong for the Church of a small minority of the Irish people (under 12 per cent by the census of 1861) to possess the position of privilege conferred by establishment. For Irish Catholics, forming about three-quarters of the population, such a situation was unjust and vexatious. The argument was readily supported by making a comparison with England. "We English", said *The Times*, "rest our Church on its popular basis—that is, on the basis of numbers." Nobody could expect the people, once represented in Parliament, to tolerate the ascendancy of a single communion which was not ascendant in numbers.[38] An Irish clergyman (though not a typical one) wrote in similar terms: "Can any one suppose that if the members of the present Church of England dwindled down to a twelfth of the population, the people would for one moment consent to that Church remaining the Established Church of the country?"[39]

The argument from numbers lay behind all the other arguments, and at a time when the principle of democracy was gaining ground it gave them added weight. It was obviously connected with the argument from the wealth of the Irish Church, one aspect of which was that funds which should properly be used for the benefit of the whole Irish people were being devoted to a small minority. Not only this, but the resources of the Irish Church were grossly disproportionate to its needs. Here the Church presented a broad target, and its assailants made the most of it. The *Freeman's Journal*, which ran its own survey of the Irish Church while the Royal Commission was at work, hammered away repeatedly at this point. In the united diocese of Cashel, the *Freeman* found 13,853 Church members, cared for by 152 clergymen with an annual revenue of £43,137 between them. In the same area there were 354,779 Catholics. In the city of Cashel itself, there was an Anglican bishop, with a cathedral and its dignitaries, amid a population of 282 Church members and 4,066 Catholics. The Archdeacon of Cashel, who held also the benefice of Thurles, received according to the *Freeman* a higher income than the Catholic Archbishop of Cashel, who happened to live in the Archdeacon's parish.[40] In the united diocese of Tuam there were 17,157 Church members, and 488,907 Catholics, and the whole structure and endowments of the established Church were devoted to the benefit of 3·4 per cent of the population.[41] This was the most extreme case, but in none of the dioceses, even in Ulster, was there an Anglican majority.[42] The *Freeman* repeatedly pointed out the vast expenditure which would be needed to endow the Catholic Church in Ireland on the same scale as the established Church, calculating per head of the membership of each. There is no need to labour the point further, or to illustrate it as contemporaries did with particular examples of benefices with high incomes and few Church members.

The wealth of the Irish Church was thus disproportionate to its membership and needs. The Church's critics also asserted that much of this wealth found its way into the hands of only a few people, clergy and laymen, even within the membership of the Church. James Godkin examined the wills of Irish bishops and archbishops dying between 1822 and 1867, and found that twenty of them had left a total of £861,868. (He did not point out that this doubtless included money which did not come from Church sources.[43]) There was a certain amount of episcopal nepotism in appointments to good benefices—though this did not always mean bad appointments. Edward Stopford, Bishop of Meath, for example, in 1844 appointed one of his sons, E. A. Stopford, as Archdeacon of Meath and incumbent of the union of Kells, with a net income of £1,211.[44] The archdeacon was an able man, and in 1869 was one of the few Irish clergy who accepted the inevitability of disestablishment; but the manner of his appointment remained.

More serious was the frequent practice by which Church lands were leased at rents and renewal fines well below the current value, to the benefit of Irish landed families, often themselves connected with, or belonging to, the episcopacy. The *Freeman's* survey of the Church emphasized this point with repeated examples. The profitable lands of the diocese of Lismore were let at an average rate of 4s. 3d. per acre per annum; among the families who held them were the Beresfords, who provided two successive Archbishops of Armagh in the nineteenth century.[45] The diocese of Armagh's profitable lands, amounting to over 100,000 acres, produced an average income of 3s. 10d. per acre; the principal tenants included the Ulster Protestant families of Vance, Archdall, Stronge, Graham, Leslie, and Maxwell, as well as Lords Caledon, Cremorne, and Belmore.[46] The Irish Church Commission itself gave similar information, reporting for example that the Duke of Abercorn, Conservative Lord Lieutenant of Ireland 1866–8 and as such the most prominent layman in the Irish Church, held 6,133 acres of the episcopal lands of Derry at a total rent of £134 12s. 1½d. per annum, and renewal fines of £678 11s. 9d.[47] For comparison, the *Freeman* noted that the diocese of Limerick leased its small episcopal lands, on the poorer west side of the country, at an average of just over £1 per acre per annum. Sir John Gray argued in the House of Commons that the landlords who took advantage of these profitable arrangements were the true spoliators of the Irish Church.[48] Gray's paper, the *Freeman*, was perhaps more to the point when it claimed that the Church was allowing its political allies to hold its lands at nominal rents.[49] Loss of revenue was simply the price paid by the established Church for political protection.

The arguments of numbers and of wealth merged naturally with the arguments from history, nationality, and religion. All these three elements were fused together in the outlook of Irish Catholics. They felt that the lands and other endowments of the established Church had been unjustly usurped in the past from Catholic owners and Catholic purposes. They felt, as an article attributed to Cardinal Cullen said, that they were "unjustly obliged to support a church which they disown and a religion which they abhor".[50] They still resented, that is, the imposition of the tithe rent-charge, even though this was since 1838 only paid directly by landlords, few of whom were Catholics. They resented too, and probably more deeply, the fact of the establishment of the Irish Church, because by its very existence it symbolized Protestant ascendancy in Irish social and political life. The facts that by the 1860s that ascendancy was no longer what it had been half a century before, or that the established Church had less political influence than the Catholic hierarchy in Ireland, were of little importance in Catholic minds. Indeed, as the substance of Protestant ascendancy diminished, so the incentive and opportunity to do away with the appearance increased.

These grievances of the mid-nineteenth century had behind them the weight of the collective historical memory of the Irish people. In the anti-establishment literature of the 1860s the familiar figure of Oliver Cromwell appeared alongside that of Adam Loftus, Archbishop of Dublin for most of Elizabeth's reign; and the Cromwellian confiscations in Ireland alongside the penal laws against Catholics of the eighteenth century. The *Freeman* held that the attempt to force the religion of the conquerors on the conquered had been "the fatal blunder of the Irish policy of England", and that the deep sense of wrong felt by Catholics against the established Church was rooted in the inherited consciousness of generations of persecution.[51] This theme was frequently supported by quotation from a charge of 1866 by William Fitzgerald, the Anglican Bishop of Killaloe, in which he said that the penal laws had been designed to crush Catholics "into a state of hopeless poverty, ignorance, discontent, and undying hostility to everything that bore the hateful name of English".[52]

Such support from the other side was welcome, especially as it fitted in with another theme of the attack on the established Church: that it was an alien Church—a phrase which Disraeli had used in 1844, and which was repeatedly cast in his teeth in 1868.* The *Freeman* was careful to refer to the established Church always as Anglican, never as the Irish Church or the Church of Ireland. It was an alien Church, imposed by English legislation in the sixteenth century and maintained by English power ever since. It was a badge of servitude, in another of the phrases of the day, and its disestablishment was an essential step along the road to the restoration of Irish nationality.

Finally, the argument from politics was that disestablishment and disendowment were certainly an essential step, possibly the decisive step, towards a general solution of the Irish question. O'Neill Daunt, at the meeting to found the National Association on 29 December 1864, moved a resolution: "That we demand the disendowment of the Established Church in Ireland as a condition without which social peace and stability, general respect for the laws, and unity of sentiment and action for national objects, can never prevail in Ireland."[53] The *Freeman* put it even more strongly: "The Church question lies at the root of all the other grievances of Ireland." The education question originated in an attempt to make the people Protestant for the benefit of the established Church; the Church's lands and its arrangements with landlords were an obstacle to a settlement of the land question. Statesmen, while dealing with the symptoms of Irish discontent must remove the *fons et origo malorum*—the established Church.[54]

The same view was expressed in English newspapers. The *Daily Telegraph* (then a popular radical paper), wrote on 17 March 1868 that the Irish Church "must cease to exist", thus tolling "the knell

---

* "That dense population in extreme distress inhabits an island where there is an Established Church which is not their Church [loud cheers from the Opposition], and a territorial aristocracy the richest of whom live in distant capitals. Thus you have a starving population, an absentee aristocracy, and an alien Church, and in addition the weakest executive in the world. That is the Irish question." Quoted in W. F. Monypenny and G. E. Buckle, *The Life of Benjamin Disraeli, Earl of Beaconsfield* (new edn, in two volumes, London 1929), vol. I, pp. 589–90.

of the last great badge of conquest and ascendancy in Ireland".
The *Pall Mall Gazette* commented on 12 March 1868 that the
Irish Church question was the test of English honesty: if you did
not destroy the established Church, no one would believe you intended to do justice to Ireland at all. It was thus the indispensable
prelude to all reform, without which no other measure could be
effective.

It must be noted that this optimistic view of the far-reaching
results of Irish disestablishment was not shared by all those who
advocated the measure. The *Saturday Review*, for example, believed that when the establishment had been given up, the Irish
would demand the revision of the land system, and then independence. Land tenure was a very difficult matter, and independence was impossible; but with the establishment gone, one could
resist further demands on firmer ground, and use force in case of
rebellion with a clear conscience.[55] *The Times* on occasion took a
similar line, identifying Irish aspirations with what it took to be
those of the whole Roman Catholic Church. A leading article
claimed that no reasonable person thought it possible to satisfy the
Irish people or Catholics generally:

> . . . as their pretensions are beyond the range of possibilities, they
> never can be satisfied. . . . Their ambition ascends to the temporal
> and spiritual ascendancy of the world; and even though they would
> not avow what they cannot at present hope for, they would find it
> impossible to point to the goal beyond which they could never
> aspire . . . There is no known, no imaginable scheme of peace and
> amity that Rome could make with this, the chief Protestant Power
> in the world. That title twenty-five millions of us still claim; that title
> five millions of us abhor . . . Let all be conceded that can be conceded
> next year, and the Irish Catholics will be neither thankful nor satis-
> fied. What of that? Who ever said they would be? . . . We shall have
> done a great act of justice, and shall feel comparatively at ease. Our
> cause will be stronger. The responsibility of discontent will not rest
> upon us.[56]

The Times, however, was far from holding this view consistently. It
argued on other occasions that disestablishment would do more
than anything else to appease antagonisms of race and class in
Ireland;[57] and again, that what was at stake in the election of 1868
was "nothing more nor less than the temper and policy of the
future government of Ireland, and, dependent upon this, the feel-

ings of the inhabitants of Ireland towards ourselves, the peaceful-ness—we may almost venture to say the unity—of the kingdom".[58]

This was a formidable case; but it in no way dismayed the defenders of the Irish establishment. Their arguments lacked the massive simplicity of their opponents' case; but they were pre-pared to dispute every inch of ground, and to produce almost innumerable arguments to justify the position of the established Church. It is clear that behind much of the argument lay the solid ground of vested interest, political, social, and financial; clear too that the protagonists on both sides dearly loved a fight—a seemingly irrefutable argument was merely a challenge to their ingenuity, to which they rose with relish. But it is also plain that most of the views advanced in argument were sincerely held, and that many of the defenders felt that great issues were at stake.

The defenders of the established Church were willing to meet its assailants on their own ground. The argument from numbers was met in different ways. Some of the attacks, notably those by Skeats for the Liberation Society,[59] were on particular anomalies. For these the explanation often was that the Church Temporali-ties Act of 1833 had preserved vested rights. Many clergymen appointed before 1833 were still alive in 1868, so that there had been no opportunity to suspend their benefices under the Act. But these were remnants of the past, and should not be used as illus-trations of normal conditions in the Irish Church. It was possible to find other mistakes of detail, and a good deal of time was spent in doing so.[60] It was also argued, on the matter of numbers, that since the rather rough religious census made by the Education Commissioners in 1834 the proportion of Church members and Methodists (taken together, as they had been in 1834) in the population had slightly increased.[61]

None of this detailed statistical in-fighting could make any im-pression on the solid fact that about three-quarters of the people of Ireland were Catholics. But this too could be met, in two differ-ent ways. One was the argument frequently used by conserva-tively minded participants in debates on the question of franchise reform: that a minority must be weighed as well as counted. The members of the Irish Church, it was claimed, included most of the people of rank and substance, industry and enterprise, in Ireland. To accept the argument of mere numbers as decisive in the question of the established Church would in effect concede the case for manhood suffrage. Alfred Lee, for example, asked: "After all, is not the democratic question of universal suffrage at the bottom of this matter? If mere numbers are to outweigh education, property, and intelligence in a country, to what are we advancing?"[62] By this line of defence, the argument could be shifted on to different ground altogether. The second way to deal with the fact of the massive Catholic majority in Ireland was by taking the Act of Union to mean what it said: that Ireland was no longer a separate State, nor the Church of Ireland a separate Church. In these circumstances, Ireland was only the same as other places in the United Kingdom where the members of the established Church happened to be in a minority—Wales and Cornwall were obvious examples. Thus again the ground of the argument could be changed, this time to the general question of establishment in the country as a whole, and the validity of a numerical test for Church establishments. As one English defender of the Irish Church wrote:

> The continuance of the English establishment is made a question of statistics alone. Our national testimony to the truth of God . . . comes to an end. All that survives in its stead is a national testimony to the doubtful result of a gigantic addition sum, which affirms that Dissenters and Romanists are still outnumbered by English Churchmen.[63]

The argument from nationality could also be met either frontally or by setting it in a different context. It was possible to take the high line: that the established Church was the true Catholic Church of Ireland, and of native growth. It was the Church of St Patrick himself: "Every Bishop of the Established Church there can trace back his Apostolic commission in clear and unbroken succession to the Apostle of Ireland himself."[64] Again, Magee, the Dean of Cork and later Bishop of Peterborough, made an ingenious reply to F. D. Maurice, who had argued that Protestantism in Ireland was anti-national.[65] Magee took up some references of Maurice's to the Church of England asserting national sovereignty against foreign interference, and declared that in this sense the Irish Church was national: it did not accept the domination of a foreign potentate, as did the Church of Rome. This would certainly have been widely accepted by Irish Protestants at the time. Magee went further. If Maurice was right to say that the Irish establishment was an English work, and the English had no right to establish their Church there, what right had they to be there at all? Or to be anywhere outside England, for that matter? To acknowledge the argument of nationality, which entailed the independence of nationalities, meant the dismemberment of the British empire.[66] It may be doubted how far Magee meant this line of argument to be taken seriously. It was doubtless another attempt to get away from the justification of the Irish establishment on Irish grounds, and to get on to wider issues of politics and consequences. A hundred years later, with the British empire in fact dissolved through the action of the principle of nationality, it is apparent that the Dean of Cork spoke more truly than he knew.

The argument from wealth was met partly by disputing the figures for the revenue of the Irish Church, by denying that those revenues were excessive for the Church's needs, and by asserting the sanctity of property. Alfred Lee maintained that the true net revenue of the Church was only about £540,000 per annum—at one point he had produced a substantially lower figure, but had been forced to amend it.[67] It was possible to argue too that even where a benefice contained only a small number of Church members, often the distances involved were so great that pastoral care could involve a good deal of time and trouble, so that comparatively high stipends were not out of place.[68]

The argument from the rights of property was much more important. The position of most of the defenders of the Irish Church was simple. The property of the Church was not national property but its own. It had its origin either in private gifts or in settlements by statute, which gave the Church as good a title as anyone in Ireland. The Church held a good deal of its property, for example, under the Act of Settlement of 1662, on which the titles of many Irish landlords also rested. To the statutory right could be added the prescriptive right of three hundred years' possession. Any measures which broke a title as good as this would endanger the whole institution of property, not only in Ireland but elsewhere. Did the Russells, as the *Quarterly Review* asked, have any better right to Woburn Abbey?[69] Sometimes the rights of property were presented as though they were total. On the other hand, it was sometimes accepted, even by defenders of the Irish

Church, that the State had rights and duties in relation to Church property. It had the duty, for example, to ensure that trusts under which property had been given were fulfilled. Disraeli in the House of Commons in March 1869 distinguished between the duties of the State in relation to private property and corporate property. For private property the State was a guardian, and had simply to protect its ward. For corporate property the State acted as trustee, with the prime duty of ensuring that the intentions of the founder of the corporation were fulfilled, as far as changing circumstances permitted. If a trustee found that the resources of the trust were extravagantly beyond what was necessary, or that the purpose of the trust was pernicious, then he must consider redistribution of the funds and property. But under no circumstances should a trustee appropriate such property to himself.[70] The *Quarterly Review* accepted that "unquestionably the State may, if there are sufficiently urgent reasons, deprive any individual or his heirs of what he now enjoys". It could deal similarly with a corporation. If it were demonstrated that the Irish Church had a larger revenue than it needed, then the State might equitably divert the surplus.[71] Both these views allowed the State some discretion in dealing with the rights of property, but the defenders of the Church held that in fact its resources were not excessive for its needs, and that it was fulfilling a trust which was not harmful to the national interest. Disendowment, therefore, was not justifiable.

The argument from the rights of property was a strong one in a society which had a high regard for such rights. Those who attacked the Irish establishment had to make a particular effort to counter it. They did this by arguing that Church property was to a large extent national property, using the arguments of Edward Miall that the tithe was a tax for public purposes; or by maintaining that in Ireland the State had endowed the Church for its own political ends.[72] This latter argument was similar to the ground taken by Lowe, the Chancellor of the Exchequer, in February 1869. Lowe wrote to Gladstone:

> I wish to make one observation on what seems to me the only principle on which we can justify the disendowment of the Irish Church. That principle is, that *the property of bodies corporate founded for public purposes is the property of the State from whatever source it may be obtained*

subject only to a due provision for existing interests of individuals. If we go behind this principle and enter into the question of the sources whence the property came we leave ourselves no simple and intelligible justification for what we do and involve ourselves in endless subtleties and technicalities.[73]

Just how simple and intelligible Lowe's justification was may be doubted, for everything depended on what one meant by "public purposes". This would presumably cover schools, colleges, hospitals, borough corporations; on a wide interpretation it might be held to cover commercial companies also. The limits might be extended almost indefinitely. Nor is it clear *a priori* why the property of bodies corporate founded for public purposes should be the property of the State. Such a bald declaration did not meet, for example, the position set out by the *Church Times*:

> What the State gave the State can take away, but we utterly deny the principle that the State can, without breach of faith, alienate property given, on the faith of the then existing laws, by men now dead—whether last year or three centuries since—for a definite purpose, religious or secular.[74]

Another justification, perhaps more intelligible but still by no means simple, was advanced by the *Saturday Review*. This was that the Irish Church had been rendered "a noxious institution" by receiving, in the course of its history, a special character from the State. The Church had become a symbol of the hatred of the conquerors of Ireland for the creed of the conquered, and as such it was incompatible with the good government of Ireland. Its noxious character was bound up with its property as well as with its establishment, but it was not in itself noxious. Therefore, just enough property must be taken away to cleanse the Church, but at that point the government must stop.[75] This had the merit of putting the case firmly on the ground of reason of state, on what was necessary for the good government of Ireland; but exactly how one was to tell when the point was reached when the Irish Church ceased to be noxious was not explained.

There was one other argument, which in Britain is often regarded as virtually decisive: such things had been done before. If one looked back to the sixteenth century, the State had confiscated the property of the monasteries. If one looked back only to the 1830s, the Irish Tithe Act of 1838 had deprived the Church of a quarter of its tithes.[76] This latter act of disendowment had been performed to enable the remaining three-quarters to be collected more easily, and as one of the steps to end the tithe war and so to restore tranquillity to Ireland. It was hard to see why the same should not be done again, on a larger scale, if it were again necessary for the sake of public order and good government. It is interesting, however, that the argument from precedent amounted only to another form of the argument from reason of state. It was a powerful argument, but not one which a Liberal government liked to have in the forefront of its case, nor one which Liberals were normally willing to accept when used by their opponents. It was one, however, which the issue of the rights of property forced into the open, for the only fully satisfactory ground on which property rights could be overridden was that of the greater public good.

These various attempts to refute the arguments of their opponents still left the defenders of the Irish establishment to make their own positive case. This could be done by defending the principle of an established Church. J. T. O'Brien, the Bishop of Ossory, took the high line:

> The true ground on which to justify an Ecclesiastical Establishment is, that the State is bound by its duty, both to God and to the people whom He has committed to its care, to provide, for all who will avail themselves of the provision, means of public worship, according to a pure ritual, and the means of public instruction, according to a sound and Scriptural confession of faith.[77]

James Byrne, one of the more serious and thoughtful writers on this subject in Ireland, also accepted as an axiom that it was the duty of the civil power to provide permanently, and for the whole country, the "beneficial influences of religion".[78] Both permanence and universality were important, in his view. Since the State had this duty, the way to fulfil it was by an established Church, defining establishment as "adoption of a Church by the State as its organ for the religious training of the nation, and the provisions made by the State for its due performance of this office".[79] The alternative to establishment, and the permanent endowment which went with it, was voluntaryism. Byrne argued that pure voluntaryism could not ensure either permanence or universality. The tide of faith ebbed and flowed, and it was necessary to provide for the lean years between the prosperous times. Equally, he argued, it was not possible for a religious body working on the voluntary principle to carry on missions to the masses in a city without abandoning its principle, because the missionaries would be paid by others than those to whom they ministered. This, of course, was an extremely narrow definition of voluntaryism, as meaning no more than the maintenance of each local church by its own members. But certainly it was widely held then and afterwards that only an established Church had the obligation, and only an endowed Church the resources, to provide its services over the whole country.

Another argument frequently advanced against voluntaryism, and put by Byrne in moderate and persuasive language, was that dependence of clergymen on their congregations had damaging effects. Byrne held that clergy in this position were bound to lower their standards to meet the demands of sectarian zeal—as, for example, Catholic priests in Ireland tended to support the demands of those on whom their livelihood depended. For this reason, he claimed, "free thought on the Christian faith cannot flourish under the congregational system".[80] He believed that government by synods, working by majorities, would have the same effect. This would have particularly serious consequences at that time, when Byrne saw the Christian faith threatened by "the spirit of physical science and the spirit of historical criticism",[81] the latter coming especially from Germany. In Ireland, in view of the attitude of the Catholic Church, the only hope for intellectual salvation was the Irish Church, and this depended on establishment, "which links the religion of the country with its intellect by making the ministry of the Church one of the professions which are naturally selected by able and educated men".[82] This view was certainly too subtle and intellectual for most Irish Churchmen, who probably had little notion of what was going on in German biblical criticism. But it is interesting to see the less intellectual parts of his argument supported by Godkin. Godkin was in favour of disestablishment; his long survey of the Irish Church was scathing on its faults and anomalies; he thought that the life in the Church came from voluntaryism, notably the proprietary churches; and he believed that the Church clung to the territorial system simply because of its interest in the tithe rent-charge. Yet he too argued that the voluntary system, if universally adopted in Ireland, would have deleterious results. In the unceasing effort to raise funds, religious zeal would be excessively stimulated, prejudices inflamed, and differences exaggerated. Superstition on the one hand, fanaticism on the other, would grow. The mass of the people, moreover, would go to church only as paupers, with no right to the services which were paid for by those above them in society. Godkin held that this was wrong; people of all denominations ought to have the right to public worship and the ministrations of their Church guaranteed by the State.[83]

By their similar lines of argument, Godkin and Byrne were both led to the same conclusion: concurrent endowment. Since Byrne believed that it was the State's duty to provide religious ministrations for the whole country, this raised the question of which Church it should choose for the purpose. He argued that in all the denominations which took the Scriptures or Christian tradition for their basis, what was good far outweighed the bad, and so the State should provide some measure of endowment for them all.[84] Godkin agreed, and thought that the funds of the Irish Church should be used for this purpose. Byrne, however, wished to retain establishment as well as endowment. He justified this on the ground that the Church to which the leading classes in the country belonged would be the most influential, and should therefore be adopted by the State as the religious leader of the nation. In Ireland, the leading classes belonged to the then established Church, which should therefore retain its social standing and dignity, while anomalies which were not connected with the principle of establishment should be swept away.[85] So endowment for all would be combined with establishment for some, and all that Byrne thought important would be secured.

All this proceeded from the premiss that it was the duty of the State to provide the means of religious worship and instruction. At the time, this view of the State's duty was widely accepted, though it remained a question whether the State should choose one Church for the purpose, on the ground that it taught the truth, or more than one on the ground of duty to all the people. O'Brien, the Bishop of Ossory, claimed the former,[86] though he also claimed that it was quite possible for the government to support the Irish Church on grounds of truth, and another Church or Churches on grounds of public policy, as it did at Maynooth and through the *Regium Donum* to the Presbyterians.[87] Whately, Archbishop of Dublin from 1831–64, described his view of the State's duty (which was in his opinion the case for concurrent endowment) thus:

> The taxes are a portion of each man's income, which the State takes from him, in order to render to him certain services, which it can perform for him better than he can do for himself. Among these, the most important is the maintenance of religion and of religious education. This service the State does *not* render to the Roman Catholics, and so far it defrauds them.[88]

Whether the duty of the State extended to one Church or more, however, did not matter for the main argument. As long as it was widely assumed that the State had this duty to promote and support religion, then a case for establishment and endowment could be made, and could be applied in some form to Ireland. Only if the fundamental premiss were rejected did the whole structure fall. For the Liberation Society, the rejection of the premiss was its own basic principle, so there was no problem for them. Rejection was difficult for the Catholic hierarchy, which over the rest of Europe accepted the union of Church and State—their separation, indeed, was condemned in the Syllabus of Errors of 1864.[89] Their need for an alliance with British Nonconformists, however, was so great that for the special case of Ireland they too rejected it.

Thus the arguments of the attackers of the Irish Church were disputed and the principle of an established Church was upheld. However, a modern reader of the controversialists who defended the Irish Church has the impression that they were happiest and most confident when they shifted the argument to the question of the consequences of disestablishment in Ireland. These consequences, it was predicted, would be religious, social, and political, they would be extensive, and they would be bad.

It was often assumed, or at any rate asserted, that disestablishment and disendowment would mean the destruction of the Irish Church. Alfred Lee wrote in 1866 that total disendowment would leave 700,000 people in Ireland without the ordinary means of grace.[90] The *Quarterly Review* described Gladstone's resolutions on the Irish Church of March 1868 as "a scheme for the demolition of the Irish Church so complete as to take away the breath of Mr

Bernal Osborne".[91] (Bernal Osborne was a noted opponent of established Churches. It may be doubted whether he was in fact left breathless.) *Blackwood's Magazine* predicted: "The overthrow of the Established Church, as proposed by Mr Gladstone, must be followed almost immediately by the extinction of Protestantism in Ireland." It would not survive for a quarter of a century.[92] Even when such total destruction was not expected, it was asserted that disendowment would mean at least the withdrawal of the Irish Church from the country districts of southern and western Ireland. The scattered Church population in these areas, working on the voluntary system, would not be able to pay their clergy or keep up the parochial system. In consequence, the gentry would move away, and the poor members of the Church would either emigrate or be absorbed into the surrounding Catholic masses.[93]

This belief rested on the assumption that voluntaryism was necessarily equivalent to a purely congregational system, with each individual clergyman dependent upon his own congregation. The experience of the Catholic Church in Ireland, of the Nonconformist Churches in Britain, and of the Anglican Churches overseas in working voluntary systems was apparently ignored, or perhaps seen as irrelevant to Irish conditions. It was true that the Irish laity were accustomed to the services of the Church being provided for them without individual effort, and that this habit of mind would be difficult to change. A phrase in a charge by Bishop Fitzgerald of Killaloe in 1860 may illustrate this. He said that people would "continue, from habit, to think themselves bound (so long at least as they can have churches and ministers without paying for them) one day in the week to attend upon the performance of the public Liturgy . . .".[94] It is interesting that Cardinal Cullen also thought, at least sometimes, that the whole fate of the Irish Church was bound up with its endowments. He wrote privately on 5 April 1868 that the Irish Protestants would resist deprivation "not so much for love of their Church, but because they have no other hope of surviving, without the possession of the riches of this world".[95] An article in the *Irish Ecclesiastical Record*, attributed to Cullen, contained the same view: "They [the Protestant bishops] know Protestantism has no other hold on its followers than the mere temporal endowments. The great motive is money. Remove this inducement, and they will become the followers of Rome."[96] This proved quite unfair to Irish Churchmen (Mr Norman comments: "It was characteristic of Cullen to think the worst of his opponents"), but the defenders of the Irish Church had by their own arguments invited such criticism.

If disestablishment and disendowment led to the destruction, or at least the grave weakening, of the Irish Church, it was clear that the beneficiary of this process would be Catholicism. The result would be the undisputed predominance of the Catholic Church in Ireland. For most Protestants this was of course a threat to the cause of true religion. It was also represented as being contrary to the political interests of the United Kingdom. The *Quarterly Review* developed this theme repeatedly and at length, arguing that the aims of the Catholic hierarchy in Ireland were directly opposed to those of the government, and that Irish Protestants had reason to be afraid of a Catholic tyranny like that in Spain. The Catholic Church was the enemy of all progressive forces (which was an interesting comment from the thoroughly conservative *Quarterly*), and its aim was ecclesiastical despotism.[97] It followed that for any British government to seek the alliance of the Catholic hierarchy in Ireland was a self-defeating policy, bound to end in frustration.

Thus the arguments about the religious consequences merged into those about the political consequences. In addition to the fear of Catholic predominance just mentioned, the political arguments were of three main types. First there were the legalistic ones: that the union of the English and Irish Churches was written into the Act of Union, and to separate them would *ipso facto* terminate the union of the two kingdoms also.[98] This was in law a wholly untenable position, but it was none the less often advanced. The other two arguments were two sides of one proposition: that to disestablish the Irish Church would alienate the Irish Protestants without remedying the real grievances of the rest of the population. It would thus in fact, whatever the legal situation, weaken the union.

The Protestants of Ireland, ran the argument, were the only people who were truly loyal to the Crown and the Union. It would therefore be folly to offend them by taking away their ecclesiastical privileges.[99] In Ireland this argument was given added point by open threats that the loyalty of the Protestants was conditional upon their privileges being maintained. One Irish Protestant told a meeting at the Crystal Palace that twenty or thirty thousand people might, in honesty and loyalty to the Queen, take up arms to defend their rights, and he wondered whether the British army would really be used against them. In the very different surroundings of the schoolhouse at Rathmines, another speaker told his audience that if a government trampled Irish Protestants underfoot it must take the consequences; they would not give up without a fight.[100]

The loyalty of the Protestants would thus be shaken, or even turned to rebellion. But for this price no real advantage would be gained, because the Church represented no substantial grievance. Its disestablishment, and even disendowment, would bring no material relief to Irish Catholics, whose rents would not be reduced even if the money went to different people. The grievance was at most sentimental, and even this was often denied. The Dean of Elphin, Warburton, for example, told Gladstone that the people were not hostile to the Church; his Catholic neighbours came to him for testimonials, their children came to him to be educated at the National School, and even when the Catholic Bishop of Elphin denounced the school he did not lose a single pupil.[101] The real grievances of Ireland were the land question, and behind that the aspirations of nationalism: "a restless craving for some visionary kind of self-assertion against the power of England".[102] To disestablish the Church would not touch these matters, except by whetting the appetite for further concessions. Richard Chenevix Trench, who became Archbishop of Dublin in 1866, set out his view in an apocalyptic vision of the half-century which would follow disestablishment. The movement, once started, would involve the land, for the possession of most of the soil of Ireland by Protestants was a much more impressive "badge of conquest" than the established Church. It would involve too the Vice-Royalty in Ireland, and eventually the position of the Crown itself. The "new ascendancy" of the Catholic Irish would grow; more concessions would be made without satisfying it; until at last the democracy of England, roused by the sufferings of the Irish Protestants and determined to maintain the unity of the Empire, would make a stand. A new struggle between "English strength and Irish weakness" would take place, with the inevitable result of an English victory. Trench's final vision was of the day when "some new Cromwell stands amid the smoking ruins of the civilization and prosperity of this land".[103] It was apocalyptic, not argument, yet it was not very wide of the mark in predicting what was to happen just over fifty years later—except that then the democracy of England, wearied by the 1914–18 war and shaken in its imperial faith, did not fight the Irish war through to its conclusion in 1922. Lloyd George, though threatening instant and terrible war, chose not to be a new Cromwell.

The social consequences which the opponents of disestablishment foresaw were less far-reaching than this. It seemed very likely, indeed, that Protestant ascendancy in society, through predominance in the professions, business, and the armed services, would continue as a result of economic and educational circumstances. However, one prominent argument was that in the country districts of the south and west, from which the disendowed Church would have to withdraw, the population would lose the valuable social asset of a resident country gentleman, in the shape of the local rector. The beneficed clergyman was a man of some means and social standing, who, if he did nothing else, at least spent money in the district. Without his presence, an area would grow poorer, especially since without him the lay gentry, if they were Protestant, might not stay either. The argument of the resident country gentleman in a black coat was taken seriously.[104]

These were consequences predicted for Ireland. It was also held that disestablishment in Ireland must be followed by the same process in England, and that therefore the English establishment must be defended even in its imperfect outworks across the Irish Sea. In part this was a natural assumption from the attacks to which the English establishment was already being subjected, and from the declared aim of the Liberation Society to secure general disestablishment, using Ireland as the best place to start. Indeed, because the position of the Church of England was felt to be in serious danger from several other directions, the reaction to the attack in Ireland was very likely stronger than it might otherwise have been. It would in any case be easy to move by logical progression from disestablishment in Ireland to the same in England. It was easy for a dealer in statistics to find within the Church of England anomalies similar to those in the Irish Church: in disparity of revenue between benefices, and between revenue received and work required; in lack of Church population in various areas; and in illogical distribution of the general revenue of the Church.[105] If it were once accepted that the Church of a minority should not be established, then it would follow at once that in Wales and Cornwall the Church of England would lose its position. It was even questonable whether the Church of England commanded a majority of adherents within England, or the Church of Scotland in Scotland.[106] Indeed, if the principle of establishment were to be abandoned in Ireland, on what ground or by what logic could it be sustained in England or Scotland?

The consequences of disestablishment in Ireland, as predicted by the defenders of the Irish establishment, would bring various forms of disaster to the Protestant religion in Ireland, to the union, and to the establishment in England. So the battle raged between extremes of argument on either side. There were also among the controversialists a few moderates. They were not widely popular at the time, but they deserve particular attention for their independence of mind and for the interest of their contribution to the debate.

Among the assailants of the Irish Church, Aubrey de Vere combined harsh judgements on that Church, wittily expressed, with sympathy for it and its members, and a solution to the Irish Church question which would have retained a part of its endowments. De Vere was a poet, a friend of Wordsworth and Newman, and a convert to the Catholic Church after being educated at Trinity College, Dublin, and intending at one time to become a clergyman in the Irish Church. As such he stood aside from the main body of Irish Catholics, and unlike some converts he did not become more Catholic than the Pope.[107] He did not deal lightly with the established Church. "What is the Ecclesiastical Settlement? It is one by which the whole of the ancient religious endowments of Ireland were, and are, taken from a nation and given to a small minority—taken from the poor and given to the rich." He termed the established Church in Connaught "the Church Invisible"—dioceses and dignitaries, cathedrals and chapters, all listed in directories but with no real existence. They were in truth ideal dioceses, and several had to be clubbed together to make one real diocese—and that with a laity no larger than the population of a single parish in an English city. "The whole system is a flight of bad poetry." The solid realities of the Irish people and their religion were surrounded by conspicuous objects with no reality, and this could not last—"Statesmanship is not a department of scene-painting".[108] (It will be seen that de Vere added to the normal attacks on the Irish Church the assets of style and imagination.)

But for all the bite of his polemics, de Vere remained to some degree detached. He had a sense of perspective: "Life is a long wrangle; and each party strings together its wrongs in lineal succession from the Reformation to the Revolution, and from the Revolution to the last election. . . ."[109] He urged Irish Catholics to appreciate the position of their opponents: "They have to deal with angry men whose weapons of war have lost their edge, and with good men whose hostility is sometimes an erring form of loyalty." Catholics must not seek revenge for the past; to deprive men of endowments because they should not have ascendancy would be to imitate the injustice which they denounced.[110] He recognized too the improved state of the Irish Church, and believed that this came from within as well as from the legislation of the 1830s.[111] His conclusion was that religious equality was undoubtedly necessary for the pacification of Ireland and for the remedying of a gross injustice, but that this should be done not by secularizing Church property but by distributing it fairly between Protestants and Catholics.[112] He thus came out for concurrent endowment, a course adopted by only one of the Irish Catholic bishops (Moriarty, Bishop of Kerry). The Irish hierarchy as a whole rejected this solution in order to secure their alliance with the Liberation Society and English Nonconformists. De Vere, like Moriarty, was uneasy about this alliance with Nonconformity and advanced Liberalism. "The policy of secularization", he wrote, "is advocated by one political party alone. That party is the one least likely to benefit Ireland in the long run, and least capable of understanding what is best in her." (Moriarty also pointed out that the principle of secularization could be used to justify depriving the Catholic Church of its endowments, as had recently been done in Italy. It was a dangerous precedent to set.[113]) De Vere felt that the natural connection of Irish Catholicism was not with advanced Liberalism but with the supporters of order and stability. He thought that there must be increasing numbers in both the great English parties who would see the folly of alienating "those who, as the children of a hierarchical Church, resting on authority and antiquity, must naturally be the friends of order".[114] De Vere had his own fears of revolution, centred on the Fenians, and he saw good reason to strengthen the fabric of government and social order—"The Fenians are our Americo-Irish Socialists—one section of a conspiracy which works its unholy catacombs beneath the civilization of the world."[115]

Like de Vere, Maziere Brady might in one way be classed simply among the controversialists. Though a clergyman of the established Church in Ireland, he was an advocate of disestablishment and a vigorous combatant in the battles of history and statistics. He wrote at length to demonstrate that the Apostolic Succession in Ireland remained with the Catholic bishops; carried on a running fight with A. T. Lee about the revenues of the Irish Church; and subjected the Report of the Irish Church Commissioners to detailed criticism.[116] But some aspects of Brady's contributions to the debate set him apart from the normal run of the controversy. He drew attention to the changed political situation of the Irish Church. "As a political machine", he wrote, "the Establishment is every day becoming less useful to the State." By the 1860s it had no function beyond that of furnishing a few rewards to government supporters.[117] He also foresaw shrewdly the probabilities of the future, arguing that, if disestablishment were delayed, it might come later with much greater risk to the Church, because the proportion of the wealthy and landed classes who were Protestants would diminish, and the attitude of the Catholics might well get worse.[118] Moreover, even if disestablishment were staved off, the Church would remain under constant attack, and would be condemned to a political struggle which would absorb energies better used in the work of the Church in other ways.[119]

Brady insisted on separating the interests of the Church from the interests represented by the establishment. He held that "no necessary connection exists either between Protestant ascendency in Ireland and purity of religion, or between the Church and the Irish Establishment".[120] The Church was a religious institution, and its endowments were valuable as a means of doing its religious work; but, if this means proved unjust or inexpedient, it could adopt another.[121] He believed that the establishment was a burden on the Church, and asserted that "in proportion as the Church Established seeks more earnestly to live as a Church, so will her position as an Establishment become less tolerable".[122] On the practical issues involved, Brady argued that Irish Churchmen should create a body of Church property and revenue which they could rightly call their own. The nucleus of a new endowment would be formed by the compensation for vested rights paid by the government at the time of disendowment, and the gifts of Churchmen could be relied on to supplement this fund. "The abolition of the Establishment in Ireland, if it led to such an issue, would be the revival of the Church."[123] Finally, like de Vere, Brady thought in terms of some form of concurrent endowment, and suggested that, after compensation had been allowed for, the property of the Irish Church might be used to endow the Catholic Church.[124]

Brady was an exception among clergymen of the Irish Church. William Bence Jones was just as exceptional among its laymen. He was a landowner of County Cork, an improving, scientific farmer, who made a point of living on his estate and seeing that it was worked thoroughly. He was a Balliol man, a friend of Tait who was successively Bishop of London and Archbishop of Canterbury. In 1868-9 Bence Jones was not yet the national figure which he was briefly to become during his struggle against a boycott in 1880, but he was a man of some reputation, consulted by ministers on agricultural matters. He was a man of ability and great independence of mind, who cared little what others thought. He always knew he was right, and often was—an irritating characteristic.[125]

It was in the nature of the man to stand no nonsense from either side. He was scathing about the credulity of Englishmen, and especially English Liberals, in dealing with Irish affairs. "Now, in no place on earth is the art of dressing up for a purpose a story founded on a modicum of facts, or on no facts at all, so well understood as in Ireland." Fenianism and the ill-will towards England which it demonstrated had taken people in England by surprise, but they should not have done, because the ill-will had always been there. They had also been taken too seriously by those who did not know their Ireland—"Nobody goes into anything of the kind without keeping one eye constantly fixed over his shoulder to secure a safe retreat. . . ." The art of the Irish was to "talk and act sedition and half sedition to perfection . . .".[126] He thought it unwise, therefore, to make Fenianism a reason for far-reaching measures in Ireland. (It may be that Bence Jones, with his practical turn of mind, failed to penetrate the mysteries of romantic nationalism.) Moreover, in his experience the ecclesiastical issue did not cause profound discontent or bitterness.[127] He thus denied some of the premisses on which the demand for disestablishment was based. On the other hand, he asserted freely that parishes with tiny Church membership were a scandal. Even those with a hundred or two hundred members were not satisfactory—"20 or 40 families do not give half work to a clergyman".[128] Such parishes were "enough to chill the life out of any man of energy. How any man of ability or vigour or earnestness, who has ever thought what it means to be a minister of Christ, can be contented to must out his life in such a position, even with the advantage of a good income, is quite beyond the comprehension of laymen of intelligence."[129] This was a favourite theme with Bence Jones. "There is a feeling in Ireland that a clergyman ought not to have hard work, and has a right to complain if he has. The work that a doctor or lawyer does for the same income would be thought too much for a clergyman. But this must be changed."[130] Bence Jones was unwilling to allow the Church to be less well run than one of his farms.

Having dealt his blows to both sides, Bence Jones offered his own solution to the Irish Church question. He thought that the true object of disestablishment should be to get rid of Protestant ascendancy, and the exclusive privileges and anomalies of the Irish Church, while leaving that Church its fair rights and a fair chance for the future. The only way to achieve this was by an equitable compromise. Bence Jones held that the plan taken up by Gladstone in 1868, to strip the Irish Church of its revenues, the Catholics of the Maynooth Grant, and the Presbyterians of the *Regium Donum*, rested on no principle but mutual hatred. No good would come of it.

That which is most wanting in Ireland is that Protestants and Roman Catholics should in matters of religion look on each other as fellow

Christians ... but the practice on both sides is to act as if it was otherwise. It would not so much matter if they would even look on each other as erring Christians, provided only they really felt each other to be Christians at all. The result is very discreditable to both religions.[131]

He too therefore advocated a form of concurrent endowment, arguing that with proper handling the revenues of the Irish Church could both provide income for a reduced number of Anglican clergy, and meet also the Maynooth Grant and the *Regium Donum*. He also proposed that glebe-houses and land should be provided for the Catholic clergy. Such a compromise would be to the benefit of the Irish Church. It would save it from falling back on the voluntary system, which Bence Jones believed would be difficult to work in Ireland.[132] At the same time the Church would have to group its parishes and get rid of the scandalous ones. "I do not put any faith in the assertions of the benefits of disestablishment; nor, on the other hand, do I believe in the extraordinary virtues Mr Gladstone is in the habit of ascribing to the Irish clergy. But I think that anything that compels the clergy to do more work will be eminently useful to the Church."[133]

Concurrent endowment was an idea common to all these three writers, who contrived to stand, even if only a little, outside the battle. It was an idea with other, and better-known, advocates, one of whom was Earl Grey. In 1866 he proposed a scheme to treat the property of the Irish Church as a general fund for the religious instruction of the Irish people, and to apply it to that purpose through the three main Churches.[134] In March 1868 he saw that the tide of opinion was setting strongly in favour of simple disestablishment and disendowment. This, he thought, would be better than leaving the position as it stood, but it would still be a great public misfortune which it was worth trying to avoid. Grey believed that it would exacerbate religious strife in Ireland, and cause lasting resentment among the Protestants. Above all he wished to preserve the principle of state concern for religion.

Disestablishment and disendowment in Ireland [he wrote to Tait] would inflict a heavy blow on the English Church as involving a distinct recognition of the "Voluntary principle". Dividing the Church property in Ireland on the contrary instead of helping to establish this dangerous principle, wd. amount to a new recognition of the duty of the State to make some public provision for the religious instruction of the people, in a form acceptable to them, the only principle on which as I think an established Church can be defended.[135]

Grey therefore tried, both in private and in public, to secure acceptance for concurrent endowment.[136] He continued to believe that it might prove politically possible, because it might attract the support of Churchmen, and because he thought it was what the Catholics really wanted, though they dared not say so for fear of losing the alliance of the Dissenters.[137]

The unanimity of these four moderates in favour of concurrent endowment is impressive. They were at one in their opinion with a number of others, including Lord John Russell, Tait, Lord Dufferin, and, interestingly, J. M. Ludlow.[138] Ludlow had, with Maurice, been prominent in the Christian Socialist movement of the early 1850s. Like Maurice, he was deeply attached to the principle of establishment. He wished to avoid voluntaryism, which he described as the application of the law of supply and demand to religion, and therefore the negation of the social need of worship, which should be met by society, just as society provided poor laws and factory laws, and was being urged to provide education. Rather than have mere voluntaryism in Ireland, Ludlow would have preferred an exclusive Catholic establishment.[139] Concurrent endowment thus had no lack of intelligent and influential supporters, and it would have made an extremely interesting experiment to be tried in Ireland. In June 1869, when Gladstone's Irish Church Bill came before the House of Lords, provisions for concurrent endowment were inserted into it by a majority of the peers. But the House of Commons would not have it, and victory went, not to the moderates, but to the advocates of disestablishment and disendowment.[140]

The arguments discussed above used up a vast amount of time and thought and print; they were always interesting, sometimes ingenious, and effective to a degree which varied according to the premisses from which an observer regarded the situation. But whichever side may be thought to have won the debate on the merits of its arguments, the question remained at bottom one of politics. It would be decided not by arguments, but by calculations of what was politically possible and politically advantageous.

This was inevitable. The Irish establishment had had its origin in politics; it had been kept in being for political purposes; if at any time it had depended on passing the test of pure reason and abstract argument, it is doubtful whether it could have done so. This did not mean that the agitation and the public meetings, the speeches and the pamphleteering, were wasted or irrelevant. Even though the question was ultimately one of politics, no serious political move on the Irish Church would be made unless there was an active public opinion on the subject, which could on the one hand make itself felt, and on the other hand could be appealed to by politicians. To raise a cry in the country, to agitate the question, to argue it out—these were essential preliminaries to action in Parliament, even though they did not make any such action certain, nor decide what form it might take.

Indeed, by the end of 1867 and the beginning of 1868, it appeared that some of the drive was going out of the agitation for Irish disestablishment without its object having been achieved. The National Association, after a successful start, suffered from internal difficulties and divisions, and from the fact that it spent its energies on three objectives rather than on one. The Irish Catholic hierarchy tended to concentrate, between 1865 and the beginning of 1868, on the question of a Catholic university, which seemed more likely to reach a practical conclusion than the question of the established Church.[141] In Britain the Liberation Society was active and vigorous, but its power was limited, as its own leaders well knew. If left on their own, these engines which propelled the agitation against the Irish Church might well have run out of steam. Certainly, if alone, they could not have reached their destination. As in the case of the Anti-Corn Law League in the 1840s, and in that of the movement for Irish Home Rule in the 1880s, the essential condition for success was to win the support of one of the great political parties. For that, the situation at the beginning of 1868 did not look hopeful.

3

GLADSTONE TAKES THE OFFENSIVE

At the beginning of 1868, the Irish Church had for some time been a centre of debate and controversy. But there was no sign of a political upheaval likely to end in its disestablishment. A Conservative government held office, and though it was in a minority in the House of Commons there seemed little prospect of its being turned out. The *Pall Mall Gazette* and the *Saturday Review* (both independent-minded papers giving general support to the Liberals) thought that the government would hold on for another year.[1] The Reform Act had been passed in the previous year, and there was bound to be an election when the new registers were ready, probably early in 1869. The Liberals were unlikely to court the expense of an extra election in 1868 as well, which they might incur if they turned the government out.[2] In any case, could the Opposition summon up enough unity and energy for an assault? The Whig grandees thought not. Granville saw no chance of a change of government. Clarendon wrote languidly to Granville: "I suppose that there will be nothing to do in England except watching the undeserved success of the Tories, and the hopeless disunion of the Whigs, which, as far as I am concerned, may be done as well at Rome as in London." He did not expect much of Gladstone by way of remedy—his party were "always suspicious of what he may devise when he gets into higher or unknown latitudes".[3] Argyll counselled Gladstone to attempt nothing, because "if the temper & discipline of the Party is still bad (which I hear it is)" there was not much he could do.

> I admit the necessity sooner or later [he wrote] of putting an end to the condition of things in which a nominal leader is regularly deserted by his men at the moment when he orders a charge. But all I say is—postpone till the new Parliament all attempts to rally, or to *test* Party allegiance—and above all choose a vote on which all the tendencies of our Party are as far as possible undivided.[4]

To which Gladstone replied on 1 February that he did not propose to test party allegiance, but neither did he intend simply to take what the government offered on all questions.[5]

The Liberals had not recovered from their defeats during the passage of the Reform Bill in 1867. Gladstone, outmanoeuvered and bewildered in that affair, seemed a baffled and helpless figure. There seemed good reason for the Conservatives to congratulate themselves on the weakness and divisions of their opponents.[6] They had, of course, their own difficulties. The Reform Act had not been welcome to all Conservatives, and Disraeli's phrase about educating his party was often thrown in his teeth.[7] None the less, the transfer of the premiership from Derby to Disraeli was smoothly managed (Disraeli kissed hands on 27 February). If there was some grumbling, an observer noted that the bark of dissenting Conservatives was always worse than their bite.[8]

What was the government to do with its apparently secure power? There was routine business to be done—Reform Bills for Scotland and Ireland, some useful legislation on minor matters. But the question of the time was Ireland, mostly because of the spectacular nature of the Fenian disturbances—by far the best way to attract attention at Westminster, then as now, was to throw bombs—but partly too because of the organized political activity of the Irish Catholic hierarchy. The *Freeman's Journal* welcomed Disraeli to the Premiership as one who "has strong sympathies with Ireland". It hoped he would deal with Ireland liberally, and that on Church reform he would go straight to the root by proclaiming the disendowment of the Irish Church. His party would follow him as it had done on Reform.[9]

Disraeli was not ready for anything as drastic as this, though he and his Cabinet recognized that they must do something about Ireland. Home Rule, the restoration of a Parliament in Dublin, was at the time unthinkable to both Conservatives and Liberals. There were other possibilities, each with a long and discouraging history: land tenure, the established Church, and education. For some twenty years there had been a succession of Bills to amend the terms of land tenure in Ireland so as to improve the position of the tenant; few had reached the statute book, and those which did achieved very little. It was still an important issue—compensation for improvements had been placed first in the list of objects of the National Association in December 1864, and the *Freeman* was campaigning vigorously for land reform at the beginning of 1868;[10] but it had become less prominent than the Church question. The established Church had become in the past few years the most prominent centre of controversy, and Irish Protestants were rallying to its defence. The Executive Committee of the Protestant Defence Association published an address on 20 January 1868 declaring that a sacerdotal conspiracy led by Cardinal Cullen was seeking to overthrow the established Church as a step towards destroying Protestantism and civil liberty; the Association held its inaugural meeting at the Rotunda in Dublin on 5 February 1868.[11] The education question was primarily a religious one, and the aspect mainly agitated for the previous three years had been the possibility of government support for a Roman Catholic University in Ireland. Finally, there was the question of improving the material conditions of Ireland, for example by developing railways, in so far as government action in such matters was thought proper in the 1860s. This might not be very far. The *Quarterly Review*, for example, argued that it was for the Irish people themselves to improve their own conditions, especially by ceasing to drive away capital investment from Ireland. Others emphasized that there were no panaceas for Ireland, and that it would be fatal to claim that there were.[12]

When the Cabinet met on 2 and 3 March to discuss Ireland, all these different possibilities were before it. Two long documents in the Disraeli Papers show the advice given by prominent civil servants at this juncture. It is significant that both believed that the ecclesiastical situation in Ireland must be changed, and that one believed that in this change lay the key to the Irish question— a panacea, in fact. This was the view of John Lambert, an official of the Poor Law Board, who had helped Disraeli with the details of the Reform Bill in 1867, and who was to be one of Gladstone's advisers in preparing the Irish Church Bill in 1869. (By 1874 he had left the civil service, and stood successfully as a Liberal candidate for Parliament.) His argument was that the two main aims in legislation for Ireland must be to establish tranquillity and to promote habits of industry among the people. Tranquillity was primary: "The mind of the nation must be pacified before other remedies can be applied with any chance of success." In this connection, "The institution, which above all others presents itself to

the Irishman as a badge of conquest, is the Established Church . . .
a standing memorial of his inferior and conquered condition." It
must therefore be the first great question to be settled, on a basis
of approximate material equality between denominations.
Lambert proposed the disendowment of the Irish Church, leaving
the clergy their parsonages and glebe lands, and giving state
grants to provide houses and land for the Catholic and Presbyterian clergy. Far-reaching results would follow. Given religious
equality, a better understanding would grow up between Ireland
and England; capital would no longer be frightened away from
Ireland; the Irish would become better labourers; and eventually
the general character of the people would be changed by a partial
amalgamation of the races. While preparing a detailed measure,
the government should give an earnest of their intentions by re-
pealing the Ecclesiastical Titles Act, or by granting a Royal
Charter to the Catholic University.[13]

The second paper was by G. A. Hamilton, formerly a Conservative politician, whom Disraeli had made Permanent Secretary to
the Treasury in 1859. He thought that the opposition would press
an attack on the Irish Church question, presenting the government with two choices.

1. To resist, either on principle or on the ground that the present
Parliament was moribund. This would risk defeat in the Commons, and also make the present Irish ecclesiastical system the
main issue in the election, which Hamilton thought would be
dangerous.

2. To put forward the principles of a comprehensive measure—
not the details, because its passing would be a matter for the new
Parliament.

Assuming that the present system could not be maintained, the
best course would be to put the three Irish religious bodies on a
rough material equality, by proposing suitable financial provision
for the Anglican and Catholic clergy all over Ireland, and for
Presbyterian clergymen where there were sufficiently large congregations. Provision should also be made for Catholic and
Presbyterian clergy houses. Hamilton did not indicate whether he
thought that there would be long-term benefits, but he hoped for

tactical advantages by dividing the Liberals on the question of endowments, and finding good ground on which to fight an election.[14]

Neither Lambert nor Hamilton thought that the Irish Church could be kept as it was; both favoured some form of concurrent endowment as the best way of changing its status. The Cabinet, after long deliberation, decided to put off making any proposals until the next Parliament. According to Disraeli's account to Derby, they were divided on the merits of the question, but unanimous for postponement—and also "that no pledge should be given of maintaining absolutely unchanged the present state of ecclesiastical affairs. . . ."[15] (It was useful that the Royal Commission on the Irish Church was still at work; its presence gave a reason for postponing a decision, and its recommendations might provide a policy.) The direction of the change, if there were to be one, was indicated by Disraeli to the Queen after the Cabinet. They had rejected as impractical the disendowment of the Irish Church in order to hand over its funds to the Roman Catholic Church; and also general disendowment, including the ending of the Maynooth grant and the *Regium Donum*. But it might be possible to make some provision for both the Catholic and Presbyterian clergy.[16] It was decided to throw out a hint of some such idea, perhaps to test reaction, perhaps in the hope of picking up some support.[17]

The rest of the government's Irish policy was summed up thus by Disraeli.

1. To wait for the report of the Commission on Irish railways, which would probably lead to an extensive measure.

2. To await the report of the Commission on primary education, and meanwhile to recommend the grant of a charter to a Catholic University, provided that it was not "a mere sacerdotal institution". (Lord Mayo, the Chief Secretary for Ireland, had earlier described this as "if not the best at least the only thing we can do".[18])

3. To introduce a Land Bill on points where there was general agreement, and on the others to appoint a fresh Commission of inquiry.[19]

The political situation at the beginning of March 1868 may be summed up thus. The Conservative government was believed to be in a strong position, facing a divided and disheartened opposition. Ireland was at the centre of political attention; but the government had decided on a policy which amounted mostly to waiting—the one positive proposal of significance was on the University question. The Church question was obviously more important, and the Cabinet as a whole did not believe that things could be kept as they were; they leaned towards a form of concurrent endowment (perhaps that proposed by Hamilton), but could not yet find sufficient agreement or chance of parliamentary support to put forward a plan. On the other hand, it was doubtful whether the opposition could offer anything more positive. They seemed incapable of united action on any issue, and they were divided on the particular question of the Irish Church, since Liberationists opposed all and any state endowments of religion, while Lord John Russell repeated his arguments for concurrent endowment in a pamphlet as late as February 1868.[20] Gladstone wrote on 10 December 1867 that to take up the cause of Irish disestablishment "may again lead the Liberal Party to Martyrdom".[21]

Yet take it up he did, and led his party, not to martyrdom, but to parliamentary and electoral victory. There was a general debate on Irish affairs in the House of Commons on 10, 12, 13, and 16 March 1868. The government's Irish policy was expounded by Mayo, and torn to pieces in debate and by the newspapers. At the end of the debate, Gladstone declared that the Irish Church, "as a State Church, must cease to exist".[22] He followed this up on 23 March by placing on the table of the House of Commons three resolutions. The first ran: "That, in the opinion of this House, it is necessary that the Established Church of Ireland should cease to exist as an Establishment, due regard being had to all personal interests and to all individual rights of property." The second was to restrict the work of the Irish Ecclesiastical Commissioners pending a final decision on the Irish Church. The third asked for an address to the Crown requesting the Queen to place the Crown's rights in Irish Church affairs at the disposal of Parliament.[23] On 30 March he moved that the House go into committee on these resolutions. As sometimes happens, a great political issue was to be decided on a vote which was technically on a matter of procedure—"That the Speaker do now leave the Chair". For the government, Stanley moved an amendment which admitted that "considerable modifications" in the temporalities of the Irish Church might be expedient, but proposed that the question should be left for the new Parliament. In the early hours of the morning of 4 April, Stanley's amendment was defeated by a majority of sixty votes, and Gladstone's motion then carried by a majority of fifty-six.[24] When the first resolution itself, with its firm declaration of principle, was put at 2.30 a.m. on 1 May, it was carried by a majority of sixty-five.[25]

These votes represented a crushing victory for Gladstone. From division and uncertainty he had conjured up unity and purpose. He had picked a political winner when no one else was willing to place a firm bet. He had done it by placing the question of the disestablishment and disendowment of the Irish Church at the centre of British politics. These events raise three questions. First, how did Gladstone come to this decision? Second, why did Disraeli and the Conservative party decide to fight him on the ground he had chosen, when, as has been seen, the Cabinet was by no means united in determination to keep the ecclesiastical state of Ireland as it stood? Third, why did the move prove to be such a success, both in Parliament and later in the general election?

Gladstone's personal decision was crucial. He found a policy for his party; he made Irish disestablishment politically possible. At the time his action was the cause of much abuse on two main grounds: first, that his attitude was inconsistent with the argument of his book, *The State in its Relations with the Church*, first published in 1838; and second, that he had changed his principles suddenly in order to seize a political advantage. Gladstone himself was sensitive to these charges—unusually so for one so long in politics—and felt bound to justify himself. As Mr W. E. Williams has written: "He baffled men by his explanations; he suffered from no more serious impediment than this. He had not learned the maxim 'Never explain'."[26] The inconsistency he did not attempt to deny; he freely admitted that his opinion on the established Church in Ireland was in 1868 the direct opposite of what it had been in 1838. It was the explanation that mattered in *A Chapter of Autobiography*, which he wrote in the summer of 1868, though delaying its publication until after the election.[27] In his earlier book he had argued that the State was by its nature moral, subject to the moral law, able to make moral judgements, and wielding moral influence. It was its duty, therefore, to acknowledge truth, and thus to profess only one religion.[28] He wrote in 1868 that this had been "the one master idea of the system"—the established Church was to be maintained for its truth, and this principle was as good for Ireland as for England. As soon as the book appeared, he had found himself "the last man on the sinking ship", and his concern in 1868 was to show "the manner in which I retreated from an untenable position".[29]

Before going on to this explanation, it must be noted that Gladstone did not give up the *whole* of his previous position. He still believed that the State had a conscience, and was obliged to follow the moral law. The question was one of the range of that conscience, whether it obliged the State to take cognizance of religious truth and error, and to give exclusive support to a particular religion because it was true. This he thought had become impossible with the establishment of popular self-government and the breaking up of Christianity into different communions. When what was meant for the nation became the private estate of a few, it became impossible for the State to uphold an established Church. It was rightly observed at the time that these conditions had already existed in 1838, when Gladstone first wrote, and it was strange that he had not noticed them.[30] Indeed, as the *Pall Mall Gazette* wrote on 24 November 1868, it was not far from the mark to say that the sum of Gladstone's essay was: "You may ask how I ever came to write such a silly book as my *Church and State*. The answer is, I was impressible and sanguine and was carried away by Puseyism, and I have been finding out ever since that it was all a mistake." This was doubtless true; but why must a man soon to be Prime Minister say so? The answer surely was that he had to find and to give publicly some reason for abandoning the particular argument that the State should uphold an established Church because of its duty to the truth, without abandoning the premiss that the State was a moral entity. This was the basis of his whole political outlook; more, it met a psychological need. Gladstone felt at his best as the leader of a moral crusade, as in 1868 or as later in the Bulgarian agitation. It was on great moral issues that he felt he made contact with the masses, in whose nobility he believed. But moral crusades of Gladstone's type presuppose the moral nature of the State, its duty to fight against evil. Religious establishments, Gladstone had come to think, should be tried "by a practical rather than a theoretic test", but not the State itself.[31]

So there was a fundamental consistency in Gladstone's attitude, even though he had abandoned the ground on which he had once defended established Churches in general and the established Church in Ireland in particular. Let us turn now to the stages by which this ground was abandoned, and Gladstone came to declare openly for Irish disestablishment.[32] There was no question of his abandonment of the Irish establishment being sudden, and even the revelation of his position was less sudden than his opponents claimed in 1868—though it is on the question of public declaration of his mind that he remains most open to charges of opportunism or deceit. Briefly, Gladstone's own explanation was that he had regained his freedom of action in 1845 by his resignation from Peel's government on the question of the Maynooth Grant. Peel proposed in that year to increase the grant and put it on a regular annual basis. Gladstone resigned from office because he had written in his book on Church and State that the Maynooth Grant was an error. He regarded his resignation purely as a demonstration of his own integrity; he did not believe that Peel could have done other than he did, and he voted for the Bill in the Commons. After this, he regarded himself as having bought his freedom of action on the Irish establishment at the great political cost of resignation. This was doubtless clear to him, though others can be forgiven for not appreciating the position. (Peel wrote when Gladstone resigned: "I really have great difficulty sometimes in comprehending what Gladstone means.") Gladstone maintained that he had made his new position plain in 1847 by declining to pledge himself on the Irish Church when first standing as a candidate for Oxford University.[33]

Though he thus considered himself free, it was over twenty years before he declared openly against the Irish establishment. He put it in a characteristic phrase, which accounts for much of the distrust which he aroused: "It is one thing to lift the anchor; it is another to spread the sails."[34] He gave various reasons for this. He told Bright that in Ireland the question had slept, and that it was best to ponder long over something which would be difficult to deal with and might lead the party to martyrdom.[35] In his *Chapter of Autobiography* he wrote that he wished to give the Irish Church an opportunity to do its work as an establishment under the improved conditions since 1834, and that no one should speak decisively on such an issue until he calculated that the time for action had come.[36] In these explanations there is a strong element of waiting until the time was ripe, until an opportunity occurred, mixed with a desire to postpone action because of the risks involved. The sense of these dangers was heavy upon Gladstone in December 1867. The day after he had mentioned martyrdom to Bright he used the same expression to Fortescue. He thought they must try to deal with the Irish question: "but I believe we shall have to go to martyrdom upon it, which is a graver consideration for men of your age than of mine".[37] (Gladstone genuinely believed that his political career was nearing its end—29 December 1867 was his fifty-seventh birthday.) When he took the question up in March 1868, he must then have done so as a calculated risk, not in the certainty of political success.

In the mid-1860s the question no longer slept in Ireland, and Gladstone gradually gave indications of his mind. As late as July 1864 he wrote privately that there was "neither hope nor fear" of the Irish Church question being opened "for a practical purpose".[38] In February and March 1865 he worked on the question with Phillimore, to whom he wrote: "I am not loyal to it [the Irish Church] as an establishment."[39] On 28 March 1865, on Dillwyn's motion on the Irish Church in the House of Commons, he spoke in such a way that Fortescue congratulated him on securing entire liberty of action for the future, and the Conservative *Morning Herald* concluded that there could be no doubt that when he became Prime Minister the destruction of the Irish Church would be part of his policy.[40] Shortly after this, he wrote to Maziere Brady that he thought the Irish Church a case where the true interests of religion were in conflict with establishment and material advantage.[41] In May 1866, Gladstone was prepared to oppose Sir John Gray's motion for disestablishment, but he wanted to argue "on the ground of time, as well as on the merits".[42] In May 1867, on another motion by Gray, his speech left the

Daily Express with the impression that the Irish Church need expect no quarter when a favourable moment came.[43]

Later in the same year, Gladstone was still uncertain that the time was right to take action about the Irish Church, and apparently about what to do when he did act. He told Gray on 22 July that he was free to support any plan, for levelling up or down, when Irish opinion became clear. This produced clear statements from the Irish hierarchy in favour of the voluntary system, and against concurrent endowment.[44] Gladstone told Gray that his own leanings had been towards concurrent endowment, but he would not let them interfere with the best way of dealing with the question.[45] On 1 December 1867, however, he was still so uncertain that the time had come that he gave only a noncommittal answer to an inquiry from Maguire (M.P. for Cork) as to whether Fortescue or he would bring in a motion for a general debate on Ireland, or whether they would prefer Maguire himself to do so. He thought it too early to make any decision about such a debate.[46]

It must have been some time between then and 16 March 1868 that Gladstone came to his decision. His letter to Bright on 10 December 1867 does not indicate any firm decision to take action, only that he was hostile to the Irish establishment:

> My own personal difficulties or preferences in this great matter are as nothing to me, compared with the evil of the present system and the advantage of altering it fundamentally. Further I think that it is better so to alter it, as to destroy the principle of State establishment in Ireland: better for the country at large, better for the members of the body itself. . . .[47]

This was not new. Writing to Fortescue the next day, Gladstone showed that he was deeply worried about Ireland, but said nothing definite about the Church:

> I am going into Western Lancashire next week, & I have just had an intimation that the *Liberal* Farmers are for maintaining the Irish Church as it is! This I suppose is the tendency which the Fenian manifestations make on stupid men. Of course I do not mean by this any of my constituents.

> The Irish question which has long been grave is growing *awful*. In my opinion this Empire has but one danger. It is the danger expressed in the combination of the three names Ireland United States

and Canada. English policy should set its face two ways like a flint: to support public order, and to make the laws of Ireland such as they should be. This is what we must try: but I believe we shall have to go to martyrdom upon it, which is a graver consideration for men of your age than of mine.

He hoped that Fortescue would come to an understanding with Maguire about a new Land Bill, but saw little means of improving on that of 1866, because "a more ultra measure" would mean a split in the party.[48]

This was on 11 December 1867. On 12 December there took place the Fenian attack on Clerkenwell prison, which killed twelve people and injured a hundred and twenty in a vain attempt to rescue some prisoners. If, as is generally believed, it was the Fenian outrages of late 1867 which were decisive in convincing Gladstone that the time had come to act on the Irish Church, it was presumably Clerkenwell which did the trick, rather than the Manchester rescue attempt of September, when a policeman had been killed, and three Fenians later executed for his murder.[49] Even if this is so, it still leaves some three months between Clerkenwell and 16 March 1868, when Gladstone declared his intention to move against the Irish establishment. Within this period there were other events which might have influenced Gladstone. It is possible that Gladstone's resolutions on the Irish Church were a reply to Mayo's plan to give a charter to a Catholic university in Ireland.[50] A denominational university—especially since Gladstone believed (wrongly) that government endowment was in question as well as a charter—ran counter to deeply held Liberal views on education. It was heavily attacked from the Liberal benches during the debate on Maguire's motion. In December 1867 Argyll had told Gladstone that if the Irish bishops got what they wanted, "we shall be compelled to aid in the worst system of Education existing in any part of Europe . . .". It was an important point of conflict between Catholics and Liberals, as it continued to be during the general election.[51] It carried with it the possibility of an alliance between the hierarchy and the government which it was worth while to break up.

From all this it may be seen that by 1868 Gladstone had long abandoned his position as the defender of the Irish establishment, and that by 1865 his opponents could deduce from his public

speeches that he would attack that establishment at some time.
As late as the beginning of December 1867 he was not convinced
that that time had arrived. By March 1868 he *was* so convinced,
largely by the Fenian outrages, partly perhaps to kill the University project by outbidding the government. There was no question
of Gladstone abandoning his principles on the Irish establishment
suddenly, or even of suddenly revealing his change. What was
sudden, and generally unexpected, was his decision to give his
ideas practical form.

Gladstone had decided that the state of Ireland was a danger to
the Empire. How far did he believe that the disestablishment and
disendowment of the Irish Church would remove that danger?
He recognized that a settlement of the land question would have
to follow; but there is evidence that the advice he received from
various people was such as to lead him to believe that to deal with
the Church would be the most important step towards the settlement of Ireland. Gladstone was at this time again in close touch
with his old friend Cardinal Manning, who was going out of his
way to remove the antipathy between the English and Irish hier-
archies by supporting the aspirations of the Irish bishops.[52]
Manning was convinced of the great effects which disestablishment would produce. "The Irish Establishment is a great
wrong", he wrote to Gladstone at the end of March 1868. "It is
the cause of division in Ireland, of alienation between Ireland and
England. It embitters every other question. Even the land question
is exasperated by it. All relations of life are tainted by it."[53] He
wrote in the same vein to his nephew, John Anderson: "The main
cause of all division, conflict, and animosity is the Irish Establishment." Manning was encouraged in this belief by Cullen, who had
written to him a year earlier: ". . . the Irish Bishops are persuaded
that peace and love for authority can never be established in
Ireland as long as the Catholics shall be obliged to support a
Protestant establishment and to submit to a Protestant ascendancy. . . . The total disendowment of the Protestant church
would put an end to a grievance and insult . . ." He went on to
add that a good system of education and encouragement for
agriculture and industry were also necessary for Ireland.[54]

Gladstone also had in his hands a letter by Moriarty, the
Catholic Bishop of Kerry, setting out to prove that "Religious

equality will remove disaffection and make the Irish people contented and loyal". The essence of the argument lay in the proposition that "The minds of the Irish people are in the hands of the Irish priests". The priests could not love a government which gave status, money, and ascendancy to the Church of the stranger and conqueror; change that, gain the priests, and you would gain the people. It would be better for a government to deal with the Church than with education, which could not be a popular issue, or with the land question, for which legislation could do little. Moriarty asserted his belief in the superiority of British institutions to all others (explaining that he had seen some others). If the established Church could be got out of the way, he believed that this sentiment would spread, *via* the priests.[55]

Gladstone had heard the same view from one who had no stake in Irish affairs, his old friend and regular correspondent Malcolm MacColl (later a canon of Ripon Cathedral). MacColl had written while on a visit to Ireland in September 1866 of his astonishment at the hatred between Catholic and Protestant. "I believe it to be impossible to make Ireland loyal till the Establishment is abolished, & Protestant ascendancy destroyed."[56]

Such private advice as this supplemented the powerful public assertions of the same belief. Disestablishment and disendowment had been one of the three great demands of the National Association, and probably the one which was most prominent. In February 1868 a Declaration was published, signed by nearly a thousand Irish Catholic laymen of good social standing, to emphasize their grievance against the ecclesiastical position in Ireland. As Fortescue wrote to Gladstone, it was a relief to turn from Fenianism and sedition to "a righteous & constitutional movement such as that inaugurated by the R. Catholic Noblemen & Gentlemen who are signing the Declaration in favour of Religious Equality".[57] It was important that such men, considered to be the natural leaders of society (along with the Catholic clergy) should choose to stress the importance of the Irish Church question.

There were thus good reasons for Gladstone to believe early in 1868 that in taking up the issue of the Irish Church he was taking certainly an important, and quite likely a decisive, step in the solution of the Irish problem. Gladstone's election address later in the year put the argument clearly, though naturally with a touch of grandiloquence. The question of Ireland, it proclaimed, overshadowed all others. The object was to make the law respected in Ireland because it was loved, and to this the established Church in Ireland was an obstacle, because it misapplied funds meant for the nation at large, was a memorial of past oppression, and embittered religious controversy. "In the removal of this Establishment I see the discharge of a debt of civil justice, the disappearance of a national, almost a world-wide reproach, a condition indispensable to the success of every effort to secure the peace and contentment of that country...."[58]

Another way of putting this was that the loyalty of the Catholic hierarchy, and its support against Fenianism, were essential for the British government. If the price of loyalty and support was disestablishment, then that price would have to be paid. It may be that such language was too harsh and crude for Gladstone's style in political oratory, but it is hard to believe that he did not make the calculation.

These were the reasons why Gladstone committed his party to the disestablishment of the Irish Church in March 1868. How was it that the Conservative government came to oppose him in head-on collision, when at the beginning of that same month they had been divided on the question, and had even been prepared to accept that some sort of change in the Irish establishment was necessary? At first, there was certainly a strong desire for a compromise on the Irish Church within the Conservative government. Lambert and Hamilton had advised some form of concurrent endowment. On 2 and 3 March the Cabinet had discussed the possibility of providing for the Catholic and Presbyterian clergy, as well as agreeing to give no pledge that the ecclesiastical position in Ireland would be maintained unchanged. What sounded like concurrent endowment was hinted at by Mayo in the House of Commons on 10 March, when he spoke of levelling up, not down, as the best solution of the question of the Irish Church: "Justice and policy may demand a greater equalization of ecclesiastical arrangements than now exists.... If it is desired to make our Churches more equal in position than they are, this result should be secured by elevation and restoration, and not by confiscation and degradation."[59] Sir John Pakington, the Secretary for War, in a letter of 14 March, pressed Disraeli to go further. "It is clear", he wrote, "that a state of affairs which no one ventures to defend cannot be maintained." He suggested that they should consent to disestablishment but not disendowment, and that an outline be sketched for:

1. disestablishing; 2. insuring a surplus by reducing the provision for the Church to the minimum of her real requirements; 3. devoting the surplus to providing glebes, parsonages, and good churches for the R.C.s; 4. extending the powers of the Commission [i.e. the Commission already sitting on the revenues of the Irish Church], if necessary, to arrange the details of such a plan.

He ended: "You will excuse the zeal which offers a suggestion to one who so little needs it."[60] There was here a calm abandonment of the Irish establishment, and a proposal for partial disendowment of the Irish Church, with a clear hint that Pakington knew that Disraeli was not averse to such ideas.

It was also open to anyone to infer from Disraeli's conduct in the past ten years that he valued an alliance with the Catholics. He had sought Catholic support during Derby's government of 1858–9, and had earned a remark from the Pope to Odo Russell: "Mr Disraeli was my friend; I regret him." In 1861 Cardinal Wiseman had recommended three Catholic M.P.s (Monsell, Bowyer, and Pope Hennessy) as a good combination on which to build up a working arrangement with Catholics in the Commons. Disraeli attacked Palmerston's support for Italian unification, supported the temporal power of the Pope, and stood ostentatiously aloof from the adulation of Garibaldi when he came to England in 1864.[61] It was always a risky policy, exposing Disraeli to the danger of provoking Protestant hostility without gaining sufficiently solid advantage to make this worth while. He defended himself against those who accused him of truckling to the priests (at the time in question it was the *Dublin Evening Mail*) by pointing to the importance of the English Catholics—a powerful body, and, he believed, naturally Tories.[62] The proposal for a charter for a Catholic university in Ireland was a natural development of this policy, and concurrent endowment to include the Catholic Church in Ireland would have been a further development.

There was thus some reason to think that Disraeli's mind was moving in the direction of compromise on the establishment, perhaps even abandoning it, and concurrent endowment. But when Gladstone sprang his mine it faced Disraeli and his government with a new situation. The Prime Minister at first believed that it could be met without wholly abandoning his earlier ideas. After Gladstone had declared on 16 March 1868 that the Irish establishment must cease to exist, Disraeli wrote to Cairns (Lord Chancellor and Conservative leader in the House of Lords) on the 19th:

> I assume, from what reaches me, that Gladstone and his party will now propose the disestablishment of the Irish Church.
>
> He seems to me to have raised a clear and distinct issue. I don't think we could wish it better put.
>
> I think we ought to hold that the whole question of national establishments is now raised; that the Irish Church is but a small portion of the question; and that those who wish to demolish it must be held to desire the abolition of national establishments in the three kingdoms.
>
> But we must detach the Irish Church as much as possible from the prominent portion of the subject, for, there is no doubt, it is not popular.
>
> I think, if the principle that the State should adopt and uphold religion as an essential portion of the Constitution be broadly raised, a great number of members from the north of England and Scotland, called Liberals, would be obliged to leave the philosophic standard.
>
> I am, therefore, at present inclined to an amendment which, while it admitted that the present condition of the Church of Ireland was susceptible of improvement, while it might be desirable to elevate the status of the unendowed clergy of that country, still declared it was the first duty of the State to acknowledge and maintain the religious principle in an established form, etc.[63]

The *Globe*, which at this time usually reflected Disraeli's views, was taking a similar line, though (perhaps significantly) without the qualifications. It argued on 17 March that Parliament had no more right to disestablish the Irish Church than to abolish the Crown and set up a Republic—it was a matter of a fundamental law of the British system, the union of Church and State and the Crown's protection of Protestantism against the Papacy.

When Disraeli appealed to the public, he too omitted the qualifications, and declared that it was the Liberals' purpose to destroy "that sacred union between Church and State which has hitherto been the chief means of our civilization and is the only

security of our religious liberty".[64] He told the Queen that Gladstone had mistaken the temper of the country. "The abhorrence
of Popery, the dread of Ritualism, and the hatred of the Irish, have
long been smouldering in the mind of the nation. They will seize,
Mr Disraeli thinks, the opportunity long sighed for and now
offered, to vent their accumulated passion." In the boroughs the
old No Popery cry would revive; in the counties the clergy and
gentry would rally to the principle of Church and State. The
Queen, to her credit, thought there was "but too much truth" in
this. She thought that Gladstone should have paused before reviving the old cries which had worked evil in the name of religion,
and she hoped the government would do nothing to encourage
retaliation by the Protestants or revive religious animosities. It
might give them a temporary party advantage, but would injure
the permanent interests of the Empire.[65]

The Queen counselled moderation, but moderation was not to
be the order of the day. When Disraeli wrote to Cairns, he intended to hedge on the Irish Church itself and to keep open the
possibility of concurrent endowment. When the actual amendment
to Gladstone's resolutions came to be prepared, however, there
was nothing in it about elevating the status of the unendowed
clergy. What remained was a mention of the possibility of "considerable modifications" in the state of the Irish Church, and the
tactics of trying to postpone the attack on the Church rather than
meet it head-on. This possibility of a compromise was kept open
too by the choice of Stanley to move the amendment. Stanley,
the Foreign Secretary, was generally known to believe that Irish
disestablishment was inevitable. His father, Lord Derby, who was
still in his retirement a frequent and frank correspondent of
Disraeli's, disliked the amendment as too temporizing, and was
nervous about the way Stanley would handle it.[66]

In the event, the amendment and Stanley's speech produced
confusion and dismay. In the course of what Cairns described as
a "colourless and chilling" performance, Stanley remarked:
"Probably there is not one educated person in a hundred who will
stand up and pretend that the Irish ecclesiastical arrangements as
they exist are of altogether a satisfactory kind."[67] There was con-
sternation among the rank and file. Irish Protestant opinion had
already been angered by Mayo's speech on 10 March, with its

plan for a Catholic university and shadowy references to levelling up—it showed only "the influence of fear . . . and the desire to trim", wrote the *Daily Express*.[68] The reaction against Stanley's speech was more widespread, and showed up markedly in contrast to the warm reception given to Gathorne Hardy, the Home Secretary. The nature of Hardy's speech, and the reputation he held, may be shown by two comments upon it. The *Daily Telegraph* (Liberal): "Mr Hardy's work is to give utterance, on any and all occasions, to the old-fashioned Conservative notions." The *Globe* (Conservative): Hardy's speech was "one of those manly, outspoken, and earnest utterances which befit the character of an English gentleman".[69] He declared firmly: "I will not be a party to a measure for disestablishing the Irish Church." He stood foursquare on the Act of Union, the rights of property, and the sacred character of Church endowments. And he was welcomed wholeheartedly by Conservative members from Dungannon to Cheltenham.[70]

The debate showed plainly that the course Disraeli had tried to set was impossible. The Conservative party could not fight on the general principle of national establishments, of the duty of the State to uphold religion, and at the same time (in Disraeli's words to Cairns) "detach the Irish Church as much as possible from the prominent portion of the subject". The battle must be waged all along the line—*including* the Irish Church itself, whatever Disraeli and some of his colleagues might think of it—or it could not be waged at all. The only thing achieved by Disraeli's tactics, his attempt to keep his hands free on the Irish Church itself, was a revival of the sort of suspicions which flourished after his conduct on Reform the previous year. Blakesley (vicar of Ware, later Dean of Lincoln) told Tait, then Bishop of London, that what he most feared was a repetition of Disraeli's management of the Reform question. He could see the Prime Minister starting with one Bill, and ending with another which disestablished and disendowed the Irish Church without saving anything—"D'Israeli will accept the decision of the H. of Commons with a grave face and his tongue in his cheek".[71] The *Freeman* on 1 April 1868 had drawn the moral from Stanley's amendment that when the Conservative party had been educated up to disestablishment, the Irish Church would be abandoned. Lord Cranborne and General Peel (who had both resigned in 1867 on the Reform question) thought the same. Cranborne said that the amendment was "too clever by half" (still a damning indictment to some Conservatives); Peel thought it meant that the party was as yet "not sufficiently educated".[72] True, Cranborne and Peel were not the Conservative party; their revolt against Disraeli during the Reform debates had been ineffectual. But the situation was no longer the same. Over Reform, Disraeli had been able to claim that the question was one only of details, and in any case he had the overriding justification of success, bewildering and outvoting the Opposition. On this occasion the question was one of principle (could even Disraeli claim to uphold all establishments and yet be prepared to let the Irish one go?), and he led his party only to defeat. The evident division and failure in argument on the government side told on the vote. Speaker Denison reckoned when the issue was first raised that Gladstone's majority might be 20 or 30—40 at the most partisan estimate. In fact it was 60; every doubtful man voted against the government, and even some who had been counted as certain to vote for it.[73]

This suspicion had therefore to be overcome. The government had to show itself to be sound not only on the question of establishments in general, but also on the Irish establishment in particular. Also if it were to raise the No Popery cry with conviction, then its connections with the Catholics must be jettisoned. Colonel Taylor, the Conservative Chief Whip, wrote to Disraeli on 19 April 1868: "The more I consider it the more convinced I am that you should let the Catholic College go, if you possibly can—it is the only drawback to the Protestant feeling in our favour."[74] So Disraeli abandoned the encumbrances and the qualifications, and appealed outright to what he hoped was the Protestant sentiment of the country and what was certainly the instinctive Conservative attachment to the established Church, including even its distant and dubious bulwarks across the Irish Sea.

In his speech to the House of Commons on 3 April (the last day of the debate on Gladstone's resolutions), Disraeli had already gone some way down the new road—not yet the whole way, for there were still some friendly references to the Catholics. The attack on the Church of Ireland would be followed by others on the Church of Scotland, the Church in Wales, and in England too.

7

He produced a famous piece of rhodomontade: "High Church Ritualists and the Irish followers of the Pope have been long in secret combination, and are now in open confederacy."[75] He took some pride in this passage. He drew the Queen's attention to it. He repeated the assertion in a public letter, adding for good measure that the Liberation Society was a mere instrument in the hands of this confederacy.[76] He drew a rebuke from Hardy, who pointed out that Conservative High Churchmen among his constituents (Hardy sat for Oxford University) were justifiably annoyed.[77] The published letter drew derision in the press. The *Saturday Review* was typical in saying on 18 April 1868 that no one would take it seriously outside Bedlam and the office of the *Record* (the main Evangelical journal). But of course, Disraeli was aiming at the *Record*; and the *Daily Express* took it seriously too, as welcome evidence that Disraeli's heart was in the right place after all.[78]

The campaign had to be fought, in fact, by assertion, by sticking things together which did not necessarily belong together but which plausibly looked as though they might. Ritualists and Irish Catholics were both good enemies for Protestants to attack. As for what was being defended, the Irish Church involved the fate of the English Church; both depended on establishment; both involved the safety of Protestantism. With the establishment and Protestantism were wrapped up the very constitution of the country, the monarchy, and the liberties of Englishmen.

The *Globe*, for example, hammered away at these themes day after day during April 1868. "Shall the Government of the British nation cease to be religious? Shall the old and revered institutions of the country be overturned? . . . There need be no fear for the Protestant faith, which is indestructible; there is great fear lest this Empire should be turned into a democracy." The attempt to disestablish the Irish Church "is a sign of revolutionary tendency". Disestablishment everywhere, the advance of Rome, and the disintegration of the Church of England after disestablishment were predicted. The question for the hustings was "Shall the Church of England be destroyed?" The disestablishment of the Irish Church "will unchristianize the Crown and demoralize the Government". Those who sought Irish disestablishment were "the revolutionists and Americanizers in our midst", for whom it was only a part of a great programme.[79] In May the *Globe* found another scare, in a resolution put down by Sir Colman O'Loghlen, that Sovereigns should cease to make on their accession the declaration against transubstantiation, invocation of saints, and the sacrifice of the Mass. This was reprinted in a special leader, in heavy type, so that the country should be informed of this new assault on the religion of the English martyrs. If the Protestant Church and Protestant Sovereign should go, it would not be long before the monarchy would be abolished and law itself suspended.[80] In July, an article by John Morley in the *Fortnightly Review* gave Conservatives a splendid handle.[81] Even the *Pall Mall Gazette* reproved him for imprudence in saying that Irish disestablishment was the first step to the redistribution of Irish land and the abolition of many English institutions, including the House of Lords. The *Globe* seized on the same points with glee, and added that to Morley all clergymen were dishonest and the Queen merely "the most highly paid official in the land". Gladstone, of course, would not approve of Morley's ideas—but then everyone knew that Gladstone's views were capable of development.[82] This was the sort of thing the *Globe* needed to play on fears of revolution, which it continued to foster to the end of the campaign. The Radicals, if they could, would "rush into a democracy ... disestablish and disendow state churches and rush into the vortex of a godless republican-ism".[83]

There was much more in the same vein to be found elsewhere. The stern and unbending *Quarterly Review* pointed out the danger of accepting the argument of mere numbers in the Irish dis-establishment question. Even if only eleven per cent of the popu-lation of Ireland belonged to the established Church, and over three-quarters were Catholics, was this to count for everything, while wealth and intelligence (deemed to be ranged decisively in the ranks of the Irish Church) counted for nothing? If so, it should be remembered that over the whole country there were few people who owned property, and many who did not.[84] The chief issue of the election, in the view of the *Quarterly Review*, was whether the country was to have a government mindful of the past, or was "to plunge headlong into the chaos of democracy". It took comfort, however, in the reflection that "whatever may be the rate of advance of the democratic theory", there would always be a large proportion of the British people opposed to innovations

imported from abroad.[85] *Blackwood's* held much the same position.
The Liberals were pledged to "a speedy, though perhaps a blood-
less, revolution in this country", though the Conservatives could
still hope, even if they lost the election, to act as a brake on the
coach as it went downhill towards "the level of pure democracy".[86]

On quite a different level from that of the respectable periodicals, with their interminable pages of close print, there were
pamphlets like the anonymous *Richard Sykes and John Rose: A
Dialogue on the Irish Church, and the approaching General Election.*
Richard explained matters to John, a simple soul who had been
bothered by the clever arguments of one Mike Green. The Protestants of Ireland must be supported, as the only ones to stand
out against the Fenians. If the Irish Church went, the English
Church would soon follow, and if the Catholics got the upper
hand they would allow no freedom. John agreed: "My vote (and
I'm right glad I shall have one) shall go to no man who won't
stand up for the Irish Church." Richard also explained why the
Irish were so troublesome. England had conquered Ireland five
hundred years before, "and somehow they've owed us a grudge
ever since; and they'd like to set up a King and a Parliament of
their own. Poor work they'd make of it—and it wouldn't suit us
either to have such a neighbour. As it is, we make the best we can
of it, as folks do of a child. Sometimes we coax and sometimes
we're obliged to punish; but we don't mean to let go, that's
certain."

The Scottish Reformation Society put out placards for the
election, advertised thus: "'Romish progress and British infatuation.' A large illustrated placard, showing the infatuation of
spurious Liberalism—the designs of the Romanists against civil
and religious liberty—the Romeward career of Ritualism—the
British lion fast asleep. A truthful and striking representation."[87]
A Protestant demonstration at the Crystal Palace on 17 August
struck the same note. "Let it be a Protestant election. Return no
Ritualist to Parliament", said the chairman, Lord Fitzwalter,
formerly a Conservative M.P. There were songs at the end of the
meeting—"Our Dear Old Church of England", and "Our Good
Old Constitution", for the latter of which the correspondent of the
Pall Mall Gazette forecast rapid popularity.[88]

The lines of this campaign were followed by Disraeli, and encouraged by the central conservative organization. The Chief Whip had letters sent out to individuals in Liberal constituencies:

> My Dear Sir,
> Are there any of the leading Liberals of your borough likely to have been annoyed at the vote of Mr. —— and who are well affected towards the Church and State?
> If so send me by return the names of three or four of them.
> Please send me also the names of such of your clergy as are against the proposed spoliation of the Irish Church.[89]

Disraeli, writing to the Queen on 1 May, might have been writing a leading article for the *Globe*, or an election leaflet. His government opposed Gladstone's policy on the Irish Church, firstly because it was retrograde, destroying the effects of thirty years of conciliation; secondly because it was an attack on property; thirdly because it dissolved the connection between government and religion; fourthly because it introduced a principle which must be applied, and probably soon, to England. There its effects would be very serious:

> The Church will become either an Imperium in Imperio more powerful than the State, or it will break into sects and schisms and ultimately be absorbed by the tradition and discipline of the Church of Rome; and the consequence will be that the Queen's supremacy, the security for our religious liberty, and, in no slight degree, for our civil rights, will be destroyed. In fact, this will be a revolution, and an entire subversion of the English Constitution.*

This was very much his language of the previous day in the House, and he kept reverting to it. His speech at the Merchant Taylors' banquet was on the connection between Church and State, which saved the State from degenerating into mere police and preserved religious liberty.[90]

Disraeli used the Church patronage which fell to him as Prime Minister to strengthen the Protestant cause. He wrote to Stanley on 16 August: "What we want at this moment is a strong Protestant appointment in the Church. I have been expecting a

---

* Disraeli to the Queen, 1 May 1868, Monypenny and Buckle, vol. II, pp. 371–2; this was his formal letter after the government had been defeated on Gladstone's first resolution, recommending a dissolution as soon as the public interest permitted, with an appeal to the new electorate under the Reform Act of 1867. Disraeli preferred to fight the election from office rather than resign.

Bishop to die every day, but there is hardly a 'good Protestant' strong enough to make a Bishop." He had, however, been able to recommend McNeile as Dean of Ripon.[91] McNeile was a strong Evangelical, a favourite of the *Record*, who at the end of July had published a pamphlet denouncing Gladstone as the dupe of the Catholic priesthood.[92] Disraeli was fortunate in the number of posts he had to fill up during the period of the campaign—he wrote exultantly to Corry, his secretary, on 9 October: "Another Deanery! The Lord of Hosts is with us!"[93] There was no doubt about Disraeli's view of this aspect of the virtues of an established Church. At the last minute, it is true, he came to think he had gone too far with his Evangelical appointments. The High Church party, which he had entirely discounted in August,[94] was apparently working against him in the counties, and he tried to appease it by some appointments for High Churchmen during November.[95]

This, however, was a last-minute aberration, perhaps a touch of panic. In general during the campaign Disraeli appears to have believed his own propaganda—he was usually an optimist. On 21 August he wrote: "The feeling in England is getting higher and higher every day; but it is Protestant, not Church, feeling at present. The problem to solve is, how this Protestant feeling should be enlisted on the side of existing institutions. I think it can be done: but it will require the greatest adroitness and courage."[96] This is presumably what Disraeli sought to do in his election address, published at the beginning of October, though it was more repetition than development of what he had said in May. If there was any change, it was an increase in the vigour of his anti-Catholicism. He declared that ministers would offer uncompromising resistance to Gladstone's proposals, which would change the fundamental laws of the realm by dissolving the union between Church and State. "The connection of religion with the exercise of political authority is one of the main safeguards of the civilization of man. It instils some sense of responsibility even into the depositories of absolute power." To destroy the connection would "lower the character of government, and tend to the degradation of society". Great Britain enjoyed religious liberty because the Church had accepted the principles of the Reformation, and recognized the supremacy of the monarch in ecclesiastical as well as in secular matters. Now, this settlement was under attack in several different ways, but there was one enemy behind them all:

> ... amid the discordant activity of many factions there moves the supreme purpose of one power ... The ultimate triumph, were our Church to fall, would be to that power which would substitute for the authority of our Sovereign the supremacy of a foreign prince; to that power with whose tradition, learning, discipline and organization our Church alone has hitherto been able to cope, and that, too, only when supported by a determined and devoted people.[97]

Stanley, commenting on the address in draft, regretted that Disraeli by implication rejected absolutely the idea of a compromise on the revenues of the Irish Church, which he (Stanley) had long favoured. He recognized that no such course could be advocated publicly then, but did not want Disraeli to say anything which would hamper him from falling back on it in the future.[98] Stanley asserted that two-thirds of the Conservative party did not believe it would be possible to save all the endowments—"to maintain the thing as it stands".[99] But he soon gave up the argument: "I regret, though I cannot dispute, your opinion that compromise on the Irish Church question is impossible."[100] Disraeli had ceased to dispute it long ago, and he surely looked sceptically on Stanley's view of what two-thirds of the party believed.

Disraeli and his party had taken up their position. It was highly vulnerable to argument. The *Saturday Review* remarked on 20 June 1868 that Disraeli dressed up his arguments on Church and State to look like principles, but they were nothing of the sort. He claimed that the State was saved by the moral influence of the established Church from being mere police—as in Canada, where there was no established Church? The connection between Church and State preserved religious liberty—as in Spain?* The *Freeman* on 7 August noted the assertion that Irish disestablishment would lead to the same result in England, and so to the ascendancy of Rome, and commented that according to this view "the whole structure would fall to pieces if half a million Irish Protestants were required to support their own Church!" But shots of this

---

* We may note in passing the remark of the *Liberator* (July 1868) that the Irish Church never had a better defender than Disraeli—"Both are shams" (p. 127).

sort, however accurate, were unimportant. The position was not supposed to be proof against logic—it was supposed to be unmistakable and popular.

It was certainly unmistakable. "The coming election is by general consent predestined to determine what shall be the national policy towards the Irish Church and the Irish people", wrote *The Times* on 3 July 1868. The Irish Church issue became the touch-stone. It was even claimed, with some justice, that without it candidates who did not belong to established Tory families would have found it hard to explain what they meant by being Conservative. There was even a candidate who was in favour of further extension of the suffrage, and of abolishing the religious tests at Oxford and Cambridge—but he was against Irish disestablishment, so he was a Conservative.[101] Another candidate, a sitting member at Canterbury, was called before a Conservative meeting to explain his votes for Gladstone's resolutions; he refused, and put himself forward as an independent Conservative.[102] The question of the Irish Church was the most prominent point in the vast majority of election addresses. There were, of course, other questions—the ballot, education, economy (not in those days *the* economy, but the issue of which party would spend less public money), army reform, legislation on trade unions.[103] But the Irish Church was in the forefront. In the apocalyptic visions in which establishments everywhere, Protestantism, and the constitution all came toppling down together, the Irish Church figured as the stone whose removal would bring all the rest down.

Whether the position was popular is another matter. At any rate the Conservatives lost the election heavily (the Liberal majority was a hundred and ten seats[104]), so the campaign failed on the one test that really mattered. The reasons for this defeat will be discussed later. Meanwhile, it must be said that there was at the time some reason to believe that the line followed by the Conservatives would be electorally profitable. (If there had not been, of course, the campaign would have been fought differently. As a West-country elector wrote to Northcote, there were, "amidst the uproar, the accents of Messrs. Tadpole and Taper".[105]) Three facts were plain: that there was anti-Catholic and anti-Irish feeling in the country to be exploited; that there was genuine belief that the Church (that is to say the English establishment) was in danger; and that the clergy of the Church of England could be mobilized for a great electoral effort on behalf of the Conservatives.

The most spectacular evidence of anti-Catholic feeling was provided by William Murphy, a lecturer (as he was called) for the Protestant Electoral Union. In 1867 he had "lectured" at Wolverhampton and Birmingham, with visual aids which included a mock confessional box, and distributing a pamphlet called *The Confessional Unmasked*. The result had been a series of riots which showed that anti-Catholic and anti-Irish feeling was there for the summoning in the Midlands.[106] There were similar riots in May 1868 at Ashton-under-Lyne, following a meeting run by the same organization, addressed this time by the Reverend Tresham Gregg, from Dublin. The meeting was on a Saturday night; there was fighting in the streets on the Sunday, and a Catholic chapel was burned. The *Pall Mall Gazette* pointed out that these riots, together with Murphy's activities the previous year, showed the feelings of a large mass of the British public, without which Murphy could not have gained his successes. The *Globe* asked self-righteously what else was to be expected when Gladstone's proposals roused passions in the country, and thought that he might regret his actions if blood were shed in every English town and Catholic chapels burned throughout the country.[107] Murphy himself was again busy in May 1868, producing riots in Oldham.[108] He appeared in Manchester at the end of August, and found himself before the magistrates charged with inciting to a breach of the peace (he had been carrying a loaded ten-chamber revolver and a knuckle-duster when he was arrested). He was bound over to keep the peace for three months, and promptly offered himself as a parliamentary candidate for Manchester (he was able to date his election address from Belle Vue gaol). "I desire", he wrote, "to stake the whole contest on this one question: Are the electors of Manchester prepared to vote for Protestantism or the tools of Rome?" He advocated the inspection of nunneries under parliamentary authority, like factories or lunatic asylums, and also, rather oddly, a statutory minimum wage of five shillings per day for every workman. His first meeting produced a riot between his supporters and a phalanx of Irishmen before he even arrived to address it.[109] On 9 May, the *Saturday Review*, commenting on a Protestant meeting at the St James's Hall in London, with the

platform party made up of bishops and peers, had written that
Disraeli had called up spirits but they had not come. But by
September and October, its conclusion was that both No Popery
feeling and the national quarrel between English and Irish were as
lively as ever; one might deplore this, and some had thought No
Popery was dead, but it was not.[110]

In fact, respectable newspapers, including the *Saturday Review*
itself, and the *Pall Mall Gazette*, which gave their support at this
time to the Liberal party, were prone to very similar sentiments.
The *Gazette* described Roman Catholic priests as the subjects,
heart and soul, of a foreign power, which was itself the incarnation
of the principle of superstition.[111] The *Saturday Review* declared that
the last thing the British tax-payer wanted to subsidize was an
ultramontane university to disseminate the principles seen in
action in Rome; he would be asked to help pay for the French
garrison there next.[112] (At this time there were still French troops
in Rome to prevent the advance of the Italian national State to
its natural capital; the regime they protected still represented the
nadir of reactionary tyranny to most right-thinking Englishmen.)
The Times wrote a heavily ironical leader on the Pope's invitation
(in preparation for the Vatican Council) to all non-Catholic
bodies to return to the fold, ending by inviting the Pope to become a
good Protestant.[113] Even *The Times* leader, of 28 October 1868 on
why the anti-Catholic line had not in fact told in the election campaign (except in Lancashire) declared that this was due to security,
not indifference. People knew that in fact they were in no danger
of papal supremacy. The Pope had no terrors—"We laugh at his
Syllabus. We scorn his Encyclical". There was no lack of hostility
here.

Take again a few clergymen of the Church of England. The
rector of Bermondsey, Mr Tugwell, wrote privately to Gladstone
the day after his resolutions were put before the House:

> I feel it to be my duty as a Protestant clergyman of the United
> Church of England and Ireland & as an honest & straightforward
> Englishman to protest against the iniquitous course that you purpose
> pursuing in regard to the disendowment of the English Church, and of
> the separation of Church and state with a view to giving Roman Cath-
> olics the supremacy in this free country, & thus again bring England
> deprived of her liberty & of the word of God, under the Papal Yoke.

He added, to show that he was not self-interested, that his own endowment was only £17 per annum.[114] Mr Tugwell wrote thus in the exact terms of a *Globe* leader or of Disraeli's later election address. That he was no mere isolated fanatic may be seen by looking at another clergyman. Girdlestone, the rector of Kingswinford, was prepared to cast his vote in favour of Irish disestablishment. Yet he wrote to Tait:

> I note however that this is only one out of several measures now before parlt. for conceding points in favour of papal aggression. And comparing our own times with those of James II, especially as pourtrayed by Macaulay, I seem to see an exact parallel between the subserviency of the H. of C., and of the press, in these days, to Jesuitical influences, & that of Jas. II and his evil counsillors: the only difference being, that the dupes who now plead for the indulgence are not privy to the plot for making it the means of introducing popery.[115]

Jelf, the Principal of King's College, London, also had his mind on James II, even in Hendaye, where he was building a house "with English arrangements and decencies, which are almost universally defective in French houses, owing to imperfect drainage". He wrote to Tait: "I am inclined to hope that Gladstone has run his head against the same wall which James the second found too hard for him. I think there can be no doubt that the disestablishment of the Church in Ireland means the establishment of Romanism. . . ."[116]

Finally, Alexander Ewing, Bishop of Argyll and the Isles, who wrote Gladstone a long and emotional letter of support for his Irish Church policy in April 1868, still wrote a month later that he would be unwilling to give up the Irish establishment if it meant that Rome was to be provided for thereby. He hated and feared the Church of Rome.[117] When writing to Tait from Palermo, Ewing reminded him that on the continent Rome was seen simply as the enemy of light and progress.[118] Dean Stanley once wrote of Ewing that he would "not touch the Pope with his little finger even to do him injury".[119]

Thus one did not need to go to the level of Murphy to find whole-hearted anti-popish sentiment. The second point, that there was genuine belief that the disestablishment of the Church of England was imminent, has already been dealt with in an earlier chapter. It is only necessary to re-emphasize here that it was natural for many people to believe that the attack on the Irish establishment would be the last straw in England also. After all, it was the avowed intention of the Liberation Society that Irish disestablishment should be the prelude to English disestablishment. Moreover, some of the arguments used in defence of the Irish Church, to show that its position was not dissimilar to that of the Church of England in Cornwall or Wales, pointed in logic to English disestablishment, if the Irish measure went through.

If the fall of the English establishment was near, as many people were saying, what should those who were concerned with it do? Here one meets an important difference between the liberal and the conservative mind—or the progressive and the reactionary mind. The liberal (or progressive) tends to say to himself, this change is inevitable, it is in the spirit of the age, it must be helped along. The conservative (or reactionary) says to himself, this change is wrong; inevitable or not, it must be opposed. The great majority of the clergymen of the Church of England felt thus about disestablishment. They felt it was wrong, by instinct, even though only a minority of them benefited materially from establishment— most of them must have been in the position of Mr Tugwell, defending the establishment and his endowment of £17 per annum, even though the same system gave other clergymen, through family connections and influence, incomes of £1,000 or more. Equalization of incomes such as would follow disestablishment (and did follow it in Ireland) would surely have benefited more poor clergy than it would have damaged wealthy ones.* Yet the English clergy in general (there were exceptions) responded to the cry of "the Church in danger" and rallied to the Conservative party.

The *Globe* sent out the call to the clergy on 12 June 1868: it was their duty to take politics into the pulpit, and not let tabernacle and tract have it all their own way. (There was of course an important point here: if the Anglican clergy were active on one side

* Cf. *The Times* leader, 4 September 1868: "The benefit of a splendid and high-titled Establishment is very much confined to places, to classes, to cliques, and to families, to the owners of patronage and the possessors of influence. Of course, they will lose something—that is, all they cannot commute into solid cash. But the many, we humbly think, will not lose so much as either the friends or the foes of the Church of England seem to anticipate."

in politics, Dissenting and Catholic clergy were equally active on the other.) The *Record* on 3 August urged the clergy to overcome their reluctance to take part in party politics (one wonders how reluctant they really were), because the real issue was not political. It was "whether the State, as a State, shall have a religion, or should look with godless indifference on all matters relative to men's souls, to the commands of God, and to the claims of another world". The latter would be "the public avowal of national atheism". From the other side, the *Daily News* on 6 August tried to warn them off; the activity of the clergy on behalf of the Irish Church might bring upon them the very fate they feared—the English establishment would not survive an offensive and defensive alliance with Toryism.

The Convocation of Canterbury, which met at the beginning of July, reflected the general opinion of the clergy by resolving that an address be sent to the Queen asking her to take measures to prevent the disestablishment and disendowment of the Irish Church. (It was not clear just what the reverend gentlemen thought the Queen could do.) This passed in both houses with very few dissentients.[120] At the same time twenty-five influential Conservatives, mostly clergymen, met to form the Church and State Defence Society, "to oppose the policy of Mr Gladstone and Dr Pusey". The Dean of York took the chair, and became President of the Society.[121] A few examples of activity in the constituencies may be noted. At Exeter, the Archdeacon preached a sermon in the cathedral comparing the Liberal party with five of the most wicked men in the Bible—not to the Liberals' advantage, which is a formidable thought. The local Liberal candidate expected thirty or forty clergymen to vote against him.[122] The Dean of Carlisle issued a long address to the electors, telling them that they had to decide on a religious principle, for or against the principle of an established Church.[123] The vicar of Christ Church, Mirfield, sought to act as a political talent scout, writing to Disraeli that he thought a Conservative would have a good chance at Ripon, and recommending a candidate—"Send this to Colonel Taylor and he can make inquiries".[124] Henry Allon, the editor of the Nonconformist *British Quarterly Review*, wrote to Gladstone: "Everywhere the Evangelical clergy have moved heaven and earth to excite fears about the Church. In my own parish the vicar has had meetings of his clergy at his house since July—& the most perfect & strenuous organisation has been brought into operation." However, the Liberals had won the seat.[125] After the election, Gladstone told General Grey (the Queen's private secretary) that he attributed the defeat of the Liberals in the counties to the work of the country clergy, and from the security of his great majority he was able to add that he was glad to see the influence of the clergy still so strong.[126]

There were exceptions. There were High Churchmen (Pusey and Liddon prominent among them) who favoured disestablishment in Ireland and would not be sorry to see it in England too. There were others who had been offended by Disraeli's wild attacks upon their party. The appointments in early November 1868 of Tait to Canterbury and Jackson to London also annoyed High Churchmen. There were reports of High Church influence working against the Conservatives. Other supporters of Irish disestablishment were the 261 clergymen of the Church of England who signed a petition presented in the House of Lords on 23 June 1868. These were only a tiny fraction of the 20,000 or so clergy in England, but they included some distinguished intellects— Maurice, Kingsley, Jowett, and the headmasters of Winchester, Harrow, Haileybury, and Rugby.[127] Dean Stanley promised his votes to the Liberal candidates in Westminster.[128] At Derby, one Evangelical clergyman worked so effectively for the Liberals that a local Conservative appealed to the Prime Minister to get a sound Tory appointed to a Lord Chancellor's living in the town.[129] At Greenwich, the vicar, J. C. Miller (another Evangelical) publicly supported Gladstone's campaign, bringing upon himself the condemnation of *The Rock*.[130] For not even all Evangelicals supported the government. There had been a suspicion abroad that under Disraeli, the Bishop of Oxford, Wilberforce, had had undue influence in appointments, and that Evangelicals had been neglected; more, that those who had voted Conservative at Oxford University at the last election had been neglected in favour of some who had voted for Gladstone.[131] There were a few brave clergymen who appeared on Liberal platforms—one, just outside Wigan, even sat not only with Lord Hartington but with a Roman Catholic priest.[132]

In these three elements—anti-Catholic feeling, a conviction that the Church really was in danger, and the willingness of the clergy to turn out in its defence—there lay some reason to believe that a campaign such as that fought by the Conservatives in 1868 might succeed. But it did not do so. The Conservative government, which had begun by being crushingly defeated in the House of Commons, went on to lose the general election by a wide margin. Gladstone won; his policy and choice of battle-ground were vindicated at the polls; with a majority of over a hundred seats, he had every opportunity to translate his policy into legislation, to disestablish and disendow the Irish Church. We must next look briefly at why this happened.

First, it is worth noting that all Disraeli's efforts did not wholly dispel the suspicions in the minds of some of his supporters. Disraeli had denied outright in the House of Commons on 22 May that his government had ever intended to endow a Catholic university or to pay the Catholic clergy in Ireland. Mayo too had explained that in his reference to levelling up he had meant no more than that the "gradual elevation of churches", which had been going on for some years, should be continued. It is doubtful how far they were believed.[133] The Archdeacon of Raphoe, for example, declared that he feared Disraeli's treachery more than Gladstone's open hostility.[134] The report of the Commission on the Irish Church, whose substance was well known long before it was published late in September 1868, kept speculation alive. It proposed the suppression of four bishoprics and several dignities, the amalgamation of small parishes, and various other adjustments. Hardy gloomily described these recommendations as "further enfeeblement before the final blow".[135] The *Globe* welcomed the report, including its recommendations, and it is easy to see how Irish Churchmen feared that the government meant to put it into operation.[136] There appears to be no indication that the government as such had any plan for the Irish Church,* though in October both Mayo and Cairns thought that one should be

---

* In October, Disraeli persuaded Colonel Wilson-Patten to become Chief Secretary for Ireland in succession to Mayo. Patten protested that he knew nothing of Ireland or the Church question, but Disraeli brushed this aside. All he needed to say was that the question would be considered by the government, which would advise the course most in the public interest (Hanham, p. 297).

devised. Mayo told Disraeli that he must have a measure ready, whether he eventually decided to introduce it or not. If he intended to carry out all or some of the Commission's recommendations, they must quickly get down to the details.[137] Cairns in fact produced a detailed memorandum, dated 19 October. He thought that the government must be prepared to legislate about the Irish Church, because it had always said that there were defects to be remedied. But he insisted that the issue of establishment raised by Gladstone did not admit of compromise. The actual suggestions he made were for minor changes—suppression of several dignities, readjustment of benefices, reduction of bishops' incomes—which left the whole substance of the Irish Church, in establishment, in organization, and in endowment, intact.[138] There is, of course, no certainty that these proposals would have been acted upon if the government had survived, but at least there is nothing in them to justify suspicion of the government.

However, the suspicion was there, both of the government's Irish policy and behind that of Disraeli himself.[139] It is not possible to deduce what effect it had, if any, on the election result, but it seems likely that it was slight. The sort of person who distrusted Disraeli for being too Liberal was likely to vote Conservative anyway—he might abstain out of pique, but local reasons, if no others, would probably bring him to the poll. Suspicion of the government may have had some influence at Belfast, where besides the two official Conservative candidates there appeared a third, Johnston, who claimed to be the representative of the Protestant working men, and who denounced the government for hinting at "levelling up".[140] Johnston won a seat, the Conservative vote was split, and a Liberal Presbyterian candidate slipped in to gain a seat for his party.[141] But there was more in this than the Irish Church question or Disraeli. One reason for Johnston's popularity was that he had been imprisoned (under the Conservative administration) for breaking the Processions Act. Mayo had known that the enforcement of the Act against Orangemen as well as against Catholics would raise the North against the government.[142] Moreover, the Irish Reform Bill was unpopular with Belfast Conservatives. The Conservative Association there objected to lowering the franchise, to changing the constituency boundaries, and to increasing the number of seats in Ulster. Mayo commented to Disraeli: "I fear we shall find our Irish supporters very unmanageable over this and many other questions."[143]

There was a far greater weakness on the Conservative side than the suspicions of some of their supporters. They left too many seats uncontested. On this point Disraeli was over-optimistic, as on other aspects of the campaign, and also surprisingly ill-informed. He wrote on 16 August: "We have our men better planted than our opponents; more numerous candidates, and stronger ones."[144] When it came to the poll, this proved quite wrong; there were 213 seats with no Conservative standing, as against 116 with no Liberal.[145] This crippled the Conservative campaign hopelessly. In more than half the constituencies there was no contest, and in these the Liberals were bound to win a majority of 92. Also, among the contested constituencies, there were many with two seats and only three candidates, two from one party, one from the other. Here in effect only one seat was being fought, and *The Times* calculated that of these additional uncontested seats, thirty-four would go to the Liberals, five or six to the Conservatives. This gave the Liberals a majority of about 120 on the uncontested seats. If the Conservatives were to win the election, they would thus have to win over two-thirds of the remaining seats. *The Times* reckoned that in fact these seats would be shared equally between the two parties, leaving the Liberals with a majority of at least 100. All this was apparent at the beginning of November, before the poll began.[146] (Disraeli, incidentally, was not dismayed—he still thought it possible that his party would win two-thirds of the contested seats.[147]) To give away a majority of 120 before the poll started was a grave handicap, which it would need a crushing Conservative victory elsewhere to overcome. It was reckoned after the election that the Conservatives could have carried several more county seats if they had put up more candidates.[148]

One reason for the Liberal victory in the country was thus that they gave themselves a good chance of victory by putting up plenty of candidates. Another important reason was that the alliance created by Gladstone in March held firm, both in Parliament and in the country. Whigs, rank and file Liberal M.P.s (who were mostly Anglicans[149]), Radicals of various sorts, Dissenters (urged on by the Liberation Society), and Catholics—all held together. There was obviously a real danger that they would not do

8

so, and the Conservatives hoped to be able to split up this combination. The Whigs, for example, might have been responsive to
arguments based on the danger to property inherent in Gladstone's Irish Church policy. Anglican Liberals might have been
alarmed at the prospect of disestablishment in England, or have
been convinced that it was wrong to disendow a Church. (In the
event, among prominent Liberals, only Roundell Palmer took the
stand that disestablishment was right, but disendowment wrong.)
Most obvious of all, the alliance between Dissenter and Catholic
appeared vulnerable. Lord Grey, for example, thought that they
could be split up if the defenders of the established Church
would accept a policy of concurrent endowment. He thought that
the Irish hierarchy could be persuaded to accept this, while the
Liberation Society, with its opposition to all state endowments,
would not.[150] This proved to have no chance of success. The Conservative government had burned its fingers once on the matter of
"levelling up", and would not touch it again. There was strong
feeling among Protestants against "endowing error". And Grey's
guess about the attitude of the Irish hierarchy was mistaken; with
the exception of Bishop Moriarty, the Irish hierarchy firmly preferred secularization to concurrent endowment.[151]

The Catholic influence on the general election was obviously
strongest in Ireland, where the hierarchy threw all its weight
behind Gladstone. They used all the very considerable means at
their disposal; circulars, letters in the press, addresses to their
clergy, organization, intimidation, and undue influence.[152] The
result was a Liberal victory in Ireland by sixty-five seats to forty,
and the crushing out of the remnants of the old "Independents",
some of whom had in the 1860s given general support to the Conservatives. Sir George Bowyer, for example, was defeated at
Dundalk, where Archbishop Kieran worked against him.[153] The
Liberal majority in Ireland before the election has been reckoned
at seven, so this represented a substantial gain of eighteen seats.
Outside Ireland, there was a considerable Catholic vote, but in
1868 where it was most heavily concentrated it brought a reaction. Lancashire returned a great majority of Conservatives,
and Gladstone himself was defeated in South-West Lancashire.
Brand, the Liberal Chief Whip, apologizing to Gladstone for this
mishap, wrote: "The truth is, Lancashire has gone mad, and the

contest there has been one of race, Saxon against Celt. This is a sad state of things."[154] Similarly, Milner Gibson, who lost his seat at Ashton, wrote that the Irish Catholics had supported him to a man, turning him into their own candidate and alienating a number of English voters.[155]

The influence of Protestant Dissent, with some few exceptions, worked alongside that of the Catholic hierarchy. The Liberation Society, which had first forged the alliance with the Irish Catholics, made a great effort in the election of 1868, and looked back on the results with satisfaction. It had concentrated mainly on propaganda, and claimed that without its efforts many areas would have been left to the supporters of the Irish Church. The Society promoted 515 lectures and addresses, employing twenty-seven special lecturers as well as their regular agents. They printed 1,070,000 of their publications, all but 12,000 of which were distributed.[156] How many of these were read, and by whom, it is impossible to tell, but the scale of the propaganda operation was impressive. The Liberation Society's most striking and immediate success was in Wales, where it provided the basis of the Liberal organization and above all the drive necessary to rouse Welsh Nonconformity into political activity. It played a vital role in giving the Liberals victory in Wales and Monmouthshire by twenty-three seats to ten, a majority of thirteen as against one of four in the previous Parliament.[157] In Scotland, the Liberals almost swept the board, with a victory of fifty-three seats to seven. The Conservative appeal to Protestant sentiment failed utterly. The Presbyterian vote was overwhelmingly Liberal—with the exception of a majority of the ministers of the Established Church of Scotland, whose votes in the University seat went to the Conservative candidate.[158] The Liberal majority in Scotland rose to forty-six from thirty-three. Ireland, Wales, and Scotland provided the Liberals with their total gains.

In England, their majority remained at twenty-six seats, as in the old Parliament. But there too the Nonconformist influence made itself felt. The Wesleyan body, previously Conservative, changed its sympathies, partly on the disestablishment issue, partly in revulsion against the growth of ritualism in the Church of England.[159] A Conservative reported to the Conservative Chief Whip from Lincolnshire that there the Wesleyans were neutral, and all other Nonconformists (who were strong in the county) were supporting Gladstone.[160] Lord Malmesbury wrote in disgust to Disraeli from Christchurch, Hampshire after the election:

> This district is a hotbed of Dissent & almost every labourer & small tradesman is a dissenter & the feeling among them is execrable. Our bill [the Reform Act of 1867] has added 800 of these to the old constituency of 420.
>
> *All* the gentry (& they are numerous) went well with Wolff [the Conservative candidate] & so did the *farmers* but their *labourers* were stolid—Men who have worked for 20 years voted agn. me, & were driven to the poll by their ministers, after promising, as if they were in Tipperary—& those who voted right told me that "it was agst. collar". The Church cannot hold its own with the new electors if it does not institute a class like the *bas clergé* in R.C. countries. They have no sympathy with *gentlemen* parsons.[161]

Against this determination Conservative propaganda beat in vain. The Protestant Association hammered away to the end at its theme that all Protestants, whether Churchmen or Dissenters, Conservative or Liberal, should unite to resist the progress of Popery.[162] It appeared barely credible to some that "the union of Cardinal Cullen with Knox and Manning with Wesley" could survive.[163] But it did. The grand alliance, however diverse its elements, held fast in face of the enemy.

The importance of this was incalculable. In the mid-nineteenth century elections were decided more by local influences and issues than by national questions. The key to the great Liberal victory in 1868 was that Gladstone's chosen national question—the disestablishment of the Irish Church—was one which concentrated important local elements on the Liberal side. National and local issues were fused. The religious groups of Catholics and Dissenters, with all the local interests and sentiments which they represented, were thrown overwhelmingly on one side. The social antagonisms which ran alongside the religious differences told in the same way. In Wales to win a Liberal victory was to strike a blow against both the Church and the landowner—against the local social order. This did not prevent, in other places, the normal influence of Liberal landowners or manufacturers being exercised in the usual way. So all the local influences which could operate on the Liberal side did so. Moreover, they did so with a zeal and fervour which could only come from service in a righteous cause. The moral element was vital, and here again the national issue raised by Gladstone was linked to local issues. A simple cry of justice for Ireland would have raised only limited support on the eastern side of the Irish Sea, as Gladstone was to find later. But when it was joined to the cause of religious equality, and presented by a master in the art of elevating politics to the plane of morality, it had a far wider appeal, because this was a question which was alive in every community. In these circumstances, the Conservatives did not lose their own local influences, exercised by landowners and the clergy of the established Church, but these were inadequate if the front against them remained unbroken. Their own attempt to produce a national issue which would rally local support, the Protestant cry, failed. It was Gladstone who produced the necessary fusion of the different elements in political life, and so won his victory.

4

THE PASSING OF
THE IRISH CHURCH ACT, 1869

Difficulties Ahead

When Gladstone first publicly raised the issue of Irish disestablishment and disendowment, Lord Derby predicted that the Liberals might be able to carry an abstract resolution condemning the state of the Irish Church, but that when it came to positive measures they would be hopelessly divided.[1] This view was widely shared. The *Saturday Review* on 11 April 1868 wrote that there could be only one opinion among Liberals on whether the position of the Irish Church was just or not, but they would have great difficulty in deciding what to do about it. Such forebodings were not dispelled even by the great electoral victory of November 1868. The *Pall Mall Gazette*, immediately after the election, thought that the Irish Church Bill was likely to take up the whole life of the next Parliament, or at least a whole session. The longer it lasted, the greater would be the difficulties of the Liberals.[2] The *Saturday Review* on 12 December gave Gladstone's new government as good a chance of surviving as not, which was scarcely complimentary when its majority was over a hundred. These misgivings were at least to some extent shared by Liberal leaders. The Duke of Argyll wrote to Gladstone on 30 November 1868: "As regards what you say of *strength* not being more than enough except in point of *numbers*—this is true enough—considering the *novelty* of the work before us—The whole idea of a Free Church is, strange to say, absolutely new to the great majority of English Politicians —and moreover it is specially feared & detested by a great section of the Liberal Party."[3] Gladstone foresaw the possibility of "minor schisms in the Liberal body, when we come to adjust details esp. with ref. to R.C.s".[4] He was well aware of the need to keep the support of the different groups in his party—or, as he himself put it, "My desires and those of the Govt. must necessarily, in matters not of strict right, have regard to the nature and coherence of the forces by means of which our end is to be gained."[5]

Two of the detailed schemes put forward in the press will serve to show the sort of ideas which were current about a disestablishment measure. *The Times*, on 17 and 18 December 1868, proposed certain obvious steps: exclusion of the Irish bishops from the House of Lords, abolition of the ecclesiastical courts, compensating the clergy for the loss of their life-interests. It dismissed as impractical the idea of a constituent assembly for the Irish Church, and thought that Parliament itself would have to regulate many matters. The property which remained to the Church, for example, should be held in trust for congregations attending episcopal churches and worshipping according to the Book of Common Prayer. The Crown might, if Irish Churchmen wished, continue to nominate bishops, and the bishops might appoint the lower clergy. The Church's property should be held subject to the clergy performing their duties according to the ecclesiastical law of England, to be enforced by the ordinary lay courts (i.e. by the Irish Court of Chancery). These proposals would have created a strange hybrid, a Church supposedly disestablished but still to a large degree controlled by the State. The *Pall Mall Gazette* thought that they would not do: Irish Churchmen would not have such an arrangement; and the lay courts would not be able to enforce their decisions if clergy and laity were against them. The *Gazette* therefore suggested that if the Irish Church could form a body representing bishops, clergy, and laity, which would submit a scheme for a voluntary religious association, then such a body should be incorporated by the Queen in Council and become the governing body of the Church. This was in substance what was actually to happen, but even the *Gazette* proposed to appropriate the remaining property to the provision of worship according to the forms of the Church of England.[6] Thus two responsible and influential journals, which both supported disestablishment and disendowment in Ireland, produced schemes which differed markedly in the principles to be applied.

The newly formed government, then, faced a difficult task. The generalities of Gladstone's resolutions on the Irish Church and of the general election campaign had to be translated into a Bill, and that Bill had then to be steered through both Houses of Parliament.

In the process, there would arise questions both of principle and of detail which were expected to test severely the new-found unity of the Liberal party.

Drafting the Bill

The Irish Church Act of 1869 was a major piece of legislation in which several different bodies were interested: the Irish Church itself, the Roman Catholic and Presbyterian Churches in Ireland, the Church of England, the Liberation Society. All acted as pressure groups, whether in the country or in Parliament, on the government directly or on persons who might influence the government. The opposition in the House of Commons was help-less if the Liberal majority held firm, as it did, but in the Lords there was a Conservative majority, and the question arose of what was the best use that majority could make of its power. The posi-tion of the Queen also became significant at one point. The whole passage of the Act can be traced, from Gladstone's first sketches and questions to the Act placed on the statute book. The Prime Minister, the Cabinet, a Cabinet committee, and civil servants all worked at it. Representations were made and pressures brought to bear on the government by outside bodies. In seeing how the Irish Church was disestablished and disendowed, one can also catch a glimpse of the organisms of Victorian government and politics at work.

The drafting of the Bill before it was presented to the House of Commons occupied two and a half months. Its progress may be briefly traced. On 17 and 18 December 1868, Gladstone wrote a memorandum of detailed questions on which he needed informa-tion, and proposals for dealing with them.[7] There are undated memoranda on general principles and various details which ap-pear to belong to the same month.[8] He also prepared a very rough sketch of a Bill, undated, followed by a full draft in eighty clauses, which was completed by 26 December.[9] Both these papers he wrote out in his own hand. He sent a copy of this draft to Fortescue, the Chief Secretary for Ireland, on 26 December; one to Granville, his principal political friend and government leader in the Lords, on the 28th; and one to Sullivan, the Irish Attorney-General, on the 29th.[10] Gladstone asked Sullivan to work on it, and arranged to meet him and Granville at Hawarden on 18 January 1869 to confer on the Bill. Granville liked the draft, though he had some trouble with its presentation: "Like some other documents in *your own handwriting* which has of late somewhat degenerated, one finds novelties on reading it a second time."[11] Gladstone brought Spencer, the Lord Lieutenant, into the secret at the New Year.[12] He does not appear to have informed his other colleagues of the scheme until it was formally submitted to the Cabinet on 8 February.

Gladstone's small working party duly met at Hawarden on 18 and 19 January.[13] Sullivan then took the Bill back to Dublin to get it in shape to be printed. Gladstone intended the Cabinet to consider the substance of the measure, and then what he called a caucus to meet daily and sift it line by line.[14] The Cabinet met on 8 and 9 February, with before it not a printed draft, which was not yet ready, but a "General View" of the Bill, prepared by Gladstone himself.[15] A Cabinet committee on the Bill had its first meeting on 17 February; it consisted of Gladstone, Granville, Fortescue, the Lord Chancellor, Kimberley, Lowe, Bright, and Sullivan, with Henry Thring, Home Office Counsel, present as draftsman.[16] By the time the committee met, the Bill had been printed in Dublin and brought over for it to work on.[17] Gladstone was by then anxious to hasten the work, even if this meant taking risks with the drafting of some minor clauses.[18] In fact an amended draft was printed on 25 February, and the Bill presented to the House of Commons on 1 March.[19] In the meantime, the Cabinet had twice considered reports from its committee, on 20 and 27 February.[20]

It is obvious even from this summary that Gladstone himself took the lead in all but the routine work of drafting. How then did Gladstone see the problems when he set about his task? First, he learned much from the precedent of Canada. In 1853 an Act of Lord Aberdeen's government, of which Gladstone had been a member, had empowered the Canadian legislature to deprive the Churches in Canada of those lands set apart for the support of the clergy. In 1854 the Canadian Parliament had passed an Act to this effect, saving the life-interests of the existing clergy. The Act allowed the Anglican clergy to commute their life interests, that is, to accept a lump sum in lieu of their right to an annuity. This they handed over to the Church authorities, which took over the payment of the annuities. Only one clergyman had refused to take this step. At the same time, the Church had been disestablished, and had set up its own system of synodical government. Gladstone had received information about these affairs from the Bishop of Montreal during 1868, and when he took office he had a paper on the subject prepared in the Colonial Office.[21]

The value of this recent experience was considerable, though it could not be taken as a blueprint for Ireland. Reflecting on the specific problem before him, Gladstone described it thus:

1. To wind up all the affairs of the present Church Establishment.

2. After the satisfaction of all proper claims, to apply the residue [i.e. of the Church's income].

In the winding up, he should be guided by the principles of justice, a friendly spirit towards the Irish Church, and equality as between it and other religious bodies.[22] What he meant by a friendly spirit is shown in his notes—that the measure "must respect the freedom of the disestablished Church; that it must make the transition as easy as possible; and that it must avoid unnecessary encouragement to change within the Church".[23]

These were generalities. Gladstone also needed large quantities of specialized information on details, and he set down a whole series of questions, ranging from a request for an approximate valuation of the whole property of the Irish Church (presumably to check on the figures of the recent Commission) to questions of how many curates there were, how many glebe-houses and from what sources they were built, and how many churches in Ireland might be considered ancient monuments and how much it cost to keep them up. A dozen pages of such "queries on the Irish Church" show Gladstone's mind probing into nearly all the problems which were to be raised in the course of the work.[24] Gladstone thus had a good grasp of what needed to be done, but he was still very glad when a chance came to get informed guidance from within the Irish Church. In general, the leaders of the Church held aloof and refused to co-operate in framing a Bill they detested. But, on 22 December 1868, Edward Stopford, Archdeacon of Meath, wrote to Gladstone to say that while he still disliked disestablishment, he was willing to accept the inevitable. It would be best to remove the Irish Church from the arena of party conflict by getting a measure through in that session of Parliament, and he offered to help to draw up a Bill which would be as little open to attack as possible. Stopford offered himself as one familiar with the details of Irish Church arrangements, and one of the founders of the Lay and Clerical Association, a body set up to discuss measures of reform within the Church. Gladstone welcomed his approach, invited him to Hawarden, and thereafter kept in close touch with him—though he did not always follow his advice.[25] A few other senior Irish clergy also offered Gladstone occasional advice—Atkins, Dean of Ferns; MacDonnell, Dean of Cashel; Woodward, Dean of Down.[26]

Such advice, offered in a constructive spirit, was welcomed by Gladstone. He received, of course, plenty of suggestions of all kinds, amounting sometimes to pressure. The Liberation Society put forward a memorandum on 23 January 1869, with a proposal that members of the Executive Committee should see the Prime Minister. Gladstone agreed to submit the suggestions to his colleagues (the Society anyway sent copies to Argyll, Bright, Bruce, and Lowe), but his reply was extremely guarded. He did not expect to have to ask more of them than to give support to the measure as a whole, without sacrificing the whole to any of the parts. He did not anticipate any special disagreement with the Society, but it would be a large and complex measure. He did not take up the suggestion for a meeting, though Miall and Henry Richard later had a talk with Bright.[27] By the end of January, of course, the preparation of the Bill was far advanced, and Gladstone obviously intended to keep the Liberation Society at arm's length, while the final details were being worked out. In fact, the broad outline of the Society's proposals was similar to that of Gladstone's Bill; but this was not the result of direct pressure. Where they differed in detail, as will be seen shortly, the Society's view was usually rejected.

From the Catholic hierarchy in Ireland there was open pressure, exerted through letters from bishops read at a meeting of the National Association on 12 January 1869. These warned Gladstone against any compromise—both disestablishment and disendowment of the Irish Church must be total. This was so blatant as to be something of an embarrassment to the government.[28] But there is no indication that the letters affected the drafting of the Bill on those matters—such as the compensation clauses or the disposal of glebe lands—which were concerned with disendowment.

In general then, Gladstone was the guiding force in drafting the Bill. He consulted close colleagues, ministers connected with Irish affairs, and finally the Cabinet as a whole; he also listened to advice from certain friendly Irish clergymen. Neither the Liberation Society nor the Catholic hierarchy appears to have influenced this process, except in so far as the Cabinet was aware that there were certain limits to Nonconformist and Catholic toleration.

In the process of drafting, important sections of the Bill appear to have gone through without leaving trace of discussion. Others raised disagreements between ministers, and occasionally attracted outside intervention. These are worth some attention.

First, there was a group of questions concerning the future organization of the Irish Church, the status of its existing clergy, and the disposal of its glebe-houses and lands. Here, the key point was established at the start by Gladstone, with some advice from Fortescue. Disestablishment was to be total. The Irish Church was to be placed in the same position as other religious bodies in Ireland, with no special position being retained by the Crown, as *The Times* had wanted. The Church was to be given the power to organize itself, and to form a body to hold property. The position of the existing clergy in the new conditions, however, proved a difficult question. There was no dispute over the principle that the clergy who were being deprived of their freehold tenure of office had the right to receive for life their incomes at the time of disestablishment. The issue was whether the clergy should receive their annuities without any obligation to the Church, or only on condition that they continued to perform their duties. Gladstone and Fortescue advocated the latter course.[29] The Liberation Society, with support from Bright, advocated compensation without reference to duties.[30] So did the Dean of Down, who argued that the new system, in order to succeed, must be congregational, and the existing parochial arrangements must disappear. It would be better to do this at one stroke.[31] The simple argument against this was that it would be scandalous to have clergymen leaving Ireland, and enjoying in England or on the continent an income guaranteed for life by the State, while their congregations were left without spiritual care—a low view of the clergy, but something which Gladstone foresaw as possible.[32] MacDonnell, the Dean of Cashel, suggested a compromise by which clergymen should not be absolutely bound to their duties in their then parishes, but be given the option of retiring on perhaps half of their annuities.[33]

The upshot of this discussion was in favour of the obligation to perform duty, as will be seen later. While the Bill was in draft, it became connected with the question of commutation. In Gladstone's first draft, he proposed to allow the Irish clergy to commute the annuity they would receive from the government for a lump sum, calculated on the expectation of life, to be paid to the representative body of the Church. Stopford strongly supported this course, and urged that inducements be held out to the clergy to make sure it was a success.[34] The potential advantages to the Church were indeed considerable. It would be a marked psychological advantage for the Church to pay its own clergy, instead of each man separately being paid by the government. Financially, skilful management might make advantageous use of the capital sum placed in the hands of the representative body. Hartington in fact thought the scheme would be considered too favourable to the Church: "Are we not under the name of compensation for life interests about to create a new endowment?"[35] Bright, too, after an interview with Miall and Richard of the Liberation Society and a deputation of Irish Presbyterians, suspected that the Church might be getting all the compensation for two thousand clergy into a fund which in the future would only have to provide for five hundred, because the Church would drastically reduce its commitments.[36] Gladstone denied to Bright that there would be any excessive liberality to the Church, and pointed out to Hartington that it would be an advantage to the government to escape as quickly as possible from the position of paymaster to the Irish clergy.[37] Fortescue took the view that the government should try to secure early and general commutation. He was willing to allow an incumbent to commute and then leave with perhaps two-thirds of the value of his life-interest, with the remaining one-third going to the Church not back to the State.[38] Again the views of Gladstone and Fortescue prevailed in the final draft of the Bill.

A question which loomed large during the drafting of the Bill was that of the glebe-houses of the Irish Church.* The discussion about the arrangements to be made for these houses remains of considerable interest, for two reasons. First, on this question Gladstone harked back to a form of concurrent endowment, which to all appearances he had given up in 1868. Second, on this issue in particular, the government felt the pressure of the various groups involved—Catholics, Nonconformists, even to some extent the Irish Church—and it was compelled to yield to the strongest of these pressures. As so often in human affairs, it was a question of houses and land which really raised the fighting spirit of all involved.

Gladstone's first thoughts on the matter, in his memorandum of 17/18 December 1868, were to recommend to Parliament that the glebe-houses should be offered to the Church in trust as residences for the clergy, free of charge. At the same time there should be offered to the other religious communions in Ireland perhaps £300 per congregation to provide houses for their ministers. If Parliament would not accept this, the glebe-houses should be offered to the Church at moderate terms, with loans to ease the process; similar loans should be made to other denominations to buy parsonages.[39] In the draft of 26 December, the proposal to offer the glebe-houses to the Church appeared again, and the amount to be offered to the other communions had gone up to £700 per house, where there was a congregation but no parsonage. No alternative was mentioned.[40] The money for the other denominations would be provided from the confiscated funds of the Irish Church, and the process would have amounted to a considerable measure of concurrent endowment.

It is not clear why Gladstone went back at this point to the sort of views he had favoured in 1867. Predictably, he ran into the opposition which had previously made concurrent endowment an impossible policy. Bright warned him on 9 January 1869 that, while he personally was willing to be generous, any proposal to give parsonages to the Catholics would cause all the fifty-three Liberal members from Scotland to revolt.[41] From the other side, Sir John Gray had been writing to Gladstone since October 1868, arguing that to hand over the glebe-houses to the Church free of

---

* The term glebe-house is here used to include all residences of clergy, including bishops.

charge would amount to re-endowment, and that the Church should be made to pay for the houses, though on easy terms. There should be a system of loans for the other denominations. Cullen agreed with this attitude, and indeed at one point he was presumably angrier with Gladstone than he need have been, because he had the idea that the intention was to leave the glebes to the established Church and give nothing to the other denominations.[42] Faced with this opposition to his plan, Gladstone was inconsistent in his attitude. To Gray he wrote on 15 January 1869 that the Scots Presbyterians and English Nonconformists "might take fire" if a system of permanent loans for glebe-houses were suggested.[43] One might think that, if they would so object to loans, they would surely also object to gifts? But Gladstone still thought he might work the oracle. His reply to Bright's objection was that the Ulster Presbyterians might play an important part—"This peculiar cross between Scotchman & Irishman has undoubtedly a very good nose for catching any scent of public money." He thought that they might come in, and draw the Catholics after them. At any rate, he was going to have the Bill drafted to include his plan— the Cabinet could cut it out at the last moment if necessary.[44]

In fact Gladstone clung to his plan as long as he could. His paper for the Cabinet on 8 February 1869 included two proposals —either to give or to sell the glebe-houses to the Irish Church.[45] The draft Bill printed on 15 February, however, simply stated that the houses should be handed over free of charge, and that sums with an unspecified upper limit should be given to the other denominations.[46] This astounded the Duke of Argyll, who wrote at once to Gladstone that this did precisely what he thought they were agreed to avoid: "levelling up" in the matter of glebe-houses. However much there was to be said for this in the abstract, it had no chance of success.[47] This was true. Stopford could put a strong case that the houses had been built out of the past incomes of the Irish clergy, and the Church should not be required to pay again for what had already been paid for. But Stopford's only means of pressure was to argue that harshness on this point would alienate moderate opinion in the Irish Church, and might compel certain bishops to vote against the Bill in the House of Lords.[48] This was inadequate against the big battalions of Catholics and Nonconformists. Fortescue was impressed by Stopford's case, which was reinforced by his own findings on the small proportion of public grants which had gone into the building of glebe-houses. He was clear that the government should deal very considerately with the Church in this matter. But he thought that this would have to be done by giving the Church the right to buy back limited areas of glebe land, with the houses thrown in, either free of charge or at a very moderate price.[49] Something like this in fact emerged in the Bill, which compelled the Church to buy back its own glebe-houses, but at various valuations which made the transaction as favourable to the Church as possible. The plan to give money to other denominations was dropped, and a separate measure providing for temporary loans to build clergy houses was introduced later. Thus the political pressures involved in the question forced Gladstone to abandon the plan he thought best, and to cloak the fairly generous terms he succeeded in giving to the Church under the obscurities of the different ways of valuing property in Ireland.

Another question to which a good deal of attention was given during the drafting of the Bill was the use to which the surplus of the funds of the Irish Church (after all claims for compensation had been met) was to be put. Gladstone expected this surplus to be large, and he thought in terms of a lump sum, which proved to be mistaken. "I shd. like a residue of at least six millions", he wrote to Sullivan on 11 January 1869. When he introduced the Bill in the Commons, he said seven to eight millions.[50] It was generally taken for granted that there had to be a surplus, though there was a perfectly good argument that there need not be. The Archdeacon of Tuam, John Cather, for example, pointed out that if any other tax on land was no longer required for the purpose for which it was levied, the natural thing would be to abolish the tax. In England, indeed, church rates had just been abolished, not diverted to national purposes. The simplest course, therefore, would be to abolish the tithe rent-charge in Ireland; this would cause much of the revenue of the Irish Church to disappear, and there would be little left for people to fight about. It would benefit the landowners who paid the tithe, and the government could thus buy their support for a measure they would otherwise oppose.[51] A writer in the *Revue des deux Mondes* had pointed out the logic of this position several months before, commenting how odd it was of the English to regard the tithe as a sort of perpetual rent owed by the land, which, if it were not to be used for the religious benefit of the people, had to be used in some other way.[52] Roundell Palmer too had argued during the election campaign that the landowners had a better claim to the tithes than anyone else.[53] It was indeed difficult to see in logic why the cost of some new benefit or service to the people of Ireland should fall just on the former tithe-payers, and not on all property-owners in the country.

The test which had to be applied to the question was, however, not logical but political. It was politically quite impossible for a Liberal government to give a substantial present to the Irish landlords. Hartington thought that even the arrangements in the Bill to allow landlords to buy up their liability to the tithe rent-charge at twenty-two-and-a-half years' purchase, with government loans to help them, would be considered unduly favourable to the landlords.* So the tithe could not simply be abolished, and some new way of spending it would have to be found. One sort of proposal was some form of concurrent endowment, which would have the advantage of keeping the revenues of the Irish Church devoted to religious purposes, rather than secularizing them. This was supported by several people, including the editor of *The Times*, a former Bishop of Norwich, and a Catholic Irish bishop.[54] As we have seen, Gladstone was willing to attempt a limited form of this by gifts of money for parsonages. Other possibilities which he considered were education, public works, the remission of the poor rate, and the relief of unavoidable suffering without adding to the poor rate.[55] Of these, Gladstone preferred the last. As early as 1 December 1868 he drafted a set of questions for a special inquiry by John Lambert, the official of the Poor Law Board who had earlier that year written a paper on the Irish Church question for Disraeli's government. Lambert was to visit Ireland to find out whether there was sufficient provision for the aged and sick poor, the blind, deaf and dumb, lunatics and idiots, and sufferers from accidents.[56] Lambert spent January in Ireland,

* Hartington to Gladstone, 12 February 1869, Gladstone Papers, 44143, ff. 22–5. Gladstone assured him that the government were asking the landlords for 22½ years' purchase when the market price was at most 20 years' purchase, so the terms were not unduly generous. They turned out to be nothing like generous enough; hardly anyone was willing to buy up the tithe at this price, and its payment dragged on when the government wanted to see it wound up and out of the way.

talked with Gladstone on 5 February 1869, and submitted an elaborate report on 8 February.[57] He found a need for more nurses for the sick poor; that the Census Commissioners in 1851 and 1861 had urged on the government the need to make national provision for the deaf, dumb, and blind; and that there were not enough lunatic asylums. He recommended that the following annual payments might be paid out of a national fund produced by the Church surplus.

Infirmaries and hospitals	£51,000
Lunatic asylums	£185,000
Deaf, dumb, and blind	£40,000
Imbeciles (training)	£25,000
Nurses	£15,000
Reformatories and industrial schools	£10,000
	£326,000[58]

Lambert proposed changes in the local tax system to relieve especially the payers of the county cess, who included (except in Dublin) all occupiers, down to the lowest value of property. For example, lunatic asylums were paid for out of the county cess, which could be relieved of this charge.

Lambert's inquiry and Gladstone's personal concern with it are worth setting out in some detail because they show how seriously Gladstone took these proposals to use the surplus, and how carefully the matter was gone into. The intention to use the funds thus was written into the Bill presented on 1 March. In the preamble it was stated that the funds "should be appropriated mainly to the relief of unavoidable calamity and suffering, yet so as not to cancel or impair the obligations now attached to property under the Acts for the relief of the poor". In clause 59 the purposes set out in Lambert's memorandum were enumerated. It would have been a humane and sensible way to spend the money, though the argument was still illogical. If these services were needed, they should be paid for in the usual way by local taxation, or even, if need be, by national taxation. To pay for them out of the Church funds would in fact, whatever the preamble might say, reduce the obligations on the poor rate and other forms of taxation.*

* A justification in the eyes of some contemporaries was that the tithe had, in its origin, been set aside for the benefit of the poor as well as of the Church,

The general picture which emerges of the drafting of the Irish Church Bill is one of vigour, speed, and efficiency. The process was very largely confined to a small circle within the government. Gladstone himself provided at almost all points the initiative and the decisions, though he consulted frequently with Fortescue on matters of detail. The function of the Cabinet and its committee on the Bill was the scrutiny of the Bill at a late stage in its development, when of major matters only the question of the glebe-houses remained to be settled. Of persons and bodies outside the government, Archdeacon Stopford provided expertise and knowledge not otherwise obtainable; he influenced details, but failed in a trial of strength on the glebe-houses. It was on this matter that the Catholics and Nonconformists showed their influence when they cared to insist. Other suggestions from these groups were ignored: for example, requests that the disused church on the Rock of Cashel should pass to the Catholic Church;[59] hints from Cullen that the transfer of some cathedrals and churches actually in use would be acceptable;[60] and the proposal of the Liberation Society that the clergy of the Irish Church should receive their annuities without any obligations. The Bill which emerged was not the Bill of any pressure group; it was not even the Cabinet's Bill or the Chief Secretary's Bill; it was Gladstone's Bill, just as the initiative for the whole operation had been his. One may think that he suffered an aberration of judgement on the question of giving funds for parsonages to Catholics and Presbyterians; one may have reservations about the logic of the use of the surplus; but for the skill with which the whole many-sided problem was handled, for the intellectual grasp reflected on page after page of Gladstone's closely-written hand, one can have only the greatest admiration.

The Subject of the Operation
The Irish Church during the Drafting of the Bill

The Irish Church as a body did not have its views represented to the government during the drafting of the Bill. This was the result

---

and in fact constituted a "national reserve", in Coleridge's phrase, to be used for such purposes. But it is difficult to see why such a concept should influence a mid-nineteenth century government, normally concerned to rationalize administration.

of the refusal of its leaders to have any part in the matter, not of
unwillingness on Gladstone's part to consult them. He was glad
to have the advice of individual Irish clergymen, and he hoped in
December 1868 and January 1869 to have discussions with the
Irish bishops on some sort of formal basis. He opened by writing
to Trench, the Archbishop of Dublin, on 14 December. He said
he wished to communicate as much and as freely with the Archbishop as the latter saw fit. The time might come when the Irish
Church authorities might wish to consider ways and means,
rather than whether disestablishment was to come about at all,
and when it came the government would give the Church facilities
for considering its position and providing for its future. "Your
Grace will, I am sure," he ended, "construe favourably the spirit
in which this letter is written, and written on my own responsibility. . . ."[61] In one way this was a tactful and a helpful letter,
offering closer relations to the Archbishop than he had enjoyed
with the previous government.* On the other hand, Gladstone
was naturally offering co-operation only on his own terms: when
the Church's leaders accepted the principle of disestablishment,
then he would give them facilities to discuss their own predica-
ment. This was a reference to the requests of the Irish bishops to
be allowed to convene the Irish Convocation, first made in
November 1862 and renewed in November 1867 and October
1868. The bishops raised the matter again at the end of December.[62] Gladstone was determined that they should not be allowed
to call Convocation to resist the government's measure, but was
willing to agree if the bishops intended to steer the body on to a
discussion of how the new situation was to be met.[63]

Trench was extremely guarded in his reply to Gladstone's letter
of 14 December. He first asked permission to consult the Archbishop of Armagh, and then replied on behalf of them both declining to put anything before Gladstone, because anything they
wrote might be misconstrued as acquiescing in the act of disestablishment. The time for this might come, but had not yet
arrived.[64] This was Trench's fixed view at this time. His old friend
Wilberforce, the Bishop of Oxford, wrote to him on 30 December,
arguing that delay would only damage the Irish Church by

* There is no correspondence with Trench in Disraeli's papers, and only one
formal letter from Beresford, the Archbishop of Armagh.

exasperating the great Liberal majority in the Commons, and sketching his own idea of a compromise acceptable to the Church. This included the retention of all churches, glebe-houses, and post-Reformation endowments; future freedom from state intervention; the Church to be a self-governing corporation capable of owning property; and compensation for vested interests out of a common Church fund, conditional on the discharge of duties laid down by the Church. These would in fact have been generous terms, especially the provision about post-Reformation endowments; but Trench forbade Wilberforce to publish them as a move towards a compromise. He claimed that he had no authority to enter into any negotiations, and that any attempt to do so would be regarded by Irish Churchmen as a betrayal.[65]

A little later, at the beginning of January 1869, the prospects for any useful contact between Gladstone and Trench were worsened still further as the Archbishop came to resent Gladstone's attitude. He wrote to friends that the Prime Minister's language was menacing, and that he entirely subordinated the interests of the Church to those of party.[66] These sentiments were confirmed when on 14 January Gladstone wrote to Trench setting out plainly his attitude on the calling of the Irish Convocation.[67] Trench was very angry, writing of "his monstrous proposal that we may meet to do *his* work, but shall not meet if we intend to do our own". News of this did not reach Gladstone, who thought a week later that "The Abp. shows no heat, nor malice: and is most righteous. But his management of the helm is not satisfactory."[68]

In part this was justified. Trench told Roundell, the Lord Lieutenant's secretary, on 21 January that terms must be come to on the field of battle, or at any rate in arms, which made little sense and understandably riled Gladstone. "A House of Commons has fought and decided—a nation has done the same, & a Ministry has run away, but the Archbishop (how militant he is) waits for 'the field of battle'!"[69] But in part too the Archbishop had a strong case which Gladstone did not give him credit for. This rested on the belief that, even if the Irish bishops opened discussions with the government, and influenced the drafting of the Bill so that they got the best terms possible for the Irish Church, they would only be repudiated by the clergy and laity behind them. General opinion in the Irish Church had not accepted defeat, and would regard any dealings with the enemy as betrayal. Yet, if the blow did fall, if disestablishment and disendowment were carried, then the bishops would be dependent on the good will and support of all the members of the Church. Thus not only Trench, but also the Bishops of Limerick, Meath, and Derry, came to say in February 1869 that disestablishment was inevitable, but in the best interests of the reconstruction of the Church they could not afford to alienate those whom they would shortly have to ask for a great deal of money and effort. In these circumstances there was little point in Gladstone deploring Trench's helmsmanship, or Spencer in Dublin appealing to the Archbishop to lead and not be driven.[70] It was by no means easy to lead a large number of belligerent Anglo-Irishmen in a direction which they did not wish to take. The consequence of this line of argument was that at the beginning of February the Irish bishops formally published a resolution that they had no authority to enter into negotiations about a Bill whose passage they would not regard as inevitable, and which they were bound to resist. They thus took up a public position from which they could scarcely retreat. Only the Bishop of Down, Knox, dissented.[71]

Gladstone was genuine in his desire for co-operation with the Irish bishops, and was disappointed not to receive it. He wrote frequently that their co-operation would be in the public interest, and also in the interest of the Irish Church itself, because men who acted like Stopford became virtual supporters of the Bill, and were entitled to have their views considered. It would enable the government to say to its supporters: "This is what the Irish Church desires, & the advantage in ease and certainty of settlement is so great a public good that you should concede it."[72] He may well have been over-optimistic in this. The nearest he got to a negotiation with the Irish bishops was a series of exchanges with Magee, Bishop of Peterborough and formerly Dean of Cork, who claimed to represent a body of moderate opinion in the Irish Church.[73] These culminated in a meeting between Gladstone and Magee on 10 February 1869, and in a further meeting on 19 February between Gladstone and the Archbishop of Canterbury, who intervened to try to follow up Magee's efforts. Both Magee and Tait requested that the Irish Church keep all post-Reformation endowments. Magee told Gladstone that the acceptance of this condition might cause Irish Churchmen to accept the Bill, but nothing else would.[74] This in fact was a demand which would have preserved so much for the Church (including all the Ulster glebes given in the reign of James I) that, given compensation for life interests, disendowment would have been nullified. If this was indeed the *conditio sine qua non* of a successful negotiation between the government and the Irish Church, then there was no point in such a negotiation starting at all, for Gladstone could never make so great a concession.[75]

So there were two insuperable obstacles in the way of any co-operation between the government and the leaders of the Irish Church: the stiff conditions even of those who called themselves moderates on the Church side, as well as a general opposition in the Church to any dealings with the enemy. The full impossibility of useful contacts is clearly seen by turning from the private exchanges to the state of public opinion in the Irish Church as, after the Liberal victory in the general election, it faced the prospect of the Bill.

A few voices were raised in favour either of compromise, of coming to terms with Gladstone at an earlier or later stage of the passage of the Bill, or at any rate of discussing and making preparations for the coming of disestablishment. For example, in December 1868, Sherlock, the curate of Bray, County Wicklow, published a pamphlet sketching the constitutions of other non-established Churches in the Anglican Communion, and using this material to make suggestions for the future arrangements of the Irish Church.[76] In January 1869, a more distinguished figure, the Honourable and Reverend William Conyngham Plunket, a member of an aristocratic Irish ecclesiastical family and Treasurer of St Patrick's Cathedral, Dublin, also published a pamphlet, *The Dangers of Silence*. He argued that the verdict of the election had gone against the Irish Church, and that it was best to prepare for the possibility of defeat. It was certainly best, for example, that there should be debate, not silence, on the question of whether the Lords should simply reject an Irish Church Bill, or try to improve it by amendment. Plunket favoured amendment, believing that rejection would ultimately produce a worse settlement. He wrote that the majority of the government were not moved by a desire to destroy or humiliate the Irish Church, and would be glad to know how they could carry the principle of disestablishment while injuring the Church as little as possible; a defiant silence on the part of Irish Churchmen would not help them. Moreover, silence would allow others to monopolize public discussion, to the detriment of the Church.[77] The Bishop of Down, Robert Knox, went further still, and advocated publicly immediate discussions with Gladstone. Dissenting from the resolution of the Irish bishops on 3 February 1869, which declined any negotiation, he declared that without forfeiting their principles they could confer with the Prime Minister in the hope of modifying the measure.[78] On 16 March he repeated the same view to a conference of the clergy and laity of his diocese, declaring that the nation had already decided the issue, and each hour of fruitless obstruction would only make matters worse.[79]

Such were three men who argued for some form of flexible policy—there were others. But they encountered a formidable volume of protest and abuse. Sherlock was told by the *Daily Express* on 30 December 1868 that Irish Protestants did not accept the inevitability of defeat. The Conservatives possessed a majority in the House of Lords and the sympathy of the Queen. So he should not give the enemy encouragement and show him how the problems of Irish disestablishment might be overcome. Plunket drew the same fire. What he showed was not the dangers of silence but the dangers of faint-heartedness—the strategy of running away before fighting. Both Lords and the Queen had obstructive powers, though timid people shrank from using them.[80] At a meeting of the Protestant Defence Association in Dublin, Lord Bandon and others continued to repeat that disendowment was robbery, and disestablishment meant replacing the supremacy of the Queen by that of the Pope. There could be no compromise on such matters. The Association circularized every clergyman in Ireland to stir up opposition to the government.[81]

The Bishop of Down saw his arguments for a compromise swept aside at the diocesan meeting at Belfast. His speech was badly received—the *Freeman* commented on the unedifying sound of clergy hissing their own bishop. Nearly all the speakers were against him, including the Dean of Down, and a resolution against compromise was carried unanimously.[82] Other conferences of clergy and laity followed, for example for the dioceses of Tuam

(23 March) and Derry (26 March), showing the same opposition to compromise.[83] In the clamour there was a persistent note demanding repeal of the Union, since the Irish Protestants gained nothing from it. A meeting of the Ulster Protestant Defence Association on 31 March in Belfast passed a resolution that if the 5th article of the Act of Union (the article providing for the union of the English and Irish Churches) were repealed, they would regard the Union as dissolved.[84] The *Dublin Evening Mail* in May 1869 maintained that Irish Protestants had been driven to support repeal.[85]

These examples of feeling among the rank and file of Irish Churchmen, both clergy and laity, were undoubtedly typical. Archbishop Trench and his colleagues were right in judging that this opinion was a serious obstacle to any compromise with the government. Indeed, it was an obstacle to the Irish Church doing anything at all while it waited for its fate to be decided. This was certainly the intention—any move to prepare for disestablishment was seen as encouragement to the enemy. Yet in fact the result was different from the intention. Even in the act of saying there should be no discussion, Irish Churchmen became involved in debate. The diocesan conferences which proclaimed "no surrender" and passed fierce resolutions against compromise with the government contained in themselves the shape of the future constitution of the disestablished Church. They had their origin in the same meeting of the bishops which passed the resolution of 3 February against negotiation. The bishops had also passed two other resolutions. The first acknowledged the right of the clergy and laity to be heard in such questions, which involved the most important interests of the Church, the second invited the clergy to meet in diocesan synods, and asked the laity to decide how best they should be represented at such bodies.[86] The Lay and Clerical Association stepped in at once, recommending that the coming Easter vestries should choose churchwardens and synodsmen to attend diocesan synods, and circulating suggestions about who should be able to vote and how many synodsmen should be elected.[87] The organisms of self-government were coming into being, even though the majority of those attending the diocesan conferences saw their function as merely to protest against the government's Bill. The Irish Church, much against its own will and to a large extent unconsciously, was preparing itself for disestablishment.

The Introduction of the Bill and its Immediate Reception

It may help the reader at this point to set out the stages through which the Irish Church Bill passed before it became law, with the relevant dates. This will provide a frame of reference for the following sections of this chapter.

TIMETABLE OF THE IRISH CHURCH BILL: (ALL DATES 1869)

Introduced, House of Commons	1 March
Second Reading, House of Commons	24 March
Committed	15 April
Passed through committee stage	7 May
Reported	13 May
Third Reading, House of Commons	31 May
First Reading, House of Lords	1 June
Second Reading, House of Lords	19 June
Committed	29 June
Passed through committee stage, heavily amended	6 July
Reported	9 July
Third Reading, House of Lords (as amended)	12 July
Lords amendments considered in House of Commons (mostly rejected)	15–16 July
Compromise terms accepted by Lords	22 July
Compromise terms accepted by Commons	23 July
Royal assent	26 July

Two days before he introduced the Irish Church Bill in the House of Commons, Gladstone wrote: "I am to begin please God at $4\frac{1}{2}$ or 5 on Monday, but when I shall *end*, I really do not know— Probably before Christmas."[88] It was indeed a very long speech, but of such clarity that it remains the best guide to the contents and intentions of the Bill.[89]

Gladstone divided his exposition into three main sections, corresponding to the three periods in which he intended the various consequences of the Bill to take effect. These were: (1) the interim period from the passing of the Act to 1 January 1871, the date of disestablishment; (2) from 1 January 1871 to 1 January 1881, during which time the arrangements for compensating vested interests and dealing with the property of the Irish Church would be completed; (3) the period after 1 January 1881, when the surplus remaining after meeting claims for compensation would be distributed.

1. *The interim period, to 1 January 1871*

From the administrative point of view, the most important act of this period would be to wind up the Irish Ecclesiastical Commission, and to set up a new body to be called the Commissioners of Church Temporalities in Ireland. There were to be three Commissioners, to be named later.* In this new Commission would be vested, on the day the Bill received the Royal Assent, the whole property of the Irish Church, some of it to be returned to the Church, some to be retained by the Commission. The Commissioners were to have full powers to decide all questions, whether of law or of fact, in carrying out the Act when passed, subject to very limited rights of appeal. They formed the key administrative body in the whole complicated operation which was to follow.[90]

Some appointments in the Church would have to be made during the interim period, to fill the places, for example, of clergymen who died or retired. The Bill proposed to allow this without creating new vested interests and rights to compensation by appointing persons with rights only until the date of disestablishment, and subject to all provisions of the Act. The Crown would nominate to a vacant bishopric or archbishopric, but only at the request of an Irish archbishop or three bishops.[91] To enable the Church to organize itself in preparation for disestablishment, restrictions on meetings of the clergy and laity were to be removed. If the members of the Church then created a body representative of the bishops, clergy, and laity, the Queen was authorized to grant that body a charter and the power to hold property. Gladstone emphasized that the only criterion to be applied for recognition was that the body must represent the three orders, and indeed even this was flexible, for the Bill allowed for the

* The Commissioners later appointed were Lord Monck (a former Governor-General of Canada), J. A. Lawson (Justice of Common Pleas in Ireland and a former Liberal M.P. and Irish Law Officer), and G. A. Hamilton (former Conservative M.P. for Dublin University). Monck and Lawson had supported disestablishment, Hamilton had opposed it.

possibility that the Church might choose to dispense with bishops. There would be no constraint to keep the Irish Church in doctrinal union with the Church of England. This idea of a representative body was acknowledged to be one of the master-strokes of the Bill. It saved the government from the infinitely difficult task of defining in the Bill the body to which property should be handed over, while retaining a final right of judgement on what was representative of the bishops, clergy, and laity. Finally, it gave the Church a most powerful incentive to press on with the work of constitution-making, because the representative body would have to be incorporated and ready to receive property by the date of disestablishment.[92]

2. *The period following 1 January 1871, presumed to last ten years*

1 January 1871 was to be the date of disestablishment. On that day the union between the Churches of England and Ireland would be dissolved, and the Church of Ireland would cease to be established by law. No Irish archbishop or bishop would be qualified to sit in the House of Lords. The Irish ecclesiastical courts would be abolished, and ecclesiastical law would cease to be binding as law. Every ecclesiastical corporation in Ireland would be dissolved. (In the eyes of the law, the Irish Church was a collection of corporations, with the power to hold property—hence the importance of the formation and incorporation of the representative body to hold property when the individual corporations were dissolved.) To ease the transition, and to ensure that any changes in government or doctrine should stem from the deliberate will of the members of the Church, the Bill provided that the existing ecclesiastical law should be deemed to be binding as if by contract between the members, enforceable in the civil courts, subject to any changes made by the future Church government.[93]

At the date of disestablishment various arrangements would come into operation to give compensation for the various vested interests involved, and to dispose of the property of the Church. These operations would all be carried out by the Commissioners, into whose hands the whole property of the Church would have passed when the Bill became law.

The greatest of the interests to be compensated was that of the clergy. All these (except curates, who formed a special case) were entitled, in Gladstone's words, "to receive a certain net income from the property of the Church", for life, on condition of performing certain duties and subject to the laws of the Church. The Bill respected this right by instructing the Commissioners to pay to each clergyman an annuity for life equal to his net annual income before disestablishment, on condition that he continued to discharge his existing duties. It was open to any clergyman to commute, that is, to capitalize his annuity as a lump sum which the Commissioners would pay to a representative body (assuming one were formed). The representative body would then assume the obligation to pay the annuity as long as the clergyman performed his duties.[94]

The position of curates presented difficulties. They had no such vested right as had incumbents; their appointments were terminable, and their stipends were paid by the incumbents who appointed them. None the less, the Bill provided for compensation. Curates were to be divided into two groups, called permanent and temporary—the task of deciding what length of service or other criteria conferred permanency was left to the Commissioners. Permanent curates were to receive for life, or until they left their curacy either freely or due to misconduct, an annuity equal to their net annual income as curates. Temporary curates were to receive lump sums, to a maximum of £200, at the discretion of the Commissioners.[95] Compensation was also provided for the holders of various lay offices—diocesan schoolmasters, organists, vergers, and others—and also for lay patrons deprived of their right to appoint to benefices.[96]

These different forms of compensation were to be paid to individuals. Certain property would pass to the Church, in the shape of the representative body, when formed. Private endowments given since 1660 would do so.[97] Gladstone stated as the ground for choosing 1660 that then the Irish Church "assumed its present shape and character", so that a man knew clearly to what sort of Church it was that he was making his gift. He guessed that the value of such endowments would be no more than £500,000, and recognized that there would be a good deal of work and expense to trace the evidence about them.

The churches in use at the time of disestablishment would also be handed over to the representative body, at its own request.* Graveyards were dealt with very simply. Those attached to a church in use were to pass to the representative body along with the church, subject to existing rights of burial and to any future changes in those rights made by Parliament. Those attached to a church not in use, when the church passed to the Public Works Commissioners, were to go to the local poor law guardians.[98]

On the question of the glebe-houses, Gladstone explained some of the difficulties in establishing the sources from which they had been built, and whether they amounted to private or public endowments. He attempted to argue that the value of the glebe-houses was immense to the Church, but very small to anyone else —a proposition which brought murmurs of dissent from the government's back benches. The Bill proposed that incumbents should be compensated for their life-interests in the glebe-houses, since a rent-free house was a normal addition to clerical income. After dealing with this, the Commissioners would be empowered to sell the glebe-houses to the representative body, at one of three valuations. Where there was no building charge outstanding,† the payment would be twelve times the value of the site (with garden and curtilage) as land alone, disregarding the value of the house. Where there was a building charge, the payment was to be either the amount of the building charge, or twelve years' purchase of the value of the house estimated at the tenement valuation, whichever was the smaller. The effect of this complicated procedure was to allow the Church to purchase the glebe-houses at very favourable terms, after the clergy as individuals had already been compensated for the loss of them.[99] The Bill also provided for the sale to the representative body of some glebe land (not more than ten acres for an incumbent's house, or thirty acres for a bishop's) to go with the house.[100] Fortescue told the House that a special Bill would be introduced later to allow the Irish Church, and other denominations too, to borrow government money on easy terms to buy or build clergy houses.[101]

* Clause 25. One section in this clause, later dropped, provided that the Commissioners should contribute to the upkeep of churches which had the character of national monuments, if it were beyond the means of their congregations to keep them in good repair.

† The building charge was an outstanding debt for building and repairs, which each incumbent was able to pass on in part to his successor.

This completed the list of compensations and of the property which was to pass, in one way or another, to the representative body of the Church, when and if formed. The importance of this body is now even clearer than before. On it depended all the arrangements for the commutation of life interests, the handing over of the churches, the sale of glebe-houses and portions of glebe land. The representative body was to be as important on the Church's side of these transactions as were the Commissioners on the government's side.

All the remainder of the property of the Irish Church was to stay in the hands of the Commissioners. This would consist for the most part of land and tithe rent-charge. The Commissioners were to sell the land, giving the existing tenants the pre-emptive right to buy. The government would advance the purchase money to tenants who chose to buy the land, on easy terms of interest and repayment, thus taking the first pioneer step in the policy of land purchase, later applied throughout Ireland.[102] The tithe rent-charge was to be offered to the land-owners who paid it at twenty-two-and-a-half years' purchase; or alternatively the landowners could borrow the capitalized value from the government and pay off the debt over a period of forty-five years. Gladstone remarked in the House that the average market value of tithe rent-charge at the time was only sixteen or seventeen years' purchase, but he still thought the Bill's terms were reasonable, and he assumed that the landlords would accept them, so that the value of the tithe rent-charge would become available as a lump sum in a fairly short time. This was a fallacy, as will be seen later. Yet it was a vital point in the Bill, because it was on this premiss that the assumption that there would be a lump sum surplus to be distributed was based. If the landowners chose not to buy up the tithe rent-charge in one of the ways provided, but simply to go on paying it, then the Commissioners would not have a lump sum, but an annual income. Moreover, the operation could not then possibly be concluded in ten years.

The Bill also put an end to the annual Parliamentary grants made to different Presbyterian bodies in Ireland (the *Regium Donum*) and to the Catholic seminary at Maynooth (the Maynooth Grant). The *Regium Donum* amounted to between £45,000 and £50,000 per annum, and the Maynooth Grant to rather over

£26,000 per annum. The *Regium Donum* consisted mostly of the stipends of Presbyterian ministers, and these were to be dealt with in the same way as the incumbents of the Irish Church. They were to receive annuities, with substantially the same provision for commutation through trustees. The Maynooth Grant was to be wound up by a lump sum payment of fourteen times the annual grant.[103] The money to provide compensation for both the *Regium Donum* and the Maynooth Grant was to be paid by the Commissioners out of the funds of the Irish Church.

After describing all these provisions, Gladstone proceeded to calculate their financial results. He put the current annual revenue of the Irish Church at about £700,000, believing that the value given in the Report of the Irish Church Commission (£616,000 per annum) was too low. He claimed that the capital value was more important than the income, and on this his figures may be summarized thus:

Tithe rent-charge sold at 22½ years' purchase:	£9,000,000
Land sold at fair valuation	£6,250,000
Money in stocks and at banks	£ 750,000
	£16,000,000

(This total was reached without placing any valuation on churches or glebe-houses.)

Of this, he estimated that between £8,000,000 and £9,000,000 would go in compensation and expenses, leaving between £7,000,000 and £8,000,000 as the surplus to be devoted to other purposes.[104] This led to the third period envisaged by Gladstone in the operation of the Act.

3. *The period after 1 January 1881*

Gladstone assumed that all these operations would be concluded in ten years, at the end of which the Commissioners would wind up their work and go out of existence, and the remaining question would be the disposal of the surplus. The Bill laid down that it was to be used for the benefit of the Irish people through the relief of unavoidable suffering, but not for any ecclesiastical purpose or the teaching of any religion. The detailed purposes named in the

Bill have already been described.[105] Gladstone said in introducing the Bill that the actual framework of the plan to distribute the help would be worked out when this third period in the working of the Act was reached.

Gladstone ended his long speech by saying: "This measure is in every sense a great measure—great in its principles, great in the multitude of its dry, technical but interesting detail, and great as a testing measure; for it will show for one and all of us of what metal we are made."* The first test was of the Bill itself and those who had drafted it, under the scrutiny of the House of Commons, the press, and the different interests involved. On the whole it came through this test well. The Conservative party in Parliament, the opposition press, and critics in the Irish Church picked on very few points of real substance to complain of (as distinct from general protests about the principles involved and demands for more generous treatment).

Of these points, only one can be called a failure in drafting—Gladstone admitted that it was "a blot: the only blot as far as I know that has yet been hit in the Bill".[106] It concerned the mode of calculating a clergyman's annuity when he had employed a curate. The curate's stipend was deducted from the incumbent's annuity, so that an incumbent whose income was £400, and who had employed a curate at £80, would have an annuity of £320. But if the curate left in the future, and a replacement were necessary, the incumbent would still have to pay the new curate out of his annuity, which had already been diminished to provide for the former curate. As several critics pointed out, this was harsh in cases where the necessity for a curate was real, and it was dealt with by an amendment moved by Gladstone. This provided that, if the curate's annuity ceased during the original incumbent's lifetime, the incumbent's annuity should be restored to its full value.[107] The point is small, but worth mentioning as an indication

* Disraeli's comment on the speech deserves to be recalled. McCullagh Torrens reports him as saying: "Perfectly wonderful! Nobody but himself could have got through such a maze of history, statistics, and computations." Then, after a pause: "And so characteristic in the finish to throw away the surplus on the other idiots." W. McCullagh Torrens, *Twenty Years in Parliament* (London 1893), pp. 67–8.

of what could go astray in drafting, and how a minor error might affect men's livelihoods.

There was considerable criticism of 1660 as the date from which private endowments should be allowed to the Church. Roundell Palmer could discover no principle behind the choice of this date. The Thirty-nine Articles of the Church of England had been accepted in Ireland in 1634. Long before that, in 1559, legislation laid down that bishops in Ireland were to be nominated by the Crown, and that the liturgy of the Church of England was to be used in all churches in Ireland. Palmer admitted that Catholics had occupied many benefices, and that there had been much intermingling with Presbyterians, but he argued that any private endowment legally given must have been given to the Church established by law, because in law no other Church existed. There could be no question of any obscurity about the Church to which people were giving property or money.[108]

The compensation to be given to Maynooth laid itself open to criticism on two grounds. One was that it was over-generous when compared with the compensation given to the Church. For instance, the buildings had been acquired out of public funds, but they were to be handed over free of charge to the College authorities, while the Church had to pay for its glebe-houses. Again, the professors at the College had a claim in equity to compensation for the loss of their life-interests; but the Bill applied the same principle to the provision made for students, who had no such life-interest to be respected. All in all, it was argued, the fourteen years' purchase to be given in compensation for the Maynooth Grant was considerably higher than the average rate of compensation which was to be given to the clergy of the Irish Church.[109] The second ground of complaint was simply that the preamble of the Bill stated, and Gladstone had repeated in his speech, that the surplus of the funds of the Irish Church should not be used for the support of any Church or clergy, or for the teaching of religion. But in fact both the Maynooth Grant and the *Regium Donum* were to be compensated for out of the surplus, and this was a direct grant for the support of Churches and the teaching of religion. As Disraeli pointed out, this device saved the Treasury from paying out a lump sum as compensation for the cutting off of a Treasury grant, but there was no good reason why the funds of the Irish Church should be used for the relief of the Exchequer and in breach of the spirit of the Bill. In this he was supported by the Liberal member for Bandon (Shaw), who was willing to support a grant from the Consolidated Fund to meet these claims for compensation.[110]

Disraeli picked on a point very akin to this, another flaw in the reasoning behind the Bill's proposals for the use of the surplus. He argued that the great bulk of the benefit of providing for pauper lunatics or any such object would in fact go to the landowners— "whatever *hocus pocus* we may be told to the contrary". If such services were not provided out of the Church funds, they would still have to be provided anyway, and the landowners would pay, as they did already in Buckinghamshire.[111]

The most dangerous weak point in the Bill was seized on by Bence Jones, who cut through Gladstone's assumption that the terms for buying up the tithe rent-charge were reasonable and would be accepted by the landlords. Bence Jones held that sale at twenty-two-and-a-half years' purchase when the market value was at best seventeen years' purchase was "harder treatment than any man were ever subject to in a country where law reigns". He could see "no just reason why, if the tithes are to be sold at all, they shd. be sold for more than they are worth in the market". They were low in the market because they were likely to fall in the future with the price of corn, and in these circumstances the landlords would prefer to go on paying. As for loans to be paid off over forty-five years, forty-five years might as well be for ever.[112] On this crucial point, Bence Jones proved to be right, and Gladstone wrong.

In general, the sight of the Bill itself did nothing to appease those who opposed disestablishment and disendowment, and it even alienated, at least temporarily, some who had been prepared to accept them as inevitable. Even Archdeacon Stopford thought that Gladstone's presentation of the Bill had caused moderate men in Ireland to be more hostile to it than before; he himself complained about a number of points.[113] The immediate effect of Gladstone's speech on Butcher, the Bishop of Meath, who had been among the more moderate Irish bishops, was to give the impression of an unjust and sweeping measure. He mournfully told Spencer that the Church would break itself up into local congregations.[114] MacDonnell, while assuring Fortescue that the Bill was "wonderfully well put together", and welcoming especially the way in which the Church was to be allowed to make its own constitution, still thought that everyone (including a moderate like himself) wanted to see greater changes in the Bill than Gladstone could concede.[115] If these were the views of moderate men, there was no chance that the resistance of the Irish Church as a whole would diminish. The *Dublin Evening Mail*, on 2 March 1869, wrote: "Mr Gladstone's Bill could not be more extreme than it is. He simply confiscates every shilling of Church property. . . . There is not a trace of moderation in his scheme of disendowment." The *Belfast News-letter*, on 3 March, called the Bill "undisguised robbery". On the extreme wing, there were doubtless many who agreed with Lord James Butler, who maintained even in private that Protestants would fight rather than pay tithe to a secular body, and that they would be right to do so. They should fight either to keep a State Church or for the repeal of the Union.[116]

The leaders of Irish Catholicism, on the other hand, gave the Bill a warm welcome. The *Freeman* found it simple, equitable, and moderate. The passage of the second reading in the Commons marked the inauguration of a new policy towards Ireland, and the people of England and Scotland were thanked for an act of justice.[117] It had reservations. It argued that the cathedrals should have been handed over to the Catholic Church, and that the Maynooth compensation was both insufficient and unjust, on the ground that England was getting rid of the commitment at the expense of Ireland (another way of complaining that the grant was to be compensated for out of the Irish Church surplus).[118] The *Cork Examiner* (Maguire's paper), on 3 March, objected to various details—it did not see the justice of handing over clergy houses and ten acres of glebe. But it gave the Bill a general welcome, and was especially pleased with the land purchase clauses. Cardinal Cullen welcomed the Bill, both in public and in a private letter to Gladstone. He thought that Maynooth would get on very well under its new conditions, but suggested that some of the cathedrals (including one of the two in Dublin) should pass to the Catholics.[119] O'Neill Daunt, who had done so much to get the disestablishment movement under way, did not share this generally favourable view. He had suspected from a very early stage that Gladstone's disendowment proposals were not drastic enough, and the Bill confirmed him in this view—commutation he saw as a plan for the re-endowment of the Church.[120] Against this jaundiced view may be set the exultation of Bishop Moriarty: "Now indeed we have reason to double our Alleluias and to sing them with notes of joy. It was at Easter time that St Patrick preached at Tara. It was at Easter we got Emancipation. This Easter has brought us our grand triumph." The penny papers which used to flatter the Fenians had ceased to do so: "Believe me that disaffection is already in its agony."[121] Moriarty had believed that disestablishment would be the crucial step in dealing with the Irish problem, and he was persuaded that he could see the cure at work.

From the Nonconformist wing of the alliance which made the Bill possible there was hearty approval. The *Liberator* wrote that the work was to be done thoroughly and completely, and noted with satisfaction "how exactly the views of the Liberationists have been adopted", which went a little beyond the truth.[122] The *British Quarterly Review* used a string of approving adjectives—complete, thorough, coherent, matured, considerate.[123] The *Scotsman*, among its praise for the Bill, was glad to emphasize that it dealt kindly with the Irish Church as a religious body, and gave it freedom to organize itself according to its actual, instead of a purely theoretical, relationship with the population of Ireland.[124] On the whole, Gladstone could be well pleased with the first reception of the Bill. His supporters had been pleased, even delighted; his opponents had revealed few flaws in the conception. But the Bill had yet to be worked through Parliament, and especially through the House of Lords, where the opposition could command a majority against it.

The Conservatives and the Bill

The hopes of the Conservative opposition in the House of Commons rested on the expectation that the unity of the Liberal party would not survive debate on the Bill. Tait and Trench visited Disraeli on 8 March, between the introduction of the Bill and its second reading, and found him "bent on doing his best to set all sections of the Liberal Party by the ears", and hoping "to play over again the game with which he destroyed Lord Russell's Reform Bill".[125] The vote on the second reading, in the early hours of 24 March, gave such hopes no encouragement. The government majority was 118.[126] Disraeli remained at least outwardly optimistic. He claimed that the government majority was merely mechanical, and that it could not be counted on for the details of the measure.[127] He thought that it was hopeless after that division to resist disestablishment, but set out to prevent disendowment by a series of amendments.

There would be little point in detailing these amendments, but Disraeli believed that, if they were all carried, there would be no surplus to divide. Gladstone thought that the amendments actually sought to restore to the Church a sum greater than that which it was proposed to take away.[128] If the opposition had had its way, the result would certainly have been a wholly different Bill. But nothing of the sort happened. The Bill rolled through the committee stage, leaving Disraeli's amendments crushed and abandoned in its wake. Gladstone wrote proudly to Manning when the Bill had passed through all its stages in the Commons: "The House has moved like an army, and an army where every private is his own general."[129] A number of minor amendments were accepted, and the government moved some of its own to deal with certain objections or defects in the wording. The form of compensation for temporary curates, for example, was changed from a lump sum with a maximum of £200 to a scale calculated by years of service, with a minimum of £200 and a maximum of £600.[130] But the substance of the Bill remained untouched,[131] and the Opposition was left facing its next problem: What attitude should the Conservative majority in the House of Lords take towards the Bill?

The answer to this question was reached only after a period of muddle and vacillation. Very early, before the committee stage in the Commons, Disraeli was apparently trying to shift responsibility for the tactics of the Lords away from himself, and ostensibly away from the Conservative party. Claiming to write not as a party leader, but as a public man anxious to maintain and strengthen the established Church, he advised Tait that the action of the House of Lords should be divested as far as possible of a party appearance, and advised him to invite perhaps a dozen peers to Lambeth to discuss what course to adopt. Of the eight names he suggested, seven were Conservatives, including Cairns, the leader in the Lords, and Salisbury and Derby, the party's two other most commanding figures in the upper House.[132] This seems a somewhat transparent device; but Tait adopted Disraeli's suggestion, and on 8 May he met eight peers at Lambeth.* All were Conservatives except Lord Grey. They reached no firm conclusion. Two (Redesdale and Harrowby) were in favour of outright rejection, but there was a more general feeling that it would not be wise to reject the Bill outright. Lord Grey especially argued that the best course was to accept the second reading, and then amend the Bill in committee. It was clear that a division was inevitable, but rejection depended on the Conservative leaders, and at this point neither Salisbury nor Cairns seems to have committed himself. It was left that Cairns would soon hold a meeting of Conservative peers, and would tell Tait of their decision.[133]

The reasons for Cairns' uncertainty are clear enough. Lord Colville, Conservative chief whip in the House of Lords, had told him on 30 April that he was not prepared to say whether or not they could defeat the Bill in the Lords. If they did, it would be by a small majority. "This is to my mind", wrote Cairns to Disraeli, "equivalent to saying that, practically, we cannot do it."[134] But, on the other hand, it was quite clear that there were passionate opponents of the Bill who would certainly divide the House against it. Cairns came to believe too that there was a growing feeling in the country against the Bill. He came to the conclusion that to accept the second reading "would seriously disorganize the Conservative party in the House, and paralyse and offend it in the country". He was afraid of even more far-reaching consequences for the position of the House of Lords itself. It would offend so many conservative-minded men that "when questions more nearly touching the privileges or the existence of the House of Lords might arise it would find no feeling existed in its favour. It might be held to have surrendered on this occasion without a struggle, and therefore to be of no use." He therefore changed his mind, and decided that rejection was the only practical course.[135]

Before the Conservative peers met as a body to discuss what to

* The eight were: Cairns, Salisbury, Bath, Grey, Harrowby, Redesdale, Marlborough, and Stanhope.

do, Tait held a meeting of bishops at Lambeth about the same problem. If the vote on the second reading was, as most people expected, a close one, whatever the Conservative party decided to do, then the votes of the bishops were likely to be crucial. They were divided, not to say confused, in their views. The Irish prelates present were naturally most concerned with opinion in their own Church, and were reluctant to appear soft or cowardly. Of the English and Welsh bishops, only seven were recorded by Tait as saying that they would vote against the second reading. Four would vote for it, two were non-committal, and the opinions of five were not recorded. There was no certainty or determination here, and the bishops were unanimous only on deciding to adjourn and hold another meeting.[136]

Meanwhile, the Conservative peers were under pressure from Ireland. Deputations from various organizations opposed to the Bill came to London at the end of May and beginning of June, and met groups of peers. They presented the usual arguments, together with a strong current of threats that the Conservative party in Ireland would not survive if the English Conservatives surrendered on the Bill, and that the Irish Protestants would cease to support the Union. They used also the argument of which Cairns was afraid: that if the Lords passed the Bill when they were known to be against it, people would ask what use their House was.[137] The arguments of the deputations were supported by Irish Conservative newspapers. The *Daily Express* wrote: "If this deed of robbery and insult be completed, the political and moral ties which bound the Protestants of Ireland to England are broken for ever."[138] The *Express* also worked hard to produce a picture of widespread protest against the Bill, in England as well as Ireland, to show that the Conservative peers would not be obstructing the will of the people by rejecting the Bill.[139]

It was against this background that sixteen Conservative peers met on 2 June, before a mass meeting on 5 June. Opinion at the small meeting was in favour of rejecting the Bill outright.[140] At the large meeting, with some 130 to 150 peers present, Salisbury, Stanhope, and Carnarvon spoke against rejection, but found little support. The Archbishop of York estimated that four-fifths of those present were in favour of rejection, and there was a warm welcome for Cairns' announcement of the decision to take this course.[141]

So overwhelming a verdict in so large an assembly appeared at last to have settled the matter. The Conservative peers had decided to challenge the Commons in open combat. Only two days later, however, the Speaker of the House of Commons was willing to venture sixpence on a bet with the Liberal Chief Whip that the Bill would pass, and he was to be proved right.[142] A great part in this change of front was played by the Queen and Archbishop Tait, working hard on both opposition and government. On 3 June, before the Tory peers' decision, Tait (at the Queen's suggestion) had offered his services to Gladstone as a mediator to prevent a collision between the two Houses, but Gladstone had been very discouraging, refusing to admit the possibility of material amendments.[143] The Queen was alarmed at the prospect of a head-on collision between the two Houses when she could see that the position of the Lords was so weak: "Carried as it [the Bill] has been by an overwhelming and steady majority, through a House of Commons chosen expressly to speak the feelings of the country on the question, there seems no reason to believe that any fresh appeal to the People would lead to a different result."[144]

The Archbishop and the Queen believed even after the meeting of 5 June that there was a chance to prevent a collision. Tait reckoned the Conservative majority in the Lords to be about eighty, and he thought that abstentions would bring this down to about twenty. Rather than have so narrow a margin, the Conservative leaders might prefer to acquiesce, if only the government would show some willingness to be flexible in its attitude to amendments.[145] So the Queen appealed to Derby, the most influential of those who favoured rejection, pointing out the dangers of this course.[146] Tait wrote to Disraeli, telling him of the Queen's wish that the Bill should be passed and then amended in committee, and arguing that this would be better for the opposition than rejection by a narrow majority. He hoped that Granville, when he opened the debate for the government, would hold out hopes for amendments.[147] The day before writing this letter, Tait had seen Granville, who had said that Ball (the member for Dublin University) would know best how to frame amendments "which it would be possible for the Gov. to accept".[148] There was, of course, a world of difference between amendments which the government would accept and the sort of large-scale reconstruction of the Bill which the Lords would undertake, and which even Tait favoured. Tait, for whatever reason, was over-optimistic on this question, and the impression given in his letter to Disraeli was distinctly misleading.

The debate in the House of Lords opened on 14 June with the issue still uncertain. The Queen had failed to move Lord Derby,[149] and there is no sign that Disraeli or Cairns had changed their minds. But there was sufficient weight of opinion in favour of passing the Bill and amending it in committee to put the outcome in doubt and make the debate of absorbing interest. It was a great question which was to be decided, both for the House of Lords and for the Irish Church. Rejection of the Bill would have meant a head-on collision between the Houses on a vital issue. The government would not have been deflected from its course, but delay and great public agitation would have been certain. The contents of the Bill might have been changed; the spirit in which it was passed undoubtedly would. Any sort of compromise would have been made much more difficult. By common consent among contemporary observers, the votes which decided this great question were actually swayed by the four days of debate (14, 15, 17, and 18 June).[150]

Of the speeches, that of Magee, the Bishop of Peterborough, caught the public eye most dramatically. Lord George Hamilton arrived ten minutes after Magee rose, and found the House packed (an unusual sight), with in its centre "a plain pigmy of a man speaking at a table". He spoke against the Bill to such effect that the House became "a pandemonium of enthusiasm", and Lord Ripon, who followed, had to wait several minutes before he could start to speak.[151] Magee stirred the emotions of the House, but the speeches which primarily influenced the division were those of Granville, Tait, and Salisbury. Granville, opening for the government, held out just sufficient hope of consideration for amendments to give colour to arguments that amendment was a feasible course.[152] Tait welcomed Granville's remarks, and gave the authority of his office and personal prestige as a known supporter of the principle of establishment to the proposition that, with some amendments, the Lords could make the Bill a good one.[153] Salisbury refused to believe that the government would reject all amendments, and argued that, even if they did, they would not get the support of the nation to destroy the House of Lords just because it had, for example, replaced 1660 by 1560 in the Irish Church Bill. Thus the peers would choose their own ground to fight on, rather than give battle on the government's terms.[154] Cairns, the Conservative leader in the Lords, remained sceptical of the possibility of amendment, pointing out that Granville had reserved the main provisions of the Bill without defining them, thus in fact leaving himself free to resist any amendment which he chose to regard as infringing those provisions. He could see no hope of serious change in the Bill, claimed to discern a movement of opinion against it in the country, and declared that he would vote against the Bill.[155]

Granville told the Queen that after Tait's and Salisbury's speeches he was sure the Bill would be carried.[156] He was proved right when the vote was taken in the early hours of 19 June. The Bill was carried on the second reading by 179 votes to 146, an unexpectedly large majority of thirty-three. The majority included Lords Salisbury, Carnarvon, and Bath, all Conservatives. One bishop (Thirlwall, of St David's) voted for the Bill, and sixteen (including three Irish prelates) against it, but several abstained, including Canterbury, York, Oxford, and Chester.[157] An immediate crisis had been averted, and the hopes of those who argued in favour of amending the Bill in committee were to be tested.

The Final Passage of the Bill

The state of the House of Lords during the committee stage and third reading of the Irish Church Bill was confused—Disraeli described it as anarchical.[158] The government, whose majority on the second reading had been fortuitous, did not control the House. Granville only rarely found it worth while to divide against hostile amendments, and then was beaten, unless he had the support of other groups in the House. For if the government could not command a majority, neither could Cairns for the opposition. There were considerable numbers of bishops, peers on the cross-benches, and even usually dependable Conservatives, who on this issue were determined to pursue their own ideas. The results were extraordinary. For example, in committee an amendment was accepted to allow the Irish prelates entitled to a seat in the House of Lords to keep their seats for their lifetimes.[159] Then on the third reading, less than a fortnight later, the House struck out its own amendment by a majority of twenty-six.[160] Stranger still, an amendment moved in committee by the Duke of Cleveland, to introduce a measure of concurrent endowment by granting glebe-houses and land to Catholic and Presbyterian clergy, was defeated by 146 votes to 113.[161] Yet on the third reading, a similar amendment moved by Lord Stanhope was carried by 121 to 114.[162] On each occasion the party leaders, Granville and Cairns, voted in the same lobby, against concurrent endowment, but most of Cairns' supposed followers, and many of Granville's, voted against them.

The outcome of such haphazard procedures was far from being a systematic and reasoned amendment of the Bill. The results of the main amendments embodied in the Bill as it was returned to the House of Commons after its third reading in the Lords on 12 July may be summarized as follows. Firstly, there were amendments which were intended to ease the transition from the established to the disestablished state. One of these postponed the date of disestablishment from 1 January to 1 May 1871.[163] Another clause was introduced to safeguard the existing clergy in case of changes in discipline or doctrine in the disestablished Church. In case of a change in the formularies of the Church, clergymen already holding their positions were given the right to dissent without loss of their annuities, provided they did so within six months of the change coming about.[164]

Another group of amendments was designed greatly to increase the amounts of property and money to be retained by the disestablished Church. An amendment moved by the Bishop of Peterborough increased the annuities to be paid to the existing clergy by reducing the deductions to be made from them.[165] A much more significant amendment was that moved by Lord Carnarvon, changing the arrangements by which the existing clergy could commute their life interests. Instead of the commutation capital being calculated on the annuities of all the individual clergymen, it was to be simply fourteen years' purchase of the aggregate of those annuities. This amount would be paid to the Representative Body of the Church, and was calculated to produce a considerable increase on the other method of commutation.[166] By another amendment, the glebe-houses of the Irish Church were to be handed over to the Representative Body free of charge, instead of on the system of payment laid down in the Bill.[167] Finally, in this group, the clause dealing with private endowments was rewritten to provide that a lump sum of £500,000 should be paid in lieu of private endowments (no date being mentioned), and also that lands made over to the Irish Church by royal grant since the second year of Queen Elizabeth's reign should be retained by the Church.[168] The principal object of this latter provision was to secure for the Church the extensive glebe lands in Ulster granted by James I.

The most remarkable of the Lords' amendments has already been mentioned: the introduction of the principle of concurrent endowment. The idea had been actively discussed for a long time, and had influential support. Gladstone himself had tried during the drafting of the Bill to introduce some measure of concurrent endowment by offering grants to other Churches. Now the peers, at the second attempt and on a motion by Lord Stanhope, laid down that the Commissioners, out of the surplus property of the Irish Church, should provide glebe-houses and lands for Catholic and Presbyterian clergy. The extent of the glebe lands was to be limited to thirty acres for a bishop or archbishop, and ten acres for other clergy, but it was still a sweeping measure.[169]

Finally, the House of Lords rewrote the preamble of the Bill and deleted clause 89, so as to remove the directions to devote the surplus to specific purposes in favour of a provision that the funds should be applied in such manner as Parliament should direct in the future.[170] Cairns argued that there would be no surplus for ten or twenty years, and that it was absurd to dispose of what did not yet exist; he hoped, too, for a future Parliament more favourable to his own party.[171]

The amendments carried in the Lords faced the government with the transformation of its Bill. Disestablishment remained, but the extent of disendowment had been drastically reduced. A careful contemporary estimate was that the Church would receive, in extra compensation and in value of property to be retained, about £2,800,000 more than was intended in the original Bill.[172] Moreover, the principle of concurrent endowment, which large sections of the government's supporters would not accept, had been introduced, and by the same stroke the disposal of the surplus had been largely, perhaps wholly, taken out of the government's hands. On the widest interpretation of Stanhope's clause on concurrent endowment, the total cost of the Lords' amendments would rise to over £8,300,000, which exceeded the maximum probable surplus. Even on a narrower interpretation of Stanhope's clause, the total cost would be over £5,000,000, which would not leave much to be distributed.[173] Instead of going to the poor, all or most of the surplus funds of the Irish Church would go to the Catholic and Presbyterian clergy.

Before the Bill went into committee in the House of Lords, on 26 June, the Cabinet had considered what amendments it would be willing to accept, and had produced an exiguous list. They were willing to give a lump sum of £500,000 in lieu of private endowments, to accept minor changes in the arrangements for commutation, curates, and glebe-houses, and to meet some of the expenses of setting up the Church Body.[174] After the Lords' amendments had been formally reported (9 July) and before the third reading of the Bill in the Lords, the Cabinet met on 10 July to consider the position. They declined to yield ground. The lump sum for private endowments they were still willing to give, and they would put forward their own amendment on curates. On the question of commutation, they would not accept Carnarvon's fourteen years' purchase, but were willing to offer seven per cent above a figure calculated from the government male annuitant life tables, and hold another three per cent extra in reserve for bargaining purposes. Otherwise, on all the financial changes, on the changed date of disestablishment, and on the disposal of the surplus, they refused to accept the Lords' amendments.[175] Gladstone noted the definitive judgement of the Cabinet that concurrent endowment was impossible, and that the majority of the House of Commons was opposed to any further concessions of property to the Irish Church.[176] They adhered firmly to this position. When the amended Bill came before the House of Commons on 15 and 16 July, its original contents were largely restored.[177]

There is no sign that the government ever showed any sign of weakening in this attitude. It was doubtless encouraged and supported in its resolve by a movement of public opinion, to some degree against the Lords' amendments as a whole, but most markedly against concurrent endowment. The Liberation Society moved very early to resist any measures of re-endowment of the Irish Church or of concurrent endowment. The Executive Committee organized a joint meeting with the Dissenting Deputies (2 July), and the Parliamentary Committee sent out letters to mobilize opinion.[178] Meetings were held to protest against the Lords' amendments at several great towns in the North of England.[179] On concurrent endowment, a much wider range of opinion was involved. A prominent Wesleyan told Gladstone that the Connexion was ready to rise *en masse* against concurrent endowment.[180] Resolutions against it came to the Prime Minister from Nonconformist bodies in all parts of the country.[181] The *Scotsman* was prepared to argue that Stanhope's amendment was the least objectionable form of concurrent endowment, and the nearest possible approach to equity between the different Churches, but came down against it on the ground that it was certainly not what the electors had voted for.[182] The *Record*, on the other hand, denounced it as the endowment of popery, which would make Britain "one of the horns of the beast".[183] The leaders of the Irish Catholics, the body which stood to gain most from the new provisions, opposed them strongly. Cullen insisted that the Catholic clergy sought no grant from the State, and he was supported by Manning, O'Neill Daunt, and the Irish Catholic M.P.s.[184] At Gladstone's request, Manning brought a little pressure to bear on certain Catholic M.P.s who were inclined to waver on the issue.[185] Majority opinion in the Irish Church had always been opposed to concurrent endowment, even as a means of saving something for itself, and this view does not seem to have changed.

On 16 July the situation, therefore, stood thus. The House of Lords had wrought far-reaching changes in the Bill, but had seen the government and House of Commons reject nearly all of them, accepting among the substantial changes only the substitution of the half-million pounds in lieu of private endowments. The question was then what the Lords would do in face of what was widely regarded as an affront to their status as an equal partner in the legislative process. Their immediate reaction when the Bill came before them once more on 18 July was to restore their amendment to the preamble, reserving the distribution of the surplus to the future discretion of Parliament.[186] They did not at the time go further; but the leaders of the opposition and the Archbishop of Canterbury were still thinking on 16 and 18 July of insisting on all the main Lords' amendments except the date of disestablishment and concurrent endowment. Disraeli was also willing to give up the attempt to retain the Ulster glebes.[187] If the Conservative leaders chose to insist, they could certainly command a majority in the House of Lords to reject the Bill altogether, because those who had voted for the second reading in the hope of amendment had seen their hopes dashed. A head-on clash between Lords and Commons, which had been avoided earlier at the time of the second reading in the Lords, again appeared possible. Gladstone considered the possibility of having to bring in another Bill in the next session of Parliament, and argued that a second Bill would be less generous to the Irish Church than the first.[188] According to both Granville and Malmesbury, Gladstone at this point seriously advocated abandoning the Bill.[189]

In fact, however, the leaders of neither side wished to precipitate a conflict if it could be avoided, and there was no lack of negotiators and intermediaries. Between 18 and 22 July there was a flurry of discussion and correspondence, involving Gladstone, Granville, Halifax, and Bessborough on the one hand; Cairns, Salisbury, and Disraeli on the other; and Tait and the Dean of Windsor, acting on behalf of the Queen, somewhere in the middle.[190] Of the various strands, that involving Granville, Salisbury, Cairns, and Tait produced on 22 July a negotiated settlement, reached in private conversation between Granville and Cairns, and announced by Cairns that evening in the House of Lords. Success was possible because both sides wanted it, and even more because the points at issue between them had been narrowed by earlier exchanges and decisions. It was vital, for example, that concurrent endowment (which Cairns had never wanted anyway) was out of the way. The principal points on which the discussions turned were limited to these: the date of disestablishment; the question of the preamble and the postponement of the disposal of the surplus; the terms of commutation; details of the arrangements about curates; the terms on which glebe-houses and limited glebe lands were to pass to the Church; and the question of the Ulster glebes. On the date of disestablishment, the government was willing to yield; but by this time the opposition did not wish to insist. Of the rest, the question was what either side thought worth fighting about. As Gladstone put it on 18 July, he did not think the peers had any arguable case for further concessions, but he was still willing to pay a limited price to avoid a quarrel.[191] On the other side, Cairns was clearly thinking of securing the best financial terms for the Church, without actually incurring the risks of rejecting the bill.

The risks involved in rejection were so great that the government's position was the stronger, and it was Cairns who yielded most ground. Granville held out on the Ulster glebes, and on the government's terms on glebe-houses and lands, and Cairns met him on these points. Granville accepted the House of Lords' amendment to the preamble in return for changes in the wording of clause 68; by this means concurrent endowment was not mentioned, and the government's main point about the use of the surplus to relieve distress in Ireland was made.* Agreement was reached on a further arrangement about curates, which would work slightly to the advantage of the Church. Finally and most important, a change was made in the terms for commutation. Cairns gave up the amendment, originally moved by Carnarvon, which had proposed to standardize the rate for commutation at fourteen years' purchase of the clergy's aggregate incomes. Instead he accepted commutation according to expectation of life, but with an extra 12% as an inducement to the clergy to commute. A further inducement was added by making this 12% dependent upon three-quarters of the annuitants in any diocese agreeing to commute.

This compromise was accepted by the House of Lords on the evening of 22 July, and by the House of Commons on 23 July.

---

* The new preamble read: "The property of the said Church of Ireland, or the proceeds thereof, should be applied in such manner as Parliament shall hereafter direct." The new clause 68 read: "And whereas it is further expedient that the proceeds of the said property should be appropriated mainly to the relief of unavoidable calamity and suffering, yet not so as to cancel or impair the obligations now attached to property under the Acts for the relief of the poor: Be it further enacted, that the said proceeds shall be so applied accordingly in the manner Parliament shall hereafter direct" (32 and 33 Vict., ch. 42).

The Bill became law on 26 July. In both Houses the mood was one of joviality and self-congratulation on both sides. The relief of some members of the government, who had worked under strain for a long time, was evident. Fortescue wrote on 23 July: "I feel like a man after a rough passage, who suddenly finds himself in harbour. The history of the last few days has been most remarkable, and the result most happy. On Thursday night and Wednesday I & most of us had almost lost hope. Cairns has distinguished himself very much by his management of the settlement."[192] Spencer in Dublin was equally relieved, writing on 22 July: "Rumour says that the opposition give way, & if so we may bless our stars & good fortune, for an autumn of agitation would have been very serious, & would have been inevitable. The news is I fear too good to be true."[193] Even John Bright, who at one point had appeared to be scenting battle and looking forward to it with relish, wrote when all was over that he was glad a conflict with the Lords had been postponed—he was getting too old for such great questions.[194] This relief is some measure of the crisis which had been avoided.

Gladstone had good reason to be pleased, for the final terms had scarcely gone beyond those which he and the Cabinet had discussed on 10 July. He had in effect yielded an extra two per cent on the terms of commutation, and accepted vaguer wording on the distribution of the surplus. There was more than mere politeness in the phrase when he told the Archbishop of Canterbury that the transactions had been "highly satisfactory".[195] The Archbishop's own feelings were mixed: "Very thankful that the matter was arranged but depressed as to the condition of Trench and the Irish Ch. generally. We have made the best terms we could—and thanks to the Queen a collision between the Houses has been averted, but a great occasion has been poorly used—and the Irish Church has been greatly injured without any benefit to the R.C. Ministry."[196] Thus Tait hankered after concurrent endowment to the end.

The Liberal press gave the details of the compromise a mixed reception. It was clear to them that the Lords had won some bonuses for the Irish Church, but there were wide differences between estimates of how substantial these bonuses were. The *Daily News* on 24 July claimed that the Lords had extracted

£1,000,000 more for the Church than the Bill had provided when it first left the Commons. The *Scotsman*, on 23 July, thought that the extra sum involved, arising from changes in the arrangements for commutation, would be at most £150,000. The *Morning Star* (24 July) agreed that the commutation terms represented the only significant concession, and believed that this would prove to be "a concession of nothing", because the necessary proportion of clergy would probably not commute. The *Liberator* thought that the Bill compensated all parties too generously and left the Irish Church too wealthy, but found this a fault on the right side.[197]

The Bill as a whole was greeted as a great achievement by Liberal newspapers. The *Morning Star* on 24 July asked its readers to reflect how impossible such an event appeared even a week before Gladstone spoke on Maguire's motion on the state of Ireland in March 1868. The *Cork Examiner* (26 July) made much the same point: the Irish Church had appeared unassailable, connected with all that was powerful in Ireland and sure of English sympathy. The *Daily Telegraph* (24 July) launched into a panegyric: the Act was "the greatest measure of modern British legislation since Free Trade. . . . Once more we have had a revolution in Britain without a blow more serious than sharp tongues can inflict. . . . It cleanses Protestantism in Ireland from a vast injustice. . . ." The leader-writer proclaimed his "glad conviction that this Act will bring peace to Ireland, strength to true religion, and a remarkable encouragement to progressive statesmen". The *Scotsman* wrote on the same date that a piece of history had been made, more important than any but one or two in two generations. With the end of the Irish establishment there disappeared "all pretence for our Irish fellow-citizens specially to complain, and for men of other countries to believe or say that Irish complaints are just". Even the *Saturday Review*, hardheaded and cautious as usual in its support for the measure, believed (31 July) that something large and generous had been done—even if the Irish had later to be disappointed about the land question.

On the other side, the English Conservative press made the most of the concessions gained by the Lords. The *Standard* argued on 24 July that the terms of disendowment could hardly have been more equitable, if they were to be consistent with the principle of the measure. The *Globe* believed that total disendowment had

been averted, but pursued its old idea about a revolution. The
Act made a deep "incision into the theory of the British constitution". Union between Church and State was now an accident, not
an essential part of the constitution. It was only the start of a
series of measures tending to place the social and political system
of the country on a purely utilitarian basis. The measure was "the
most important and extensive which the nineteenth century has
witnessed", and with it the Liberals had passed from reform to
revolution.[198] Across the Irish Sea, the *Dublin Evening Mail* (23
July) considered its cause betrayed—"Cairns has sold the Church."
The Bill accepted by the Lords was as hardfisted and unjust as
when it first left the Commons. "The Irish Protestants—as we a
hundred times warned them—have nothing to hope for from any
English party." Not all Irish Conservative papers took this line.
The *Cork Constitution*, for example, argued on 24 July that the
terms had been made, and that there was no point in quarrelling
over them or in accusing people of betrayal. There was work to be
done, and unity would be needed to do it.

That was for Irish Churchmen themselves to work out. On the
wider issues, what of the talk of revolution, of the greatest measure
since Free Trade—was this nothing but hyperbole? The Irish
Church Act of 1869 is not now looked back upon as a revolution
in the affairs of nineteenth-century Britain. But the scale of values
and modes of thought of the mid-nineteenth century were different, and, while revolution is too strong a word, something of
real importance had happened. The question of the relations
between Church and State had been a prominent theme in
ecclesiastical history, and frequently in political history too,
throughout the first half of the century. Ireland had repeatedly
played a predominant part in this: in the 1820s over Catholic
Emancipation, in the 1830s over the reorganization of the Irish
Church, in the 1840s over Maynooth. Now in 1869, with the
passing of the Irish Church Act, it was admitted for the first time
in the United Kingdom that there need be no relationship
between Church and State at all, other than that which exists
between the State and any other institution, such as a limited
company, or a public school. This was the end of a long era of
history. The necessity for an established Church in all parts of
the country had been accepted for so long, and the question of

relations between Church and State was so important to the politically and ecclesiastically conscious, that this break in Ireland was, as a matter of principle, very significant. On this, contemporaries judged rightly. It was also true, on the Irish aspect of the measure, that this was the first time since Catholic Emancipation that an attempt had been made to deal with one of the fundamentals of the Irish problem. Here too the Act marked a break with the past, by recognizing the scope of the problem. However, it still remained to be seen whether the actual consequences of the Act would fulfil either the fears of its opponents or the hopes of its supporters.

5

THE IRISH CHURCH AFTER DISESTABLISHMENT

The State Bows Out

The Irish Church Act became law on 26 July 1869. The date of disestablishment was 1 January 1871. At the time these events came as a shattering blow to most Irish Churchmen. William Alexander, then Bishop of Derry, wrote later in life: "I can never forget the summer night just after the division when I reeled out into the cool air almost hearing the crash of a great building."[1] His wife, the prolific (and still popular) hymn-writer Mrs C. F. Alexander, wrote a hymn for the occasion of disestablishment which echoes this feeling. It was sung in Derry Cathedral on 1 January 1871:

> Look down, Lord of heaven, on our desolation!
> Fallen, fallen, fallen is now our Country's crown,
> Dimly dawns the New Year on a churchless nation,
> Ammon and Amalek tread our borders down.[2]

Archbishop Trench, never an optimist, looked gloomily ahead. "I oftentimes augur the very worst for our future", he wrote to the Archbishop of Canterbury. "Certainly nothing but an inspiration from on high of more wisdom and moderation than we have ever shown signs of possessing can save the Irish Church from a very dismal catastrophe."[3] That was in August 1869. By the next October he thought that the Irish Church was doomed because the laity were not raising enough money.[4] He was afraid too that the Church would cut itself off from other Anglican Churches, and itself split, "first into two or three, and then probably in a thousand fragments".[5] Some were more cheerful, like Graves, the Bishop of Limerick, whom Spencer, the Lord Lieutenant, found at the end of August zealous and hopeful—"quite excited as to his new work with a free Church".[6] Whether gloomy or hopeful, the leaders of the Church had to prepare for disestablishment, for the end of a system of government, almost a way of life, to which they had long been accustomed.

The State too had to deal with the last remnants of the long connection with the Church. Most of the winding-up operations which the State had to perform (other than the work of the Church Temporalities Commissioners in the disposal of the secularized property) were straightforward. The episcopal members, for instance, continued to attend the Irish Privy Council until they died, when their successors were not appointed to the Council. By this time, the Council was concerned mostly with matters of local government—fisheries, lunatic asylums, lodging houses, and the like—and it may well have been some relief to future Archbishops of Armagh and Dublin, and Bishops of Meath, not to be members of this body.[7] The machinery for making Crown appointments in Ireland went through its motions during 1870 as usual, except that appointments were made in accordance with the Irish Church Act, so that newly appointed incumbents had no freehold, and their rights to the incomes of their benefices would end on the date of disestablishment. The Chief Secretary's Office also continued to exact the usual fees (£16 11s. 8d. on appointment to a rectory, £19 16s. 9d. for a vicarage and rectory), which one or two new incumbents protested was rather steep for an appointment valid for only a few months instead of for life. The Office remained adamant.[8] The Ecclesiastical Affairs Book in the Chief Secretary's Office, in which the formal correspondence about appointments to bishoprics, dignities, and Crown livings had been copied out, was closed after a last entry on 27 January 1871. The Chief Secretary and Lord Lieutenant were thus relieved of at least one of the functions which involved them in the delicate personal relationships of Irish patronage. They did not escape, however, without a last complication. By a strange fatality, the see of Kilmore fell vacant twice during 1870 through the death of its bishop. The filling of this see on two occasions within five months of each other is worth a little attention. It provided the government with its last problems of Irish Church patronage, and it illustrated clearly some of the problems which the Church in future would have to resolve for itself.

The Irish Church Act laid down that the Crown was to fill a vacant bishopric on the requisition of the Archbishop of the

Province, or of three bishops.[9] Gladstone had said in the Commons on 1 March 1869 that the intention was that the archbishop or bishops concerned should nominate a candidate, whom the Crown would then appoint. As he wrote to Fortescue when the first vacancy occurred, "we were to wash our hands of the matter & to look substantially to the sense of the Church as it might be declared thro' the Prelates named in the Act".[10] But what was the sense of the Church? The Archbishop of Armagh, Beresford, suggested Leslie, a little-known man from within the diocese of Kilmore. Spencer, with Gladstone's support, pressed the claims of the Dean of Cashel, MacDonnell, as a much more distinguished man, but was told that MacDonnell was a southerner and would be unacceptable to the diocese. Gladstone thought this a melancholy state of affairs, but acquiesced.[11] Leslie was appointed, but died three months after his consecration. So in August 1870 the same problem arose again, and this time the question about the sense of the Church became really difficult. Spencer was confronted by a deputation from the diocese of Kilmore, bearing a memorial asking that no appointment should be made before 1 January 1871, so that the new form of election by Diocesan Synod might be used; or else, if the appointment were to be made at once, that the Synod-to-be should be consulted. The argument was that the churchmen of the diocese should not be deprived of the right which would be theirs automatically the following January. But there was more to it than that. A member of the deputation told Spencer that there was ill-feeling within the diocese. The Irish dioceses, as has already been mentioned, were unions of small ancient dioceses. In this case, the union was of the dioceses of Kilmore, Elphin, and Ardagh. Leslie had been from Kilmore, and Elphin and Ardagh were jealous.

In these circumstances, Spencer urged Beresford to choose the best man from all Ireland, but had to admit that this would not be tolerated in the diocese. This left only two available candidates: Carson, the Dean of Kilmore, and Darley, the Dean of Ardagh. According to Beresford, Darley had canvassed for the appointment as soon as the see first became vacant, and was the prime mover behind the deputation to the Lord Lieutenant. In the Convention which was drawing up the Church's constitution during 1870, he had voted steadily against the bishops, and Beresford described him as an extreme Low Churchman. These facts alone would have made Darley a popular candidate with the powerful elements pressing for a revision of the Prayer Book in a more Protestant direction. After some delay, Spencer accepted Beresford's recommendation and appointed Carson.[12] He died in 1874, when Darley was finally elected Bishop of Kilmore under the new procedures.

These two episodes in one diocese in the interim period before disestablishment presaged the problems which were to recur frequently in arguments about the election of bishops in the disestablished Church. Would dioceses want "safe" men, which would usually mean known, internal candidates, rather than strangers from another part of the country? If they chose internal candidates, would this bring out internal rivalries, regional or personal? Would extreme Evangelical, "revisionist" views carry too much weight as against other characteristics? How much scope would be given to canvassing or personal animus? The omens from the see of Kilmore were not favourable on any of these matters. They are, of course, the sort of questions, *mutatis mutandis*, which occur in any Church with an electoral system, but they were present in Ireland at the time of disestablishment in an acute form.

With these affairs, the State, which from Whitehall and Dublin Castle had so long dominated the Irish Church, quietly bowed out of its long role. The Church had now to cope with great problems which the State had previously settled for it. It had to create and work its own form of government. It had to organize its own finances, and repair the damage done by disendowment. In the circumstances of Ireland at that time, it unavoidably had also to face questions of doctrine and Church order: whether the Book of Common Prayer so long by law established really embodied the sort of Church its members wanted. These questions affected each other. The debates on the form of the constitution were conducted in the knowledge that revision of the Prayer Book was certain to come before the central legislative body. The question of what forms of legislation would best promote or obstruct revision was therefore in everyone's mind. The constitution, once settled, had its effect on the course and conclusion of the revision debates. The form of government, and the pressures which formed the constitution, helped to shape the financial organization adopted by the Irish Church. The prospect of revision of the Prayer Book also affected the finances of the Church, though probably only in a small degree, by discouraging subscriptions from those offended by the revision debates. Such interactions must be kept in mind when studying separately the problems of government, doctrine, and finance.

Government

At the Lambeth Conference of 1878, when enough time had passed to get some sort of perspective, the Archbishop of Armagh looked back over the changes in the Irish Church during the first half of the nineteenth century, and concluded that the improvements of that period, especially in eliminating non-residence among the clergy, had been such that "at no period of our history were we in so good a condition to bear the heavy blow and great discouragement of disestablishment, as at the time when that calamity came upon us".[13] This was surely true. Certainly the crisis drew out reserves of ability, self-reliance, and cohesion, as well as of money, which were highly creditable to the Irish Church. But it was not how things looked at the time. In January 1869 the *Irish Ecclesiastical Gazette*, the most moderate and sound of the Irish Church journals, deplored the efforts of those who sought to prepare constitutions to take the place of the establishment, not only because this was doing Gladstone's work for him, but also because it was "a hopeless thing to expect uniform action amongst all the extensive and variously circumstanced dioceses of the Irish Church, supposing it reduced to a Voluntary Society".[14]

Fortunately, there was some discussion of the future of the Irish Church, and the *Gazette*, despite its proclaimed views, gave it some encouragement. One of its reviewers, for example, even in January 1869, commended a pamphlet on *Diocesan Synods*, which declared that bishops need not be wealthy, that they did not need an ornamental framework of deans and chapters, and that they would be better employed sitting in their own diocesan synods than in the House of Lords. In February the *Gazette* printed a paper suggesting how the constitution of the American Episcopal Church might be adapted to Irish needs. When the die was cast, from August 1869 onwards, the discussion gathered momentum, with frequent reference to the American and Scottish systems of Church government. Interestingly, along with this increasingly earnest debate on possible constitutions there went a changing view of the effects of the Bill. In April 1869, while still deprecating it, the *Gazette* admitted that it might prove a blessing in disguise, which would call forth the latent energy of the Irish Church.[15] In June, when the eventual result seemed certain, it was insisting that Irish Churchmen would want a truly free Church, not the sort of disestablishment which would leave it still subject to "State trammels"—a phrase straight from the propaganda of the Liberation Society.[16]

There were plenty of other suggestions besides those aired in the *Gazette*. Three are worth brief notice as examples. Sherlock's substantial pamphlet on reorganization has already been mentioned.[17] It carried the approval of Selwyn, Bishop of Lichfield and formerly Bishop of New Zealand, who had read the proofs and added comments. It was designed to ensure a conservative attitude towards questions of doctrine, proposing a declaration of agreement with the Church of England in the same Christian faith, and that the assent of all three orders (bishops, clergy, and laity) should be necessary for all acts of the General Synod. Sherlock's constitutional suggestions, for the creation of a General Synod and Diocesan Synods, for the mode of election of bishops, and for the appointment of parochial clergy by boards of parochial and diocesan representatives, with the bishop in the chair, were often closely similar to the arrangements actually adopted.[18]

The opinions of Bence Jones, if not usually acceptable to his contemporaries, always commanded attention. He published a forceful and detailed pamphlet in August 1869, having collected a good deal of information about the self-governing Anglican Churches.[19] He thought the practice of the three orders debating together and voting separately should be adopted by the Irish Church. Recent Canadian experience made him wary of electing bishops, and he suggested that the Synod might choose three names, from which the Archbishop of Canterbury or another outside figure would select one. For the parochial clergy he favoured private patronage in the country, and appointment by the bishop in the towns. These ideas on appointments were individual, and perhaps not disinterested—Bence Jones was a personal friend of the then

Archbishop of Canterbury, and a strong-minded country gentle-man. They had no chance of acceptance. But his individuality also made him willing to strike ruthlessly at a problem with which in fact the Church was only to tinker for the next fifty years, by which time it had grown into a considerable crisis. This was the problem of the union of parishes. He had written about this in 1868, and still believed that in the debates on disestablishment parishes with very few Anglican inhabitants and large clerical incomes had counted heavily against the Irish Church. He thought this an abuse which, if continued, would do the Church great harm. In Connaught, because of the distances involved, and Ulster, because of the large numbers of Churchmen, unions of parishes might not be possible. But in Bence Jones's own diocese of Cork, for example, there were 180 parishes, while in the same area the Catholics had only ninety; the Irish Church could surely manage with ninety too. He was sure that unions of parishes would be workable, though difficult. One may wonder how far his stern, practical Balliol mind took into account the real difficulties, the local loyal-ties and traditions, the unfamiliarity and jealousy which deter people from attending any other parish church than the one to which they are accustomed. Still, the Irish Church had to face this problem in the end, just as the Church of England at the present time is slowly having to face its own similar problem.

Finally, in these examples, a brief polemical pamphlet repre-senting a strongly held point of view: W. H. S. Monck, *The Irish Church and the Order of Bishops*.[20] Monck argued that the key issue in the future constitution of the Irish Church was the position of the bishops, and in particular whether they should form a separ-ate house in the legislative body, thus holding a veto over the other two houses. The pamphlet was inspired by distrust of bishops in general (Churches which had dispensed with them had shown no tendency to relapse into Romanism as episcopal Churches had), and of the Irish bishops in particular (they were working against the laity, many had been appointed by political enemies of the Irish Church, and some even came from the University of Oxford). Apart from this distrust, the author advanced three reasons why the bishops should not be allowed to form a separate house. The old order in the Church had given great power to the laity in the shape of the State; the laity should therefore have at least half the authority in the new constitution. Secondly, the laity would bear nearly all the financial burden of the Church, which again entitled them to at least half the power. Thirdly, it depended on the first steps of the new body whether the Church would be Protestant or Catholic, and the laity wanted security against crosses, candles, processions, and exorcisms. To allow the bishops a veto would obstruct the fulfilment of this aim.

These are only selections from the widespread discussion on the future government of the Irish Church carried on during 1869. It was not discussion in a vacuum. Decisions had to be taken before 1 January 1871, and a body had to be created to take them. In practice the initiative lay with the bishops, as the only persons of acknowledged authority in a position to take action. Their actions were much criticized and suspected, but they were accepted, and in the event produced a workable arrangement.

On 4 August 1869 the Irish bishops published a resolution that a General Synod, in which clergy and laity should be "fully and equally represented" should meet as early as possible. Provincial Synods of the clergy (for Armagh and Dublin) should meet to consider the representation of the clergy.[21] The question of how the laity were to be represented was not dealt with, which caused misgivings and criticism. On 18 August the two archbishops summoned their Provincial Synods of clergy, and in this letter they broached the question of the representation of the laity in a future General Synod. They hoped that the laity would arrange this for themselves, offering full co-operation if they wished to use the parish system and diocesan conferences (which had sprung up during the campaign against disestablishment) as their framework.[22] This method of proceeding by holding separate clerical and lay meetings was criticized because it made for delay and suspicion between clergy and laity.[23]

The Provincial Synods of the clergy of Armagh and Dublin met in St Patrick's Cathedral, Dublin, on 14, 15, and 16 September 1869. They were not themselves a constituent assembly, but only made preparations for the calling of one, to be termed the General Convention. None the less, they made two negative decisions of real importance, because they set a pattern which was not changed. A proposal by Archdeacon Lee of Dublin that consideration of doctrine and discipline in future synods of the Church should be restricted to the clergy alone was brushed aside. It was also decided, by an overwhelming majority, that there should be no *ex officio* seats for deans or archdeacons in the General Convention. They also settled on a franchise for the clergy.

The Lay Conference then met on 12, 13, and 14 October 1869, again in Dublin. This body was brought together by holding meetings in individual parishes, which sent representatives to a diocesan conference, which in turn elected representatives to the Lay Conference.[24] This Conference too expressed important opinions. It agreed that clergy and laity in the future General Synod might vote as separate orders; the more contentious question of whether the bishops might do the same was left aside. It was decided that the proportion of lay to clerical representatives should be two to one, on the ground that laymen would often be unable to attend synod meetings, so that this proportion would be necessary to produce approximately equal numbers actually present. The difficult question of how these representatives should be distributed among the dioceses was raised. A scheme was carried which would give weight to population in the election of the General Convention. This angered Bence Jones, and doubtless other representatives of the southern and western dioceses. "They carried a resolution that puts us at the mercy of the North", wrote Bence Jones to Tait. "6 other dioceses together have fewer votes than the 2 dioceses of Armagh and Down." He tried to secure voting by dioceses in the Convention, on the ground that each diocese was independent and should positively agree to all rules of the general body before it was bound by them, but he failed. This conflict of interest between the thickly and the sparsely populated dioceses was to recur. Finally, the Lay Conference proposed a lay franchise for the Convention of simple Church membership, established by declaration by men (but not women) over twenty-one years old.[25]

One further proposal of the Lay Conference was that a committee should be created to prepare the ground for the meeting of the General Convention. This was a crucial job, because no body of over 600 members could conceivably have drafted a constitution from scratch. The preparatory committee was to have sixty members: the twelve archbishops and bishops, and two clergy and two laymen from each united diocese. They co-opted a number of lawyers as advisers without votes. The lay members were to a large extent drawn from the peerage and the gentry.[26] The predominance of the landed and professional elements ensured that a competent group of men was available to grapple with the task ahead. The Irish Church as a body was unaccustomed to self-government, but its members were drawn in large part from the Protestant ascendancy, which was certainly used to exercising authority. There were laymen with experience of local government, the law, finance, and Parliament. The clergy came from the same social milieu, and often shared the same background in Trinity College, Dublin; some of the bishops had experience in the House of Lords. Such men can never have doubted their capacity to govern themselves. Indeed, once launched into it, they took to the business of constitution-making and self-government, of committees and synods, with efficiency and zest, as to the manner born—which, of course, they were.

So rather more than sixty like-minded men met together in Dublin on 5 January 1870. They promptly divided into seven sub-committees on different subjects, and in about three weeks produced a complete draft constitution. Accounts agree that the proceedings were amicable and free from party spirit. Even on the most contentious matter, the position of the bishops, the committee was able to recommend without a division that the bishops should be recognized as a separate order, though they should normally sit and debate with the clergy and laity.[27] There is no point in examining the draft constitution put forward by the preparatory committee, which was substantially amended by the General Convention, but it is necessary to emphasize the importance of its work. It was difficult enough for the Convention to amend a document already drawn up; it would have been virtually impossible for it to write the document itself. One of the most distinguished members of both the committee and the Convention, Professor Salmon of Trinity College, wrote that the committee's draft gave many members of the Convention their first idea of the work they had to do.[28]

After this valuable preparation, the General Convention first met on 15 February 1870. It had two sessions, the first of some seven weeks, and the second, starting on 18 October, of just over a fortnight. Its members (666 if they were all present) met in "a cold, half-underground cellar, badly lighted, and with no ventilation except that caused by draughts, the effect of which on the health of its more assiduous members was disastrous. . . ."[29] Its work received much praise. Archdeacon Stopford, Gladstone's old ally in the drafting of the Irish Church Bill, was fulsome: "Our Convention", he wrote to Gladstone, "is a grand & noble assembly, sometimes noisy and impulsive—untrained of course, sometimes wasting time—but with strong sense and great discrimination. . . ."[30] Even Bence Jones approved, after his fashion: "We talked more nonsense than was ever before talked in the same time, but when it came to acting we did very reasonably & well as any right minded man could wish."[31] The Lord Lieutenant, looking on from outside, agreed: "There was a great deal of bluster and nonsense spoken at the Convention, but scarcely anything they settled was badly done. They came to sound practical results."[32] The praise was surely justified. Any large deliberative body will talk a lot, as will most small ones, but not all of them will at the end of the talk produce an elaborate constitution out of difficult and controversial matter. This the Convention did. The constitution it prepared may be outlined as follows.[33]

The *General Synod* was the supreme legislative body, meeting annually. It had two Houses, the House of Bishops and the House of Representatives, the latter made up of the clerical order (208) and the lay order (416). The two Houses would normally sit together, but the bishops could withdraw to deliberate separately if they so decided. A vote by orders could be demanded by ten members, clerical or lay; if this was called for, then a measure before the General Synod would only pass if it received a majority from clergy and laity voting separately, and from the House of Bishops. Bishops, clergy, and laity could thus each exercise a veto on legislation. The veto of the bishops was limited in one respect. If a measure rejected by the bishops were passed again at the next annual meeting of the General Synod by not less than two-thirds majorities of the clerical and lay representatives, then it could only be rejected a second time by the bishops if two-thirds of their whole number voted against it, giving their reasons in writing. This was the "Abercorn compromise", famous in its day, which resolved one of the most difficult questions at the Convention. Some of the lay representatives, led by Lord James Butler, were

anxious to prevent so much power being given to the bishops. Indeed, they did not wish to see the bishops recognized as a separate
order at all, which had implications for the nature of the Church
as well as for its form of government. This group put a motion
that the bishops should have no second veto over a measure receiving two-thirds majorities from the lay and clerical representatives.
This put their views in their most moderate and limited form, and
it was accepted by a small majority of the laymen but rejected by
the clergy. Then on 25 February 1870 the Duke of Abercorn's motion was carried by 346 votes to 110. 164 clergy and 182 laymen
voted for it, twelve clergy and ninety-eight laymen against.[34]
This was presumably the full strength of the strongly anti-episco-
pal school, but the fight had been carried on with such gusto and
in so hot a tone that English newspapers sometimes assumed that
the Irish Church was well on the way to Presbyterianism.

This decision on the bishops' veto was hard fought, and the
centre of absorbing interest at the time. Attendances at the Convention were at their highest while it was being debated, and fell
off later. How important was it? Salmon thought in one way not
at all important. Judging by the observable influence of the
bishops on the Convention, and assuming that in the future, when
bishops were elected, they would be in harmony with opinion in
the lower House, he thought that the contingency of a majority of
the bishops being permanently opposed to two-thirds of both
clergy and laity was "as improbable a one as six hundred rational
men ever spent time in providing against".[35] This was doubtless
true. But still all the oratory and the ink represented something
real, a point of decision which the Irish Church had to negotiate.
Lord James Butler and his allies had to try their strength. The
gloomy Archbishop Trench had to be convinced that the Church
was not going to cut itself off from the rest of Catholic Christen-
dom. More important than either, the great majority of Irish
Churchmen who stood between these two positions had to make
up their minds about the importance of bishops in the Church.
Were they so vital an element in it that the will of a few men, because they were bishops, ought to prevail against that of a great
majority? It was very important that this question, as a purely
theoretical matter, was answered in the affirmative, even if in
practice the issue was unlikely to arise. It was the kind of question

which disestablishment forced upon Irish Churchmen. What sort
of Church were they? What sort of Church did they want to be?
It is also the kind of question which many Christians will have to
ask if schemes of union between episcopal and non-episcopal
Churches are to come to fruition.

Because it was concerned with the nature of the Church, the
question of the constitutional position of the bishops was closely
bound up with questions of doctrine and the revision of the
Prayer Book. The bishops were widely regarded as a conservative
group, who might in the future use their powers to resist revision.
On the question of revision, however, the Convention was itself
conservative, writing into the constitution a severe restriction on
the power of the General Synod. There was to be no modification
in the "articles, doctrines, rites, rubrics or formularies of the
Church" except by two-thirds majorities of each order at two
successive annual meetings of the Synod.

Any clergymen ordained as a priest was eligible for the General
Synod, and any layman over twenty-one who declared himself a
communicant. The clergy were to be elected by clergy of their
diocese and the lay representatives by the Diocesan Synodsmen.*

The *Representative Church Body* was the other central organ in the
new constitution. Its creation was compulsory under the Irish
Church Act, which also laid down that it must be appointed by
the bishops, clergy, and laity of the Church. It was incorporated
by royal charter, and its function was to hold and administer the
property of the Church. In this capacity it was to receive back
from the Church Temporalities Commissioners the churches,
private endowments, and other items of property which the Commissioners were to return to the Church on the date of disestablishment. It was thus the one element in the constitution which of
necessity had to be in full working order before 1 January 1871.
The make-up of the Representative Church Body was: the archbishops and bishops *ex officio*; one clergyman and two laymen
elected by each Diocesan Synod (twelve clergy and twenty-four
laymen in all); and twelve co-opted members (lay or clerical)
chosen for their financial abilities. The Representative Church
Body was responsible to the General Synod, to which it was to

* For the Diocesan Synods, see below, pp. 171-2.

present its accounts. Its importance in the government of the Church proved to be considerable, over and above its natural importance as the controller of property and finance. For instance, it had to give its consent to the creation or union of parishes or dioceses, because these operations had financial effects. More important, it was a comparatively small body, meeting frequently, and made up of the ablest administrators in the Church. Such a body was bound to wield great influence, whatever its formal powers might be.

As well as these central bodies, *Diocesan Synods* were set up in each united diocese. With the powerful local loyalties which existed in the Irish Church, it was taken for granted that this would be so—indeed, they had come into existence, almost spontaneously, before the Convention met.[36] Local feelings were so strong that even the small ancient dioceses which made up the united dioceses had never wholly lost their identity. D'Arcy, when he became Archbishop of Armagh in 1920, had had twelve enthronements in his lifetime, though he held only five episcopal appointments; he was enthroned in the cathedrals of each of the ancient dioceses concerned—three times in the united diocese of Ossory, Ferns, and Leighlin, for instance.[37] In 1886, to take another example, local pressure succeeded in reviving the diocese of Clogher, united to Armagh since 1850.[38] In these circumstances, the creation of Diocesan Synods was inevitable; local patriotism demanded local self-government, though this was later sometimes judged to have been a mistake, because it produced administrative and financial difficulties.

These Synods consisted of: the bishop; all beneficed and licensed clergy; and normally two lay synodsmen for every clerical member. Their functions included the election of the bishop of the diocese, and uniting or dividing parishes, with the consent of the Representative Church Body and of the sitting incumbent. Subject to trusts, the law of the Church, and the overriding control of the Representative Church Body, it administered the property and revenues of the diocese. Finally, it appointed a nomination board to help in the choice of parochial clergy.

The question of the power of the bishop in the Diocesan Synod was a subject of controversy, like that of the House of Bishops in the General Synod. The solution reached was to give the bishop a

veto, and to provide that, if a vetoed measure were brought forward again at the next annual session and carried by two-thirds
majorities of the clerical and lay orders, but was still objected to by
the bishop, it should be referred to the General Synod. The Diocesan Synods were to meet annually, and could delegate their
powers to Diocesan Councils, consisting of the bishop and a number of clergy and lay synodsmen, to meet more frequently and
ensure continuity of administration.

At the base of the structure lay the parish. To be a registered
vestryman in a parish (i.e. to have voting rights) it was necessary
to be male, twenty-one years old, to declare oneself a member
(not necessarily a communicant) of the Church of Ireland, and to
be either (a) an owner of property in the parish, or (b) a resident
in the parish, or (c) an accustomed member of the congregation.
Vestrymen had three principal functions: to elect a select vestry
for parochial affairs; to elect diocesan synodsmen; and to elect
parochial nominators to serve on the board when a new incumbent
was to be appointed.

In describing the separate organs of the constitution, the system
for making appointments within the Church has been mentioned
on a number of occasions. The creation of this system was in many
ways the most important and difficult aspect of the reorganization
of the Church. In the past, appointments to bishoprics and dignities had been made by the Crown, and appointments to incum-
bencies by a variety of nominators—the Crown, private patrons,
Trinity College, bishops. It had been a patchwork affair; many of
the appointments had been frankly concerned with political or
family interests; but the tradition was old, and people knew how
it worked. They might dislike it if it worked against them—if one
were a Tory Dean hoping for a bishopric but faced with a long-
lived Whig government, or a clergyman without connections
resenting the promotion of others less able or worthy but with influential friends. But no one expected the system, or rather lack of
one, to be fair. No one claimed that it was designed for the benefit
of the Church as a spiritual body. But after disestablishment, a
whole new system had to be devised to meet this exacting criterion, and it would be correspondingly open to more severe
criticism. Moreover, it had to be a system in which open democratic processes replaced the arcane influence of Dublin Castle in

the most important appointments, those of bishops. Last but not least, an appointments system is involved with personalities at all points: the feelings and interests of the candidates, and the natural concern of those who will have to listen to a man's sermons Sunday by Sunday, or to be subject to his authority as a bishop. Such matters had to be taken into account.

The arrangements devised were rather complicated. Bishops, and the Archbishop of Dublin, were to be elected by the Synod of the diocese concerned. First, a vote established a short list of three names. Then, on further voting, a candidate receiving two-thirds of the votes of each order would be elected. Failing this, the appointment lapsed to the House of Bishops. The bishops would then choose from the first two candidates, having before them a full record of the voting at the Diocesan Synod.

To this procedure there was an exception for elections to the archbishopric of Armagh, which carried with it the Primacy of All Ireland. When the see of Armagh fell vacant, the Diocesan Synod elected a bishop, termed the Bishop-elect of Armagh. He would then sit with the rest of the bishops to elect from among themselves a Primate. If not himself elected, the Bishop-elect of Armagh would go to fill the see of the man elected to the Primacy. An account of what happened in 1895 may help to make the procedure clear. The Diocesan Synod of Armagh first elected Archdeacon Meade of Armagh as Bishop-elect, and he thus joined the House of Bishops. The bishops then met, and elected the Bishop of Cork, Gregg, as Archbishop of Armagh, and Meade went to Cork.[39] The reasoning behind this somewhat tortuous procedure was that elections to the Primacy were the concern of the whole Church, not just of the diocese of Armagh; yet it would be unfair to deprive the Synod of Armagh of the privilege of electing a bishop. However, by 1897 it was felt that the diocese of Armagh was in fact electing too many bishops for other dioceses. A change was made, providing that, if there were already two bishops on the bench elected by the diocese of Armagh (or appointed by the bishops from names sent by Armagh), the House of Bishops should first elect one of its number to the Primacy, and then the Diocesan Synod of the newly vacant see should meet in the usual way to elect a bishop.[40]

Parochial appointments were made by a board of nominators

representing both the parish and the diocese concerned. Each Diocesan Synod appointed a board of nominators, two clergy and one layman, to serve for three years. In each parish, the general vestry every three years elected three parochial nominators. When a benefice became vacant, the diocesan and parochial nominators were to meet as a board, with the bishop in the chair, and these seven persons would make the appointment. The bishop had both an ordinary and a casting vote, and also the right to object to a nominee, in which case an appeal could be made to the General Synod.

Finally, the old system of ecclesiastical courts was abolished by the Irish Church Act, and had to be replaced by a new system to administer the internal law of the Church. Diocesan courts were set up to try offences which did not involve doctrine or ritual. Normally the bishop was judge, with the chancellor of the diocese as assessor and one layman and one clergyman as judges of fact. If the bishop himself instituted proceedings, the chancellor was to act as judge. A right of appeal lay from this court to the court of the General Synod, which was also the sole court in cases involving doctrine or ritual. This consisted of the three members of the House of Bishops first in order of precedence and able to attend, and of four laymen from a list of ten, elected by the General Synod and of high legal standing. Decisions were to be by majority vote, except that in questions of doctrine or involving expulsion from Holy Orders the concurrence of at least two of the bishops was required for a condemnation.

The constitution of the Church of Ireland was drawn up in about nine weeks of hard work, ending in November 1870 with just a few weeks to spare before the date of disestablishment. It remained to be seen how well the institutions would work, and whether they would prove flexible enough to meet changing circumstances. This may best be discussed by looking first at the system of government, and next at the working of the system of appointments.

The structure of the General Synod proved satisfactory. The prediction that having two laymen to one clergyman would produce roughly equal attendances from each order proved correct. Attendances in the early years were high, with the debates on the revision of the Prayer Book and the novelty of self-government to stimulate interest. After that they fell off. To take an example at random, attendance at the General Synod of 1891 was:

	CLERGY	LAYMEN	TOTAL
1st day	164	135	299
2nd day	174	149	323
3rd day	157	127	284
4th day	156	144	300
5th day	72	67	139

This was out of a total composition of 208 clergy and 416 laymen, so that on this occasion the laymen mustered barely a third of their full numbers. *The Irish Ecclesiastical Gazette* observed at the time that during the past three years ten clerical and ninety-two lay representatives had not attended any meeting of the General Synod.[41] These figures may be compared with those for May 1920, when by general consent the Irish Church was facing a crisis in its affairs, affecting especially the whole position of the clergy:

	CLERGY	LAYMEN	TOTAL
1st day	191	180	371
2nd day	189	173	362
3rd day	184	163	347
4th day	143	69	212[42]

In general, the exercise of self-government in the supreme legislative body produced attendance in Dublin of a good majority of the clerical representatives, though (after the first flush) rather less than half the lay representatives. On the whole this must be reckoned a fair record for a voluntary body, and the General Synod certainly proved to have marked value as a meeting-place for Churchmen from all over Ireland.

Of the devices adopted for voting in the General Synod, the bishops' veto lay unused. Some prelates tried to use it during the revision debates, but failed to get enough support from their fellows.* Much later, J. A. F. Gregg, then Archbishop of Dublin, told the English Archbishops' Commission on Church and State in 1932 that the bishops hardly ever voted at all at meetings of the

* The House of Bishops voted separately in 1875 on the question of the Athanasian Creed, but the Bill was carried in their House by eight votes to three. The House again voted separately on the Preface to the Prayer Book in 1877, but again the Preface was carried by five votes to four. *I.E.G.* (May 1875), p. 101; ibid. (April 1877), p. 196.

General Synod.[43] Thus it came about that what had been seen as an indispensable safeguard of the Church, or as an instrument of episcopal tyranny, proved instead to be a dead letter. That is not to say, of course, that it was unimportant, or that it did not exercise by its very existence a steadying effect in the early years. Voting by orders, on the other hand, was invoked quite frequently, especially in the early years, when a number of important divisions in the revision debates were taken in this way.

The real tests of the system of government came in the two substantial crises of the half-century after disestablishment. The first of these was the revision controversy, which will be discussed in the next section. The second was the problem of reorganization, which came to a head in 1919 and 1920 but had been developing for years before then. It reached a climax at that time through a combination of a long-standing failure to adjust the Church's organization to the changing shape of the Irish population and the sudden impact of wartime taxation and inflation on the financial position of the clergy. The problem is worth discussing in some detail, because it was a severe test of the government of the Irish Church, revealing something of the inflexibility into which it had fallen and demanding a great effort of will from its representative bodies.*

That the distribution of parishes, churches, and clergy in the Irish Church did not correspond with the distribution and needs of the Church population was already clear to some observers at the time of disestablishment. Bence Jones had advocated regrouping in 1869. In 1870 C. P. Reichel had believed that the authority given to Diocesan Synods to unite and divide parishes would release the Church from the paralysis of its parochial system.[44] In the event, these powers were used to some extent to group parishes in the south and west of Ireland, but they were not used sufficiently to prevent serious difficulties arising. The committee of the Representative Church Body which examined the problem in 1919–20 reported that a Diocesan Council had told them that they could always agree that parishes ought to be amalgamated, but, when

---

* It is also interesting to trace a number of resemblances to the problems of the Church of England at the present time and for some time past. Sometimes in studying the Irish Church's crises of 1919–20 one might be reading Leslie Paul's *The Deployment and Payment of the clergy* (London 1964), and the debates upon it.

it came to deciding *which* particular parishes should lose their identity, local influences prevailed and nothing was done.[45] The problem of distribution was heightened by the rapid growth of the population of Belfast, a large proportion of which claimed member-ship of the Church of Ireland. The problem of Belfast, and the contrast between that city and other parts of the country, was a staple of discussion in the Irish Church for many years. One example will serve to bring out the main lines. In February 1910 two articles appeared in the *Church of Ireland Gazette*, pointing out that in Belfast there were over 90,000 Church-people and fifty-six clergymen. In one parish alone there were 10,000 Church-people and, when it was fully manned, four clergy. This parish had a greater Church population than the united diocese of Cashel, Emly, Waterford, and Lismore, which had a bishop, fifty-five rectors, and seventeen curates. The ancient diocese of Kilfenora had a Church population of 162, with four clergymen; that of Kilmac-duagh 216, also with four clergymen. Yet there were streets in Belfast where twenty houses contained over 216 Church-people. From evidence of this kind the articles argued the need for re-distribution of labour in the Church, which was too much divided into watertight compartments.[46]

The writer was careful to say that he was not disparaging the work done in the south; but his articles naturally drew some sharp replies. There was indeed a problem in the south and west of Ire-land as well as in Belfast, a problem of declining numbers and long distances. The Church had a duty to all its members, and there was a strong argument that the smaller and more scattered the Church population, the greater the need for a resident clergy-man. Moreover, these small Church populations had to pay heavily for their clergy; their diocesan assessments per head were far higher than those in the north. They were able to claim that they valued their clergy highly, and also that they were entitled to services for which they were willing to pay so heavily.[47] The Bishop of Down, Crozier, who had formerly been Bishop of Ossory in the south, intervened to deplore comparisons; from his experience he would not reduce the numbers of clergy in the south, but he did ask for help from other dioceses to meet the needs of Belfast.[48]

But in fact little was done, just as little had been done during the previous forty years. One obstacle was that the financial arrangements of the Irish Church were very rigid. Practically all its capital was held under trusts linking it with particular dioceses, so that it could not be used for other purposes. Sometimes funds were tied not even to the united dioceses, but to the small ancient dioceses—the Irish Church began its disestablished career with twelve united dioceses, but twenty-one diocesan financial schemes.[49] Quite apart from this, strong local loyalties and influences militated against change. Disestablishment and the power of self-government in themselves did not provide the energy and flexibility to deal with the problem. Indeed, the reaction after the great efforts of the early years after disestablishment, and a justifiable self-satisfaction at the results, helped to encourage the inertia which prevailed afterwards.

How long this creeping paralysis would have gone on untreated it is impossible to say. In the event, the 1914–18 war came, with effects so dire that the Church was jolted into action. Heavy taxation and inflation together put the clergy, with their fixed incomes, in an impossible position. There was a desperate need for the Church to save money, which at last gave the necessary impulse to the regrouping of parishes. The *Church of Ireland Gazette*, indeed, ran a campaign for changes going beyond financial reorganization and union of parishes, advocating union of dioceses as well, and changes in the constitution of the General Synod to prevent its being dominated by the aged. Its campaign made two particularly valuable points. One was that an answer to the problem of distance in the country districts was now available: the internal combustion engine. A car or motor-cycle could enable one clergyman to do the work of two.[50] (The *Gazette* for 5 November 1920 carried an advertisement for Chevrolet—"the car that will eventually settle the amalgamation and many other problems".) The second point was that the problem of amalgamation was not confined to the country districts, but was severe also in a number of towns, where there were no geographical obstacles to its solution. In the centre of Cork, for example, there were three parishes, whose combined Church population in 1870 had been 2,820; in 1905 it had declined to 650, and by 1919 to perhaps half that, but all three parishes were still in existence, though distance would not prevent their congregations attending another church.[51]

The seriousness of the situation was fully realized, though not everyone shared the *Gazette's* ideas about how it should be dealt with. The Bishop of Cashel, Miller, for example, thought that in his diocese amalgamation of parishes had reached its useful limit —the number of benefices had been halved since 1868—and suggested some form of permanent diaconate as one solution to the problem of manning.[52] In October 1919 the Representative Church Body set up a committee of inquiry, to report to the next session of the General Synod. Its report, published at the end of April 1920,[53] found that the Irish clergy were seriously underpaid, and recommended minimum stipends of £400 for incumbents and £200–250 for curates. This would demand an extra £140,000 per annum, which the Committee saw no chance of raising through increased giving (annual contributions to the Church at that time averaged about £100,000 per annum). Nor was there any large sum available from the general funds of the Church, and there seemed little chance of creating one financial organization for the Church instead of the several diocesan schemes. If the trusts under which the money had been given were to be broken, parliamentary consent would be necessary unless the agreement of every individual interested in the funds were secured. It was not thought worth while to attempt this. The Committee accepted that there was great waste of men and money in keeping up a parochial organization beyond requirements, especially in the towns of the Province of Dublin. It considered that there was still room for more amalgamation of rural parishes too. The Committee linked the two aspects of the crisis together. Only by amalgamations could money be raised to increase the stipends of the clergy. It therefore proposed that the General Synod should appoint a Commission to visit every diocese and make recommendations on amalgamations, which would be carried out by the standing committee of the General Synod. Measures of compulsion were necessary in the circumstances.

This report was prepared with commendable speed; but what followed was even more remarkable. Disestablishment and self-government had not saved the Irish Church from a stiffening of the joints and natural inertia. But, confronted with a crisis, it had the immense advantage of possessing a single representative body with the power to act and commanding widespread respect. The

General Synod accepted in May 1920 that a *prima facie* case had been made out for reform on the lines recommended, set up a committee to prepare legislation, and decided to hold a special session in November.[54] At this session, the General Synod accepted all the major bills put before it, and in five days made the following provisions: (1) that the minimum stipends should be £400 for incumbents and £200 for curates; (2) that a central fund for the Church be created, even though it could only be built up slowly; (3) that a commission be set up to prepare schemes for amalgamations, with powers to overrule diocesan authorities if necessary; (4) that nominations to the first vacancy in any benefice be placed in the hands of the bishops, after consultation with the boards of nominators; (5) that if a parish failed to raise enough money to pay the new stipends, it could not have a rector, but only a curate-in-charge, appointed by the bishop.[55]

These measures did not please everyone. The *Gazette* was disappointed that there were to be no fewer bishops, and that the territorial system had been everywhere retained, instead of having some areas worked by teams of priests with motor-cycles. The steps to provide a central fund were criticized as inadequate.[56] But nothing can diminish the size of the achievement. Thirteen months from the setting up of the committee of inquiry, legislation putting into effect the main recommendations of that committee had been passed, even though they meant heavy new financial commitments and action running counter to deeply felt local loyalties. It was a remarkable feat, not least in its speed. It may be that the Irish Church had waited too long before acting; but, when it came to the point, it showed that it had both the will to act on a large scale, and a system of government which enabled it to do so. Self-government in the Church had been severely tested and triumphantly vindicated.

The general system of government thus stood the test of taking a drastic decision. The strains and difficulties of the system of making appointments in the Church were less violent but more persistent. The method of appointing bishops was subjected to a continuous grumble of criticism on a number of grounds. Some of these arose from the alleged unseemliness of the system. For example, Salmon wrote to John Bernard in August 1897, when there was some question of Bernard being nominated for election to the see of Meath: "The process of popular election is hateful, having your merits discussed in the newspapers, unduly depreciated by the friends of a rival and, what is still more disagreeable, over-pressed by your own injudicious friends."[57] George Seaver, a clergyman of the Church of Ireland and biographer of J. A. F. Gregg, Archbishop of Dublin and Armagh successively, wrote that under the Irish electoral system "the rein is given to invidious gossip in the interregnum and, if it be unduly prolonged (as is generally the case), to canvassing also. The system is also an encouragement to the ecclesiastically ambitious."[58] It is doubtless true that there are these unpleasant aspects to the process of electing bishops. But Crown appointments too, when they were a matter of public interest (as in the nineteenth century), were also the subject of discussion in the press. It was only when most people ceased to care who was made a bishop that this ceased. Where the inside story of Crown appointments is known, it is clear that a certain amount of discreet canvassing of those who might influence the choice was not unknown. Such things are part of human nature, and will be present whatever the form of appointment. The questions are only of degree—how much gossip, how much canvassing; and of how far publicity in these matters is likely to be harmful.

More serious were questions as to whether the system fulfilled its purposes properly. It was supposed to put the choice in the hands of the Diocesan Synod, with an appeal to the bishops if the Synod could not elect by the prescribed majorities. But in sixty years after disestablishment, the Diocesan Synods only succeeded in electing on fifty per cent of occasions. The other half had to go to the House of Bishops. This could sometimes result in an appointment which the majority of the Synod had clearly not wanted. There was an early example of this at Ossory in 1875. The Dean of Cashel (Walsh) secured a two-thirds majority of the lay representatives, but fell a few votes short of it in the clerical order. The choice went to the House of Bishops, who chose R. S. Gregg, Dean of Cork, who had not approached these numbers of votes. He proved a successful choice, moving back to Cork as Bishop, and ending his career as Archbishop of Armagh. But was this really the way the system should work? The bishops' action was criticized, for example, by the strongly Protestant *Irish Church*

Advocate, on the ground that the plain will of the Diocesan Synod had been overridden on a technicality, and that the bishops had been unduly influenced by the opinions of the two candidates on the revision question.[59] There was similar criticism of the system, for example, in the Dublin Diocesan Synod in 1911, when it was said that the system was degenerating into co-option by the bishops.[60] However, there was no strong movement to change the law, so presumably most of the bishops' choices must have been found reasonable.

It was repeatedly asked whether the system produced the right men; but this was virtually an impossible question to answer. It was often said that it produced "safe men". As a criticism, this seems to presuppose some other system capable of picking out good, bold individualists who would never succeed in an election. This doubtless can happen—the two Temples may be examples in England. But such methods too can go wrong, and a bishop can be worse things than "safe". There was certainly in the Irish system a bias against younger men; in the first forty years after disestablishment only two men were elected to bishoprics while they were under fifty years old. The field of choice was also often restricted to the diocese concerned, partly from a natural desire to choose a local man, partly because the electors did not know enough about clergymen in other dioceses.[61]

There was enough dissatisfaction with the system for the General Synod in 1919 to set up a committee to examine a proposal to hand over the election of bishops to an elective council of the whole Church, including all the bishops and representatives of each diocese.[62] The *Church of Ireland Gazette*, in its zeal for reform of all kinds, favoured a very small electoral college of fifteen members.[63] But nothing happened. Archbishop J. A. F. Gregg, in 1932, spoke of continuing discontent with the system, and of interest in the Welsh electoral colleges, but emphasized that it would be difficult to persuade the Diocesan Synods to give up their rights.[64] Whatever the defects of the system, it had at least given to the clergy and lay synodsmen a privilege and voice which they valued. Only in 1959 was the system changed, by an amendment which placed elections to sees other than that of Armagh in the hands of an electoral college representing the diocese concerned, the province, and the whole Irish Church. Elections to Armagh were to be by the House of Bishops, choosing from its own members.[65]

There was also persistent criticism of the method of making parochial appointments. This, it will be recalled, was for three parochial nominators, three diocesan nominators (two clerical and one lay), and the bishop, to choose an incumbent for a vacant parish. This naturally produced canvassing of nominators in ways often felt to be unseemly. Alexander, as Bishop of Derry and later as Primate, would not willingly appoint a candidate known to have canvassed.[66] The main criticisms, however, were that the parochial nominators had undue influence on the boards, that in their choices they ignored certain sorts of merit among the clergy and took no account of the interests of the diocese as a whole, and that the result of their domination was to diminish the numbers and lower the qualifications of those entering the ministry.

When the new system was introduced, some parochial nominators at once assumed control of the proceedings, advertising for applications on their own initiative. An attempt in 1872 to check this by modifying the procedure failed, and the practice continued for many years. It was generally recognized that the choice of the parochial nominators was rarely obstructed by the bishop and the diocesan nominators. It could well happen that one of the men from a parish—a local landowner, for example—could influence the other two, and thus be in effect *the* nominator.[67] It was claimed that the parochial nominators who thus found themselves with the practical power of choice neglected the claims of service in favour of those of youth (a strange charge, when one reflects that the Diocesan Synods were attacked for doing the exact opposite in their election of bishops). The *Gazette* calculated that between 1880 and 1890, out of 206 appointments, eighty-five were of men with four years' service or under.[68] This caused discontent among clergymen with some years of work behind them who wanted a change of parish. It was also argued that the outlook of the parochial nominators was too narrow—each appointment was considered separately, not as part of a series which affected the whole diocese. The bishop and the diocesan nominators thus failed to develop a policy for appointments, which might have proved one of the advantages of the new conditions.[69] Even the diocesan nominators, when they made themselves felt, proved to be in their way parochial, so that it was unusual to get an appointment from outside the diocese. D'Arcy, when Archbishop of Dublin, remarked that some Irish dioceses were close corporations.[70] In the early years after disestablishment it was said that the parochial nominators were also narrow in a doctrinal sense—they tended to be strongly revisionist and Evangelical, so that Bishop Fitzgerald of Killaloe wrote that if there was even a whisper that a man believed in baptismal regeneration no office was open to him.[71]

In the decade after disestablishment there was a decline both in the numbers of men ordained in the Irish Church, and also in the proportion of graduates among them. There was some movement of divinity students from Trinity College to England. Several explanations were advanced for this, including uncertainty about prospects after disestablishment, low stipends, and the assertive attitude of laymen on theological questions during the revision debates.[72] A committee appointed by the General Synod in 1878 to investigate this problem concluded that the new appointments system was more important than any of these reasons. It believed, and this view continued to be held much later, that men without academic qualifications were preferred to those with them.[73]

However, the system was never without its defenders. William Conyngham Plunket, while Bishop of Meath, described it as admirable, and certainly much better than the position before disestablishment.[74] The *Irish Church Advocate* too thought it compared very well with what had gone before, asking whether there had been no canvassing before, and no injustice under a system by which bishops used their powers to provide for their families.[75] According to Archbishop J. A. F. Gregg, by the 1930s things had settled down and the system was working well in the majority of cases. The caprices of what had amounted to lay patronage had passed away, and a working relationship between the different elements in the system had been attained. He still, however, found that there was little scope to plan for the diocese as a whole, and that there was little interchange between dioceses.[76] It seems to be true, as Bishop Bernard wrote in 1914, that the fundamental difficulty was the *uniformity* of the system; a variety of methods would, he thought, serve the needs of the Church better, and he advised the Welsh Church, if it were disestablished, to seek a variable method.[77]

There is no such thing as a system of appointments without defects, or one that can satisfy everyone involved. But methods devised by a Church for itself deserve to be judged by high standards, and it does appear that the Irish system suffered from an undue rigidity resulting from the emphasis on local choice. In one way this provided the stimulus and interest which gave life to the system; but in another it prevented the proper recognition that the appointment of a bishop is a matter for the whole Church, not for just one diocese, and that the appointment of a parish priest is a matter for the diocese as well as for the parish.

Doctrine: the Revision of the Prayer Book

The coming of disestablishment and self-government meant that the Church of Ireland gained control over its own statements of doctrine, forms of service, and ritual. There was no reason inherent in the fact of disestablishment why this power should necessarily be used at once; but circumstances made it inevitable that it should. The main tradition of the Irish Church was Protestant, in natural reaction against the predominant Roman Catholicism by which it was surrounded. James Godkin was exaggerating when he wrote that the Church was "committed to the mortal struggle with Romanism under such conditions as exist nowhere else in Europe",[78] but most Irish Churchmen would surely have agreed with him. This meant that in Ireland the Ritualist movement in England was received with dismay and anger, as being the betrayal of the citadel of Protestantism from within.

It so happened that disestablishment in Ireland came at the height of the Ritualist controversy in England. The case of *Martin* v. *Mackonochie* opened in 1867, and that of *Hebbert v. Purchas* in 1869. In 1867 the Ritual Commission was appointed. The differing verdicts of the courts, and the need to set up the Commission, showed that the law of the Church of England on some of the matters at issue—candles on the altar, the mixed chalice, the use of vestments, the position of the priest when celebrating Holy Communion—was doubtful. It was perfectly possible to argue, for example, that rubrics in the Prayer Book actually demanded the use of vestments and the eastward position during the celebration of Holy Communion. This ambiguity of the law about the

13

outward forms of worship was matched by ambiguities in the doctrines of the Church of England which had been revealed during the previous thirty years by the work of the Oxford Movement. It had been shown that the forms of service, and even the Thirty-nine Articles of Religion, could bear meanings which were very different from those accepted by Protestant Churchmen. There had arisen controversies about the doctrine of the Holy Communion, about confession and absolution, about the nature of the Church, and about the tradition of the Church as against the unique authority of the Bible. By the time of Irish disestablishment, divergent views on such matters were held by well-developed schools of thought in the Church of England, with their own party organizations and organs of opinion. The Church was profoundly divided into High and Low, and Irish Churchmen saw with alarm that the High Church school not only remained within the Church of England but claimed it as their own.*

Fear of Ritualism in England mingled with political resentment against England in the period immediately after disestablishment. Many Irish Churchmen felt that the Church of England, and especially the bishops in the House of Lords, had betrayed them. In these circumstances, they saw every advantage in breaking away from a Church which combined Romish tendencies with political treachery. Revision of the Prayer Book to excise those portions which were used as cover by High Churchmen, and to fortify the Irish Church in its true Protestant purity, was an obvious step to advocate. The argument for revision also drew strength from a desire to remove obstacles which prevented Protestant Nonconformists from joining the Church. This wish for Protestant solidarity led some Churchmen to seek to remove the marks which distinguished Church from Dissent, especially the peculiar offices of bishop and priest. There were ample motives here to set a movement for the revision of the Prayer Book under way. Once

---

* The Broad Church too, though much less significant to Irish minds, aroused some fears. The *I.E.G.* in December 1869 (p. 279) wrote that election of bishops would save the Irish Church from an appointment like that of Temple to Exeter. (Temple was under heavy attack as a rationalist because he had contributed to *Essays and Reviews*.) Salmon wrote (*Irish Church Convention*, pp. 5–6) that it had been seen how far English clergymen could go towards either Rome *or* Infidelity and still keep their positions in the Church.

started, other points arose because they were already under discussion. The status and content of the Athanasian Creed, for example, were being debated at that time throughout the Anglican Communion, because of a widespread reluctance to accept the "damnatory clauses" at its beginning and end.

There was a further argument for revision. Disestablishment placed the Irish Church in a new position, and in face of the vast Roman Catholic majority an exposed position. It needed solidarity and certainty about where it stood. C. P. Reichel wrote in 1870 that the Prayer Book had to be revised to meet these conditions. "Its illogical comprehensiveness renders it unfit for a communion which will have to depend on internal coherence, instead of on external pressure. . . ."[79] There was substance in this argument. It is the custom for apologists of the Church of England to make a virtue, even a glory, of its comprehensiveness. But there is virtue too in knowing where one stands in matters of doctrine, and in having a recognized standard in ritual, enforced, if necessary, by courts whose authority is generally respected. This eventually is where the Irish Church arrived, and it was a desirable end—a Church in its position could not afford the luxury of anarchy. It is doubtful whether this end could have been achieved without the revision of the Irish Prayer Book in the 1870s, even though it proved that the actual changes brought about by that revision were miniscule.

Thus the circumstances were such that an attempt at revision was almost inevitable. There was both a reasonable case and powerful emotional forces in favour of it. At the time, the emotion was more important than reason. Fear of ritualism was probably the strongest single force for revision, and, as far as ritualism in Ireland itself was concerned, this fear was largely baseless. As Bence Jones wrote scornfully. "Ritualism is their bugbear, tho' there are only 2 [ritualists] in all Ireland."[80] The manifestations of anti-ritualism could be extreme, as was shown in the Maberley affair, which is worth brief mention as an illustration of the state of feeling in Ireland at the time. In March 1870 a Dublin layman, Maberley, wrote to Archbishop Trench to complain that a clergyman had given to one of his domestic servants a booklet entitled *Short Prayers, etc., for those who have little time to pray*, by the Reverend G. R. Portal, which Maberley found full of dangerous doctrines.

The Archbishop replied in April that he saw no reason to disapprove of the booklet. Among the points on which he agreed with Portal were the following: that it was wrong for members of the Church to be present at Roman Catholic or Dissenting services; that baptism involved the forgiveness of sins—if Maberley objected to this, Trench pointed out, he must also object to the Nicene Creed and to the baptism service; that absolution from sin could be given by priests—Trench again referred to the forms of absolution in the Prayer Book, to be pronounced by the priest alone. This correspondence was published in the *Daily Express*. It produced a fierce controversy, and a wave of attacks on Trench himself. "Puseyite Trench" was scrawled on walls all over Dublin. Eighty-two clergy in his diocese signed a protest against the booklet and Trench's approval of it, on the ground that it contained Romish teaching. Seventy-eight others signed a letter regretting that the Archbishop's refusal to condemn the booklet should have been construed as approval of doctrines they were sure he did not maintain, and hoping that the Irish Church would not narrow her statements of doctrine so as to exclude fair differences of belief. All over Ireland vestries passed resolutions condemning Trench. The most important point in all this was that the form of Trench's letter to Maberley invited his opponents to cast their arguments in the form of demands for revision of the Prayer Book, which Trench himself wished to avoid. If the Archbishop could so easily quote the Prayer Book in defence of a booklet so obviously Romish in its tendencies, then the Prayer Book must be altered. Thus were the arguments against ritualism given concrete form.[81]

The affair itself was trivial, taken up and exploited by those anxious for revision. Maberley himself was a self-appointed watchdog for Protestant truth, who later took part in agitations against retreats and for the removal of the rood screen in Christ Church Cathedral, Dublin.[82] On the other side, Trench's handling of the matter might have been more skilful. But personalities apart, the affair touched a sore nerve in the Irish Church, and illustrates the state of feeling which made revision almost certain. It was this feeling which made the process of revision dangerous to the Church, because it was expressed in demands which Churchmen far removed from ritualism felt would change the nature of the

Church.* One revisionist pamphlet concluded that the Church of Ireland was "a religious co-operative society, established for the benefit of its members and of all the world. . . . The Church of Ireland is invested with no authority by God, directly or indirectly. . . . The Church is of mundane construction, but the religion is divine." It stated too that the Bible contained "the complete and only rule of faith and conduct", the Prayer Book being only a record of the bye-laws and resolutions of the committee of management for the time being; that the absolute control of the Church had been before disestablishment in the hands of the laity; that the clerical office and ranks in it were the creations of the Church as a society, and in particular that bishops could not be distinguished as a separate order, but were just another sort of clergy.[83] This was an extreme example, in that all these assertions were made together, and the language was somewhat crude. But all its points were matched in other revisionist writings. The unwillingness to acknowledge the bishops as a separate order, and the importance of this issue, has already been noted. There were plenty of objections too to acknowledging the special position and powers of the priesthood. As one writer put it, "You do not believe that Priest or Minister can remit sins", so why should the bishop in the ordination service be allowed to say, while laying his hands on those about to be ordained, "Whose sins thou dost forgive, they are forgiven; and whose sins thou dost retain, they are retained"? Nor should the Church use the form of absolution laid down in the order for Visitation of the Sick—"I absolve thee from all thy sins".[84] Again, the Protestant Defence Association, with Lord James Butler as its chairman, argued that Churchmen could not consistently deny any priesthood except that common to all believers, and yet accept the ordination of priests; they could not protest against the confessional and absolution by a priest, and yet provide for both in their services and rubrics. To admit these inconsistencies was to encourage Romanism in the Church.[85]

In such views there could be found a programme which, if

---

* For example, Bishop Alexander of Derry wrote that the report of the Revision Committee set up by the Convention (below, p. 192) "would have made a position in the Irish Church untenable, not only by moderate High Churchmen but by several Evangelicals" (Alexander to Disraeli, 11 May 1871, Hughenden Papers, B/XXI/A/139.)

carried out in all its implications, would certainly have changed the nature of the Church of Ireland. It was, of course, not the programme of all revisionists. There were moderate, scholarly men such as C. P. Reichel and William Conyngham Plunket, who had more limited objectives. Plunket's definition of moderate revision may stand as an example. He wanted first the removal of difficulties caused by the damnatory clauses of the Athanasian Creed; second the recognition in the Prayer Book of the liberty in interpreting the baptism service, particularly the idea of regeneration, which had already been legally authorized in England;* third, in the Communion service to forbid eucharistic adoration, to omit the ornaments rubric, to enjoin celebration at the north end, and to forbid any bowing or making the sign of the cross; fourth, that as a safeguard against the introduction of the confessional, the sentence conveying authority to forgive sins should be omitted from the ordination service. In spite of their relative moderation, Plunket's biographer points out that these changes would still have involved important matters of doctrine, as well as fundamentally unimportant details of form.[86]

Such demands for revision, even the more moderate, presented two kinds of danger to the Church of Ireland. First, there was the possibility that some drastic measures might be carried, so that the Church would cut itself off from its own history and from its fellow-members of the Anglican Communion. There were genuine fears that this might happen. Archbishop Trench, when giving a generous sum to the Church's sustentation fund, took the precaution of spreading the payments over five years and reserving the right to suspend payment, lest "the Church of Ireland turn out after all to be no Church, but only a Protestant sect".[87] During the Maberley affair, a Broad Churchman and moderate revisionist, John Jellett, remarked that he had no fears for the Protestantism of the Irish Church, but her Catholicity was in some danger.[88] Some highly placed people in England, including Magee, the Bishop of Peterborough and formerly Dean of Cork, as well as some High Churchmen, also took the danger seriously. But in the event the clause in the constitution demanding a two-thirds majority of each

---

* Presumably a reference to the Gorham case, in which the Judicial Committee of the Privy Council finally ruled that it was not necessary for a clergyman of the Church of England to hold the doctrine of baptismal regeneration.

order in the General Synod twice over in successive years was a formidable obstacle to any change in the Prayer Book. The fears of a drastic revision severing the Church of Ireland from the rest of the Anglican Communion, while not wholly baseless, were not realized.

Second, there was the possibility of schism within the Church of Ireland, whether or not far-reaching changes came about. There were those who thought that the extreme revisionist group would break away if there were no changes.[89] Their representatives mentioned this possibility on occasion,[90] and the virulence of the language used by extremists outside the General Synod lent colour to the threat.[91] The *Gazette* was more worried than it cared to remember afterwards, and wrote in September 1870 of a possible division in the Church which would leave one part of it as the Church of England in Ireland.[92] Salmon, who was no alarmist, wrote at the end of the same year that the great question was whether unity could be preserved; if not, it would be a triumph for the Roman Catholics, who had always said that state protection was the only prop of the Irish Church.[93] Again, in the event no schism materialized, though a few individual clergymen did refuse to accept any revision of the Prayer Book—a minor secession at the opposite end of the scale from the extreme revisionist group.[94] But even though schism was avoided, the revision controversy still endangered the unity of the Irish Church in a more general sense. It tended to set the clergy against the laity in the General Synod, because the laity generally favoured revision while the clergy obstructed it, leading to protests that voting by orders and the two-thirds rule were nullifying the will of the majority.[95] This held ugly possibilities for the future of the Church. Another danger to unity lay in the fact that the debate was sometimes conducted in terms of personalities rather than of principles. This should not be exaggerated, and *odium theologicum* was kept within reasonable bounds for the time; but it remains true that blows were struck which were not easily forgotten. Archbishop Trench was often at the centre of these personal storms. According to Bence Jones, this was because he was tactless and obstinate about trifles;[96] if so, he suffered disproportionately for his faults. Bishop Alexander wrote that during the Maberley controversy Trench had been "condemned in language that ran up the whole scale of vituperation. . . . He has been baited in his own Synod, scoffed at by the Protestant Press generally, and furiously denounced in the Convention."[97] When he wrote this letter, Alexander was plainly under the stress of great emotion and sympathy for Trench; the feelings of others, on both sides, may be guessed at. Allowance must be made for the conventions of the time. Abuse was the normal small change of political and ecclesiastical controversy, in both England and Ireland. Irish bishops were certainly not the only ones to suffer. At the Lambeth Conference of 1878, Plunket said that English bishops caught in the crossfire between the *Rock* and the *Church Times* might even find life more peaceful in Ireland.[98] Even with due allowance, however, the controversy was fierce, and gave rise to personal bitterness and rancour at a time when good will and unity were more than usually desirable.

These, then, were the reasons why disestablishment in Ireland was followed at once by a revision of the Prayer Book, and why this process involved dangers for the Church. The process, once begun, was long and stormy, but only the outline of the story need concern us here.[99] It began during the Convention of 1870, which made clear the strength of the demand for revision, and set up a committee (generally known as Master Brooke's committee*) to consider how revision of the Prayer Book might check the introduction of novel doctrines and practices. This committee reported to the General Synod in 1871, in a strongly Protestant document.[100] One of its proposals was put before the Synod, and was beaten only because it did not receive a two-thirds majority of the order of clergy. It thus became clear that revision of some kind was inevitable, and Salmon moved for the setting up of a strong committee of the General Synod, on which the bishops should be represented, to undertake the work of revision in a systematic and responsible manner. This was accepted, and the Revision Committee reported to the General Synod in 1873.

The ensuing debates in the General Synod went on until 1878, and the resulting revised Prayer Book did not come into use until 1879. When all was over, only two changes of substance were made, and only one of those arose out of the anti-ritualist cam-

---

* William Brooke, Master of the Irish Court of Chancery, moved the setting up of the committee. It consisted of twenty-six members, half clerical and half lay. The bishops refused to serve on it.

paign. This was the change in the form of absolution used in the service for the Visitation of the Sick, the form of prayer from the Communion Service replacing the straight "I absolve thee". This was carried in 1873 without a division.[101] The second change concerned the Athanasian Creed. In 1875 a Bill was passed by the required majorities for the second successive time, and so became law, to omit the rubric before the Creed (which enjoined its use on certain days) and to have only portions of it recited on Christmas Day, Whit Sunday, and Trinity Sunday. The verses to be omitted were the first two and the last (the "damnatory clauses"), and that running "Furthermore, it is necessary to everlasting salvation, that he also believe rightly the Incarnation of our Lord Jesus Christ" (which was treated on the same footing as the "damnatory clauses"). On this Bill the House of Bishops voted in both years, the vote of 1874 being the first time they exercised their right to vote as a separate House, but on each occasion a majority of the bishops present voted for the Bill. Archbishop Trench warned the General Synod that, if it persisted in its intention, he would use his right under the Irish Church Act to refuse to accept the change. He would not use a Prayer Book containing a mutilated Athanasian Creed. In the event, he did not have to carry out his threat. In 1876 the statute of 1875 was repealed, and an arrangement substituted by which the Creed was retained in its entirety, but the rubric directing it to be publicly used on certain days was omitted. This was accepted by overwhelming majorities of both orders (108 clergy and 103 laymen to eight clergy and four laymen). This Bill became law on its second passage in 1877.[102] This decision was scarcely logical, for the Irish Church continued to retain the eighth Article of Religion, which lays down that the Athanasian Creed "ought thoroughly to be received and believed", so it is hard to see why it should not also be said. However, even to Bishop Alexander, who opposed the change to the last ditch, the decision came to seem one of consummate wisdom. It was certainly no worse than other proposals made, and sometimes adopted, in other Churches in the Anglican Communion.[103]

On all the other major points at issue, no change of any importance was made. The ordination service was left as it was, including the words spoken by the bishop to the ordinands around which controversy had raged. The baptism service, including its references to regeneration, remained intact, and no further explanatory rubric was added to it. Similarly, the Communion service and the rubric at the end of it were left as they stood. On all these matters, paragraphs were inserted in the new Preface to the Prayer Book, which undertook to explain why certain changes had been made but not others. It thus became a commentary on the process of revision, or, as some thought, a compendium of explanations to conciliate disappointed revisionists. It was subjected to some scathing criticism by Bishop Alexander, and the House of Bishops divided on it; but it was passed in 1878.[104]

While the Prayer Book came through the revision debates largely unaltered, the General Synod in 1871 and 1872 had already taken certain steps against ritualism by other means. The new canons of the Irish Church forbade the use of vestments (Canon 4); forbade the use of lamps or candles except when needed for light (Canon 35); forbade the placing of a cross on or behind what was carefully referred to as the Communion table; and instructed the celebrant at Holy Communion to stand at the north side of the table.[105] These canons laid down standards of ritual which, as Archbishop J. A. F. Gregg pointed out long afterwards, "would have been imposed in England had the Church of England been free to make its own laws at that time".[106] They were restrictive, they were clear, and they commanded general acceptance.

On the whole, the results of the revision controversy were very different from those which many had feared or hoped. The general effect was undoubtedly beneficial to the Church. This was apparent even while it was going on. The *Gazette* wrote in 1874 that there was in the Irish Church no longer a "calm, easy dead level of theological opinion".[107] The debates had brought about an unexpected strengthening of High Church opinion, and revealed also (especially in discussion on the Athanasian Creed) more Broad Church or rationalist opinion than had been thought to exist in the Irish Church. The Protestant majority, too, had been forced to think about fundamental matters which they had previously taken for granted, and had increasingly come to recognize that there was another view beside their own. Its educational effect was indeed one of the great results of the revision controversy. Previously most members of the Irish Church had taken their religion without much question. The revision debates forced many of them to examine the doctrines and principles of their Church, and ultimately to reaffirm them. Traill, the Provost of Trinity, looking back in 1910, thought that the laity had learned more about the history and tenets of their Church than they had ever known before.[108] This was no small gain.

That there was a price in rancour and ill-will has already been seen. But ultimately the work was done, as Bishop Plunket proudly told the Lambeth Conference in 1878,[109] without breaking ranks, and without damage to the fundamental position of the Church. Bishop Alexander, who, as has been seen, disapproved of many aspects of revision while it was going on, voting against the arrangements for the Athanasian Creed and against the new Preface, said afterwards: "Our Prayer Book has not admitted into its text enough anti-Catholicism to drown an ecclesiastical midge."[110] Bernard, while Dean of St Patrick's, assured a mainly English audience that "no single principle of Catholicity was abandoned or denied".[111] There was nothing in the make-up of the Irish Church to prevent one of its most distinguished Primates, J. A. F. Gregg, holding a very high view of the Church, though he was far from being an Anglo-Catholic in an English sense. On questions of reunion, for example, Gregg emphasized the importance of continuity and Church order, and once remarked that "The Church of South India is not a Church, it is merely a society"—which could not be capped by any Anglo-Catholic.[112] The Irish Church emerged from the revision controversy stronger than before: with its Catholicity intact; with firm (perhaps excessive) safeguards against ritualism embodied in its canons; and with a body of law which was understood, respected, and obeyed.*

* It is worth mentioning the case of the cross in the church of St Bartholomew, Dublin, which went on from 1888 to 1895. This involved the interpretation of Canon 36, which forbade the placing of a cross on or behind the holy table. The details of the case cannot be gone into here, but it was noteworthy that the incumbent obeyed the instructions of the Archbishop of Dublin that the cross should be moved from where he had placed it, and that both accepted the ultimate ruling of the Court of the General Synod. The contrast with the state of anarchy in England in the late nineteenth century, when neither bishops nor courts were obeyed, could not be more striking. See How, *Plunket*, chapter XXI, and Phillips, vol. III, pp. 403–5. Canon 36 was amended in 1960 to allow a cross to be placed on the Communion table, or to be depicted behind

This last was more than could be said about the Church of England at that time or since.

Finance[113]

The Irish Church, though ill-prepared, took readily to the ways of self-government, and plunged eagerly into the waters of theological debate and emerged safely on the other side. For the financial problems created by the Irish Church Act the Church was even less prepared, and the dangers here were probably greater than any others. The Irish Church had lived comfortably for many years, with resources which were greater than its needs, even if they were inequitably distributed. The only serious economic difficulties in living memory were the tithe wars of the 1830s, which had arisen from the problem of how the tithes legally due to the Church could be collected; the situation had been grave, but it had been essentially a problem for the clergy, not the laymen of the Church. The lay members, with comparatively few exceptions, were accustomed to having clergy, buildings, and services provided without any deliberate financial effort on their part.

After disendowment the situation changed completely. The Irish Church Act deprived the Church of all its property, with an annual value of between £619,000 and £680,000,[114] with the exception of (1) churches, certain graveyards, church plate and other furnishings, if claimed by the Representative Church Body from the Commissioners for Church Temporalities in Ireland; and (2) a sum of £500,000, the estimated equivalent of private benefactions. The Act made provision for the payment of life annuities to the archbishops, bishops, incumbents, and permanent curates appointed before the passing of the Act so long as they continued to discharge their duties. It also gave the right to the Representative Church Body to buy back from the Commissioners the clergy houses and a limited amount of glebe land at what proved to be advantageous prices.[115] Everything else was lost, though the terms of compensation for the clergy were favourable

---

it, provided that a faculty was obtained with the approval of the incumbent and a majority of the select vestry.

to the Church and provided a basis for its new financial structure. The clergy of 1869 (except for temporary curates) had their incomes guaranteed while they performed their duties, and the twelve per cent bonus offered on commutation was a further advantage. However, the clergy of 1869 would die and have to be replaced, and within a measurable period of time the Irish Church would have to provide for its own needs out of its own resources.

Within this breathing-space provided by the lives of the existing clergy, then, the Church had to organize itself and make the best use of the financial resources remaining to it. This was done chiefly in two ways: first, by the capitalization of the money provided by the annuities of the existing clergy, in the processes known as commuting and compounding, and second, by the raising of money by gifts and subscriptions.

Under the Irish Church Act, the archbishops, bishops, incumbents, and permanent curates were to be paid life annuities equal to the net amount of the income they lost through the Act. The Act also allowed any annuitant, with the consent of the Representative Church Body, to commute this annuity for a lump sum, which would be paid to the Representative Church Body, which would then assume the obligation of paying the annuity. The amount of the lump sum was calculated on current government male life annuity tables, and on the assumption that the capital would be invested at three-and-a-half per cent. As an inducement to the clergy to commute, the Act also provided that in each diocese or united diocese where three-quarters of the clergy commuted, the capital sum thus payable to the Representative Church Body would be increased by twelve per cent. This was worth while from the point of view of the government, and of the Commissioners of Church Temporalities in Ireland who acted as the government's agents, because, if generally adopted, it would greatly simplify their administrative tasks. Instead of having to pay some two thousand individual annuities, some of which might continue for fifty years or more, they could hand this work over to the Representative Church Body, excepting only those who declined to commute. It would be worth while to the Church, because, even though it would inherit the administrative work, it would also secure two advantages. One was financial—the bonus of twelve per cent, and the possibility of investing the commutation capital at a rate of interest higher than the three-and-a-half per cent calculated upon. There was some dispute at the time as to the effect of commutation and the bonus. This was an actuarial problem. The commutation scheme was based on the government male annuitant life tables which fell short of the actual life expectancy of the Irish clergy, and it was possible to argue that in view of the longevity of the clergy, a more appropriate life table should have been found. However, it was almost certain that the twelve per cent bonus added to the tabular values would outweigh the disadvantages of the government table, and leave a surplus when all demands had been met.[116] The second advantage was psychological—the unifying effect of having the clergy paid by the Representative Church Body instead of by the Commissioners, or rather, as would quickly come about, the old clergy being paid by the Commissioners and the new by the Representative Church Body. Moreover, by commuting, the clergy would openly express their confidence in the Irish Church in its new form.[117]

The whole process of commutation, indeed, depended on whether the individual clergymen of the Irish Church had this confidence. From their point of view, commutation was not necessarily so attractive as it was to the Representative Church Body. The Dean of Down, for example, writing in the style of one who distrusted those who manipulated statistics, remarked that it was bad enough to have been robbed of one's freehold and turned into a government annuitant, but even so "it might be far worse by a voluntary act to become the annuitants of a popular assembly". A government annuity was secure, but one from an untried representative body might not be.[118] The Dean of Cashel, MacDonnell, who came down on the side of commuting, still pointed out that the clergy had a right to security, and that the commutation capital might be dissipated by bad management.[119] However, when in March 1871 the Representative Church Body gave its formal opinion that general commutation would be safe for the clergy and profitable for the Church, this was almost unanimously supported by the clergy in the way that really mattered. They commuted.[120] By the end of 1875, only seventy-one clergy of those entitled to commute had not done so.[121]

A sum of rather over £7,500,000 in commutation capital paid

in respect of the clergy was thus placed in the hands of the Representative Church Body, the first charge on which was the payment of annuities to the clergy.[122] The Act also gave the Representative Church Body power to make such further arrangements as seemed suitable with annuitants who had commuted. The Representative Church Body was anxious to save some of the commutation capital, and was also aware of the need to make changes in the parochial system. One way to achieve both ends was by the device known as compounding. The Representative Church Body provided in November 1870 that an annuitant who wished to be relieved of his obligation to the Church (which was the condition of his annuity) could do so by compounding, i.e. by taking a portion of his commutation capital for his own free use and leaving the rest with the Representative Church Body. The proportions of this division were to be as follows: clergymen of sixty-five or over would receive two-thirds of their commutation capital; those of thirty-five or younger would receive one-third; and those between those ages would receive a proportion on a sliding scale between the two figures. Thus a clergyman aged forty-five would compound by taking five-ninths of his commutation capital, leaving the Representative Church Body with four-ninths not charged with an annuity—though, of course, unless the parish concerned were amalgamated with another, they would also have to pay another clergyman.[123]

Compounding proved popular. By November 1874, 736 clergymen had compounded. By 1890, when compounding was virtually at an end, the yield in what were termed composition balances to the Representative Church Body was £1,624,000.[124] It was on the whole beneficial to the Church, though there was controversy over some cases of abuse where clergymen compounded and took a lump sum from the Representative Church Body when moving to some more lucrative post within the Irish Church.[125]

Commutation, compounding, and the judicious use of the capital thus provided were of some use to the Church, but, however skilful the operations of the Representative Church Body, the future of the Church really depended on the generosity of its laity. Only this could prevent the Church from finding itself in a few years' time with a balance in hand from the commutation capital quite unequal to meeting its necessary expenses. The task fell on a body which was not numerous—just over 690,000 in all in 1861 and steadily if slowly declining thereafter—though it included many of the wealthiest people in Ireland, as well as a solid backbone in the professional and business communities. Even allowing for this social composition, the performance of the Irish Churchmen of that generation was highly creditable. The subscriptions to the sustentation fund raised by the Representative Church Body were as follows for the first twenty years:

1870	£229,754	1880	£147,768
1871	£214,709	1881	£153,818
1872	£248,445	1882	£154,487
1873	£230,180	1883	£178,445
1874	£257,021	1884	£190,612
1875	£218,499	1885	£137,117
1876	£212,095	1886	£167,011
1877	£197,739	1887	£136,963
1878	£174,404	1888	£148,381
1879	£165,008	1889	£170,724

TOTAL FOR TWENTY YEARS: £3,733,180.[126]

It has already been mentioned in the section on government that these funds were mostly tied to the dioceses or even to the parishes where they were raised. The amount available as a central fund, entirely at the disposal of the Representative Church Body, was very small. This was not the original intention. The Representative Church Body at first wanted a general fund for the whole Church, but the psychological obstacles proved too great for this policy to succeed. On this question even Bence Jones and R. S. Gregg, a Bishop of Cork of whom Bence Jones had a low opinion, were at one. Bence Jones argued that the only plan was to make each parish provide for itself, if necessary with some help from a general fund.[127] Gregg, when he went to Cork as bishop, took the same view, and put assessments on a parochial, not even on a diocesan, basis. He argued that, under a diocesan system, the poorer parishes would leave it to the richer to contribute, because what is everybody's business is nobody's business.[128] In the event, the scheme for a general fund for the whole Church was abandoned in favour of a series of local funds.[129]

This change was doubtless inevitable. It was again a matter of local loyalties; people would subscribe to sustain their own parish and its clergyman when they would not do so for a general fund raised by a body in Dublin. The approach was psychologically sound, but its long-term results were highly inconvenient. The Irish Church put itself into a strait-jacket. The laces were tightly tied by trust-deeds limiting the use of funds to parish or diocese, and escape was extremely difficult. The situation was made worse by the fact that the commutation capital was paid to dioceses and continued to be administered by them. This was not necessarily done by a united diocese as one unit. For example, within the united diocese of Cashel, Cashel and Emly worked as one unit, Waterford and Lismore as another. It so happened that many annuitants in Cashel and Emly died early, leaving those dioceses with substantial sums of commutation capital intact, while Waterford and Lismore, with a separate financial scheme and longer-lived annuitants, were worse off.[130]

The financial system of the Irish Church, then, contained this great flaw, whose effects grew with time. But the main point at the start was that the money came in. The Church was not doomed but saved. The general financial position of the Irish Church in the twenty years after disestablishment, and the use it made of its money, may now be summarized. Dr Shearman has calculated that the Representative Church Body received compensation payments from the Commissioners amounting to £8,548,447, of which £500,000 was in lieu of private endowments and the remainder commutation capital.[131] The sums given annually to the Church by its members have already been set out. The situation was simple; as more money was subscribed, so more of the commutation capital could be saved for permanent investment. By Dr Shearman's estimates about £4,000,000 of the compensation payments were still in existence in 1895. This was the year in which the interest on the commutation capital was first sufficient to meet the payment of annuities without drawing on the capital. This may be accounted the amount of the compensation payments saved by the voluntary efforts of Irish Churchmen and by the good management of the Representative Church Body.[132]

By gifts and skilled handling of its funds the Church was able to accumulate a gradually increasing total of invested capital: £6,475,000 in 1885; £6,952,000 in 1895; £7,858,000 in 1905.[133] When the Representative Church Body first began to invest its capital, it put it mostly in railways and mortgages on Irish land, at interest rates of between four and four and a half per cent. The agricultural depression which set in about 1875, Gladstone's Irish Land Act of 1881, and the agrarian disturbances of the 1880s all tended to reduce both rents from land and its capital value. As the early mortgages were paid off, the Representative Church Body found itself unable to reinvest at such favourable rates of interest— in 1904–7 it was reinvesting at about three and a half per cent.[134] The agricultural depression and agrarian crime had more immediate effects on the income of the Church from subscriptions. Landowners were among the principal supporters of the Irish Church, especially in the south and west, and when their incomes declined, or later when they sold their estates to tenants under the Land Purchase Acts, the Church suffered accordingly. In 1881 it seemed that the stipends of the clergy in the dioceses of Tuam and Killaloe would have to be reduced because the assessments were not being met, and the diocese of Down came to their help.[135] It is highly likely that, if the Church had not been disendowed, it would have suffered even more from the depression and from the boycotting and violence of the 1880s. It was a bad time for landlords in Ireland, and if the Church had still been a great landlord it would have fared as badly as any—perhaps worse than most. It was better to be drawing interest from investments than to be trying to collect tithe rent-charge or rents in the Ireland of the 1880s. The sort of property the Church held before 1869 would have fallen markedly in value twenty years later, so it is possible to argue that it would scarcely have been better off even if it had avoided disendowment.

The income of the Church proved sufficient to make adequate provision for its new clergy—those appointed after the passing of the Act, who were not entitled to annuities. One important change which the disestablishment of the Church introduced was the standardization of incomes as between benefices, which greatly reduced the gross disparity of clerical stipends under the old regime. The proposed incomes for benefices, to take effect when the incumbent at the time of disestablishment died or left, were normally between £150 and £250. There was an occasional £100 or £300. Cork proposed the most generous scheme, with nothing below £200, most of its parishes at £250, and as many as twenty-six at £300–350. There was some discussion as to whether there should be more prizes in the Church, well-paid posts to attract men of intellect and distinction, and there were those who believed that the loss of wealthy benefices was serious.[136] But with the decline in giving during the 1880s, the real question became whether the figures already proposed could be paid, and later whether the Church could raise enough money to enable its stipends to keep pace with the falling value of money—a problem not peculiar to the disendowed Church of Ireland. At least under the new order the ordinary clergyman received his income regularly, from the Representative Church Body if he commuted or was appointed after the passing of the Act, otherwise from the Church Temporalities Commissioners. He was relieved of the task of collecting it himself in tithe rent-charge or rents, which was cumbersome and could be unpleasant or even dangerous.

There are two points of detail arising from the administration of the Act which deserve mention. The first is the matter of compensation to curates. Under the Act a "permanent curate" was entitled to an annuity on the same terms as an incumbent, while other curates were to be paid a lump sum gratuity. The Church Temporalities Commissioners were the sole judges as to whether a curate was "permanent" or not. The only necessary qualification for compensation was that a curate must have been serving before the date of disestablishment, 1 January 1871. After disestablishment it was freely asserted that the Church had taken advantage of these compensation provisions by "manufacturing" curates in numbers far beyond its needs, getting them declared to be "permanent", and securing annuities for them. It was stated that the number of permanent curates had been increased from 400 at the passing of the Act to 900 by the date of disestablishment. In fact, the number of stipendiary curates on the passing of the Act was 563, and the Commissioners accepted as permanent 201 curates appointed between the passing of the Act and the date of disestablishment. This brought the total number of permanent curates to 764 at the most. Some confusion arose, however, because the total number of permanent curates at the time of disestablishment was sometimes given in returns as 921; this figure included incumbents who held curacies in addition to their benefices, and who appeared twice in lists under different headings, though they were compensated as incumbents, not as curates. So the true increase in the number of curates entitled to an annuity was not 400, but at most 201. Some of these appointments were doubtless necessary; but in general the Irish Church was over-manned rather than the reverse, and there was obviously a strong desire both to acquire clergymen who would be paid by the Commissioners, and also to extract as much compensation money as possible from the government. The Church gained a certain amount from the operation, both in terms of commutation capital and through the services of clergymen entitled to annuities. There was thus some exploitation of the terms of the Act by the Church, but much less than the gigantic jobbery depicted by opponents of the Church. However, exaggerated accounts of the scandal of the curates in the Irish Church influenced the debates on Welsh disestablishment, and were the direct cause of curates in the Welsh Church being denied any compensation.[137]

The second point of detail concerns the glebe-houses, about which there had been so much discussion when the Irish Church Bill was being drafted. The terms of the Act on this matter proved extremely favourable to the Church. In cases where the incumbent agreed to commute, there was included in the lump sum payment to the Representative Church Body the value of his glebe-house and land calculated at twelve and four fifths times the letting value. The Representative Church Body could then buy back from the Commissioners the house and a certain amount of land at the lowest of three different methods of valuation. The result was that the Commissioners consistently paid compensation for the glebe-houses and land at one rate, and then received payment for those they sold at a lower rate. The Commissioners estimated in 1875 that they would have been £264,000 better off if the glebe-houses and gardens had simply been given to existing incumbents for their lifetimes and after that to the Representative Church Body.[138] Gladstone had intended to be generous to the Church in this matter, but presumably not to be as prodigal as this.

Disendowment was the severest blow to fall on the Irish Church through the Act of 1869. The compensation clauses, especially the provision for commutation, gave the Church an opportunity to recover, though they did not in themselves provide re-endowment.

It was through the generosity of its members and the good management of the Representative Church Body that this opportunity was taken, and the finances of the Church re-established on a sound footing.

Relations between the
Churches of Ireland and England

On the whole, the Church of England fought the battle against Irish disestablishment with vigour, if not always with discernment. Such at any rate is the view of an Englishman a hundred years after the event. It was not the view of many Irish Churchmen at the time, betrayed as they saw it by the bishops in the House of Lords, first at the Second Reading of the Bill, and then again at the final compromise. They resented the treatment they received at the hands of English Conservatives and the Church of England as well as of the Liberals and Nonconformists. Some of them for a time threw in their lot with the Home Rule movement.[139] The *Daily Express* summed up the feeling when it declared that "The people of England have inflicted a grievous wrong upon the Irish Church".[140]

The two Churches, in fact, had never been close together, even when they were legally the United Church of England and Ireland. English Evangelicals were sympathetic to the Irish Protestant tradition, but had little knowledge of Irish conditions. High Churchmen disliked the tone of Irish Protestantism, and saw Ireland as a place where lone members of the Tractarian movement struggled against ignorant abuse. In general, when the flurry of the disestablishment campaign was over, English Churchmen tended to return to their normal state of ignoring the existence of the Irish Church. When an article on the Church of Ireland appeared in the *Church Quarterly Review* in 1885, the author remarked that since the journal began in 1875 it had printed only two articles on this subject, which was quite as many as English readers wanted. He thought that this was a mistaken attitude; but his own article was still patronizing in tone and deprecatory in content.[141]

These attitudes of resentment on the one hand, and misunderstanding and condescension on the other, further worsened a relationship which had never been close. Yet there was some consciousness in Ireland of a need for English support, moral and financial. Archbishop Trench's fear of the Irish Church being cut off, a lonely fragment, has been noted, and while it was exaggerated, he did have some cause to be uneasy. Bence Jones, himself of English origin, just as Trench was English in upbringing and outlook, felt strongly that the Church of England could play a useful role in the financial arrangements of the Irish Church. Time and again he impressed on Archbishop Tait the desirability of an English fund expressly tied to the needs of the poor Irish parishes, especially in the south and west.[142]

However, whether the Irish wanted it or not, there was little help forthcoming from the Church of England. The Archbishops of Canterbury and York sent a formal letter of sympathy and offer of help to the Irish Church Convention in February 1870.[143] But soon afterwards Tait, who might have got something done, fell gravely ill, and Thomson of York was hesitant. He was afraid that revision of the Prayer Book in Ireland would give it a Presbyterian character, and felt that people in England ought to be sure to what ends their money would be used. He and other bishops whom he consulted were encouraged in this mistrust by the Archbishop of Dublin.[144] Tait thought at the end of June 1870 that the time was ripe to start raising funds in England, but when he had the bishops of his province circularized, he received some very dubious replies. The influence of Trench was clear, as was also that of Magee at Peterborough, who held the view that there was serious danger of schism in the Church of Ireland, and that it was in any case bound to have a new Prayer Book, which made its future state an unknown quantity.[145]

Not until February 1871 did the English bishops decide to give a lead by making their own gifts to the Church of Ireland, and a lay committee for a general appeal was formed with the public approval of the two Archbishops.[146] The appeal did not do well. Its first full year, 1872, produced £13,500. By July 1880 only just over £62,000 had been raised.[147]

All this uncertainty and reluctance to give financial help did not go unobserved in Ireland, where it was clear that the Irish Church was getting the cold shoulder.[148] The running commentary by English High Churchmen on the revision debates was also unwelcome in Ireland. The comments were sometimes courteous and sympathetic, as was for instance the advice given by Beresford Hope to leave the Prayer Book alone.[149] Sometimes they were neither, as when the *Church Times* in 1873 referred to "the drunken Helots of the General Irish Synod".* The most unfortunate episode occurred in May 1875, when Archdeacon Lee of Dublin (who had refused to recognize the authority of the General Synod) publicly appealed for help in England to build a new church in Dublin where only the unrevised Prayer Book would be used. Pusey and Liddon, the acknowledged leaders of the High Church movement in England, at once offered contributions. Liddon was particularly agitated about the decision to drop the damnatory clauses of the Athanasian Creed, which was later reversed. He spoke of "the evil spirits of Puritanism and unbelief" at work in the Irish Synod. This intervention led nowhere, but it was naturally deeply resented in the Irish Church, where Pusey and Liddon were not popular at any time.[150]

It was small wonder, then, that Irish Churchmen felt that their Church was either ignored or disparaged in England.[151] Some personal ties survived, notably between some of the Irish bishops and Archbishop Tait, whom they rightly regarded as a true friend of their Church. He even visited Ireland in 1877—the first known visit by an archbishop of Canterbury, according to the address of welcome presented to him at Armagh.[152] But these ties were bound to weaken, when Irish bishops no longer came to London to attend the House of Lords and when they no longer went to the informal bishops' meetings at Lambeth.[153] Primate Beresford and Bishop Plunket attended the Lambeth Conference of 1878, where Plunket appealed for a more understanding attitude towards the Irish Church;[154] but such great meetings were no substitute for small, frequent, and informal ones.

In general it is fair to say that English Churchmen only showed keen interest in the Church of Ireland during the struggle about disestablishment, when they believed their own interests to be at

* A "drunken helot" was one made drunk as a warning to young Spartans, so presumably the *Church Times* meant that the Irish Synod was an awful warning to the English Church. The technical meaning of the phrase probably escaped many in Ireland, where it gave serious offence. Cf. *I.E.G.* (July 1873), p. 422.

stake as well as Irish ones. Afterwards there were fitful flares of interest in the more exciting passages of the revision controversy, and a continuing concern by some few individuals. For the rest, the Irish Church receded into its own unfamiliar Irish world, which there was little incentive for Englishmen to understand—after all, it was a time when they heard more than enough about Ireland in other contexts, most of it displeasing to them. Only later, when it was thought that experience in Ireland might be used to prove something in the debate about Welsh disestablishment, was some interest rekindled—again when there was something at stake besides the Irish Church itself. Irish Churchmen for their part resented criticism from England, and were glad and proud to stand on their own feet, a national Church in one sense though no longer established.

Losses and Gains of Disestablishment

It is not easy to sum up the consequences for the Irish Church of the Act of 1869. George Salmon wrote in 1886 that he was often asked by Liberal correspondents about the experience of the disestablished Church. Whatever his answer, it had been used to justify the Act. If he reported that the Church was thriving, then how fortunate it was to be released from the trammels of the State; if not, what a weak Church it must be, only sustained in the past by its connection with the State.[155] It was a fair point—the evidence can be used to argue both ways. Then there is the question of *post hoc* or *propter hoc*. No one is likely to deny the vigour of the Irish Church after disestablishment. But was this due to the stimulus of the crisis itself, or to a revival of faith and sense of duty earlier in the century?[156] Nobody can know the answer. Disestablishment happened, and how the Irish Church would have developed without it no one can tell. All one can reasonably guess is that, if the blow had fallen on a weak and ailing body, it might well have been fatal—disestablishment of itself could scarcely confer life and energy, though it might well stimulate powers already present. The task, then, of summing up is difficult, but it must be attempted.

Chief among the losses was money. How much the Church lost it is impossible to say, but the loss was important and was not fully redressed by the efforts of the Representative Church Body and the generous giving of Church members. Reduced resources were bound to mean reduced effectiveness; the problems both of Belfast and of the sparsely populated parishes in the south and west would have been more easily dealt with if more money had been available. The financial loss, together with the new methods of making appointments and the loss of prestige through disestablishment, caused the loss of many clergy in the first ten years of disestablishment. The educational standard of some of those who were recruited also fell.

Other disadvantages were less material in kind. It was often said that the form of government of the Irish Church and its prevailing methods tended to suppress individuality and diversity. Archbishop J. A. F. Gregg in 1932 spoke of the undue rigidity of the system of government: "The individual tends to be submerged beneath the committee."[157] Much earlier, in the decade or so after disestablishment, it was more a matter of the undue influence of the prevalent revisionist opinion, especially asserted through parochial nominators, which bore hard upon individual clergymen who did not share that opinion. It was this pressure which caused Gladstone to say in the House of Commons in 1873 that there was less freedom of religious thought in the disestablished Church of Ireland than in the Church of England.[158] It may be that this tendency has been overrated; at any rate in the present century such men as Bernard, D'Arcy, and Gregg himself have not lacked individuality, and yet each reached an archbishopric.

There was also the danger of isolation. This was always present for the Church of Ireland, geographically cut off by the sea and heavily outnumbered by the predominant Roman Catholic community. Disestablishment made the situation worse by dissolving the formal structure of unity with the Church of England, by bringing to an end the informal meetings of Irish and English bishops, and by ending attendance at the House of Lords by certain Irish bishops. It was possible to counteract this to some degree, but it demanded a positive effort on the part of leaders of the Irish Church, such as was made, for example, by Archbishops Bernard and D'Arcy.[159]

Finally, it was argued, by Bernard for example, that disestablishment meant a "loss to the country at large, which is due to the complete abandonment of religious observance in public life". He instanced the abandonment of religious services at institutions to the Order of St Patrick, and argued that, if there were an Irish Parliament, there could be no prayers to open its days as at Westminster. He admitted that the amount of vital religion represented by such observances may not be great, but asserted that their elimination made for secularism.[160] This argument is used sufficiently frequently in favour of retaining an established Church to make it worth quoting among the losses, though its validity is highly dubious. It is hard to claim that over the past century there has been greater secularization of life in Ireland, where there is no established Church, than in England, where there still is one. The sort of argument advanced in all seriousness by Bernard was surely a piece of wishful thinking by one who hankered after an established Church.

It is not wholly clear whether the defects of the system of making appointments in the Church should go on the debit side or not. Such defects existed, but no system is perfect, and there is little doubt that the new Irish methods, with all their faults, were better than those prevailing under the establishment.

To turn to what may be regarded as clear gains it must first be pointed out that there was material gain to set against the undoubted financial loss. The Church's income was lower, but it was more reliable in its sources, better administered, and more equitably distributed. The clergy could rely on reaching £200 fairly early in life, even if not many would go higher.[161]

The gains of self-government far outweighed the disadvantage of the rigidity of the system. The Irish Church provided itself with a government which was generally respected and obeyed, even if everyone did not agree with all its details. Even Bernard accepted this as one of the advantages of disestablishment: "We know what our laws are, and we all alike recognize the authority of the body which makes them."[162] Complicated though the system was, its workings and the distribution of power within it were simple compared with those of the established Church in England. Even rigidity has some advantages. Order and discipline are not necessarily undesirable in a body which often chooses to liken itself to an army. Moreover, self-government and the crisis of disendowment meant giving laymen real responsibilities within the Church. It may be that these were in some ways abused in the early years, but it was generally agreed that the giving of responsibility had tapped an immense source of energy. A lady in County Down wrote to a prominent English Nonconformist in 1874: "Even in our own Parish since the Disestablishment everyone seems stirred to feel that their own individual help & strength avails something in aiding it, whereas before the Church was vaguely supposed to be upheld by some immovable power with which the units of a congregation had nothing in common."[163] She cannot have been alone.

A most important and advantageous result of disestablishment was the removal of the Irish Church from the political firing line. Irish Churchmen, knowing the establishment to be a part of the Protestant ascendancy, and by no means averse to a fight, would surely never have withdrawn voluntarily. From time to time, indeed, they even rashly tried to put their Church back into the front line. The first two special meetings of the General Synod were held in 1886 and 1893, not on some vital Church matter but to protest against the first and second Home Rule Bills.[164] Many clergymen of the Church, including, for example, D'Arcy when he was Bishop of Down, signed the Covenant and actively supported the Ulster Volunteers during the Home Rule crisis before 1914.[165] These were reflex actions, produced by deep and abiding loyalties, prejudices, and interests. As it happened, the Irish Church escaped political attack in spite of such gestures; but they serve to illustrate the risks the Church would have run if it had remained an obvious target for Irish nationalists in the half-century after 1870. As it was, Gladstone effectually took the Church out of politics by the Act of 1869, and thus enabled it to escape with only slight damage from the activities of the Land League and Sinn Fein, and even to survive partition as one of the very few bodies which span the border.*

* Gregg told the Archbishops' Commission on Church and State (*Minutes of Evidence*, vol. III, p. 522) that partition had made no difference to the Church— the General Synod, for instance, continued to meet in Dublin. He himself, interestingly enough, did feel the difference between North and South. When wondering whether to accept the Primacy and move to Armagh in 1938, he wrote in his diary: "Nor did I think that at 65 I should ever be able to find N. Ireland anything but a strange land spiritually and politically" (Seaver, *Gregg*, pp. 217–18).

Finally, and it may be most importantly, disestablishment compelled the Irish Church to accept the reality of its own position. Fifty years after the passing of the Act, the *Church of Ireland Gazette* wrote the epitaph of the establishment—and it was significant that even amidst the troubles of 1919 the writer could recollect the great crisis of his Church in tranquillity.

> The Establishment was an artificial thing, with no real roots in the soil. The conditions which make an Establishment defensible cannot be said to have existed in the case of our Church; and, as democratic ideas became increasingly dominant, the arguments adduced in its defence became decreasingly cogent. The idea underlying a State Church is, not so much that it is the dominant religious community within the frontiers as regards numbers, nor the most ancient religious organisation, nor the most perfect embodiment of Christianity, but rather that it represents and expresses the greatest common measure of the religious life of the people. In Ireland the Church of Ireland cannot be said to have fulfilled this essential condition. It was the Church of a small, though important, minority. In no sense can it be said to have been broad based upon the people's will, nor to have attempted to express the religious experience of the vast majority of the Irish people. It was in direct and active opposition to the religious belief, practice and allegiance of the race whose name it bore . . . the Church of Ireland was not in fact the Church of the Irish people.[166]

Some might say that it had taken an unduly long time for this truth to dawn on the minds of Irish Churchmen. But fifty years in Irish history is a mere moment of time, and once the facts were accepted the Irish Church was able to work out its own vocation untroubled by the pretensions and the frictions of the establishment.

The Church was not even burdened by an historical grievance, which cannot always be said in Ireland. The first sentence of Archbishop J. A. F. Gregg's evidence to the Archbishops' Commission on Church and State in 1932 ran: "Few members of the Church of Ireland today would be found to regret Disestablishment. The losses inflicted by Mr Gladstone's Act have been more than outweighed by the gains which have accrued."[167] This seems an acceptable verdict.

6

THE IRISH CHURCH ACT:
EXPECTATIONS UNFULFILLED

It is almost certainly true that if the Irish Church Act had been expected to produce no other result than the disestablishment and disendowment of the Irish Church, then it would never have been passed, nor would the issue have been the centre of such intense political activity. On the contrary, the measure carried with it hopes and fears of far wider scope than the fate of the Church of Ireland and its property. Gladstone took up the question because he saw it as a vital step in resolving the Irish question. He never saw it as the only step, recognizing the importance of land and education, but he put the Church first. Spencer wished in March 1869 that the government could pass a land bill in that session of Parliament.[1] Gladstone, rightly in view of the complexities of both operations, would not try, and he was clear that they had the order of priority correct—"a compound controversy is like a compound fracture; & the Church is enough for today. Moreover if we are right in our Church policy, the passing of our Bill will of itself soothe the general sentiment of Ireland."[2]

To Gladstone's supporters in Ireland—the Catholic hierarchy, Irish Liberals, the *Freeman's Journal*—the Act was a vital measure of justice to Ireland, removing one of the great obstacles to the proper working of the Union. Justice to Ireland, of course, was not a process which was expected to stop with the Church question. The *Freeman* declared firmly that the land question would come next;[3] and for the hierarchy the issue of denominational education remained to be settled as they wanted it. None the less, the Irish Church Act was both a great stroke in itself and an augury of great things for the future. It remained to be seen whether these expectations of further English concessions aroused by the Act either would or could be fulfilled. If they were not, the Act would surely have failed in its most important purposes.

Much less important, but still an expected consequence of the

Act in Ireland, was the distribution of a large capital sum for the benefit of the Irish poor and the various institutions in which the sick and lunatic poor were cared for. This was a matter over which Gladstone himself had taken a good deal of trouble, and on which he had aroused by his speeches considerable expectations.

In England, for the Liberation Society and militant Dissent in general, the Irish Church issue had been not so much important in itself as a step towards general disestablishment, and equally it had been largely for this reason that the Conservative party and English Churchmen had flung themselves so vigorously into the defence of the Irish establishment. Another expected consequence of the Irish Church Act, therefore, whether this were a matter for hope or fear, was a further strong movement towards disestablishment in Britain.

None of these expectations connected with the Irish Church Act was fulfilled. The point hardly needs to be laboured that it did not resolve the Irish question, or even bring about a significant improvement in the situation. It may be worth emphasizing, however, how rapidly Gladstone met serious difficulties in Ireland which the Church Act did not assuage. It is true, of course, that the measure was widely welcomed in Ireland, and that Spencer was at first optimistic about the state of opinion. The O'Donoghue told Spencer in August 1869 that the Act had "won many discontented Irishmen to England", and enabled Irish Liberals to appeal with confidence to constitutional rather than to violent ways of redressing grievances. Spencer agreed, and thought he saw "a change of disposition towards Government in this part of the World".[4] But the welcome was not universal, and not everyone was persuaded that mere constitutional pressure produced the Irish Church Act. "The fenian plough has upset the establishment", wrote the *Irishman*,[5] a nationalist newspaper, with much justification. Moreover, Fenianism was still very much alive, in the explosive issue of the Fenian prisoners.

In the last stages of the election campaign of 1868 there was already on foot a movement asking for an amnesty for the eighty-one Fenians in prison. When in February 1869 forty-nine were released, leaving the remainder (including the principal leaders) imprisoned, this was for the British government a generous gesture, but for Irish nationalist opinion it was quite inadequate. The prisoners who were released were greeted as national heroes, and a great amnesty campaign was launched on behalf of the remainder, culminating in the election of one of the imprisoned Fenians, O'Donovan Rossa, at a by-election in Tipperary in November 1869.[6] To the *Irishman*, Gladstone's refusal to give an amnesty to all the prisoners proved him to be a cheat.

> How could it have been otherwise? He was, and is, a Minister of England whose business it is to rule Ireland for the benefit of the empire. He is the inheritor of a traditional policy of misrule, the high priest by succession of the Temple of Terror, at whose altar, life and liberty, and land, have been the bloody sacrifices for centuries.

Gladstone himself had said that Ireland was in a state which justified revolt, and yet those who had attempted a revolt were kept in prison. An amnesty was asked "of him who had written and spoken their justification, who had acknowledged his indebtedness to them as the authors of the act of legislation on which he builds his chance of fame". Yet the appeal had been rejected, because it was peacefully presented. Force was the key when dealing with the British government.*

So, while the Irish Church Bill was still going through Parliament, a widespread popular movement arose in Ireland on the question of the Fenian prisoners, and only four months after the passing of the Act a Fenian actually in prison won Tipperary against a Catholic Liberal who supported land legislation, denominational education, and an amnesty.[7] Even before this by-election, on 3 November, Spencer wrote: "I confess that I am staggered by the amnesty meetings, & with men like Moore and Butt inviting the people to arms it is a matter of surprise that they are as quiet as they are." He was disturbed by the nationalist newspapers—"The abominable press is one of the Plague Spots of the country"—and by terrorism in the countryside.[8] Fortescue

---

* *Irishman*, 23 October 1869. A copy was sent to Gladstone—Bruce to Gladstone, 25 October 1869, Gladstone Papers, 44086, f. 50. Compare this with a letter from Lord Sligo to Spencer, 27 October 1869. Sligo supported disestablishment, but thought there was "a belief, all but universal except in the highest class, that it was passed in terror of Irish agitation and for the sake of Parliamentary support. Hence arises a popular conviction that by violence, by murder, by intimidation, by keeping the people on the verge of rebellion, the so-called popular will *simpliciter* will be forced on the Govt" (Spencer Papers, Misc., 1869).

too, in October, was disturbed by the amnesty demonstrations, and by continuing agrarian crime, and suggested to Gladstone the suspension of habeas corpus to deal with agrarian murders.[9]

There was nothing particularly remarkable in all this. It was the common state of Ireland for much of the nineteenth century. But it was an unhappy state of affairs so soon after a great new departure in Irish policy, a measure which was to remove the *fons et origo malorum*, or at least to soothe the general sentiment of Ireland. Gladstone himself remained optimistic. He wrote to Spencer on 4 December 1869:

> I own that at present I do not understand the great excitement about the state of Ireland, or rather do not sympathize with it. If the Fenians mean an outbreak, then indeed I have something to say. But if they only mean to insult law & authority without disturbing order, that, however scandalous and however inconvenient as a fact, is not in my eyes bad as a symptom. They fear lest they should some day soon find their occupation gone.[10]

This was precisely the same hope as before: that the Irish Church Act, with a Land Bill to come, would cut the ground from under Irish agitation and deprive it of its force. Others took a different view of the results of the Irish Church Act. Lord Monck, one of the Irish Commissioners and a supporter of disestablishment, wrote to Spencer on 3 September 1869 that there might have to be strong measures against agrarian crime. "Happily we can now declare war on the disturbers of the public peace with hands more free, and our consciences more clear, than was possible formerly."[11] This was just what *The Times* and the *Saturday Review* had said, at least occasionally, before the Act was passed.

Thus the storm signals were flying in Ireland even before the end of the year in which the Irish Church Act was passed. By March 1870, Spencer was convinced of the necessity for special legislation to deal with agrarian crime, which was increasing by leaps and bounds.[12] All this was before the failure of the Land Act of 1870, declared unsatisfactory even by moderate Irish opinion before it reached the statute book, and proved to be largely unworkable after it had done so. It was before Isaac Butt's Home Rule movement got under way in 1870. It was long before Gladstone's Irish Universities Bill of 1873 was first denounced by the Irish hierarchy and then in consequence defeated in the House of Commons. The Irish Church Act was itself only a limited success in political terms, and it was the prelude to a run of total failure in Ireland, culminating in the general election of 1874, when "home rule destroyed liberal unionism as a political force in Ireland".[13]

In the collapse of Gladstone's Irish policy, the opponents of the Irish Church Act found some vindication for their attitudes during the controversy. The *Quarterly Review* had rightly assessed the far-reaching aspirations of Irish nationalism. The alliance between Liberalism and the Catholic Church proved indeed to be unnatural and short-lived. The rights of property in Ireland, as predicted, came under further attack, though the rights of landlords were treated much more gently in 1870 than those of the Church in 1869. It even happened that some Protestant Conservatives, as they had threatened, turned against the Union, and supported Butt's Home Government Association in 1870, as did, for instance, Major Knox and his newspaper, the *Irish Times*. The strange alliance did not last, but it was for a time a remarkable feature of the Irish political scene.[14] On all these points Gladstone's opponents were able to claim the fulfilment of their prophecies. It by no means followed that the Irish Church Act was a piece of mistaken legislation, or that it brought no benefit either to Ireland or to the Church. But it was true that the Act's effects were severely limited, and that even in the political sense the greatest beneficiary was probably the Church itself.

It was the intention of the Act that the material beneficiaries of the disendowment of the Irish Church should be the Irish poor. Introducing the Bill, Gladstone had held out the prospect of a lump sum of £7m. or £8m. which would become available ten years after the date of disestablishment. This estimate, generally accepted at the time, proved to be ill-founded. Firstly, the amount to be paid in compensation was more than the £8m. or £9m. which Gladstone at first thought. The total paid in compensation for Church of Ireland interests up to 1923 was over £10,200,000.[15] There were in addition other big compensation payments: £622,741 for commutation of *Regium Donum* annuities; £778,880 in compensation for lay patrons; £372,331 to Maynooth College.[16] Secondly, the assumption that the annual income from the secularized property could be capitalized was not fulfilled. The offer

of redemption of tithe rent-charge at twenty-two and a half years'
purchase was not attractive enough for landowners to take it up.
The Church Temporalities Commissioners were left, not with a
large capital sum available for distribution in the near future, but
with an annual income from tithe rent-charge and rents, out of
which their first tasks were to service and repay the loan raised to
make the commutation payments to the Representative Church
Body, to pay such annuities as had not been commuted, and to
defray their own administrative costs.

In these circumstances, the expectations aroused by the passing
of the Act were bound to be disappointed. As early as July 1869,
the house surgeon at the North Charitable Infirmary, Cork, wrote
to Gladstone to ask what his hospital might receive from Church
funds.[17] In December 1870, Maguire, M.P. for Cork, wanted
Fortescue to provide a letter which could be read to hospital
boards on the matter of the Church funds. After consulting the
Commissioners, Fortescue replied that there was no prospect at
that time of applying the surplus to that purpose; the repayment
of loans would take up the resources for some time to come.[18]

In the event, neither the North Charitable Infirmary, Cork, nor
the other beneficiaries specifically envisaged by Gladstone and so
carefully analysed by Lambert, received any of the secularized
funds of the Irish Church. Though the intention to use the funds
for the relief of unavoidable calamity and suffering was expressed
in the Act, it was also provided that they should be applied as
Parliament should direct. In fact this meant that they were used,
as Asquith said in 1894, as an "emergency reservoir", drawn upon
by successive Chancellors of the Exchequer for various Irish
purposes.[19] These purposes, and the sums spent up to March 1923
were as follows:[20]

Intermediate Education (Ireland) Act, 1878	£1,962,029
National School Teachers (Ireland) Act, 1879	£1,664,598
Royal University (Ireland) Act, 1881	£560,000
Irish Universities Act, 1908	£265,000
Relief of Distress (Ireland) Acts, 1880 and 1881	£3,671,839
Arrears of Rent (Ireland) Act, 1882	£2,494,513
Relief of Distressed Unions (Ireland) Act, 1883, and Poor Relief (Ireland) Act, 1886	£66,547
Sea Fisheries (Ireland) Act, 1883	£548,124

Poor Relief (Ireland) Act, 1886—Piers and Roads Commission	£43,850
Seed Potatoes Supply Act, 1890	£17,564
Purchase of Land (Ireland) Act, 1891	£950,226
Seed Potatoes Supply Act, 1895	£3,738
Seed Potatoes Supply Act, 1898	£4,770
Agricultural and Technical Instruction (Ireland) Act, 1899	£4,780,940
Irish Land Act, 1903	£345,114

Gladstone himself wrote in 1892: "The Church surplus has been used for all sorts of Irish purposes, especially by the Tories. I do not know whether that old hack will carry any more."[21] It was a sorry descent from the high hopes and hard work of 1869. Gladstone had not intended to disendow the Irish Church in order to provide a hack for Chancellors of the Exchequer and Irish Chief Secretaries. (Indeed, but for the Lords' amendment on the disposal of the surplus, this would probably not have come about.) A bad joke went the rounds at the passing of the Irish Church Act, that Gladstone was robbing the clergy to give to lunatics. He did not rob the clergy—at any rate, certainly not those of 1869—but, sad to say, the lunatics gained nothing either.

The *Saturday Review*, which advocated disestablishment in Ireland and had little sympathy with those who prophesied calamity as a result of it, yet wrote on 27 March 1869 that the event "cannot fail to affect the English Church. The minds of men have been turned in the direction of leaving all religious bodies to themselves". This was a view widely held—that disestablishment in Ireland would bring on disestablishment in England, towards which events seemed to be moving in any case. The fear of disestablishment certainly continued within the Church of England —almost inevitably, because the alarms of the 1860s were unlikely to die away at once. Indeed, crises for the Church recurred frequently, and with them the spectre of disestablishment.

The year of the Irish Church Act was not yet out before the appointment of Frederick Temple to the see of Exeter raised a storm, which was perhaps the greater because his contribution to *Essays and Reviews* had been followed recently by support for Gladstone's Irish Church policy. The *Record* fulminated virtually without pause for most of October and half November.[22] Pusey again wanted to choose freedom: "For us, who believe, there is nothing left but to pray and strive that the Church should be delivered from this tyranny of the State at any cost. . . . Disestablishment appears to me now our only remedy."[23] The *Guardian* was generally favourable to Temple himself, and thought that disestablishment in England, brought about by the Church and preceded by bitter divisions, would be far more calamitous than in Ireland; but still it believed that it was not an impractical aim.[24]

Temple's appointment caused five clergy of the deanery of Tamerton to petition Gladstone to bring before Parliament the unfairness of the system of appointing bishops, in which neither clergy nor laity were consulted, and asking for more effective representation of the Church in the process of appointment. It was at once apparent that ministers thought that what was right and beneficial for the Irish Church would not do at all in England. Lord Halifax wrote that "This wd. be the beginning of the end". Fortescue commented heavily that the existing system secured the representation of enlightened and reasonable opinion better than any other that could be foreseen. Clarendon thought that there could be no worse service to the Church than to comply with the request, and Kimberley agreed. Hatherley noted that it would mean disestablishment, and did not think that the memorialists represented the clergy.[25] He was doubtless right, and it was not an important episode; but it deserves to be remembered that even a few English clergymen could raise the question of the Church being granted a voice in the appointment of its own bishops, and that high-minded Liberal cabinet ministers recoiled in horror from the prospect.

After Temple's appointment came the Purchas case, and the judgement of the Judicial Committee of the Privy Council against certain vestments, the eastward position, wafers, and the mixed chalice. This time Gladstone himself commented that: "in its practical effect the recent judgement may advance us another step in a course too likely to end not only in disestablishment but in schism"—though his own view was that there was no doctrinal issue involved, and that limitation to a surplice was a hardship which clergymen could well bear with.[26] The *Daily News* thought that the Church was moving towards anarchy, and wondered how long the establishment could be maintained in such conditions.[27]

To Bishop Magee, on the other hand, the Purchas judgement had saved the establishment for another two or three years.[28]

Magee was one who speculated repeatedly on how long the establishment in England would last. In 1870 he thought ten years, in 1871 he thought five or ten. He also argued that the Church of England was so comprehensive a body that it would not hold together as the Church of Ireland had done. "You are homogeneous enough to make a good compact sect", he wrote to MacDonnell in 1870.[29] Another bishop who was perennially anxious about disestablishment was Ellicott at Gloucester. In 1871 he held that the cathedrals must be reformed, or else "it will be the Irish Church over again";[30] in 1872 the question of the Athanasian Creed must be settled at once, or it would be exploited by those who sought disestablishment.[31]

The Public Worship Regulation Act of 1874 caused a further flurry of talk about disestablishment. Archbishop Tait, pressing Disraeli to get the Bill through in that session, told him that both violent Dissenters and Romanizing High Churchmen wished to keep up the agitation. "The result may be perilous politically & cause the disestablishment of the Church."[32] Lord Salisbury, on the other hand, thought that one of Tait's drafts for a Bill was dangerous for precisely the opposite reason: that it proposed to give bishops too much power, which if used throughout a diocese against one Church party would lead to disestablishment, as men found that the establishment was an oppression rather than a privilege.[33] He thought that there was real danger from the High Church party: "It is earnest, to fanaticism: it sits loosely to the Establishment as matters stand: & if driven by any act of serious aggression will listen to its most reckless advisers, & throw itself on the Free Church side."[34]

These were the opinions of individuals, but they were well-informed and responsible individuals. Thomson, the Archbishop of York, thought the uneasiness was widespread. "I am persuaded", he wrote to Tait on 5 August 1875, "that the great mass of this people, if they cannot get rid of ritualism in other ways, will gladly vote for disestablishment in order to wash their hands clean from this whole question. . . . There is a crumbling of the edifice around us, and all our efforts at reform will not touch it, I fear."[35] It may be that there were too many cries of wolf. The *Liberator* once told a story: "'Friend,' said a Quaker to an episcopalian alarmist, 'I had rather not belong to a Church which is so often in danger as thine is.'"[36] It was a story which made its point. Yet, as the *Globe* adjured its readers to remember on 8 December 1869, even twenty false alarms of the Church in danger did not preclude the possibility of a real crisis. It seems that many prominent Churchmen believed that the establishment was passing through a real crisis in the early 1870s, a crisis made worse by events in Ireland.

Those dedicated enemies of the establishment, the leaders of the Liberation Society, took a more sober view of the prospects after the victory in Ireland. The *Liberator* welcomed it as a decisive victory, a mortal blow to all establishments, after which the separation of Church and State all over the kingdom had become a practical possibility. But it recognized that the strength which had proved sufficient to destroy the Irish establishment would not suffice for the remaining tasks. It would not even be available. The Liberation Society had for two years been one wing of an army, aiming at one objective but with different motives. With that objective achieved, the Society would again be left alone, and its allies would even turn against it. In Parliament, the time of future sessions was already pledged, and there would be no room for disestablishment measures. In the country, it was doubtful whether public opinion was prepared for disestablishment. The next step must therefore be to resume the work of propaganda, with the advantage that the public mind had moved in the last twenty-five years and that further results would not be too long delayed.[37]

This shrewd and balanced view of the situation reflected that taken by the Parliamentary Committee of the Liberation Society. This was that the attainment of Irish disestablishment gave an opportunity for "a new movement of a distinctly aggressive character", and thought that the state of public opinion would facilitate this. But they dwelt at length on the difficulties. The issue of disestablishment roused insufficient interest in Scotland as yet. In Wales, popular feeling would favour a movement which might soon be successful, if the Welsh question could in practice be separately dealt with; but the Committee thought it could not, and was opposed to any attempt to press the question at once, as Watkin Williams was proposing to do by a motion in the Commons. This left as the best course to aim at the disestablishment of the whole Church of England, not as a matter for immediate parliamentary action, but by a period of propaganda, combined with support for legislation on specific issues such as university tests or burial grounds.[38]

The pessimistic parts of this analysis were quickly borne out by events. Watkin Williams, in spite of much advice to the contrary, brought forward his motion for Welsh disestablishment in April 1870. It was defeated by 211 votes to forty-seven; Gladstone spoke strongly against it, asserting the identity of the Church in Wales with that in England; and even the Welsh Liberals were divided, seven voting for the motion and eight against.[39] It may be that on this question the very attitude of the Liberation Society produced the defeat it predicted. The Society provided the political organization and much of the impetus of Liberalism in Wales,[40] and its opposition to Watkin Williams's motion was enough in itself to ensure division amongst Welsh M.P.s. But there were other more general conditions which made the attempt premature. There was as yet no acknowledgement that Wales could or should be treated separately from England for purposes of legislation. Secret voting by ballot had not yet been introduced, and evictions (such as those which took place in some areas after the election of 1868) were still a weapon of which Welsh Liberals were afraid. Despite the work of the Liberation Society, Welsh Liberal M.P.s were not yet sufficiently self-conscious, organized, and united to form an effective pressure group. Not until these conditions changed was it possible to make Welsh disestablishment a matter of practical politics.

The predicted dissolution of the grand alliance of 1868–9 also occurred within two years. The breach between the Liberation Society (indeed militant Nonconformity in general) and Gladstone and his government came in 1870 over the Education Act, which was felt to be much too favourable to church schools. The old Nonconformist leader, Miall, and a new one, Joseph Chamberlain, led the National Education League in a campaign of resistance in the provinces, especially Birmingham. Gladstone and Miall met in open conflict in the House of Commons. It is true that the education controversy stimulated demand for disestablishment among militant Dissenters, but it was more important that it divided the Liberal party and contributed to its defeat in 1874.[41]

The breach between militant Dissent and the Liberal party was also obvious in May 1871, when Miall proposed a motion for the disestablishment of the Church of England. Gladstone intervened early in the debate, arguing that there was no parallel between the positions in England and Ireland, and opposing the motion. Moreover, on this occasion an appeal by the Liberation Society to the National Association for support went unanswered, marking the end of the alliance between the Irish Catholics and the Liberation Society.[42] This breach too was further confirmed in 1873, when Nonconformists supported Gladstone's Irish Universities Bill, which was opposed by the Irish hierarchy. The army which won the campaign for Irish disestablishment in 1868–9 was scattered, and in the general election of 1874 the Liberal party, which had provided the central corps of that army, was heavily defeated.

The leaders of the Liberation Society, who had predicted these divisions, remained confident of success in the long run. They could take encouragement from the activities of John Morley and Joseph Chamberlain, coming men on the radical wing of the Liberal party, who in 1874–6 took up disestablishment and placed it with the extension of the county franchise as the prominent points in a new radical agitation.[43] The Bulgarian agitation of 1877–8, in which Nonconformity was very prominent, gave further encouragement, Miall seeing its success in the country as the pattern for a later campaign on disestablishment.[44] Support for disestablishment grew in Scotland during the 1870s. There was thus good reason for Miall's confidence in planning, in 1874, a five-year policy to prepare for the introduction of a scheme for disestablishment and disendowment.[45] The disestablishment movement had indeed yet to reach its peak in terms of success at elections and strength in the House of Commons—a peak which came in 1885. In the longer term still, however, it became clear that the movement was losing its vitality. It failed to establish contact with the working classes in the great towns,[46] as was seen by Chamberlain in 1874. He then predicted the consequences unless this could be changed: "Such questions as Disestablishment and Disendowment will be indefinitely postponed, as the Artisan voter ... looking at the whole affair as a squabble between Church and Chapel, will take no interest in the matter."[47] In

England, this proved increasingly true from the 1880s onwards. In Wales, matters were different, because there the "squabble between Church and Chapel" was more than a squabble, embodying and symbolizing deep social and political conflicts. In Wales, therefore, though not elsewhere, the impetus of the campaign for disestablishment was maintained, and in the 1880s conditions became steadily more favourable for its success.

Thus, in the irony of history, little actually materialized of all the aspirations and fears involved in the Irish Church Act of 1869. A badge of conquest was removed from Ireland; but the Irish question was far from settled. The Irish poor received some benefits, but not in the ways foreseen. Disestablishment elsewhere in the United Kingdom did not follow, except much later in Wales. The only substantial consequence of the Irish Church Act was indeed the disestablishment and disendowment of the Irish Church, about which alone no great political battle would have been fought.

7

WELSH DISESTABLISHMENT
THE BILLS

The Welsh Church Question to 1892

Disestablishment in Ireland gave an impulse to a movement for disestablishment in Wales, but brought it nowhere near to achieving success. The conditions in which such a success was possible came about in the dozen years between 1880 and 1892. One necessary preliminary, if the question of the established Church in Wales were to be detached from the same question in England, was the acknowledgement by Parliament that Wales could be treated as a separate unit for purposes of legislation. This came with the passage in 1881 (under a Liberal government) of the Welsh Sunday Closing Act, and in 1889 (under a Conservative government) of the Welsh Intermediate Education Act. The issue of a government grant for the Welsh University Colleges raised similar questions, though not in the form of legislation, and here again a Liberal government gave a grant in 1883, which was increased by a Conservative government in 1885. Thus both parties, at any rate on some issues, accepted the principle of separate legislative and administrative action for Wales.[1]

In the same period there also came about the almost total domination of the parliamentary representation of Wales by Liberal members demanding disestablishment. In 1880 the Liberals won twenty-nine seats out of thirty-three in Wales (including Monmouthshire). In 1885, on the new and wider franchise of the Reform Act of 1884, they won thirty out of thirty-four, and in 1886, when the Liberal party was divided and England swung decisively against the Gladstonian Liberals, the latter still won twenty-five Welsh seats out of thirty-four. In 1892 their victories rose to thirty-one out of thirty-four, many of them by what were in those days very large majorities. Disestablishment always figured prominently in Liberal election addresses and campaigns,

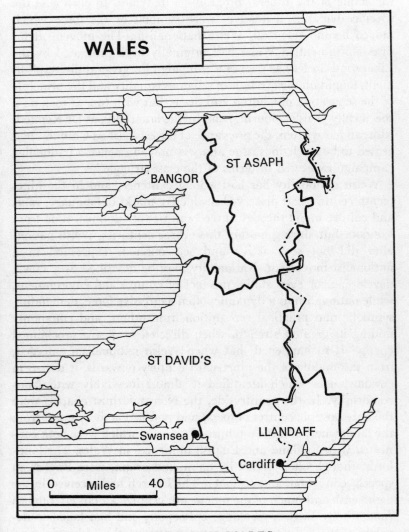

CHURCH IN WALES

Diocesan Divisions at the date of Disestablishment

and along with proposals for land tenure and education formed the staple of the Liberal programme in Wales. In each case the specific demands themselves were symbols of the force which moved behind them all, Welsh nationalism. The movement for disestablishment in Wales had originally been promoted by the Liberation Society as part of a campaign for general disestablishment, fought on the grounds of religious equality and the principle of the separation of Church and State. But with time it took on a specifically Welsh colouring, and by the late 1880s, as Dr Kenneth Morgan has written, the grievance of the established Church "had ceased to be a religious issue and was now in essence a nationalist campaign expressed in terms of the class struggle".[2]

Welsh nationality has had a long existence, and in the nineteenth century had preserved distinctive marks of language, race, and culture intact through three centuries of administration from London. But, during most of these three centuries, Welsh nationality did not seek active and self-conscious expression in a nationalist movement. Nationality may be described as a slowly developing, or even static, product of culture and environment, while nationalism is a dynamic, often aggressive force, demanding symbolic and practical recognition from others, and commonly finding its greatest strength when directed against a proclaimed enemy. It so happened that when Welsh nationalism emerged, from the middle of the nineteenth century onwards, it did so in circumstances which identified it almost inevitably with Nonconformity. In the countryside, the Nonconformist chapels were the only possible centres of social and political activity apart from the landowners and the established Church, which were both connected with England and English influences in Wales. The landlords, though often Welsh by name and origin, were English in speech, education, and outlook.[3] The Church had received in the eighteenth and much of the nineteenth centuries a largely English (and wholly English-speaking) episcopate, and had failed to develop a Welsh-language religious press. In the industrial and mining towns of South Wales, the new form of Welsh society was predominantly Nonconformist,[4] and no other significant organized influence made itself felt. These conditions prevailed during the formative period of the Welsh nationalist movement in the nineteenth century, between 1847 (the publication of the report of the

Education Commissioners) and the 1880s. So Welsh nationalism and Welsh Nonconformity came to be identified with one another, and the natural enemies of both were the landlords and the established Church. Enemies are of prime importance to any nationalist movement, and once an enemy has been defined and given a prominent place in the propaganda and ritual of nationalism, it is very hard for the impression so created to be changed. Even though, as will appear later, the position of the established Church was changing even as the attack on it developed, the new facts took a long time to efface the old impressions.

The demand for disestablishment in Wales was thus one of the symbolic claims of Welsh nationalism, put at Westminster by the solid phalanx of Liberal M.P.s from Wales. By 1886 the movement had emerged from its old political framework, which had been provided by the Liberation Society. In that year, two Liberal Federations, for North and South Wales respectively, were created, so that Welsh Liberalism at last provided its own political organization. At the same time the older demand of the Liberation Society for general disestablishment was pushed aside by the rising force of Welsh nationalism. The majority of Welsh Liberal M.P.s, led incongruously but with tact and skill by an Englishman and an Anglican, Stuart Rendel, were being shaped into a Welsh pressure group within the party. Rendel chose to put Welsh disestablishment as the first of the demands of this group, as "a clear and effective issue with all anglicising influences in Wales, and a practical declaration of the case for Welsh Nationalization outside Wales".[5]

It still remained, however, for this pressure group to persuade the whole party, and especially its leader, Gladstone, to take up the cause. Here the situation was closely akin to that in Ireland in the early 1860s. No amount of agitation, however powerful and successful, in the individual country concerned could produce legislation on the Welsh Church question. Only the Liberal party —indeed, only a Liberal government—could do this. The years 1884–5 seemed to show that the Liberal party was on the point of taking up either general, or at least Welsh, disestablishment. Joseph Chamberlain, then by far the most popular radical politician in the country, included general disestablishment in his "unauthorized programme". Gladstone, little though he approved either of Chamberlain himself or of Chamberlain's tactics, was moving towards some acceptance of disestablishment. He said in his election address of 1885 that disestablishment in England was far off, and the question was not ripe; but if ever the people decided that it should come, it would have to be done. Salisbury at once pointed out that the last time Gladstone had said that a question of disestablishment was unripe, the Irish Church Act had been on the statute book in two and a half years.[6] Disestablishment was a prominent issue in the general election of 1885, which was probably the high water mark for the movement for general disestablishment.[7] In March 1886 a new motion for Welsh disestablishment (the first since 1870) was introduced by the veteran Liberationist, Dillwyn, who had moved a similar motion on the Irish Church in 1856. It was defeated by a majority of only twelve votes—241 to 229, a massive change from the forty-five votes for Welsh disestablishment in 1870.[8]

At this point in time the Liberal party split over Gladstone's attempt to give Home Rule to Ireland. Among the Liberal Unionists who broke away from the Gladstonians were most of the aristocratic Whigs, and also Chamberlain and his radical followers. This had a number of effects, which worked themselves out in subsequent years. Firstly, Wales remained substantially Gladstonian, and in a weaker Liberal party, with its base in England gravely narrowed, the Welsh group could exert pressure more effectively than before. In October 1887, Welsh disestablishment was formally placed on the programme of the Liberal party at a meeting of the National Liberal Federation. Motions on the subject in the House of Commons in May 1889 and February 1891 had the support of the party, and on the second occasion Gladstone spoke in favour of the motion. Finally, the Liberal programme which Gladstone announced at Newcastle in October 1891 placed Welsh disestablishment second after Irish Home Rule in its list of objectives.[9] In the circumstances, after the general election of 1892, when Gladstone's last Liberal government had, with the support of the Irish Nationalists, a majority of only forty over the Conservatives and Liberal Unionists, the position of the thirty-one Welsh Liberals was stronger than ever. As Gladstone said to Archbishop Benson, in a fit of unaccustomed straightforwardness of speech, "The Welsh vote *is* a heavy vote, and they are right to try what they can do with it."[10] This pressure was felt, for example, in the introduction of a Welsh Church Suspensory Bill (that is, a Bill to prevent the creation of any new vested interests in the Welsh dioceses by the exercise of public patronage—the Crown, for example, would go on making appointments, but they would carry no right of compensation under a future disestablishment Bill). In an early sketch of measures for the 1892–3 session, a Suspensory Bill appeared only as the first in a list of Private Members' Bills to be supported by the government.[11] But pressure from Rendel, and from T. E. Ellis, the Welsh M.P. who had become a deputy Liberal Whip, ensured that time was found for a government Bill, and that it was introduced before the government wanted it.[12] The Suspensory Bill proved wholly abortive, not even going to a second reading because the Irish Home Rule Bill took up so much parliamentary time, and Welsh pressure was again exerted on the government to give a disestablishment Bill priority in 1894.[13]

Secondly, among the effects of the Liberal split was the restoration, in effect if not in set terms, of the alliance which had carried Irish disestablishment. The Gladstonian Liberals were committed to Irish Home Rule, and the Irish Nationalists were bound in their turn to support Welsh disestablishment, in which they had earlier shown little interest. British Nonconformity, Irish nationalism, and Gladstonian Liberalism were again in harness together. The partners were no longer what they had been in the 1860s; Nonconformity was less solid and less powerful, and Gladstonian Liberalism was in decline rather than in the ascendant. However, it was still a strong alliance, and its restoration did something to make up for the damage which the split over Home Rule brought to the cause of Welsh disestablishment.

For next among the effects of the division over Home Rule must be noted the abandonment of disestablishment by the Liberal Unionists. It took Chamberlain a long time to change his public position on the issue. As late as 1892 Salisbury was complaining about his "ostentatious disestablishment proclamations". But in fact by then Chamberlain had ceased to care. He told Balfour: "I am ready to go on voting for disestablishment as long as such a vote is inoperative and to stay away so soon as it becomes dangerous."[14] This was the withdrawal of a formidable political force from the campaign for disestablishment. Other Liberal Unionists, such as the Duke of Argyll and Goschen, found themselves opposing Welsh disestablishment after helping to carry through the Irish Church Act. They defended their change of position by arguing that the integrity of the United Kingdom had become the prime issue in politics, an argument which was the antithesis of the Gladstonian Liberal position—that the national status and demands of both Ireland and Wales should be conceded.

It followed from the defection of the Liberal Unionists from Gladstone and his party, and from the trend of opinion in England against Irish Home Rule, that the position of the Gladstonian Liberal party was much weakened. The Welsh group carried more weight within the party, but the party itself found it difficult to achieve political power. During the period from 1886 to 1914 the Liberals held office only from 1892 to 1895 and from the end of 1905 to 1914. Moreover, during this period the Conservatives used their majority in the House of Lords with unprecedented ruthlessness, at least partly as a result of the embitterment of political life by the Irish issue. Liberal legislation was regularly rejected or amended out of recognition, so that Liberal governments found themselves in office but without effective means of legislating until the Parliament Act of 1911 restricted the powers of the House of Lords. These weaknesses in the position of the Liberal party had serious effects on the issue of Welsh disestablishment, making it a long-drawn-out process, involving four separate Bills between 1894 and 1914, instead of the short, sharp, decisive campaign of 1868–9 which dealt so effectively with the Irish establishment.

The Liberal split of 1886 thus had important effects, which in the short term strengthened the position of the Welsh Liberals and the campaign for Welsh disestablishment, but in the long run made their task extremely difficult. However, the immediate situation in 1892, when Gladstone formed his last government, was that over the previous twelve years the conditions in which Welsh disestablishment could become a serious political issue with a chance of success in the House of Commons had been fulfilled. The case for separate legislation for Wales had been conceded by both parties—though the Conservatives were to deny the relevance of the precedents to the particular question of the Church. There had emerged a distinct and persistent demand for disestablishment in Wales, expressed through Welsh Liberal M.P.s holding a great, and sometimes overwhelming, majority of Welsh seats, and in a position to put powerful pressure on the Liberal leaders. The Liberal party itself had adopted Welsh disestablishment as part of its programme, and Gladstone had spoken in favour of it. A serious offensive in Parliament against the established Church in Wales could be begun. It is time to turn to the object of this offensive, and to examine the position of the Welsh Church.

In 1906 the Liberal government under Campbell-Bannerman appointed a Royal Commission to investigate the position of the established Church and other religious bodies in Wales. The proceedings of this Commission were the subject of much controversy, but its report remains the most convenient and authoritative basis for a summary of the organization and property of the established Church in Wales.[15]

The geographical organization of the established Church in Wales contained a complication which had not been present in the case of the Irish Church. The boundary between Wales (including Monmouthshire*) and England did not coincide with diocesan boundaries, or even on occasion with parish boundaries. Twenty parishes were situated partly in England, fourteen of them belonging to English dioceses. Ten others, though situated wholly in Wales, also belonged to English dioceses.[16]

There were in all 1,014 parishes lying wholly or in part within Wales, distributed between dioceses as follows:

THE FOUR WELSH DIOCESES

Bangor	142 parishes
Llandaff	256 parishes
St Asaph	191 parishes
St David's	401 parishes

THE ENGLISH DIOCESES INVOLVED

Chester	3 parishes
Hereford	20 parishes
Lichfield	1 parish[17]

Thus, the four Welsh dioceses contained 990 parishes. The dioceses of Bangor and St David's lay wholly within Wales, but St Asaph

* Henceforth, Wales will be taken to include Monmouthshire.

16

had eighteen parishes, and Llandaff two parishes, wholly or partly in England.[18] The problem of which area was to be dealt with in legislation about the Church in Wales was minor but irritating. It also raised problems in discussing the property of the Church in Wales, so that minor differences occurred according to the particular area which was being examined at a given time.

Turning to property, the Commission found that there were 1,527 churches (not counting the four cathedrals) in the four Welsh dioceses, distributed thus:

Bangor	254
Llandaff	451
St Asaph	227
St David's	595

There were also nineteen churches within Wales which belonged to English dioceses.[19] In the four Welsh dioceses there were 811 parsonage houses.[20] More important when the question of the disendowment of the Church in Wales was under discussion was glebe land, the total area of which in Wales was 39,017 acres. This was distributed as follows:

THE FOUR WELSH DIOCESES

Bangor	4,283 acres
Llandaff	7,776 acres
St Asaph	3,985 acres
St David's	22,313 acres
	38,357 acres

THE ENGLISH DIOCESES INVOLVED

Chester	28 acres
Hereford	564 acres
Lichfield	64 acres
	656 acres

The total rental of glebe land in Wales was returned as £43,459 per annum.[21]

Other forms of property and revenue owned and received consisted principally of tithe rent-charge and income received from Queen Anne's Bounty and the Ecclesiastical Commissioners. The total position was summarized thus:[22]

| | QUEEN ANNE'S BOUNTY | | | |
ENDOW-MENTS BEFORE 1703	ROYAL BOUNTY FUND	PARLT GRANTS FUND	ECCLESIASTICAL COMMISSIONERS	PRIVATE ENDOW-MENTS SINCE 1703
Rents of land and houses				
£19,861	£17,705	£1,929	£791	£3,173
Tithe rent-charge				
£157,573	£1,490	£424	£24,837	£5,627
Other sources				
£7,567 +£452	£12,431	£3,970	£8,605 +£23,228 These include payments from general funds of Commissioners	£12,639

The sums received from Queen Anne's Bounty and the Ecclesiastical Commissioners raised questions on the issue of disendowment which had not occurred in Ireland. The Welsh dioceses had long been treated for administrative purposes on exactly the same footing as other dioceses in the Church of England. Payments were made to the funds of the central bodies, and other payments received from them. For example, all the property once attached to the Welsh sees and cathedral churches (except the cathedrals themselves, and certain residences) was managed by the Ecclesiastical Commissioners, who received from them for their Common Fund a net income in 1906 of £33,759. The Ecclesiastical Commissioners in their turn made payments from the Common Fund to the Welsh dioceses, including the incomes of the four Welsh bishops, all or part of the incomes of certain dignitaries, and grants to augment the incomes of certain benefices. In 1906, these payments amounted to £59,366, so that rather over £25,000 was found for the Church in Wales out of the English resources of the Commissioners.[23] The Ecclesiastical Commissioners also made grants towards the stipends of curates in the Welsh dioceses, amounting in 1907 to £14,770.[24] The finances of the four Welsh dioceses were thus bound up with those of the rest of the Church of England, and there was no such clear line of separation as had existed in Ireland, which had had its own Ecclesiastical Commissioners and distinct financial structure.

The exact value of the property and revenues of the established Church in Wales was not easy to estimate. It depended on the value of tithe rent-charge, which was variable; on the value of houses and glebe land; and on the disentangling of finances which were bound up with those of the whole Church of England. The Royal Commission divided its survey of the endowments of the established Church in Wales into parochial and diocesan endowments. It concluded that the total gross income from parochial endowments, taking tithe rent-charge at the 1906 value, was £242,669.[25] Diocesan endowments, with minor exceptions, were either owned or managed by the Ecclesiastical Commissioners. These endowments—houses, land, and tithe rent-charge—produced a net revenue in 1906 of £35,609.[26] But this came back to Wales in different ways, some of which were included in the previous total for parochial endowments. McKenna, the then Home Secretary, introducing the fourth Welsh Disestablishment Bill in 1912, estimated the total net income from endowments at approximately £260,000 per annum.[27] An exact sum would be misleading, and this figure will serve to show the order of magnitude of the sums involved.

It will be observed that these figures are much lower than those for the revenue of the Irish Church before its disendowment. The established Church in Wales came under attack partly because of its endowments, but more because it was accused of being an "alien Church", and was therefore a target for Welsh nationalism. This was a charge much resented by Welsh Churchmen, and vigorously disputed in terms of the history and character of the the Church in Wales. Without wishing to prejudge this issue, it is necessary to say here that during the eighteenth and early nineteenth centuries the established Church in Wales lost effective religious contact with the great majority of the people of Wales. The census of church attendance taken on 31 March 1851 showed that in Wales about eighty per cent of attendances at places of worship were at Nonconformist chapels, while nearly forty-eight per cent of the population did not attend at all.[28] These figures are open to question on various grounds, and should not be taken at their face value, but the general fact that the Church was in a small minority is plain.[29] The explanation of this most heavily emphasized in the nineteenth century was that the Church had received its bishops from England—no Welsh-speaking bishop was appointed to a Welsh see between 1714 and 1870—and had paid insufficient attention to the Welsh language in its ministry. A good deal was said, too, of ecclesiastical neglect and spiritual torpor in the eighteenth century—of non-resident bishops, pluralist clergy, underpaid and ill-educated curates, dilapidated churches.

These explanations for the loss of contact between Church and people doubtless embody a good deal of the truth, but must be subject to some comment and qualification. First, the general picture may be subject to amendment in detail; there is evidence even in the eighteenth century of some concern in the Church for its pastoral work and care for the Welsh-speaking population.[30] Next, there is a case to be made out that some of the difficulties of the eighteenth century were due less to inherent spiritual torpor among the clergy than to economic and social circumstances. The poverty of the clergy made pluralism in many cases essential to produce a reasonable income, while the gentry combined their powers as patrons and lay rectors with neglect of their duties towards the Church.[31] Similarly, when the Church faced the rapid growth of a new industrial society in South Wales at the turn of the eighteenth and nineteenth centuries, it did so under handicaps of poverty and an inflexible parochial system, which, while they arose from the nature of the Church's establishment and endowments, were certainly not the responsibility of that generation of clergy.[32] The rigidity of the parochial system, indeed, hampered the response of the Church of England to industrialization everywhere, not only in Wales. The failure of the established Church to keep in touch with the majority of the population, especially in the great new towns, was widespread. The Church in England, though it had English bishops and had no language problem as it had in Wales, also failed to hold the people, so that the emphasis sometimes placed on the language issue in Wales may be exaggerated.

In the middle of the nineteenth century, a revival of spirit and a new vigour in administration was felt in the Church in Wales. Bishop Thirlwall of St David's was a man of great intellectual distinction and strong character, who did much to reorganize his diocese, and also took the trouble to learn Welsh so that he could preach and confirm in that language. He even received some grudging approval from Lady Llanover, fiercely Welsh and caustic-tongued, self-appointed adviser to Gladstone on Welsh Church matters.[33] Bishop Ollivant of Llandaff (1850–83) has been described by Canon Davies as one of the greatest holders of that see, and the creator of the modern diocese. He stimulated the building of churches, created a small group of priests to work as missionaries without parishes, and brought laymen more into the work of the Church.[34] In North Wales, Vowler Short at St Asaph administered and visited his diocese carefully, and did much to deal with the problem of non-resident clergy.[35] In addition to the work of bishops, the Evangelical revival and the Oxford Movement had their effect in Wales, as in England, and it is possible that the developments in ritual by the Anglo-Catholics had a particular influence in Wales in their appeal to the imagination and to the eye.[36]

The three bishops just named were all Englishmen, and the great movements in the Church spread from England. So it may well be that the appointment by Gladstone of a Welsh-speaking Welshman, Joshua Hughes, to the see of St Asaph in 1870 was less of a turning-point for the Welsh Church than the Prime Minister thought at the time.[37] However, a turning-point in one sense it was. The precedent, once set, was followed, and Welsh-speaking bishops became the rule—a rule which much later and in very different circumstances it was to prove hard to break. Moreover, the quality of the men appointed improved markedly in later years. Hughes's main qualification for St Asaph was that he spoke Welsh, not that he was in other respects well fitted for a bishopric.[38] The appointments of A. G. Edwards to St Asaph in 1889, and of John Owen to St David's in 1897, showed that it had become possible to find men whose Welshness was beyond cavil and who were also generally well qualified to become bishops. In the course of the thirty years after 1870 it became impossible to speak of an English episcopate in Wales. This was a point of great psychological importance, even though the change in the temper and activity of the Welsh Church began before it came about.

The change in the character of the Welsh episcopate was accompanied by evidence of intensified activity on the part of the Church, in terms of increasing numbers of communicants, the building of churches and church schools, and voluntary giving.[39] In the political context of the last quarter of the nineteenth century, however, it was too late for the Church to retrieve its position. Whatever Welsh bishops were appointed, whatever vigour the Church showed and whatever progress it made, the proposition that Welshness was identical with Nonconformity was too firmly established to be shaken within one or even two generations. The demand for the disestablishment and disendowment of the Church was a vital part of the Welsh Liberal-cum-nationalist programme. The Church had its fixed place in the demonology of Welsh nationalism.

There were indeed two events in the 1880s whose immediate effect was to embitter the controversy about the Church. The first was the problem of the tithe rent-charge. The Tithe Commutation Act of 1836 had laid down that tithe was to be paid in money instead of in kind, and that the yearly payment was to be calculated on the average market price of certain cereals (wheat, barley, and oats) over the previous seven years. The Act worked comparatively smoothly until the collapse in cereal prices in the late 1870s destroyed the basis of the system. The value of tithe rent-charge worth £100 in 1835 stood in 1875 at £112 15s. 7d.; in 1901 it stood at £66 10s. 9d.[40] Thus the income of clergymen who were heavily dependent upon tithe rent-charge might fall by a third or more, even if the rent-charge itself could be collected. For farmers too might have their incomes reduced sharply by the fall in cereal prices. Inevitably payments fell into arrears and resentment against the tithe rent-charge itself grew. During the late 1880s the situation became intolerable to both sides. Both country clergy and farmers were suffering real hardship. The legal rights of the clergy were clear, but could only be enforced at excessive cost, in terms both of money[41] and (more serious) of local hostility. In Wales the situation was made worse by the already existing resentment of Nonconformists having to pay tithe rent-charge to the Church, and of Welshmen having to pay to an institution they felt to be English. From 1886 onwards attempts to distrain the goods of farmers who were in arrears in the payment of tithe were sometimes met with violence, mostly in Denbighshire and Caernarvonshire. Anti-tithe Leagues were formed, in association with the Welsh Land League. The younger Welsh radicals exploited the situation to add force to the disestablishment campaign and bring Wales to the attention of Parliament.[42] The immediate effect of the tithe question in embittering the controversy over the Welsh Church is clear. The ultimate effects, however, proved to be quietening. Parliament was compelled to attend to the problem, and after a number of attempts a Tithe Act was passed in 1891 placing responsibility for the payment of tithe rent-charge on the landlord, not the tenant. Though the payment would naturally be passed on as part of the rent, this meant that there was no longer any direct contact between tithe-owner and tenant farmer—"tithe-owners got their rent-charges more regularly and from a class of men more generally friendly and amenable", as Dr Best writes,[43] and nowhere can this have been more true than in Wales. The Act took effect, and the wave of violent incidents in Wales came to an end. The grievance of Nonconformists against the principle of the tithe remained; but the change in the mode of payment took the bite out of this grievance just before Welsh Disestablishment Bills came before the House of Commons. The controversy over these Bills was not accompanied by the use of force to exact or resist the collection of tithe.

The second event which affected the Welsh Church question was the passing of the Local Government Act of 1888, creating elective county councils to administer rural areas. In the elections under this Act in January 1889 the Liberals won sweeping victories all over Wales. The exclusive authority of the gentry in the countryside was ended, though of course their influence was far from being totally removed. The Church saw its old allies in local government replaced by enemies. For example, Thomas Gee, a great Nonconformist champion and the leader of the campaign against tithe, became the first chairman of the Denbighshire County Council, while Sir Arthur Griffith-Boscawen, chairman of quarter sessions, a Conservative and a Churchman, was only just elected, and other landowners were defeated.[44] There could be no doubt of the spirit in which the new masters entered into their power. The *North Wales Observer and Express* proclaimed at the time of the elections (11 January 1889): "We are in the midst of a fight with a corrupt Church and a bloated aristocracy." Afterwards it asserted triumphantly that "the greatest struggle for LIBERTY which Wales has experienced for the last six or seven hundred years has ended in the defeat of the Classes by the united action of the Masses".[45] The Conservative *Western Mail* wrote that the bulk of the members of the county councils had been elected for the purpose of abolishing the Church in Wales, though it also looked hopefully to the responsible men, well known at quarter sessions, who had survived the elections, to exercise a moderating influence.[46]

It was important that it was to the county councils that the successive Welsh Disestablishment Bills proposed to hand over the bulk of the Church's endowments. These would thus pass, not to the government in London or its representatives (which would still have been resented by Churchmen) but to prominent local opponents of the Church, who might well be personal enemies of the local rector or churchwarden. For Nonconformists, justice would be satisfied in that national property would be restored to the nation; but there was also the prospect of a tangible victory over the local representatives of the Church. There was a particular savour in the prospect of controlling the former revenues of the Church so soon after overthrowing the long-standing power of the gentry. The Local Government Act of 1888 thus added an extra dimension of bitterness to the controversy over the established Church. However, as with the tithe question, in the long run the effect was to bring a measure of appeasement. The disestablishment question was in large part a symbol of a national and class struggle, and by the Act of 1888 that struggle was in one important respect decided. The affairs of the Welsh countryside passed out of the control of the landlords and into that of the Welsh electorate. This gradually removed the national and social aspects from the campaign for disestablishment, even though at first it gave them a new impetus.

The movement for disestablishment in Wales thus had its origins in circumstances prevailing in the middle of the nineteenth century. At that time the Church was at its lowest ebb,[47] having lost contact with the great majority of the Welsh people and being alienated from the chief sources of life and vigour in Welsh society. These were to be found in the Nonconformist Churches, powerful both in the countryside and in the new industrial areas, and about to become as active politically as they were socially. At the same time the leadership of the Church was English; the Church as a whole made inadequate use of the Welsh language; and the

Church was closely bound up with an anglicized gentry. It thus became inevitably an object for attack by a movement whose objects were social and nationalist more than religious, though a desire for religious equality played some part. During the latter half of the century the situation of the Church changed considerably; it acquired a new vigour and became more Welsh in character. But its status as a symbolic enemy for Welsh nationalism could not be changed, and during the same period the movement for disestablishment achieved overwhelming momentum in Wales and a position of great power within the Liberal party as a whole. During the Liberal administration of 1892–5, the movement for Welsh disestablishment gained a position of political power from which its desires could be translated into Bills, and the Welsh Church question took on a new aspect.

The Welsh Disestablishment Bills, 1894–1914

There were in all four Welsh Disestablishment Bills placed before Parliament, only the last of which went through all its stages and reached the statute book. There was also, in 1893, the Welsh Church Suspensory Bill. An account of the campaigns by which these Bills were promoted and resisted has already been written.[48] All that need be said here, before moving to an analysis of the Bills themselves, is that during the twenty years between 1894 and 1914 circumstances changed a great deal. The change may be seen partly in terms of the politicians who were concerned with the Bills, and partly in terms of the forces behind them.

There was a marked distinction between Gladstone on the one hand, and other Liberal politicians who were concerned with the issue on the other. While Gladstone remained leader of the Liberal party, with his vast prestige and personal authority, his adhesion was vital to the cause of Welsh disestablishment. It was while he was Prime Minister that the Welsh Suspensory Bill of 1893 was introduced, and the first Disestablishment Bill prepared. This conversion to the support of Welsh disestablishment, after he had vigorously opposed it in 1870 with the declaration that the Church in Wales had "a complete constitutional, legal and . . . historical identity with the Church of England"[49] was open to the charge of trimming for the sake of mere political expediency. Gladstone had his answers to this charge: that in 1885 he had said that the question of disestablishment must depend on public opinion; and that the principle of disendowment, the treatment of Church funds as national property, had been accepted in the Irish Church Act.[50] There was indeed no change of principle, except in Gladstone's recognition that Wales, like Ireland, could be treated as a separate entity, though there were clear signs that Gladstone resented the pressure put on him by Welsh members in 1892–3, and that he disagreed with important aspects of the disendowment clauses in the Disestablishment Bill of 1895. (He cancelled his pair to secure freedom of action on the clauses dealing with the cathedrals, burial grounds, and commutation.[51]) But whatever may be thought of Gladstone's change of mind, and of his justification for it, there is no doubt of his deep concern with the question at issue. The problem of the relationship between Church and State lay near the heart of Gladstone's political philosophy; his whole life was based on a religious foundation. The fact that he only took up Welsh disestablishment when the Welsh Liberals were in a position to force their wishes upon him does not detract from the importance of what were the attitudes of a lifetime.

Gladstone stands here in complete contrast to Asquith, who was responsible for the preparation and piloting of the early Welsh Disestablishment Bills, and under whose premiership the Act of 1914 was passed. It is true that while still at school Asquith attended a meeting in favour of Irish disestablishment, and that while a rising politician he made gestures towards Nonconformity and addressed Liberation Society meetings.[52] But he was not deeply engaged in the issue of the relations between Church and State. Nor, it appears, was he particularly attracted by the cause of Wales or Welsh Nonconformity. His latest biographer, Mr Roy Jenkins, has written that "a certain antipathy towards the Welsh temperament, which in later life (even before 1916) he never made much effort to conceal, may well have begun with his troubles over the Disestablishment Bill".[53] However, circumstances cast him in the role of champion of Welsh Nonconformity, and he played the part like the good barrister he was. The change from Gladstone to Asquith was that from a man deeply concerned with the issues involved to a lawyer handling a brief.

The fourth Welsh Disestablishment Bill was introduced in 1912 by McKenna, who also piloted it through its long parliamentary circuit. McKenna, like Asquith, was a barrister by profession. His nephew and biographer presents him as a man who dealt with questions unemotionally, in terms of administrative advantage, of facts and figures. He happened to sit for a Welsh seat (North Monmouthshire), and was associated with the Welsh party in the House of Commons, but he appears to have had little affinity with his colleagues, and was on bad personal terms with Lloyd George.[54] It appears that Owen, the Bishop of St David's, regarded McKenna as the villain of the piece in the late stages of the disestablishment question—"viciously hostile to the Church", he wrote in 1915.[55] It is more likely that McKenna was in charge of the Welsh Disestablishment Bill because he was Home Secretary at the time, and that he saw it simply as a job to be done—it might well have been Winston Churchill's job if he had not changed places with McKenna and gone to the Admiralty shortly before the Bill was introduced in 1912.

For the English politicians connected with the Welsh Bills, then, the matter became one of routine, of making a case in order to satisfy the Welsh Liberals. But even the most prominent and famous of the Welsh Liberals themselves, Lloyd George, had only dubious concern for the issue of disestablishment as such. Dr Morgan has written that even in the 1890s Lloyd George regarded disestablishment "as a stalking-horse for other objectives, such as land reform and home rule".[56] As time went on, even these issues became less important to him—it is impossible to imagine the Lloyd George of 1906 and afterwards limiting himself to being Prime Minister of Wales. His immense energy was turned to other and more important matters—strikes, social questions, the House of Lords, and later the war. Even by 1906 Welsh disestablishment had become for Lloyd George something to be got out of the way by a quick compromise.[57] In October 1907 he went to a public meeting at Cardiff not to stimulate but to damp down agitation for a Disestablishment Bill. On his return he wrote to the Prime Minister: "The Government will not be worried much more on the subject of Welsh Disestablishment until the time comes to arrange the programme for 1909. You will then be pressed very hard to give the question a look in and as it ought not to take time ... I think it would be worth while getting it out of the way then." (His letter then went on, for six and a half out of its eight pages, to discuss the possibility of averting a rail strike.[58]) Lloyd George kept up his connection with the Liberation Society, of which he was a Vice-President in 1909, and he continued to contribute to disestablishment literature,[59] but this was a façade. The issue was no longer important for a vigorous, successful, and ambitious minister, first President of the Board of Trade and then Chancellor of the Exchequer, though for the sake of his reputation in his native land it would not have been wise for him to say so in public.

By the time a Welsh Disestablishment Bill was placed on the statute book in 1914, it had become for the leading politicians involved a matter with which they were not deeply concerned. They continued to observe an old commitment in response to pressure from Nonconformist bodies in Wales, and from the rank and file of Welsh Liberal M.P.s, who continued to demand a Bill and to support rigorous conditions of disendowment. On the question of disendowment, however, there were in 1912 serious signs of a decline in support for the Welsh viewpoint by English Liberals and Nonconformists. Sir Henry Lunn, himself a Liberal and an ordained Nonconformist minister, formed a conciliation committee at the end of 1911, and convened a round table conference which in May 1912 suggested compromise terms on endowments.[60] As the Disestablishment Bill of 1912 went through the committee stage in the Commons, a number of amendments on endowments were moved by Liberal members; some were carried, and on others the government's majority was small. Welsh Liberals and Nonconformists were conscious of a lack of support from across the border. The *South Wales Daily News* wrote on 7 March 1912 that Welshmen were indignant at the "apathy and indifference" of English Nonconformists, only a handful of whom had spoken in public in favour of the Welsh Bill. At a meeting addressed by Lloyd George at Caernarvon on 18 May, a Welsh Nonconformist minister wanted "more iron in the veins of English Liberalism", and claimed that the Welsh would split the party and wreck the government rather than see lukewarm English Liberalism override the will of Wales.[61] This can hardly have been music to Lloyd George's ears at a time when the government already had to deal with the naval race with Germany, a coal strike, the militant suffragettes, and an incipient crisis in Ireland.

There were even some signs of uncertainty within Welsh Nonconformity itself. In October 1912 Henry Radcliffe, a Cardiff ship-owner, a Methodist, and a former Liberal parliamentary candidate, chose the occasion of the opening of a Calvinistic Methodist bazaar to oppose the disendowment clauses of the Disestablishment Bill.[62] He later asserted, in a Conservative newspaper, that, if there were a referendum of the religious people of Wales, ninety per cent of them would vote against the transfer of funds from religious to worldly purposes.[63] In 1914 there were petitions in Wales protesting against disendowment, which purported to bear the signatures of 103,224 Nonconformists. As with many petitions, their exact value is doubtful. Questioning by a select committee of the House of Lords on the mode of their organization and the status of the signatories revealed some dubious practices. However, there is no doubt that numbers of prominent Nonconformists were willing to sign the petitions, and this in itself indicated some wavering on the issue of disendowment.[64]

This declining impetus behind the Welsh Disestablishment Bills on the part of the Liberal party and Nonconformity was in part a reflection of the fact that the issue itself was only of the second rank in politics. The circumstances were quite different from those of Irish disestablishment. In 1868–9 Ireland was at the centre of politics, and the Irish Church was the most prominent feature of the Irish question. At no time between 1894 and 1914 was Wales the centre of political life, nor was it obvious that even for Wales the Church question was more important than the land, education, or labour questions. This fact was noted, for example, by two very different Welsh observers in April 1909. Owen, the Bishop of St David's, wrote to the Bishop of London:

> ... from what I can learn, though Disestablishment is still a Radical political cry in Wales, there is nothing like the real solidarity of conviction of it that there was twenty or thirty years ago. Free Trade, Labour and Land, the Navy and the House of Lords, are the real living issues now, though the old flag of Disestablishment is still kept flying, out of Welsh Nonconformists' regard for a cause for which their fathers fought. The Disestablishment Movement is dying at its roots from old age.[65]

This was strikingly similar to an analysis in a Liberal paper, the *North Wales Observer* (30 April 1909) where it was admitted that the demand for disestablishment was less clamorous and enthusiastic than before. The *Observer* held that this was not because the Church was more popular, but because people had become more conscious of the need for social reform—a land bill or a leasehold bill would command more support. (This was, of course, the voice of North Wales, not the industrial South, where social reform had other connotations.) The *Observer* therefore sought to argue that a Welsh Church Bill was in fact an aspect of social reform, diverting a sizeable sum of money to the needs of society. The glory was indeed departed when the old cause of religious equality and national feeling was defended in such terms.

In the country as a whole the Welsh Church was a minor issue, and the Liberal government had many other preoccupations. Among Conservatives, many doubtless felt strongly about disestablishment, which touched sentiment, and disendowment, which touched the rights of property. Bonar Law, who appears to have cared little about the Welsh Church question himself, told Asquith in 1913 that a majority of his followers in the House of Commons "would, if they had to choose, prefer Home Rule [for Ireland] rather than disestablish the Church".[66] But this may have been a mistaken view of the scale of priorities held by Conservative and Unionist M.P.s. It may be nearer the truth to see the question of Welsh disestablishment and disendowment as one aspect of what Conservatives saw as an assault upon the whole established order, constitutional, political, and social. The Union with Ireland, the House of Lords, the rights of property and of employers, were all threatened between 1910 and 1914, and the Conservatives fought all along the line with all the weapons at their command.

With these circumstances in mind, let us turn to the Bills which came before Parliament. The Welsh Church Suspensory Bill of 1893 deserves brief mention before an examination of the Disestablishment Bills proper. This was a Bill of one clause, introduced in February 1893, providing that in all new appointments by public patrons in the four Welsh dioceses, the new incumbent should hold his emoluments subject to the pleasure of Parliament—that is, he would have no claim to compensation under a future Disestablishment Bill. In essence this Bill was a mere gesture. It is hard to believe that anyone, on either side of the House of Commons, believed that it could secure three readings in that House, and it would certainly not have passed the Lords. In fact, the Bill never received a second reading, because the Irish Home Rule Bill took up the whole session. So the Bill was essentially an assurance to the Welsh members that the government was serious about disestablishment. It was defended in principle, however, on the ground that it was desirable to prevent the creation of vested interests which would later be a charge on the Church funds instead of going to secular purposes.[67] Behind this lay the belief that in 1869 the Irish Church, by manufacturing vested interests before the passage of the Irish Church Act, had secured far more compensation than was justifiable. The *South Wales Daily News*, for example, asserted that by this means the Irish Church had secured for itself £13,000,000 out of £16,000,000 capital value of its estates. It was vital to prevent "a similar disgraceful trafficking in Church livings" in Wales.[68] It is difficult to see how the figure was arrived at;* but the impression was widespread, and it affected the content of the Disestablishment Bills themselves. Lastly, it must be said that the device of a Suspensory Bill was not used again. Whatever justification it had in 1893 it seems to have been lost in later years. The significance of the Bill was as a gesture to the Welsh Liberals, and as a symptom of a tough, exacting attitude towards the question of disendowment.

Of Welsh Disestablishment Bills, there were in all four: those of 1894, 1895, 1909, and 1912. The first never got as far as a second reading in the House of Commons. The second passed the second reading, and went into committee, but never emerged because Rosebery's government fell in June 1895, at least in part because of difficulties caused by its own Welsh supporters over the Disestablishment Bill. The Bill of 1909 was introduced, and then vanished at once in the struggle over Lloyd George's budget of the same year. That of 1912 passed all its stages in the Commons, being read for a third time on 5 February 1913. It was promptly rejected by the House of Lords on 13 February, and then went steadily through the procedure laid down by the Parliament Act of 1911. It passed the Commons again in June and July 1913, and

---

* The actual figure for compensation paid to the Irish Church was approximately £8,500,000—see above, p. 201.

was again rejected by the Lords. It came round the circuit for the third time in 1914, leaving the Commons finally on 19 May. As a last delaying action, the peers set up a select committee to look into certain aspects of the Bill. This committee was still at work when war was declared on 4 August 1914, so that the Bill finally received the royal assent on 18 September, in peculiar circumstances which must be discussed later.

These four Bills were broadly similar in content, and can well be examined by considering the elements common to them all and discussing the differences in detail in the course of the analysis.[69] These elements may be distinguished as follows:

1. Provisions for the interim period between the passage of the Act and the date of disestablishment.

2. Provisions for disestablishment.

3. Provisions for disendowment: (i) property to be left to the Church; (ii) property to be secularized; (iii) the disposal of the secularized funds.

4. Provisions for compensation.

5. Provisions to allow the Church to reorganize itself.*

1. There were special provisions for the interim period between the passing of the Act and the date of disestablishment. No appointment made during this time would carry with it any life-interest or right of compensation. If a bishopric fell vacant, it was to be filled by the Crown on the recommendation of the Archbishop of Canterbury or three Welsh bishops; other vacancies were to be filled in the existing manner. These provisions remained the same in all the Bills, and ultimately proved to be important, because the interim period was in fact prolonged from 1914 to 1920.

2. On disestablishment the provisions of all the Bills remained broadly the same. All rights of patronage, public and private, were to cease, and all ecclesiastical corporations were to be

---

* It should be noted that under the Disestablishment Bills the area affected was geographical Wales, not the four Welsh dioceses. Special provisions were made for the parishes which straddled the national boundary. See below, p. 305.

17

dissolved. Ecclesiastical law would cease to exist as law in Wales; the ecclesiastical courts would cease to have coercive power; and appeals to the Judicial Committee of the Privy Council would end. The bishops of the Welsh dioceses would cease to be summoned to the House of Lords.* The dioceses themselves would cease to be represented in the Convocation of Canterbury.

3. In the disendowment clauses, there were considerable differences between the various Bills, the movement being towards a less severe treatment of the Church.

(i) *Property to be left to the Church.*   Strictly speaking, as under the Irish Church Act, all property was to be removed from the possession of the Church on the date of disestablishment, and vested in Commissioners, who would at once restore certain categories of it to the Church. For these latter categories, these two acts of transfer, to and from the Commissioners, amounted to a legal fiction; but the fact that all property was at one point to pass in law to the Commissioners disturbed some Welsh Churchmen. Again, as under the Irish Church Act, all the Bills provided for the appointment by the bishops, clergy, and laity of the Church of a Representative Body to receive and administer the property which would be returned to the Church.

Under the first Disestablishment Bill, that of 1894, the only items of property to be left to the Church were the following: (a) the churches—excluding the four cathedrals, for which special arrangements were made; (b) moveable items of property—for instance, communion plate and furnishings of various kinds; (c) the glebe-houses, or parsonages, which were to be handed over to the Representative Body outright. (This interesting divergence from the provisions of the Irish Church Act arose from the fact that the Irish Commissioners did so badly out of this aspect of the Act of 1869. It will be recalled that the Commissioners estimated that they would have been over a quarter of a million pounds better off if the Irish glebe-houses had been simply handed over to the Church.[70]); (d) private benefactions to the Church since 1703. In 1894 Asquith estimated that these amounted to £13,600

* The clergy of the Church in Wales would become eligible for membership of the House of Commons, from which they were debarred while the Church was established.

per annum. The date, that of the foundation of Queen Anne's Bounty, appears to have been arbitrarily selected, and was later changed.

The Bill of 1895 was at its introduction identical with these terms, but in the committee stage three concessions were made. Cathedrals were to be treated in the same way as the other churches, and handed over to the Representative Body. Closed burial grounds were also to go to the Representative Body, though not burial grounds which were still in use. The date for leaving private endowments to the Church was changed from 1703 to 1662—a rather less arbitrary date, being that of the Act of Uniformity.[71] (It transpired that this altered the financial situation very little, because the Church had received only small benefactions during those forty years.)

The Bill of 1909 retained the amended terms of 1895. That of 1912, as introduced, included the same provisions, the Church retaining its churches and cathedrals, closed burial grounds, moveable property, glebe-houses, and private endowments since 1662 (calculated in 1912 as being worth £18,500 per annum). The Bill of 1912 also made special provision about the income received by the Church in Wales from English sources of the Ecclesiastical Commissioners and Queen Anne's Bounty. This income was estimated in 1912 at £68,600, and the Bill authorized the Ecclesiastical Commissioners and the Governors of Queen Anne's Bounty to transfer to the disestablished Church the capital from which this income was derived. The bodies concerned agreed to this arrangement, so this revenue was secured to the Church.[72] While the 1912 Bill was in committee, an amendment was accepted which allowed the Church to retain income received by Queen Anne's Bounty from Welsh sources and from the Welsh share of parliamentary grants made between 1809 and 1824. These amounted to a total of £15,000 per annum (£9,000 from the Welsh sources, £6,000 from the parliamentary grants).[73] When this was added to the private endowments since 1662, and the revenue from English sources of the Ecclesiastical Commissioners and Queen Anne's Bounty, this last Bill in its amended state preserved to the Church in Wales just over £102,000 per annum. This was out of property estimated in 1912 at £260,000 per annum.[74]

There was also a provision in the 1912 Bill which, while not dealing with the actual property of the Church in Wales, affected the Church's financial position. Both the Ecclesiastical Commissioners and Queen Anne's Bounty had for some time appropriated capital sums to various dioceses, Welsh and English, keeping the capital in their own hands and paying the interest to the diocese concerned. Over the seven years before 1912, the sums paid to the Welsh dioceses in this way averaged £31,000 per annum. The Bill permitted the Commissioners and Queen Anne's Bounty to continue these payments if they so wished, which would increase the assured income of the disestablished Church from £102,000 to £133,000.[75]

(ii) *Property to be secularized.*   As the changes just described were made between the Bill of 1894 and that of 1912, so the amount of property to be secularized diminished. Under the Bill of 1894 all the property of the Church except the churches, moveable items, glebe-houses, and private endowments since 1703 was to be confiscated. Even the four Welsh cathedrals were to be removed from the control of the Church and retained by the Commissioners set up to administer the secularized property. They were to be treated as national monuments but still to be used for the same purposes as before. All burial grounds too were to pass out of the possession of the Church, as were all other kinds of property, including glebe land and tithe rent-charge, unless it fell into the very narrow category of private endowments since 1703. The revenue paid to Wales by the Ecclesiastical Commissioners and Queen Anne's Bounty from English sources was not to be appropriated by the government, but retained by the Commissioners and the Bounty and used for English purposes.[76] It would thus be lost to the Church in Wales without being secularized.

In 1895 the property to be secularized was diminished by the amendments restoring the cathedrals and closed burial grounds to the Church, and by the change in the date for retention of private endowments from 1703 to 1662. In the Bill of 1909 these provisions remained unchanged, as they did in the Bill of 1912 as originally introduced. In 1912 the property to be secularized was estimated as follows. Ancient endowments (i.e. before 1662, mostly tithe and glebe) amounted to about £116,000. Income from the Welsh sources of the Ecclesiastical Commissioners amounted to about £41,000; from the Welsh sources of Queen Anne's Bounty, £9,000; and from the Welsh share of parliamentary grants made between 1809 and 1824 going to Queen Anne's Bounty, £6,000. The total revenue to be secularized amounted in all to £173,000 per annum.* The later amendment about Queen Anne's Bounty and the parliamentary grants reduced this figure by £15,000 to £158,000 per annum to be secularized out of an estimated total of £260,000. This was the final arrangement embodied in the Disestablishment Bill which finally reached the statute book in 1914. It marked a great change from the proposals of 1894, which would have secularized all but £13,600 per annum of the Church's revenues.

Of the property to be secularized, the burial grounds deserve particular mention. They were of course of no economic value, but they were a centre of vocal Nonconformist grievance. T. E. Ellis once told Asquith that Welshmen would accept unpalatable points in a Disestablishment Bill if "the people's right to the *burial grounds* were made secure and real".[77] The background to this was one of disputes over the erection of tombstones, obstacles raised by incumbents about the burial of Nonconformists, and questions about the payment of fees to incumbents for various purposes. The final provision in the Act of 1914 was that burial grounds which derived from private benefactors should pass to the Church; those which had been closed should do the same, if the Church wished; and those which were not from private gifts and were still in use should pass to the various local authorities—parish, borough, or urban district councils. This was later to cause much difficulty.

(iii) *The disposal of the secularized funds.*   The detailed provisions on this point varied a good deal between different Bills, though the general principle remained the same. Under all the Bills, Commissioners† were to be created to receive the secularized property, and to administer it until it was put to the ultimate uses envisaged

* The figures given for the different sources of revenue (£116,000, £41,000, £9,000, and £6,000) add up to £172,000. The difference between this and the total of £173,000 is accounted for by the fact that the individual figures have all been rounded to the nearest thousand.

† Their title was to be "The Commissioners of Church Temporalities in Wales". They will be referred to as the Welsh Commissioners.

for it. In the Bills of 1894 and 1895 it was assumed that these Commissioners would have to exist for a long period; but in 1909 Asquith believed they would complete their work in five years, and in the Bill of 1912 the existence of the Commissioners was specifically limited to three years, with a possible extension to five years.

Under the Bills of 1894 and 1895 the secularized funds were to be divided into two parts. The first, arising from the parochial endowments (mostly tithe and glebe) was to pass (after all compensation had been paid) to the Welsh county councils. The second part, arising from the former diocesan property then administered by the Ecclesiastical Commissioners, was to remain in the hands of the Commissioners and be used for the needs of Wales as a whole. The purposes, whether local or national, to which the money was to be put were specified thus: (1) hospitals, dispensaries, and convalescent homes; (2) trained nurses for the sick poor; (3) parish or district halls, institutes, and libraries; (4) labourers' housing at reasonable rents, and allotments; (5) technical and higher education, including a National Library, Museum, or Academy of Art; (6) any other purpose of local or general utility not provided for by statute out of the rates. This mode of dealing with the secularized property was in part adopted in the light of the fate of the Irish Church fund, which as Asquith noted had "offered irresistible temptation in almost every emergency".[78] The Bills of 1894 and 1895 therefore sought to define the uses to which a Welsh Church fund would be put, and to ensure that local authorities had the administration of the greater part of it.

However, this method brought its own difficulties, arising from disparities between population and parochial endowments in different counties and parishes. Asquith noted in January 1895 that Glamorgan, with a population of nearly 700,000, would have access to Church revenue of £26,000, while Pembrokeshire, with a population of only 90,000 would have £25,000.[79] There would be obvious causes here of discontent and jealousy, and a strong case could be made out that the greater part, or even the whole, of the secularized property should be placed in the hands of a central body and distributed according to need instead of according to the incidence of parochial endowments. On the Bill of

1895, an amendment was moved by a Welsh member, D. A. Thomas, to allocate the proceeds of the tithe on a national basis; it was lost by seven votes.[80]

In the Bill of 1909 various changes were made in the provisions for distribution. One tenth of the net revenue derived from the parochial endowments was added to the sum to be used for general Welsh purposes, which went a small way to meeting the argument described above. The whole sum to be used for national purposes was to be administered not by the Commissioners but by a body called the Council of Wales. Some of the specified purposes for which the funds were to be used were dropped—the provision of labourers' housing and allotments, and of a National Library, Museum, or Academy of Art. These had already been provided out of public funds between 1895 and 1909.

In the final Bill of 1912 these provisions were changed again. The secularized property was again to be divided into two parts. One, the sum paid by the Ecclesiastical Commissioners to Welsh bishoprics and chapters, estimated at £27,700 per annum, was to be paid to the University of Wales, the National Library, and the National Museum. The other was to be divided between the various county councils, each receiving the parochial endowments existing in its own county. The county councils were to use the funds for any eleemosynary, charitable, or public purpose of local or general utility. The councils' schemes were to be submitted for the approval of the Home Secretary, and should have regard to the needs of the individual parishes to which the endowments had been appropriated. During the committee stage two changes were made in this plan of distribution. First, the National Museum was removed from the list of institutions to receive part of the secularized funds; and second, the mention of public purposes of local or general utility was dropped, leaving only eleemosynary or charitable purposes as permissible uses of the money by county councils. Under the Bill of 1912 the Council of Wales disappeared, McKenna explaining that its duties under the proposed scheme of distribution would be insufficient to justify the creation of such a body. It will be noted that the list of specific purposes for the use of the funds also disappeared in this Bill.

The final provision for the disposal of the secularized funds, therefore, in the Bill as it reached the statute book, was that a portion should go to the University of Wales and the National Library, and the larger portion to the county councils, to be used for unspecified charitable purposes which should have the approval of the Home Secretary.

4. On compensation the Bill of 1894 was markedly less generous in its provisions than the Irish Church Act had been. Anyone holding an office with freehold in the Church, including all bishops, dignitaries, and incumbents, was entitled to receive the net endowments of that office at the time of disestablishment as long as he performed the same duties. He might, with the consent of the representative body which the Bill allowed the Church to set up, exchange this assured income for a smaller compensation annuity, with the freedom to leave his duties. There was to be no commutation, as there had been in Ireland—no provision for a lump sum to be paid to the representative body, which would then assume the responsibility of paying the individual clergymen their annuities. Asquith advanced two reasons for this difference from the Irish Church Act. One was that, since one could not compel a man to commute, it was necessary for commutation to work to offer an inducement, such as the twelve per cent bonus offered to the Representative Body under the Irish Church Act. This would make the process too expensive. The second reason was that there would be insuperable administrative difficulties in combining a scheme for the local distribution of the secularized funds with a scheme for commutation, because it would be too hard to arrange that each parish should bear its part of the capital cost of commutation.[81]

A second difference between the compensation provisions of the Welsh Bill of 1894 and the Irish Church Act concerned curates. Under the Welsh Bill curates were not to receive any compensation, whereas under the Irish Act some had been allowed a life interest and others a gratuity. Asquith argued that, since curates had no freehold, they had no vested interest to be compensated; and that in practice they would not immediately be affected by disestablishment and disendowment. He also cited what he described as the exorbitant payments made to curates in Ireland, and repeated the assertion that there had been in the Irish Church "an extraordinary and unprecedented multiplication" of curates, their numbers increasing from 563 to 921—which was a misreading of the facts.[82]

Finally, among the provisions for compensation, lay patrons of benefices were to be compensated for the loss of their right of presentation at the low rate of not more than one year's revenue of the benefice in question. This again differed from the Irish Church Act, when compensation was left to the Temporalities Commissioners with an appeal to arbitration, the ultimate result being on the whole favourable to the lay patrons.

The Bills of 1895 and 1909 showed no changes from these terms for compensation, nor did the substance of the compensation clauses of the Bill of 1912. In that Bill there was still no provision for commutation, and no compensation for curates. During the passage of the Bill through the House of Commons an amendment to grant compensation to curates was rejected. An amendment providing for commutation of life interests, however, was accepted.[83] In this scheme no option was given to individual clergymen, as in the Irish Church Act; the Representative Body was to choose, within one month of the date of disestablishment, whether or not to accept commutation. Special provisions were made in the tables of mortality to allow for the longevity of the clergy. This was a strange amendment for the government to accept, since the principle of commutation had been resolutely rejected in previous Bills. Whatever administrative difficulties Asquith had envisaged in 1894 presumably still existed, since the means of disposing of the secularized funds remained in principle the same. At one stage McKenna told the Bishop of Hereford, Percival (who supported the main lines of the Bill and voted for it in the House of Lords, but wanted to secure commutation), that the resources of the Welsh Church were not sufficient to make a commutation scheme workable.[84] What was workable in February 1913, when the government made the amendment, was presumably workable before that date; and the only conclusion is that at this point the government abandoned its determination to deny the Church the limited advantages of a commutation scheme. Welsh Liberal M.P.s objected to this concession, as they did to others made at the same time, but in general it was a sign of the movement of opinion in favour of greater leniency towards the Church.

5. The provisions allowing the Church in Wales to reorganize itself and to administer its remaining property after disestablishment were in substance the same as those in the Irish Church Act, and remained the same from one Bill to another. They laid down that existing law and doctrine should be considered binding on members of the Church as if by mutual contract, until altered by the newly constituted authorities of the Church. The Church was given power to hold Synods and to create a new constitution for itself. In particular, the Bills authorized the Church to set up a representative body, which might be given a charter and receive the powers of a corporation to administer the property of the disestablished Church.

To sum up, the salient points of the Welsh Disestablishment Act as it finally reached the statute book in 1914 were as follows:[85]

1. In the interim period before the date of disestablishment (which was to be six months or, if approved by Order in Council, twelve months after the passing of the Act), no new appointment would carry with it a life-interest or right of compensation.

2. The Church in Wales was to be disestablished: that is, the privileges conferred on it by the State and the powers held by the State over the Church were to be abrogated. This meant principally the end of state sanction for ecclesiastical law; the removal of the Welsh bishops from the House of Lords; the end of the existing system of patronage; and the assumption by the Church of control over its own appointments, discipline, services, and doctrine.*

3. The disendowment clauses left to the Church its cathedrals and churches, its glebe-houses, and property worth £102,000 per annum,† while secularizing property worth £158,000. The secularized property was to pass in part to the University of Wales and the National Library, but mostly to the Welsh county councils, to be used for charitable purposes.

* The provisions of the existing Marriage Acts relating to marriages in registered buildings were to apply to marriages in churches of the Church in Wales.

† To this was to be added £31,000 per annum from the capital sums to be transferred by the Ecclesiastical Commissioners and Queen Anne's Bounty.

4. Life-interests were to be respected, and commutation permitted, for bishops, dignitaries, and incumbents; but no compensation was provided for curates.

5. The Church was to set up a representative body to receive and administer the property it was to retain; apart from this, it was to be free to create its own constitution.

8

WELSH DISESTABLISHMENT
THE ARGUMENTS

The struggle over Welsh disestablishment was a long one. The four Bills placed before the House of Commons spanned twenty years, and there was a period of agitation in Wales before that. It was a struggle fought with great persistence on both sides. It is true that the attack on the establishment declined in force and enthusiasm with the passage of time, but the hard core of Welsh Nonconformity, expressing itself through Welsh Liberal M.P.s, held on its course, and had sufficient influence (assisted by political circumstances) to carry the Bill of 1912–14 through all its stages. Similarly, on the other side, if the responses of the Conservative leaders became increasingly mechanical, the leaders of the Welsh Church itself, apparently with the widespread support of the clergy and many laymen, vigorously opposed all the Bills, using every available device of propaganda and obstruction. In this campaign they were supported by at least a solid core of English ecclesiastical opinion.

Of the two sides involved in this struggle, the forces of Welsh Nonconformity and the Liberal statesmen whom these forces drove along have already been sketched. A good deal of the pamphleteering for the cause of disestablishment was also still done by the Liberation Society, though as a political pressure group the Society's importance was much diminished by the turn of the century.

On the other side, the Church of England, as represented by the bishops and other leading clergy, and by the Church press, was almost united in resistance to Welsh disestablishment. The two Archbishops of Canterbury who held office while Welsh Disestablishment Bills were being promoted were Benson and Davidson, both profoundly attached to the idea of establishment. Of Benson, a friend (Henry Sidgwick) wrote that his conviction of the importance of the union between Church and State "was not due to any belief in the special value of Establishment to the English Church. . . . he was quite alive to the advantage which the Church would gain through disestablishment. . . . But he thought that this gain was entirely outweighed by the loss that the whole English people would suffer through the secularization of its public life." Benson said publicly that if the Church of England were disestablished, "he would prefer the establishment of another sect, holding the essentials of Christian doctrine, to a State formally irreligious".[1] As for Davidson, almost the whole of Bishop Bell's massive biography shows how fully he accepted and upheld the existing connection between the Church of England and the State. At the age of eighty, when these assumptions and traditions of a lifetime were put to the test of the rejection of the revised Prayer Book by the House of Commons in 1928, Davidson (in a joint statement with the rest of the bishops) declared the inalienable right of the Church, in the last resort, to formulate its own faith and arrange its own worship. But in presenting this statement to the Church Assembly, Davidson declared that he did not regard that principle "as in the least inconsistent with . . . the national position which the life-history of England has, thank God, accorded to our Church and has steadily maintained under all the changes of Parliamentary conditions".[2] Both these Primates, their minds impregnated with the traditions of the establishment and convinced of its value, threw their weight against disestablishment in Wales. Benson in particular, at a meeting at Lambeth in March 1893, set on foot a campaign in the country against Welsh disestablishment, and followed this up in 1894 by playing a prominent role in the creation of the Central Church Committee as a standing body to influence public opinion.[3]

Of the Church press, the *Record* was diminished in size and influence from its great days in the middle of the century, but still proud to call itself the watchdog of the establishment. It even tried on occasion to strike the same note as in the Irish Church controversy, writing for instance that the Welsh Suspensory Bill of 1893 could only pass by virtue of Irish votes—that is, by "the power of Rome".[4] Its opposition to Welsh disestablishment could be counted on. It is more interesting that the *Church Times* and the *Guardian*, which gave Gladstone general support over the Irish Church in 1868–9, opposed him over the Suspensory Bill of 1893 and continued to oppose the later Disestablishment Bills. There does not appear to have been nearly so great a measure of sympathy for Welsh disestablishment from the High Church party as there had been for Irish disestablishment. Lord Halifax in 1893, for example, addressed the English Church Union in support of the establishment in Wales, and appears to have met no opposition.[5] It is true that later Gore, as Bishop of Oxford, supported the Bill of 1912–14, making up in the quality of his own character and advocacy whatever was lacking in quantity, but on this issue it does not appear that he spoke for the High Church party as a whole.

The reasons for this change of attitude since 1869 are not wholly clear. They were probably in part ecclesiastical, in part political. Even at the height of the Anglo-Catholics' conflict with the jurisdiction of the State, between about 1874 and 1882, when clergymen were going to prison for their principles, the *Church Times* did not declare wholeheartedly for disestablishment in England and Wales. By the turn of the century it considered that the battle with Erastianism had been won, so that the establishment could be retained without pernicious effects. In 1895 it commented that one of the victories of the English Church Union had been "the death of Erastianism, as a living principle"; in 1913 it was confident that, if the Church knew its own mind, it could go its own way, State or no State.[6] On the political side, the *Guardian* broke with Gladstone on the issue of Home Rule for Ireland, and at least in part saw Welsh disestablishment as an extension of the Home Rule policy, tending to the separation of Wales from England.

In these circumstances, there were few among the prominent Anglican clergy who dissented from the prevailing attitude of opposition to Welsh disestablishment. Gore has already been mentioned as a distinguished dissentient. Another was Percival, Headmaster of Rugby and later Bishop of Hereford, whose churchmanship was of the Protestant variety but who was a Liberal in politics. (Many boys who had their names down for Rugby had them withdrawn after Percival wrote to *The Times* in May 1894 supporting the first Disestablishment Bill.)[7] But in general the support among the Anglican clergy was smaller in numbers and less distinguished in character than the minority which had followed Gladstone on Irish disestablishment. Looking at laymen as well as the clergy, the Liberal Churchmen's Union, whose secretary in 1895 was G. W. E. Russell, Under-Secretary at the Home Office under Asquith, was a small body which accepted the principles of disestablishment and disendowment, but sought to influence Liberal governments from within on points of detail.[8] During the committee stage of the 1912–14 Bill, Liberal Anglican M.P.s moved a number of amendments designed to moderate the terms of disendowment, including the acceptance of commutation. Thus Liberal Churchmen, though they could not exert as much pressure as Welsh Nonconformists, did have some constructive influence on the course of events.

The most active opposition to the Disestablishment Bills came from within the Welsh Church itself, led by two bishops who were skilled and belligerent in controversy, A. G. Edwards (Bishop of St Asaph from 1889) and John Owen (Bishop of St David's from 1897).[9] Edwards made his name by his activity in statistical polemics in the 1880s and 1890s; he later formed contacts and even some personal friendship with Lloyd George, and in 1906 and 1911 was inclined to accept disestablishment and seek a compromise on disendowment.[10] Owen was an effective pamphleteer, with a gift for the striking simplification of an issue—as when he hammered away at the slogan that the 1909 Bill would leave only 1s. 4d. in the pound of the endowments in his own diocese.[11] He was a pungent public speaker, stumping the country from Exeter to Middlesborough in the spring of 1912— though it appears that some English audiences had some difficulty in understanding him because of his strong Welsh accent.[12] He was also active behind the scenes in preparing the Church's case for the Royal Commission set up in 1906.[13] In the last years of the campaign against disestablishment, and during the period of suspense between 1914 and the Amending Act of 1919, personal relations between Edwards and Owen deteriorated somewhat, but in general they succeeded in presenting a united front.

One important point on which they differed was the question of the best tactics to adopt in 1911. The Parliament Bill, which deprived the House of Lords of its veto and left the power to delay a measure for two years, became law in August 1911. In March 1911 Asquith assured a deputation of Welsh M.P.s that after the passage of the Parliament Bill a Welsh Disestablishment Bill would be introduced in time to become law in that Parliament.[14] The Welsh Church thus faced for the first time the near certainty that the next Bill would succeed. It was actually before Asquith's undertaking that Owen and Edwards discussed by letter the question whether to fight to the end or to attempt a compromise. Edwards claimed to prefer to fight, but between the lines was clearly veering towards a compromise. He felt the Unionists to be weak, and the country as a whole apathetic on the issue of Welsh disestablishment. He wrote: ". . . if we are certain that the Bill will pass, shall we fight to the death and be 'flayed' or by terms save £40,000 a year for the Church? Personally I lean to the first alternative but it is a grave decision to make when the time comes." Owen had no doubt that they should fight: "The issues raised in Welsh disestablishment are too fundamental to admit of any compromise." Moreover, he thought they could win. He counted on the possibility of another election (even though there had already been two in 1910) and a Unionist victory, to be achieved partly by stirring up English opinion by making "a real good fight in Wales."[15]

In the event, both agreed to fight, and the struggle was kept up even in the very last stages of the Bill. When it had passed the House of Commons in three successive sessions, under the terms of the Parliament Act, and came to the House of Lords for the last time, the Welsh Disestablishment Bill was bound to become law whatever the Lords did. But Owen opposed any idea of accepting the Bill by allowing it to pass in the Lords, and instead suggested to Lord Lansdowne that the Lords should set up a select committee on certain aspects of the Bill, to secure a further delay of perhaps three weeks.[16] In fact this committee, accepted by the government on 25 June, was still in session on 4 August 1914.[17] (The proceedings of its last days make strange reading, as witnesses gave evidence about the collection of signatures on petitions against disendowment while Europe moved towards war. For those who had long seen Welsh disestablishment as the most important thing in life it was difficult to adjust their perspective, so that Bishop Owen wrote on 29 July: "The European situation absorbs everyone today, and we must watch lest it make the passing of the Bill easier."[18])

In thus keeping up the fight from 1912 to 1914, and using every device for delay, it appears that Welsh Churchmen were sustained by two possibilities. One arose from the extremely disturbed political situation, notably the great Irish crisis of these years, which made it possible that the government might be forced into a general election at any time. The second possibility was that of repeal, or partial repeal, of a Welsh Disestablishment Act. Bonar Law made remarks in the Commons on 28 April 1912 which offered hope of repeal;[19] and in a letter to Owen on 7 November 1913 he referred to the repeal of disendowment, and the return to the Welsh Church of the funds of which she would have been robbed.[20] Whatever the nature of repeal, whether total or partial, it could only be expected if Welsh Churchmen went on fighting, and refused to accept their fate under the Bill. In the event, in ways wholly unexpected by anyone involved at the time, the long fight and the delaying tactics brought some success. The war intervened to delay the date of disestablishment, and to necessitate a recasting of the financial provisions of the Act in ways which were on the whole favourable to the Church.

The attack on the Welsh establishment was maintained over a long period with the same tenacity as the defence. It is time to examine the arguments which were used, the justifications for so long a struggle. In a debate which lasted, on and off, for over thirty years, there was inevitably a vast amount of repetition, which seems to have palled even on some of the protagonists. The *Church Times* wrote about the debate on the second reading of the 1912 Bill that "the tame repetition of old arguments in the House of Commons produces a feeling of unutterable weariness".[21] Bishop Edwards in 1912, and Dr Kenneth Morgan from the perspective of fifty years later, have detected changes in the emphasis of the arguments, with the Liberals and Nonconformists making decreasing use of the argument that the Church in Wales was alien, and of old Liberationist arguments about the general question of establishment, while Conservatives and Churchmen relied decreasingly on the denial of a separate entity to Wales.[22] There is something in this view; but it remains true that all the arguments except those resting on some particular point of detail remained in use during the whole debate—the *South Wales News* even spoke of ending "the insulting dominance of an alien sect" on 31 March

1920, the day of disestablishment. As in dealing with the arguments on Irish disestablishment, therefore, an analytical summary appears the clearest way to present the substance of the debate.

The arguments may be grouped under headings as follows. First, the argument that disestablishment and disendowment were the national demand of the Welsh people. Second, the question of whether the Church in Wales was an alien Church. Third, the argument of numbers—that the Church in Wales was that of a small minority of the population. Fourth, the issue of whether an established Church was valuable or objectionable in itself—this was of course a general question, not confined to Wales. Fifth, the question of "dismemberment"—that the Church in Wales, when disestablished, would be forcibly separated from the Church of England and the Convocation of Canterbury, of which the four dioceses had long been part. Sixth, the argument about whether the State might justly appropriate Church property. Seventh, the question, following on from this, of how much damage the Church in Wales would suffer from the proposed measures of disendowment. Eighth, the comparison between the disestablishment measures in Ireland and Wales, which was used in argument by both sides. Finally, there were points of detail, which by sharpening bitterness affected the general character of the debate.

It was a fundamental argument on the Liberal and Nonconformist side that the Welsh people, through their parliamentary representatives, consistently and overwhelmingly demanded the disestablishment and disendowment of the Church in Wales. The evidence for this was plain in the parliamentary returns. In only one general election between 1880 and 1910 (that of 1895) did the Conservatives, the supporters of the established Church, return more than six M.P.s in the thirty-four Welsh constituencies. The Liberal party in Wales stood for disestablishment, and it followed therefore that the public demand thus expressed should be met. As Gladstone put it in debate in 1893: "I have an old Parliamentary habit . . . of looking to the constitutional representation of a country as the proper and legitimate organ of the expression of public opinion."[23] Similarly, Rosebery in 1894: "The case of Wales is the judgement of a country—a judgment so great as to be almost unanimous—for the removal of a branch of the Church of England which is alien to it. . . ."[24] Asquith too, introducing the

1909 Disestablishment Bill, argued from the consistent Liberal victories in Wales since 1880—at the time of his speech the Unionists held not a single seat in Wales, for the election of 1906 had given the Liberals a clean sweep.[25] Even when doubts arose on the extent of the disendowment, it could still be argued, as by the *British Weekly* on 11 January 1912, that "it is for Wales, which has so long and gallantly fought for religious equality, to decide what terms shall be offered".

This argument rested on the premiss that Wales was a distinct country, with a right to separate legislation to meet its special demands. Here the importance of the Welsh Sunday Closing Act of 1881 and the Welsh Intermediate Education Act of 1889 was firmly grasped. Precedents had been set which should be followed in the Welsh Church question.[26]

This argument from the will of the Welsh people expressed through their elected representatives was met in different ways. First, it was possible to dispute the premiss that Wales was a distinct country, as, for example, Hicks-Beach (by then an elder statesman in the Conservative party) did in 1894. He denied that "historically, Wales has any claim to be considered as a separate nationality at all. . . . Wales has not got the essentials, and never had the essentials, of a separate national existence"—which he defined as a recognized boundary, a capital city, and a single government for the whole country.[27] The *Church Times* (26 April 1912) was quite prepared to admit that: "If it [Wales] were a separate country with a separate legislature, there would hardly be room for any discussion at all; Disestablishment would be effected straightway by an overwhelming majority." But Wales was not a separate country. Even though there had been some special legislation for Wales in the past, the Parliament of the United Kingdom retained its responsibility for the whole country, and had not delegated any of it to Wales. Since there were good grounds for opposing the Bill for Welsh disestablishment, it remained right to resist it despite the demand in Wales.[28] This was essentially the position taken up by Davidson, the Archbishop of Canterbury, when he spoke at Caernarvon (in the heart of enemy territory) on 22 April 1912. He was variously reported as saying that the Welsh dioceses had a distinct character of their own, and that Wales was a national entity—which was not the same thing.

At any rate, he accepted that some change in the position of the Church was favoured by a vast majority of the Welsh people. But he went on to say that the case against disestablishment remained overwhelming on other counts.[29]

This was in fact a tenable position—to admit the strength of the demand for disestablishment in Wales, but to argue that this was not the decisive consideration. It appeared possible, however, to some defenders of the establishment to dispute even the fact of an overwhelming Welsh demand for disestablishment. It could be argued that the number of seats won by the Liberals in Wales was out of proportion to the number of votes cast, so that support for the establishment was greater than appeared by simply count-ing seats in Parliament.[30] It could also be said that the issue of disestablishment was not as prominent as previously in the general elections of 1900, 1906, or 1910.[31] As F. E. Smith asked in May 1912, did no one in Wales vote on the issues of Home Rule, the House of Lords, free trade, or industrial questions? Were the South Wales miners "really palpitating with the desire to transfer £170,000 from curates to museums?"* By 1914, petitions organized against disendowment could also be called in evidence. This argument could be extended if it were assumed that not only Welsh opinion, but that of the rest of the country, should be taken into account. The Bishop of Truro, for example, denied that there was any mandate in 1910 from the country as a whole for Welsh disestablishment.[32] The great issue in both the elections of 1910 was the position of the House of Lords, and Bishop Owen too could claim that in those elections disestablishment had been little debated in Wales and scarcely at all outside it.[33]

There was indeed a serious difficulty here, in the question of what exactly constituted a mandate for Welsh disestablishment, either in Wales itself or in the whole country. It is a problem in-herent in the whole system of British parliamentary democracy, for it is impossible to tell how far those who vote for a party actually support any given point in that party's programme. But

---

* *Parl. Deb.* fifth series, Commons, vol. 38, col. 803. This speech, which ended by claiming that the Bill had "shocked the conscience of every Christian community in Europe" (col. 820), has been remembered because G. K. Chesterton wrote a devastating poem on this last phrase. But taken as a whole it was a good debating speech, which scarcely deserved to be thus singled out.

it has never been contemplated that there should be a referendum on each individual Bill, and in fact the working assumption of British politics has long been that the electorate knows what each party stands for, and that a party with a majority in the House of Commons has the right to pass the legislation it thinks fit. In the terms of this assumption, there could be no doubt that Welsh Liberalism stood for Welsh disestablishment, and that successive Liberal governments included it in their programmes. The party, inside and outside Wales, naturally stood for many other things as well, and the prominence of Welsh disestablishment varied at different times, but these considerations were not important. In the parliamentary system as it worked, and still works, there was as much a mandate for Welsh disestablishment as for most items of legislation. It may be that the system should be made more directly and continuously democratic; but it would be hard to envisage the Conservative defenders of the established Church actually promoting a form of government by repeated referendum.

To dispute the mandate, then, was not a useful exercise. It was best to oppose the argument from the consistent demand of Wales through its M.P.s by acknowledging the demand, but holding that this could not in itself be decisive because other aspects of the question were more important. One way of doing so was to claim that there was simply no Welsh Church as such, only four dioceses in a wider Church. Therefore the question of Welsh disestablishment was not one in which Welsh demand alone could be met; it was a matter for England and Wales together, treating the Church as a single whole. This position had considerable support in both history and sentiment, and it also had the merit of turning the argument of self-determination against the Liberals, who were seeking to divide a body which wished to remain united. But this argument was open to the opposing contention that, if there was not a separate Church in Wales, then there ought to be, because the close union with England had been a source of weakness to the Church, putting it in the position of an alien body in Welsh society. This was, in fact, the argument for disestablishment on the ground that the established Church was an alien Church, and more than that, a positively anti-national force.

When the first Welsh Disestablishment Bill was introduced in

1894, the *South Wales Daily News* welcomed it with the pronouncement that "the offensive dominance of an alien sect" was to be ended.[34] Speaking on the Bill in the Commons, Lloyd George declared that:

> He could not conceive any deeper injury which [men] could inflict than to destroy that individuality of character, that sense of self-respect, that true manliness of spirit, which was the possession of every nation which had traditions, literature, and a language of its own. Yet that was what had been attempted by members of this Church from the 12th century downwards. Its consistent policy had been to destroy Welsh nationality; to use their [*sic*] spiritual position for the purpose of Anglicising the national sentiment of Wales.[35]

McKenna too, in 1912, went back to the twelfth century, invoking the authority of Giraldus Cambrensis to assert that the Churches in Wales and England had been united by the power of the Crown.[36] Others appealed to the seventh century and the Synod of Whitby; others again to the period of the Reformation. Most appealed to the eighteenth and early nineteenth centuries, when, it was held, the Church had been most heavily anglicized and when it had most obviously neglected its duty, allowing the people to lapse into irreligion until Nonconformity arose to take the place abdicated by the Church. The Church thus put itself outside the mainstream of Welsh life, isolated and alien. Even though there had been a revival of activity in the Church in Wales after about 1850, this was more among the English inhabitants of Wales than among the Welsh themselves.[37] Morgan Gibbon, a Congregationalist minister and a member of the Royal Commission on Welsh religious bodies from 1907 onwards, summed up a vast body of opinion when he wrote that the great Nonconformist Churches, taken together, were "the true national Church of Wales", reflecting Welsh national character and culture.[38] Vyrnwy Morgan, a Nonconformist minister who became an Anglican priest, in a book generally favourable to the Church of his second allegiance, accepted that to Welshmen the Anglican system represented English modes of thought and government.[39] This could be put more strongly, as by Sir Osborne Morgan, for long M.P. for East Denbighshire, who claimed that Anglicanism was incompatible with the Welsh temperament—"too cold for an emotional people, too aristocratic and Bishop-ridden for a democratic people".[40] Statistics bore out the strong connection between Nonconformity and the use of the Welsh language. Of the members of the four great Nonconformist denominations in Wales in 1906, three-quarters were monoglot Welsh-speaking or bilingual, and only a quarter monoglot English-speaking.[41]

The label of "an alien Church" was one which Welsh Churchmen resented, and they challenged its accuracy in all respects. They took up the historical arguments with vigour, reaching back into the mists of the early history of the Church in Wales to show that the Church of the nineteenth and twentieth centuries was the direct successor to the Church of the early Celtic saints, and thus truly indigenous to Wales.[42] The eighteenth and early nineteenth centuries were seen as an unhappy period from which recovery was well under way. They denied that the Church had at any time been anti-national, and Vyrnwy Morgan argued that on the contrary, without the translation of the Bible and Book of Common Prayer into Welsh in the second half of the sixteenth century (for which the Church was responsible), the fate of the Welsh language would have been the same as that of Cornish, into which these works were never translated.[43] They pointed to the number of services in Welsh provided by the Church, often out of proportion to the needs of the populations they served. The Bishop of Llandaff, for example, told the Royal Commission that in Glamorgan there were each Sunday 114 Welsh services and 657 English, though the population included only 37,000 monoglot Welsh against 369,000 monoglot English.[44] They counter-attacked on the issue of the Church's connection with England by arguing that of the Nonconformist denominations only Calvinistic Methodism could claim to be of native Welsh growth—the others were of English origin.[45] This was very much a debating point; but more serious was the fact that the four Wesleyan districts in Wales came under the authority of the British Wesleyan Conference in the same way as other districts.[46] The Wesleyan organization, like that of the four Welsh dioceses, was part of a larger whole, yet this did not prevent the Wesleyans from being accepted as a part of Welsh Nonconformity and the Welsh way of life.

The whole question of an "alien Church" turned, indeed, on what was meant by the Welsh way of life, on whether there were distinctive and exclusive characteristics of Welsh nationality and culture with which the Nonconformist Churches were identified while the Church in Wales was not. As Welsh society developed in the nineteenth century, there was no doubt that a great proportion of it, in the tenant farms and country towns of North Wales and in the industrial valleys of the South, was permeated with Nonconformity, on which social and cultural life was based. Nonconformity was thus identified with the most prominent and influential Welsh ways of life. Whether it was possible to say that nothing else could be Welsh seems very doubtful. There were different aspects of Welsh life and culture—North Wales, for example, differed in many respects from the South—and surely among these aspects there existed Church Wales as well as Chapel Wales. The Church in Wales showed a different kind of Welshness, but could scarcely be called alien except by some extremely rigid and subjective standard of purity.

Vyrnwy Morgan was willing to go further, and to claim superiority for the nationalism of the Church over that of Nonconformity, on the ground that it was less narrow. He held that it was a weak nationalism which tried to ostracize the stranger, and to keep out foreign culture, while a strong one welcomed and assimilated them. Popular nationalism in Wales, he wrote, tended towards "Celtic centralization and Celtic absolutism", whereas the nationalism of the Church rose above the racial level. Vyrnwy Morgan positively welcomed the union with England, as "politically the greatest blessing that has ever been conferred upon Wales". Subjection to England had been "subjection to a nation with a higher capacity for government".[47]

It can well be understood that some Welshmen would see in these remarks a denial of the Welsh national feeling which Vyrnwy Morgan claimed both for himself and the Church. None the less, the general point was an important one. Was not the assertion that the Church in Wales was alien tantamount to saying that the Church was not *narrowly* Welsh, not *merely* Welsh? The Church was alien to a particular Welsh way of life at a particular point in time, but it had roots in the country and was capable of growing more. Moreover, while in the nineteenth century there had been great strength for Nonconformity in its identification with that particular way of life and with the Welsh language, it was already clear at the beginning of the twentieth century, with the declining use of Welsh and the breaking up of that way of life, that this identification might be a source of weakness.[48]

It is difficult for an outside observer to see the Church in Wales in the years around 1900 as alien, except by criteria which are excessively rigid and exclusive. Yet it may well be that enough was proved in the case against the "alien Church" to make a valid argument for disestablishment. If the Church represented only one element in Wales, one aspect of a many-sided society, did it have the right to be the established, the national Church? To deny that right it was not necessary to prove that the Church was alien in any real sense of the word, only that it was not representative of the life of the nation, or even of the religious life of the nation. If the other parts of Welsh society did not accept the claim of the Church to represent the nation in its religious aspect, on what did that claim rest? As Gore, the Bishop of Oxford, said in 1913: "You cannot be the religious organ of the nation if the nation is standing against you and saying, 'We do not want you for our organ'."[49] In the first decade of the twentieth century, a large proportion of the population of Wales was indifferent to any form of religious observance; another large proportion was Nonconformist, and by that very fact repudiated the claim of the Church in Wales to be the national Church. The assertion that the Church was alien could not be made good, but it contained sufficient truth, when combined with the political demand discussed earlier, to make a powerful case for disestablishment.

In varying degrees both the issues so far discussed (the question of a national demand for disestablishment in Wales, and the question of the Church in Wales being alien) turned upon the question of numbers. During the whole long campaign the question of numbers absorbed vast energies and filled innumerable pages of print.[50] They were taken extremely seriously at the time, in one sense rightly, because figures provided the nearest thing to objective evidence in a sea of opinion. Even though it is to the present-day reader perhaps the most tedious and irritating element in the debate on disestablishment, the argument about numbers must be discussed here.

When Asquith introduced the Disestablishment Bill of 1894, he led off with the statement that "The Church of England in Wales is the Church of a comparatively small minority of the people."[51] This in itself, he believed, was a strong argument for disestablishment. Certainly it had been an important count against the Irish Church that it included only just over a tenth of the population of Ireland. A Conservative M.P. asserted in the same debate that Asquith's statement was false, and that Church members amounted to nearly half the population of Wales.[52] Various sets of figures were produced, purporting to make good these different positions.[53] Church defenders repeatedly demanded a religious census like that in Ireland in 1861, that is, the addition of a question on religious affiliation to the ordinary decennial census form. Nonconformists rejected this, on the ground that people who were not active members of any religious body, but who had been baptized or married in an Anglican church, would put themselves down in a census as Anglicans. A number of controversialists on the side of the establishment indeed made play with figures about baptisms and marriages, for example that between 1900 and 1908 nearly one-third of the children born in Wales were baptized into the Church, and that for the same years, of weddings in Wales, an average of 31·55% took place in churches, against 27·98% in chapels (the figure for registry offices was 37·52%, which might be thought more significant than either of the other two).[54] The value of such figures is very doubtful. Baptisms doubtless showed something about the residual connection of many Welsh people with the established Church. Weddings certainly showed that parish churches provided attractive surroundings for an important ceremony. A Liberal Anglican clergyman, J. Frome Wilkinson, in a pamphlet in 1894 supporting disestablishment, declared roundly that "to seriously count every man and woman whose marriage takes place in an Anglican church as Church folk would be unworthy of notice, if it were not dishonest".[55]

A more acceptable test was that of numbers of communicants. For communicant members, the Royal Commission produced the following figures for the year 1905:[56]

Baptists	143,835
Calvinistic Methodists	170,617
Congregationalists (Independents)	175,147
Wesleyans	40,811
Smaller denominations	19,870
NONCONFORMIST TOTAL	550,280
CHURCH OF ENGLAND	193,081

No organization providing figures for a Royal Commission in such circumstances as prevailed at the time would have understated its case, and it may safely be assumed that these figures are not too low. Nonconformist and Church members of the Commission alike thought that their opponents had inflated their numbers. Morgan Gibbon held that 160,000 was nearer the truth for Church communicants; Sir John Williams questioned the Church figures in an elaborate statistical appendix of his own to the *Report*.[57] Another Nonconformist member, J. H. Davies (the Registrar, University College of Wales) raised the question of the definition of a communicant in the Church. This had been left uncertain, so that some incumbents had returned regular communicants, some those who fulfilled the Church rule of three communions a year, some Easter communicants, some the numbers on a communicant roll. Davies remarked with justice that proof of one communion a year by a given person was an insufficient answer to a question about the use of provision for worship.[58] Archdeacon Evans and Lord Hugh Cecil raised similar points about the Nonconformist figures, in which there were problems of the distinction between "members" (taken as the equivalent of communicants) and "adherents", and of differences in the statistical methods used by the various denominations.[59] Evans and Cecil also pointed out that 1905 was a particularly favourable year for the Nonconformists because of the influence of the Revival of 1904–5, after which membership began to fall.[60]

Much skirmishing of this kind went on around the figures produced in the Royal Commission's *Report*, mostly by Church defenders, who were obliged to take the offensive. The advocates of disestablishment could content themselves with reiteration of numbers of communicants to show that the Church, despite its admitted progress in recent years, was still that of a small minority of the people of Wales. Often they added another set of figures given in the *Report*, those for accommodation:

Baptists	381,405 sittings
Calvinistic Methodists	447,907 sittings
Congregationalists (Independents)	446,932 sittings
Wesleyans	180,897 sittings
Smaller denominations	81,213 sittings
TOTAL NONCONFORMIST	1,538,354 sittings
CHURCH OF ENGLAND	458,917 sittings[61]

As the *Report* pointed out, there was in fact an excess of accommodation for public worship, given that the population of Wales at the 1901 census was 2,012,917. The very large accommodation provided by the Nonconformists gave them a better claim to be fulfilling one of the functions of a national Church than did the smaller number of sittings available in the established Church.[62]

The statement of figures of communicants and accommodation brought various replies from Church defenders. Bishop Edwards asserted that variations and discrepancies in the numerical arguments had surrounded it with an air of untrustworthiness[63]—as though discrepancies, which could certainly be found on both sides, were sufficient to cancel out a Nonconformist majority in communicants of nearly three to one. Another writer brought out figures which might perhaps, from the Church's point of view, have have been better left in obscurity: for example, that the percentage of the population in the diocese of St David's making their Easter communion in 1906 was 8·68, while the average for all dioceses in England and Wales was 6·28 per cent.[64] This was undoubtedly a good mark for St David's, but the logical conclusion would appear to be, not that the Church there was numerically strong, but that it was a little less weak than over the whole of England and Wales—presumably a point to those in favour of general disestablishment.

It was also stated that in the early years of the twentieth century the trend of Church communicant figures was upwards, while that of Nonconformist figures was downwards. The *Guardian* calculated that in 1912 the communicants of the four great Nonconformist Churches totalled 493,717, a decline of 36,693 from 1905. Easter communicants in the Church in Wales in 1912 were 159,252, an increase of 25,018 over those for 1905.[65] However, this process, even assuming it would continue, had a long way to go to make up the difference in numbers of communicants. What is interesting about these arguments is that they were used at all; Church defenders felt that they must try to meet the numerical argument in some way. Without much hope, they continued also to try to get away from the number of communicants by demanding a religious census in Wales.[66]

There was one argument advanced against the numbers of communicants which deserves more serious attention. It was one which linked the question of numbers with the issue of establishment as such, by holding that the significance of establishment outweighed that of numbers. Bishop Edwards estimated the total number of the four main denominations in Wales (members and adherents together) in 1911 at just over one million. Since the population of Wales was rather over 2,400,000, there were some 1,400,000 people unclaimed by the four leading Nonconformist Churches. Some belonged to smaller denominations, some were Roman Catholics; but after allowing for these there remained a large number. The Bishop did not claim all these for the Church, recognizing that many people in Wales went to no place of worship. But he did claim that these people were those in greatest need of pastoral care, and that they were more likely to receive it from the established Church than from other religious bodies. If religion entered at all into the lives of the indifferent, it would probably be through the Church—this, he argued, was the significance of the figures for baptisms and weddings in churches. Edwards asserted that particularly in the slum areas of big towns, only the Church could and did work permanently among the people. Essentially, however, he made the claim for the whole country: that as a result of the Nonconformist systems, which did not always provide a minister resident on weekdays in all areas, the clergy of the Church did "most of the real pastoral work of the ministry in Wales". The essence of this service was the parochial system, which covered the whole country, which the Nonconformist ministries did not. Edwards summed up his claims in the sentence: "The Church in Wales is everywhere; the Nonconformist bodies are only somewhere."[67]

The assumption among Church defenders was that the obligation to maintain the parochial system, and to care for the whole country, was connected with the fact of establishment: that these were responsibilities conferred by the fact of being the national Church. Lord Robert Cecil and H. J. Clayton, for example, held that while the establishment involved more restraints than privileges for the Church, these restraints were accepted because they accompanied the great privilege of "being able to render service to the whole of the nation".[68] This was certainly one of the most important arguments for the continuance of an established Church, and it has continued to be used since the controversy now under discussion.[69] It embodies a great conception: that the national, established Church has a mission to the whole of society. It has been claimed by Archbishop Garbett as "one of the glories of the Church that its clergy minister not only to a congregation but to all who live within the parish".[70] But it is open to serious question on at least two counts.

One was put by Bishop Gore in 1913. "The argument that an Established religion, an endowed religion, ministers to the relief of the poor is one which from my heart I wish I could accept." But he could not:

> ... it is impossible to have an intimate acquaintance with our country districts or our towns without recognising that the Church of England has not succeeded in becoming the Church of the poor, as is the Roman Catholic Church in so many parts of Europe, or the Salvation Army, or Primitive Methodism. ... the argument about the Established religion being the religion of the poor, and being enabled by its established and endowed position to provide for the religious needs of the whole community, is an argument that, when looked at in the light of experience, we ought to use indeed with very bated breath. In England it is an argument which we can only use with profound humiliation, whether we think of the country or of the towns.[71]

Gore may have overestimated the success of other Churches, and of Churches in other countries, but his point about the Church of England remained sound.[72] The second objection is that it is quite possible for an unestablished (or a disestablished) Church to have the same conception of a ministry to the whole of a people, to the whole of society.[73] Conversely it is perfectly possible for clergymen of an established Church to become in practice, if not in theory, simply priests and pastors to a congregation.

None the less, this defence of an established Church was constantly used and deeply held. The archbishops and bishops, in a public letter of May 1894, wrote that the Welsh Disestablishment Bill would deprive the poor in Wales of their legal right to a free place in the parish church and to spiritual services from a clergyman.[74] The *Church Times* in 1913, though recalling that the Tractarians had inclined towards disestablishment, held that the real issue was "whether it is for the eternal welfare of a large part of the population to be deprived of the ministrations of religion".[75]

The second great argument used by Churchmen on behalf of the establishment was held with equal depth of conviction. This was the importance of the national recognition of religion embodied in the fact of establishment. Vyrnwy Morgan, acknowledging the position of his opponents on the question, wrote that something essential underlay the case of each side: "on the one hand spiritual independence, and on the other the national recognition of religion".[76] An English Nonconformist clergyman, Fovargue Bradley, who wanted disestablishment without disendowment in Wales, was ready to admit that the idea of a national Church represented an ideal—"the preserved and perpetuated identity of the State with the nation's religion".[77] It has already been noted how Archbishop Benson shrank from "a State formally irreligious",[78] and this view was widely shared by Churchmen. Two further examples may illustrate it, one from outside the Church in Wales and one from within it. First, Welldon, the Dean of Manchester (formerly Bishop of Calcutta, and before that Headmaster of Harrow), believed that "the maintenance of a national Church is a matter of high and sacred principle", affecting the character of the State in the eyes of other countries, the position of religion in education, and the parish system.[79] The second example is Owen, Bishop of St David's, who held that disestablishment meant setting national life on a secular basis, which was "a violation of the Divine principles of Society".[80] He argued that since religion was the greatest power promoting morality, and the State was concerned with the morality of its citizens, then the State was clearly concerned with religion. A national act such as Welsh disestablishment would set the tone in society; and at a time when the forces of materialism were strong, as Owen felt they were before 1914, then a repudiation of the national recognition of religion would be particularly dangerous. He even hoped for some recognition of this view from Nonconformists, and put forward the idea of "a broad readjustment of the relations of the State to religion as a whole as would give Nonconformist denominations as well as the Church of England such a just recognition from the State as they might each desire . . .".[81] This presumably amounted to a suggestion for some form of joint establishment.

It is doubtful whether any Nonconformists would have been interested in such a solution. The gulf which history had placed between them and the idea of establishment was too great. The arguments usually used against establishment were those of the Liberation Society. They were summed up by the *South Wales Daily News* (28 February 1895): that a State Church secularized Christianity and degraded the Church; and that it conferred special privileges on its members, and so inflicted injustice on those who were not. The arguments of David Caird in 1912 were essentially the same. He put first the demand for religious equality, "for impartiality and justice on the part of the State towards all citizens irrespective of religious belief or practice", which he argued could not be satisfied "until the State assumes a position of complete neutrality towards all Churches and all creeds". He held too that establishment was inconsistent with the nature and dignity of a Church. State control robbed a Church of its liberty and weakened its influence, because no Church could be true to itself while allowing a secular body to order its affairs.[82]

The views on disestablishment of Fovargue Bradley, who was a rare moderate in a debate which bred extremism, are of particular interest. He was not convinced by the argument against disestablishment that it would break up the parochial system and so do harm to the poor and the religiously indifferent. He argued that, if it required the force of law to secure a clergyman's services to any particular class or person, then those services were no longer spiritual. In fact, the parish system had already broken down in the cities, and the establishment had certainly not saved it.[83] He thought the establishment worked against the interests of religion by making the ordinary layman a man without rights, dependent for his parson on the patron of the living, and for his bishop on the Prime Minister.[84] The history of the establishment, moreover, had left on Dissenters scars which they could not easily forget. The Church had never conceded to them any liberty as of right, only under compulsion.[85] He found, indeed, no matter-of-fact argument for the union of Church and State, and felt it was defended only by "that same antiquarian sentiment which holds all national relics dear, whether a decorative part of our constitution, a Crosby Hall, a Cranmer Bible, or a first edition of Shakespeare".[86] This was not enough, and he held that the Church should be disestablished, in England as well as in Wales, but left its endowments and allowed to get on with the good work he knew it was doing.

It was a powerful case, with behind it a tradition and outlook wholly different from those which formed the minds of Archbishop Benson and Bishop Owen. (Benson, for example, was well aware of the dangers and abuses of the patronage system,[87] referred to by Bradley, but saw them as much less important than the imponderable benefits of the union of Church and State.) The whole question was one in which most men were guided less by rational argument than by instinct, tradition, or prejudice. But it would appear that the weight of rational argument lay with Bradley, and with Bishop Gore.

It was commonly said by Welsh Churchmen that they faced not only disestablishment but dismemberment. The Welsh dioceses were part of the province of Canterbury, a union which was the product of a long history and which was to be broken against the will of the whole body. Gladstone had said in 1870 (and his words were kept green by controversialists for the Welsh Church) that: "There is a complete ecclesiastical, constitutional, legal, and . . . for every practical purpose historical identity between the Church in Wales and the Church of England."[88] It was argued strongly that to compel the Welsh dioceses to sever their connection with Canterbury, and to set themselves up as a separate body, was a violation of the religious freedom which Liberationists claimed to be promoting.[89] It was pointed out that Nonconformists sought to impose on the Church in Wales a separation which they did not all accept for themselves. For example, a Wesleyan witness to the Royal Commission said that separation of the Welsh districts from the Wesleyan body in the whole country would be injurious to them.[90] Again, Sir Henry Lunn noted that the Free Church Council opposed the establishment of a separate Free Church Council for Wales, while supporting the separation of the Welsh dioceses from England.[91]

Bishop Owen, with a rather surprising lack of confidence in his fellow-countrymen, looked forward with foreboding to the prospect of separation. He wrote to the Archbishop of Canterbury in 1909: "What I dread most is the dreadful apparition of a Welsh Synod, messing about with the big, complex, and far-reaching questions which now perplex all the combined wisdom of the Church of England." He feared too the growth of "tribal jealousies" and "nationalistic vanities" in a separated Welsh Church.[92]

19

Archbishop Davidson, from his side, told a select committee of the House of Lords that Convocation and its committees were "the real workshops of the Church"; that the Welsh contribution in them was valuable; and that to remove the Welsh members would impair the work of the Church.[93]

To the advocates of disestablishment, these complaints and forebodings were exaggerated. After all, the dioceses of the province of York were also cut off from the Convocation of Canterbury, and yet they managed their affairs well enough. The Church in Wales after disestablishment would still be in communion with the Church of England, and could work out some free or informal association with it—if it wanted to. The Welsh Church might find instead that it stood better on its own feet, clearly a national body and able to deal with the problems of Wales.[94]

The various Welsh Disestablishment Bills intended not only to disestablish the Church in Wales and detach it from the province of Canterbury, but also to disendow it, to an extent which varied with the different Bills. The case for and against disendowment, the question of whether the State had the right to divert all or part of the property of the Church to other purposes, was vigorously argued. It is likely that there was more movement of opinion on this issue than on most of the others; certainly a number of English Nonconformists pronounced against substantial disendowment between 1911 and 1914. The conclusions of the conciliation committee convened by Sir Henry Lunn, which worked from December 1911 to May 1912, were particularly notable. This committee, composed of thirty-two members, Church and Nonconformist, clerical and lay, recognized that there were differences of opinion on the justice of both disestablishment and disendowment, but was able to agree (with only four dissentients, two Church and two Nonconformist) on recommendations for moderating the disendowment provisions of the Bill of 1912. These included proposals that glebe land should be left to the Church; that burial grounds be left, subject to equal rights for use by all parishioners; that commutation be permitted for life-interests derived from the tithe rent-charge (which was still to be secularized); and that there should be some protection for the interests of curates.[95] It has already been noted that the disendowment provisions of the 1912 Bill were in fact amended, though not to the extent suggested by

Lunn's committee. This movement of opinion, however, does not appear to have been widely shared in Wales. Welsh Liberal M.P.s protested against the concessions, and a deputation visited McKenna to warn him against further compromise.[96]

The case for disendowment was primarily that of the Liberation Society, taken up and echoed by others.[97] The fundamental issue was not one of the power of the State to disendow a Church, because the power of the State when working through statute law was unlimited, and had in fact frequently been used to appropriate or redistribute the property of both individuals and corporations. The Irish Church Act of 1869 was an obvious precedent for secularizing the property of a Church. More recently, the Churches (Scotland) Act of 1905 had distributed property, which by a ruling of the House of Lords as late as 1904 belonged to the Free Church, between that body and the United Free Church.* The power of the State in such matters could not be doubted, and it was in fact exercised. The question was whether the exercise of this power in any particular case was just or not.

In the Liberationist view, 1662 and the Act of Uniformity marked an important dividing line in the question of endowments. After that date, any person who gave an endowment to a Church, of whatever denomination, knew that he was giving to one body among several. Before that date, only one Church had existed in the eyes of the law, and gifts had been made to a body which in law included all the people in the country—to the nation in its religious aspect, in fact. These latter endowments, intended for

---

* In 1900 the United Presbyterian Church joined with the majority of the Free Church (formed in 1843) to form the United Free Church. A minority in the Free Church refused to accept the union, and appealed to the courts on the ground that they, not the majority, represented the true Free Church. In 1904 the House of Lords ruled in favour of the minority, who therefore had good legal claim to all the property of the Free Church. The Act of 1905 divided the property and funds of the Free Church between the two parts, in an attempt at an equitable solution. See A. J. Campbell, *Two Centuries of the Church of Scotland, 1707–1929* (Paisley 1930), pp. 304–7; J. R. Fleming, *A History of the Church in Scotland, 1875–1929* (Edinburgh 1933), chapter V; J. N. Figgis, *Churches in the Modern State* (London 1913), pp. 18–22, 32–9. As Figgis pointed out, the Lords, though claiming not to judge matters of theology, in fact did so on the question of seeing whether or not the trust deeds of the Free Church had been violated. In upholding the trust deeds, the Lords in effect denied to a "free church" the power of self-development.

the benefit of the whole people, remained in the hands of a Church which in Wales included only a minority of the people. It was therefore just that they should be restored to the service of the whole people.* A particular historical argument was built up about tithe, to the effect that in Wales it had always been a tax enforced by the civil power for the benefit of the Church, introduced as a result of the Norman conquest of Wales. This argument was not, however, essential. The essence of the position was that all ancient (pre-1662) endowments, given for the benefit of the whole people, were national property, and therefore the State had every right to regulate its use and transfer it to new ownership in order to ensure that it was used for the benefit of all.† This was a line of argument which was accepted even by a few Anglican clerics, notably by Bishops Percival and Gore, and by Frome Wilkinson.[98]

In addition to this general ground for disendowment, Caird also chose to challenge the moral right of the established Church to its pre-Reformation endowments on the ground that these had been given to a Church different in doctrine and organization from that of the nineteenth and twentieth centuries. He held that this undermined the moral value of the Church's prescriptive right arising from long possession.

These arguments were essentially those which had been used to justify disendowment in Ireland. The replies by Church defenders were also similar to those used in the earlier controversy, but with less emphasis on the rights of property as such. Broadly, the defence of the endowments of the Welsh Church took three main lines. The first was historical, disputing the Liberationist argument about the origins and nature of ancient endowments. Bishop Edwards, for example, argued that the tithe neither originated as a tax nor with the Norman conquest, holding that law had only

---

* Cf. Lloyd George, preface to Wilson, *Welsh Disestablishment*, pp. ix–x: "If the Church ceases to be the National State religion of Wales, it will no longer be justifiable that endowments and impositions which were designed for the benefit of the whole nation should be diverted to the use of a comparatively small minority of its people."

† This was sometimes put in a more extreme form, for example, by the *South Wales Daily News*, which wrote (13 March 1893) that church property "is property impressed with a public trust, and its trust deeds are Acts of Parliament. . . . It is held by State officials for public uses. . . ."

confirmed custom and secured payment of what originated as voluntary gifts. More important, he produced evidence to show that early and medieval endowments were as much private as those of later date, made by individuals to particular parish churches. He also sought to prove that the Church in Wales received its endowments either before it acknowledged the supremacy of Rome or after it renounced it, so that they were not granted to a Church identified with Rome.[99]

The second line of argument was from the Church's contemporary use of its endowments. The claim of the established Church was that the endowments were being used for the purposes for which they had been given. They were not abused nor mismanaged; there was no damage to the public good; and they were not too large—indeed they were insufficient—for the work that had to be done. It was indeed the fact that the Church in Wales (unlike the Irish Church before 1869) had to raise large sums by voluntary giving. Bishop Basil Jones, Owen's predecessor at St David's, started a diocesan fund to increase stipends in rural parishes. Owen continued this work, and by 1903 had brought all stipends in the diocese up to a minimum of £200 per annum, which was by no means excessive.[100] The Church was therefore fulfilling the trust on which the endowments were given, and there was no valid reason for the State to interfere with the property.[101] On this matter numbers were held to be irrelevant. As a Conservative M.P. put it in 1894, "The property was honourably held and properly administered ... whether the numbers be small or great ... no case had been made for touching these endowments."[102] Outside the ranks of the ordinary Church defenders, Fovargue Bradley, who advocated disestablishment, opposed disendowment fundamentally on this ground. He thought that the main question was whether the Church in Wales was in such a state—religious, moral, and in its influence upon the public good of Wales—that it justified drastic disendowment in the public interest. He was clear that it was not in such a state, but that on the contrary it was doing effective work for the spiritual and moral welfare of the Welsh people—and he was able to quote Welsh Nonconformist opinion in his support.[103]

Bradley also used the third line of argument against disendowment, which was based on the uses to which the secularized funds

were to be put. Bradley thought that it was wrong, and an acceptance of mere materialism, that man's physical environment should
be improved "at the sacrifice and loss of a Church".[104] Others
argued that the improvements in environment would themselves
be marginal, of a kind which might well be provided out of the
rates or out of general taxation. It was indeed a fact that some of
the purposes for which the secularized funds were to be allotted in
the Bills of 1894 and 1895 had already been provided for out of
public funds by the time the next Bill was introduced in 1909.[105]
It would be equally possible for the Exchequer to provide the sort
of sums which would be released by disendowment and scarcely to
feel the expense. Bishop Owen put it, with his usual pungency and
particularity, thus: that, when Lloyd George said that national
endowments would be restored to national purposes, he meant
that the United Kingdom Exchequer would be relieved to some
small extent, and that all tax-payers (not just Welsh ones) would
be spared to the extent of perhaps one-thirteenth of a penny in the
pound. This did not mention that sums of money were intended
to pass into the hands of Welsh local authorities, presumably to
the benefit of the Welsh ratepayer; but the general point was sound.
Public funds could provide with ease the sort of sums involved,
but their loss to the Church would be serious. Or, as the Bishop
wrote, "The State does not need this money. The Church does."[106]

All in all, these were strong arguments. The Church had the
better of the historical debate, though questions about the Celtic
Church and the Middle Ages were too remote to influence opinion
widely. The argument that the Church was fulfilling the trust on
which the endowments had been given, doing its work effectively
and without abuse of its funds, was the most significant point
against disendowment. If it was held to be true, then the government's moral right to interfere with trust property being properly
used was highly dubious. What this argument did not deal with,
however, was the opposing point that what had been given for the
benefit of the whole people was being used for only a minority. A
judgement on the relative weight of these opposing arguments,
each with its own validity, was difficult to make. In making it, it
was fair to take into account not only questions of moral right but
that of the use being made of the funds by the Church and that to
which they would be put when secularized. Here it seems that the

Church had at the time the better of the argument. It could point to work, spiritual and material, actually being done, as against unspecified charitable purposes to be devised in the future by Welsh local authorities.[107]

There was another issue involved in disendowment: that it meant the secularization of property and funds devoted to religious purposes. Even if one accepted the view that the ancient endowments of the Church had been given for the benefit of the whole Welsh people, it could still be held that they had been given to a Church, and should not be diverted to secular bodies and purposes. One possible answer to this by the advocates of disendowment, at any rate for the earlier Bills, was that at least some of the purposes specified for the use of funds were what Frome Wilkinson called "gospel purposes"—the care of the sick and the poor.[108]

It was arguable that a better solution would be concurrent endowment, an idea much discussed during the debates on the Irish Church. The Bishop of Hereford, Percival, argued consistently for a scheme to distribute the ancient endowments of the Church between the various denominations—a task which he maintained would have to be done afresh from time to time, to keep endowments in fair proportion to numbers and work done. But he got little reponse from Convocation when he spoke about it in 1895, nor from McKenna in 1912. McKenna insisted that concurrent endowment was out of the question because the Nonconformists would not have it—as neither Nonconformists nor Catholics would in the case of Ireland.[109] It was possible to argue, as did a correspondent of *The Times* in 1910, that in fact the poorer Nonconformist chapels in Wales would welcome a redistribution of endowments, whatever their leaders said, but this was hard to prove. Certainly this particular letter, which suggested leaving the Church with £100,000 per annum from its endowments and distributing the remainder to the other Churches, evoked little response.[110]

In the report stage of the fourth Welsh Church Bill, in February 1913, an amendment was moved to allow the revenue of the Church to be used for the advancement of the Christian religion through the various denominations in Wales. It was lost by 278 votes to 167.[111] The vote in its favour was large, but this probably amounted for the most part to a party move to obstruct the Bill or to save endowments for the Church. There was little life in the idea of concurrent endowment, which did not receive even the same degree of support as in the case of Ireland in the 1860s. Welldon, who would himself have preferred concurrent endowment to secularization, recognized that antipathy to the idea was deep-rooted in Britain.[112] One difficulty, of course, was that the idea was only brought out, in Wales as in Ireland, when the endowments of the Church were under attack, so that it had all the appearance of being merely a device to save some of the Church's property, however sincere many of its advocates undoubtedly were. It may well be that in any case the religious, social, and political differences between the different Churches were too great to allow the idea to work.

The most serious aspect of the discussion about disendowment was thus on the question of whether or not it was justifiable. There was a further subsidiary controversy about disendowment, concerning the extent of the damage which the Church would suffer from it. This was mainly an argument conducted by Churchmen, who predicted disaster. The *Record*, for example, between 23 February and 6 April 1894, printed the views of 188 Welsh clergymen, the vast majority of whom asserted that disendowment would bring disaster on the religious life of Wales by crippling the Church's parochial system. The *Record* itself assumed that the effect of disendowment as embodied in the Bill of 1894 would be to close churches in many parishes where funds could not be raised to maintain them.[113] About the disendowment clauses of the Bill of 1909, Bishop Owen wrote that 511 benefices in Wales would be left without any endowment, and another 132 with less than £10 per annum each.[114] The *Church Times* asked in 1913 "whether it is for the eternal welfare of a large part of the population to be deprived of the ministrations of religion"[115]—a question again based on the assumption that disendowment would mean the break-up of the parish system.

On the other side, it was customary to describe the terms of the various Bills as fair, or even generous. Sir David Brynmor Jones, a Nonconformist member of the Royal Commission on the Church and other religious bodies in Wales, said in 1911 that the Church could not expect greater mercy on endowments than was shown in "the reasonable proposals" of the Bill of 1909[116]—which were the same as those of 1895. Asquith described the Bill of 1912, as originally devised, as "a very generous measure to the Church".[117] McKenna, introducing that Bill in the House of Commons, argued that its financial effects would be much less severe than its opponents made out, and would in any case be gradual in their impact, so that the Church would have plenty of time to provide for the transition. Only at the end of perhaps forty years would the full effects of disendowment be felt. He calculated, indeed, that including the endowments to be left to the Church, the capital sums which the Ecclesiastical Commissioners and Queen Anne's Bounty were willing to hand over, and the value of life-interests (which he put at £62,000 per annum), the Church would still retain the equivalent of £180,000 per annum.[118] A similar calculation was made by Caird. He ignored the life-interests, calculated that the Church would retain £118,000 from endowments and capital sums, and added £296,000 for voluntary contributions (taking the figure for 1906). He thus arrived at an income after disendowment of £414,000 per annum.[119] It could thus be argued that while the income of the Church in Wales would be diminished by disendowment, it would be far from vanishing altogether. Amendments to the Bill of 1912, indeed, gave further concessions to the Church.*

One point about these differing views is that they often referred to different Bills. McKenna and Caird were discussing the Bill of 1912. The correspondents of the *Record* in 1894, and Bishop Owen in 1911, were discussing earlier proposals, which had been far more severe. The Bill of 1909, along with its predecessor in 1895, left to the Church only private endowments since 1662, estimated by Bishop Owen at the time as worth nearly £20,000, and by McKenna in 1912 as worth £18,500.[120] There was little discrepancy here, and these provisions were indeed very severe. So Churchmen denounced these swingeing measures; then, later, Nonconformists remarked on the generosity of the Bill of 1912. It is fair to say that Churchmen were unduly pessimistic as to what they could achieve by a voluntary system. Equally, Noncon-

---

* The revenue of which the Church would be deprived under the original Bill of 1912 was £173,000; under the Bill as amended, £158,000—see above, p. 253.

formists and Liberal ministers were too blithe about the effects on
the Church of losing what, even when all concessions were made
and all sources of income taken into account, amounted to over
a quarter of its total revenue.

Churchmen also argued that disendowment meant, as well as
loss of money, loss of valuable independence, because it would
mean the reliance of clergymen on their congregations. They used
again the argument advanced in the Irish Church controversy,
that endowments allowed clergy to be independent, free if need
be to take issue with their people. Bishop Edwards compared this
alleged freedom with the position of Nonconformist ministers in
Wales, subject, he wrote, to "the petty tyranny of ignorant
elders".[121] The argument is worth mentioning simply to show that
it was still being used. It ignored the fact, plain in the reorganized
Irish Church, that a system could be devised by which a clergyman could be paid, not directly by his congregation, but by a
central body not susceptible to local pressures. It also begged the
question of the significance of independence—of whether a country
rector was really more likely to cross the local squire than a
minister his elders. This was surely a matter of temperament more
than anything else.

On this point the experience of Ireland was ignored. On some
other matters, however, the precedent of Ireland was frequently
cited by both sides in support of their own positions. For advocates
of Welsh disestablishment, the Irish Church Act obviously
demonstrated the power of the State to deal with an established
Church, and it provided useful practical guidance. Apart from
this, they tended to use the case of the Irish Church in two somewhat contradictory ways. Firstly, they claimed that the results
of disestablishment and disendowment on the Irish Church had
been beneficial. There had been a new surge of life and activity,
and substantial voluntary giving. The laity had taken a full part
in church affairs, without becoming tyrants. Caird thought that
the ministry was of lower quality and less independent, but saw no
other adverse effects.[122] A source frequently cited in these arguments was an interview which the Archbishop of Dublin, Plunket,
gave to the *Western Mail* on 3 November 1892, in which he gave
an account of events in the Irish Church since disestablishment
which was on the whole favourable—though the Archbishop was

careful to say that this was no reason to subject the Church in Wales to the same treatment.[123] It followed from this line of argument that the disasters predicted by Church defenders were figments of the imagination; disestablishment and disendowment could almost be made to seem a stimulating and refreshing experience to which the Welsh Church ought to be looking forward.

But secondly, advocates of Welsh disestablishment also held that the financial arrangements of the Irish Church Act had been too generous. In particular, accusations of the wholesale manufacturing of curates in the Irish Church on the eve of disestablishment were frequently repeated, and were the main ground for refusing any compensation for curates under any of the Welsh Disestablishment Bills.[124] Also it was said that the terms for commutation in the Irish Church Act had been too generous, so that until a very late stage commutation was refused in the Welsh Bills. There seems to have been some misunderstanding about the procedures of the Irish Church Act. An article in the *South Wales Daily News* on 2 December 1910, for example, confused commuting and compounding, and gave the impression that the proceeds from compounding went entirely to the Representative Body of the Irish Church, whereas they were in fact divided between the Representative Body and individual clergymen. Opinion on these points was so strong that the first three Welsh Bills were more severe in their financial provisions than the Irish Church Act. The fourth (the Bill of 1912) was probably less severe than the Act of 1869, because of the funds it allowed the Church to keep from the Ecclesiastical Commissioners and Queen Anne's Bounty. It also ultimately allowed commutation. This argument about overgenerosity in the Irish Church Act took some of the force out of the assertions about how the Irish Church had flourished after disendowment. For if the Welsh Church were to be dealt with less generously, there was presumably less chance that it would thrive so well.

On the other side, the main tactic of Welsh Churchmen was to tackle the comparison with Ireland at its root by denying that there was any proper analogy between the two situations. Bishop Edwards argued the case thus. Ireland was an island, in which the Church of Ireland included only a fraction of the people, confronted by a great homogeneous Church which had some right to call it alien. Moreover, before 1869 the Irish Church was rich, with endowments far too large for its work. Against this, the four Welsh dioceses were not separated by any physical barrier from the English dioceses, and indeed included parishes in English counties. The Church in Wales formed the largest single religious body in Wales, and was faced not by one Church but by several different ones. Finally, the Church in Wales was comparatively poor, and already had to make considerable voluntary efforts to sustain itself. There was therefore, Edwards claimed, no effective point of comparison.[125] To this could be added the historical argument that the Welsh and English dioceses had grown together far in the past, whereas the union of the Churches of Ireland and England had been brought about artificially by statute, and was therefore more easily and justifiably reversible.[126]

As well as denying the analogy, Church defenders denied that disestablishment and disendowment had benefited the Irish Church. If their opponents could quote Archbishop Plunket, they could produce other quotations. Bishop Edwards in 1895 collected letters from other Irish bishops on the ill effects of the Irish Church Act, about decreasing numbers and crippled work.[127] In 1912 the Archbishop of Armagh (Crozier) spoke to M.P.s at the House of Commons to deny that his Church had benefited from the Act. He pointed to the fall in the numbers of clergy; explained how the numbers of Churchmen had fallen in the country areas; and, perhaps most important, asserted that the undoubted activity and vigour of the Irish Church had been part of a general movement, common to England and Wales as well as to Ireland—to attribute it to disestablishment was therefore misleading.[128]

In general, the protagonists on each side merely took from the case of Ireland what they needed to support their own arguments. Nonconformist controversialists propagated misstatements about curates in the Irish Church, and underrated the tremendous difficulties caused by disendowment. Church defenders made effective replies to their opponents' specific points on Ireland, but do not appear to have considered how the Irish precedent affected some of their own general arguments. Did Bishop Owen, for example, examine Ireland to see whether disestablishment there had really meant setting national life on a secular basis; or did Archbishop Benson seek to discover what difference it had made in Ireland when the State became "formally irreligious"?[129] The Irish experience might have shown too that some of the forebodings about the consequences of disestablishment and disendowment were wide of the mark: that it was possible, for example, to keep up a parochial system so that people were not left without pastoral care.

Looking on from Dublin, the *Church of Ireland Gazette's* main reflection on the Bill of 1909 was that the Irish Church had received better terms than were proposed for the Welsh Church, and that there was an apparent desire to damage the Church beyond repair.[130] Such a view, arising from all the first three Bills, was widely held by Welsh Churchmen also. The impression that there was hatred and vindictiveness behind the Bills affected the whole controversy from the Church side. The impression arose from two main sources. One was simply the very severe disendowment clauses of the first three Bills. The other was a variety of events and statements, mostly in the 1890s. There was, for example, a draft scheme for disestablishment and disendowment produced in 1893 by Thomas Gee, the North Wales Nonconformist leader. This was extremely drastic, not recognizing life-interests, and proposing to secularize the cathedrals (and in one version to deprive the Church of all churches built before 1820).[131] In the Commons in 1894, Lloyd George too attacked the provisions in the first Welsh Disestablishment Bill for compensating the clergy.[132] He was supported by the *North Wales Observer* (4 May 1894), which thought that there should be a fixed term of ten or fifteen years, after which the Church's funds should automatically be turned to secular purposes.

In the same Commons debate it was noted that Bryce, winding up for the government, refused when pressed to say that the cathedrals (which were under the 1894 Bill to be treated as national monuments) would continue to be used *exclusively* for the services of the Church.[133] Carvell Williams, acting for the Liberation Society, argued that if they were national monuments they should not be used by only one religious body. He also wanted all churches to remain in the hands of the Welsh Commissioners, and be used only on condition of being kept in good repair.[134] In the event, the government did not take this advice, and indeed allowed an amendment to the Bill of 1895 which allowed the Church to keep the cathedrals. But the impression created by the incident was not effaced.

Fovargue Bradley, himself a Nonconformist, wrote in 1911 that the circumstances of the nineteenth century, and the once justifiable bitterness of Dissenters against the Church, had caused Welsh Nonconformists to seek disendowment (as well as disestablishment) as the best means of striking at their old enemy, of inflicting on the Church the poverty which they themselves had suffered in the past.[135] Most Nonconformist controversialists denied this, insisting that they had no animus against the Church but only against the establishment. Their opponents felt that this was too high-minded to be true, in view of Welsh demands for extensive disendowment, and protests from Welsh M.P.s when in fact concessions were made on financial points during the committee stage of the 1912 Bill. Nor did such protestations square with statements such as that by Llewellyn Williams, that "Disestablishment without Disendowment is not worth asking for, much less fighting for".[136]

This fear of vindictiveness on the part of both the government and of individual opponents of the Church showed itself in some discussion of the reorganization of the Church after disestablishment. For example, C. A. H. Green (then vicar of Aberdare, later Archbishop of Wales), whose writings on the general controversy were able, clear-headed, and in no way alarmist,* pointed out in 1911 that the Bill of 1909 had only stated that the King in Council *may* grant a charter to the Representative Body constituted by the Church. This, he argued, would admit of infinite delay in the restoration of property to the Church. All Church property was legally to be vested in the Welsh Commissioners at the date of disestablishment. Until the Representative Body was incorporated, the Commissioners would hold the property, and the clergy would not even have assured right of entry into their churches. The Bill thus gave opportunity for delay and harassment, which Green believed the Church had reason to expect.[137] The *Church Times*, too,

---

* For example, Bishop Edwards wrote that the 1912 Bill would "leave the whole organisation, the discipline, and the standards of the Church in Wales in a state of chaos" (*Landmarks*, p. 261). Green held that, whatever Bills said, there would remain the fundamental order of the Catholic Church—episcopacy could not be abolished—Green, *Disestablishment*, p. 6.

pointed out that the Representative Body was to represent the laity as well as the clergy of the Church. It was quite possible to define a layman as a baptized Christian living in Wales (the *Church Times* claimed this was the only definition it knew), which would include all the enemies of the Church, including, for instance, Brynmor Jones, who was reported to have said that he would seek election to the new controlling body of the Church.[138]

Certainly, as far as the government was concerned, these fears seem to have been without foundation. The Church was allowed the same freedom as the Irish Church had been to frame its own constitution, and the condition that the Representative Body should be representative of bishops, clergy, and laity meant no more than it had in Ireland. Indeed, on another occasion even the *Church Times* pointed out that McKenna himself had more regard for the true interests of the Church than some of the Church's defenders in the House of Commons. Lord Hugh Cecil, for instance, wanted more parliamentary intervention in the process of forming a body to draw up a constitution than the Bill provided.[139] Yet there was some reason for the fears to be found in the past attitudes of Welsh Nonconformists—attitudes which were themselves built up over generations of national, social, and religious conflict with the established Church.

In all this protracted and bitter controversy there were few who paused to consider whether both Churchmen and Nonconformists were not spending on the battle energies which they needed for other work. During the long years of the disestablishment campaign, Wales was entering the post-Christian era; yet Christians found it more important to fight one another than to grapple with their common problems. Miss Eluned Owen records an episode in 1888–9, when a few Churchmen (including the future Bishops Edwards and Owen) and Nonconformists began to meet privately to discuss the problems of combating doubt in Wales. When they planned a public conference to discuss their ideas, newspapers attacked them on the ground that the movement was a device to hold up disestablishment. The conference was not held, and the group died.[140] Perhaps an indirect defence of the establishment did form a motive on the Church side; yet there was here a tentative move towards co-operation which might have had wider results if it could have survived. Much later,

Bishop Owen was to assert that if the gospel was to retain its power in Wales, then "those who believe in it, Churchmen and Nonconformists alike, will have to stand, shoulder to shoulder, against our common enemy".[141] (The enemy he had in mind was materialism.) He appealed to Nonconformists to consider disestablishment and disendowment in the light of their agreement with Churchmen as Christians, and to reflect that their conflicts were a grave hindrance to Christian work in Wales.[142] The trouble was that these appeals, however sincere, were in fact produced in the course of a campaign to protect the Church's position and endowments—a campaign in which Owen was one of the toughest protagonists, a fighting bishop who enjoyed the fight. However sincere Owen was, it was virtually impossible for him to *appear* sincere in such circumstances.

Sir Henry Lunn was in a different position. Ordained a Wesleyan minister in 1886, and later nominally a minister of the Methodist Episcopal Church of America, he worked for much of his life for Christian unity. From 1891 he was editor of *The Review of the Churches*; he sponsored the reunion conferences at Grindelwald; and he was already conscious in 1911 of the significance of the Edinburgh Missionary Conference of 1910, which he mentioned when he proposed a conference on the Welsh Church. When Lunn claimed that the motive for his attempt at conciliation was the damage being done to religion, no one could doubt his sincerity, and his personal prestige helped to gather a distinguished conciliation committee together. But even so it was an English committee. The Welsh Nonconformist leaders refused to join, as did Bishops Owen and Edwards, Owen explaining that he was opposed to disestablishment on principle and therefore could not discuss a compromise.[143] Both sides in Wales were committed to the battle, and wanted no peace without victory. It may be that in the actual situation in Wales they were right, in the sense that perhaps co-operation between Christians could not come about there until the issues of establishment and endowment had been fully worked out and cleared out of the way.

9

WELSH DISESTABLISHMENT
ANTI-CLIMAX

The Welsh Church Question during the War, 1914–18

The British declaration of war on Germany on 4 August 1914 occurred while the fourth Welsh Disestablishment Bill was being held up by the select committee set up by the House of Lords to examine certain of its aspects. Archbishop Davidson and Bishop Owen feared at first that Parliament would be prorogued, which would result in the automatic passing of the Bill under the terms of the Parliament Act.[1] This did not come about, but the Bill was still placed on the statute book in circumstances which left a lingering bitterness in the minds of Welsh Churchmen.

On 10 August Asquith moved the adjournment of the House until 25 August, hoping then to introduce proposals on outstanding business which might meet general acquiescence.[2] The two great controversial issues were Home Rule in Ireland and the Welsh Church, and it was for these that he sought to reach an arrangement. On 14 September he gave notice of a Bill "to provide that no steps shall be taken to put either of the two Acts [Irish Home Rule and Welsh Disestablishment] into operation for twelve months in any event, and if the War is not then terminated until such further date, not later than the date of the termination of the War, as may be fixed by Order in Council".[3] However, when the Suspensory Bill was introduced on 15 September, its terms differentiated between the Home Rule Bill and the Welsh Bill. The operation of the Home Rule Bill was simply postponed, but for the Welsh Bill only the date of disestablishment was postponed.[4] This meant that all the major provisions of the Bill for disestablishment and disendowment were postponed, but other clauses which took effect before the date of disestablishment would come into force at once. These included the provisions for the interim period, notably that no new appointment in the Welsh Church should

20

carry with it a life-interest. The Commissioners of Church Temporalities in Wales would also be appointed, and would carry out the early stages of their work. Moreover, during the interim period, the Church would have to create its Representative Body, ready to receive property on the date of disestablishment and to decide the question of commutation.

Archbishop Davidson protested against this arrangement as soon as he saw a copy of the Suspensory Bill on 15 September. He believed that it was contrary to assurances he had received privately, as well as to Asquith's statement of 14 September. He wrote to Asquith:

> With regard to the Welsh Bill the proposal now before me differs altogether from what I quite clearly understood to be the arrangement you intended to make, an arrangement communicated to me by the Ld. Chancellor [Haldane] a few days ago. What I had understood—& I markedly pressed the Ld. Chancellor on the subject— was that *everything* was to be hung up for a year, i.e. all the work which has got to be done prior to the "date of disestablishment".

But, he continued, all the Bill did was to put off the date of disestablishment, leaving all the Church's preparations for that event to go on during the war, when its best men would be away. "Can this really be what you intend? If so—well, I do not know what to think or say. I write of necessity in utmost haste, having only *this moment* received the Bill."[5] It is a measure of the effect of the Suspensory Bill that it so disturbed Davidson's normal massive calm. He wrote again later the same day to apologize for the confusion and abruptness of his letter, but he held to the view expressed in it. He hoped that there was simply an error, and that Asquith would allow an amendment to the Suspensory Bill.[6]

There was at the least here a grievous muddle, made by the government. It appears that, by a failure to use words precisely, Asquith and others said they intended to postpone the whole Bill when in fact they meant to postpone only the date of disestablishment. Haldane indeed told the Archbishop of Canterbury that he thought it had been understood that the whole of the Welsh Bill was not to be postponed, but Davidson denied it.[7] Certainly Asquith's statement in the Commons on 14 September was misleading unless it was intended to suspend the operation of the whole Bill.* Some Welsh Churchmen believed that there was not muddle but deliberate deception. Bishop Edwards said in December 1914 that "The Government has dealt very treacherously with the Welsh Church", and he had not changed his mind when he came to publish his memoirs in 1927.[8] In all the press of events in August and September 1914, when the government was grappling with the problems of war and anxiously watching the German invasion of France, muddle was a more likely explanation than deception. Whatever the explanation, the government's deeds certainly differed from Asquith's words of 14 September, and new resentment was added to a subject which already suffered from a surfeit of it.

The Welsh Church Act and the Suspensory Act together placed the Welsh Church in a difficult position during the war. There were the problems of working in wartime conditions, and also uncertainty about when the war would end and bring the date of disestablishment with the peace. On this question, people often predicted an early victory, and so believed that the time available for reorganization would be short rather than long.[9] On the other hand, the leaders of the Church made their situation even more difficult by refusing to accept the *fait accompli* of the Welsh Church Act, and so not settling single-mindedly to prepare for the date of disestablishment. They continued to seek further postponement, with in the background still the hope of repeal.

During the war, in fact, the leaders of the Welsh Church followed two lines of action which were to some degree self-contradictory. On the one hand they sought by political means for postponement or even repeal, and on the other they were impelled by common prudence to frame a constitution in case the Welsh Church Act did come fully into operation. These courses were contradictory because to prepare for disestablishment was by implication to accept the Act, and so to prejudice the chance of repeal. Watkin Williams, the Bishop of Bangor, felt the contradiction very strongly, and opposed making preparations, writing

---

* Cf. Asquith to King George V, 11 August 1914: "It was considered as at least possible that a settlement might be arrived at on the basis of passing the two Bills (Welsh and Irish) into law, accompanied by a Suspensory Act preventing either of them from coming into operation for a specified time. . . ." Asquith Papers, vol. 7, f. 161.

to Frank Morgan on 12 May 1916: "The greater the chaos on the date of Disestablishment the better our case for Repeal."[10] Frank Morgan, a history don at Keble College, Oxford, who was a close friend of Bishop Owen and later to be the Secretary of both the Representative Body and the Governing Body of the Church in Wales, disagreed profoundly. He foresaw only danger if, through the fault of the Church, the Welsh Commissioners were unable to transfer property to a constituted body on the date of disestablishment. He believed, moreover, that by that time the Welsh Church question was *chose jugée*, and that even a future Conservative government would do little to change matters.[11]

However, despite the contradiction, and despite the views of Williams and Morgan in their different ways, the dual policy was followed. In 1915 it seemed that there was a real chance of the postponement of another portion of the Welsh Church Act. On 9 March 1915 the government introduced in the House of Lords a Bill to fix the date of disestablishment at six months after the end of the war, and, more important, to allow appointments made during the interim period to carry with them a life-interest. This was to relieve the Church from the diminution of its compensation payments which would occur by the death, retirement, or departure of incumbents with life-interests, and their replacement by new men with no claim to compensation under the Act. The Bill was introduced subject to an agreement between Asquith and Bonar Law that, before the new date of disestablishment, there should be no attempt to repeal or amend the Welsh Church Act without the consent of both parties.[12] The government thus sought to secure itself against total or partial repeal in the future by yielding the point about compensation rights.

The Postponement Bill, as it was called, passed all its stages in the Lords in one day. Lord Beauchamp, for the government, told Lord Lansdowne that the Commons could take it with similar speed the next day, 10 March,[13] but in fact amendments to the Defence of the Realm Act occupied the House on that day, and the Bill did not come up until 15 March. There was at this point a strange, almost grotesque, revival of the Welsh Church controversy in the midst of war. It had already begun in January and February 1915, when Sir Henry Lunn sent Asquith two memorials signed by Nonconformists, one asking for the repeal of disendowment, the other supporting an attempt by the Duke of Devonshire to postpone the whole operation of the Welsh Church Act. Lunn argued that, when the country could spend £350,000,000 in a week on the war, it was absurd to take less than £2,000,000 from the Welsh Church.[14] He was at once assailed by the *South Wales Daily News*, which told him that the demand for disendowment was "the demand of a people", and that the Church had "through the centuries been anti-national". It asked why "Free Churchmen in England assume to have a voice in this matter", and told them to mind their own business.[15] However, help was not refused when English Nonconformists took the right side. It happened that on 10 March 1915 the National Free Church Council was meeting in Manchester, and (rather surprisingly in view of the movement of English Nonconformist opinion before the war) protested against the Bill, and sent a deputation to call on McKenna.[16]

In the Commons Asquith and Lloyd George spoke for the Bill, Lloyd George telling his fellow-Welshmen that after the war the nation would be occupied with great questions of reconstruction and would be impatient of sectarian controversies. But despite this the Welsh Liberals protested against the Bill, both on financial grounds and because they feared that six months after the end of the war would be long enough to allow a Conservative government to take office and repeal the Welsh Church Act. The Bill was put off for further consultation, and withdrawn on 26 July 1915.[17] Lord Robert Cecil thought that the government had broken an absolute undertaking to get the Bill through the Commons. Asquith, however, had taken the precaution of writing on 9 March, that, while he did not think the Welsh members would oppose the Bill, they might ask for time for further consideration. Balfour thought that Lord Beauchamp had certainly made a muddle.[18] So had McKenna, who only on 21 January had given an assurance that there would be no interference with the Welsh Church Act of 1914.[19] So both Welsh Churchmen and Welsh Nonconformists felt they had been let down, with much justification.

The procedures of the Welsh Church Act and the Suspensory Act of 1914 thus remained in force. An order in Council of 14 September 1915 postponed the date of disestablishment until the end of the war.[20] During 1917 attempts were made by Lord

Robert Cecil and Bishop Owen to secure a further postponement of the date of disestablishment. They led nowhere, though they once again revealed confusion in the government when on 15 May Lord Crawford accepted postponement, to be disavowed by Bonar Law (speaking for the coalition government) on 17 May.[21] Bishop Owen, in a letter to Bonar Law of 13 March 1917 asking for postponement of the date of disestablishment, showed that behind this request there still lay wider hopes. He reminded Bonar Law that in 1913 he had undertaken to repeal disendowment, and expressed confidence that Law's influence would secure an equitable reconsideration of the Welsh Church Act before it came fully into operation. Bonar Law did not commit himself.[22] Postponement of the date of disestablishment, then, remained for Owen at any rate a stalking-horse for a far-reaching amendment of the Welsh Church Act. This was a legitimate aspiration, and it was equally legitimate for Welsh Nonconformists to try to prevent its achievement.

Efforts to modify the Welsh Church Act and the Suspensory Act thus came to nothing. The second strand in the policy of Welsh Churchmen was to prepare for this very eventuality, and to organize themselves for disestablishment. As in the case of the Irish Church, the most urgent task was the creation of a Representative Body to which the Welsh Commissioners could return the property which the Church was to retain under the terms of the Welsh Church Act. It was less urgent, but would ultimately be necessary, to devise an organ to which the Representative Body would be responsible.

The initiative for action lay with the Welsh bishops, who in November 1914 decided to call a joint meeting of the four Welsh diocesan conferences, which should be asked to set up a committee to do the preliminary work on a constitution, and to report back to the diocesan conferences. The meeting took place at Shrewsbury on 19 December 1914, and a joint committee was duly appointed, consisting of the four bishops, eighty representatives of the dioceses, and sixteen co-opted members.[23] The committee secured the services of three judges, Sankey, Bankes, and Atkin, who gave invaluable help in planning the work of the committee and drafting the elements of a constitution. The unwieldy body divided itself up into sub-committees to deal with various aspects of the problems before it.[24] The broad decision was reached to create a Representative Body to hold and administer the Church's property, and a Governing Body to exercise general legislative and administrative authority in the Church.[25]

The work of preparation thus went systematically forward, but it was none the less bedevilled by the question of how far the process should go so as not to prejudice the chances of repeal. The Bishop of Bangor adopted an extreme position in November 1916. The joint committee was under instructions to report back to another meeting of the four diocesan conferences; but the Bishop of Bangor stood out, refusing to call his diocesan conference. He gave way only in May 1917, after the government had again rejected the postponement of the date of disestablishment.[26] It was then agreed to hold a Convention at Cardiff in October 1917, to which the recommendations of the joint committee would be submitted. This Convention, on which the diocesan conferences conferred plenary powers, consisted of a hundred representatives from each diocese—the bishop, thirty-three clergy, and sixty-six laymen. Bishop Edwards, as the senior bishop, presided.[27]

This Convention was the decisive point in the preparations for disestablishment. It faced still a difference of opinion on how far the constitution-making should proceed, and also a cleavage between North and South Wales. It had before it the proposal of the joint committee to create the two main organs of the new constitution, the Representative Body and the Governing Body. But the Bangor representatives recommended that a final decision on the Governing Body should be postponed, and only the Representative Body be set up at that meeting. This arose partly out of the question of prejudicing repeal, but more out of the problem of the relations of North and South. The proposal put before the Convention by Sankey was that representation on the Governing Body should be according to numbers of communicants and clergy, in the following proportions: Llandaff 6, St David's 5, St Asaph 4, Bangor 3. There were protests against this plan from both the northern dioceses, which were in danger of being in a perpetual minority. A compromise was reached, by which the equal representation of all dioceses on the Governing Body was accepted in return for Bangor withdrawing its opposition to the creation of the Governing Body at that meeting. The proposals for setting up the Representative Body, on which all dioceses were to be equally represented, went through smoothly.[28] At this meeting too the title of the Church in Wales, which had been used in the Welsh Church Act, was adopted.

A real point of difficulty was thus successfully passed, and the main lines of the new constitution were laid down. The Convention also proved decisive in that it marked in practice the point at which the Church accepted disestablishment. It is true that Bishop Owen before the meeting, and both Owen and Edwards afterwards, were emphatic in their denials that this was so; but in fact a change of attitude was visible to both friends and enemies of the establishment.[29] From that time on, the tempo of the work quickened markedly. In January 1918 the first meetings of both the Representative and Governing Bodies were held, and in September 1918 there was an important meeting of the Governing Body, which accepted a recommendation from the Representative Body to accept commutation.[30] The Governing Body also decided on a confirmation franchise for voting in the Easter vestries, the lowest of the electoral bodies. Questions of modes of appointing clergy and the form of their tenure of office were discussed; but decisions were postponed, except for the important decision of principle that bishops were to be elected in some way by the whole Church, and not by the diocesan conference of the diocese concerned, as was at first proposed.[31] This was an important difference of principle from the method adopted in the Irish Church, reflecting the fact that the Church in Wales, despite the suspicions between North and South, was a smaller and more cohesive body than the Church of Ireland.

It is interesting to see the view taken of the consequences of disestablishment by Bishop Owen during the year 1917–18. In an article in the *Western Mail* of 26 September 1917, he still maintained that disestablishment was damaging to the nation, but he went on: "The mission of the Church to the nation, remember, was given it by its Divine Head. Parliament neither gave this mission nor can take it away in the least degree." He repeated this a year later in an unsigned article in the same paper on 23 September 1918, and he also wrote in the same month that, if the Church applied wisely the principles for its structure to be found in the Prayer Book, it had before it "the greatest opportunity in all its history".[32] This was different from his position before 1914.

The fighting bishop was accepting disestablishment, and moreover denying that the establishment itself was necessary to enable the Church to fulfil its mission to the nation.

While the Church was thus gradually framing its constitution and preparing for the date of disestablishment, the Welsh Commissioners pursued their own work in readiness for the same event.* They collected information on the nature and extent of the property of the Welsh Church, and on exactly which parts were to be secularized and which restored to the Church.[33] They carried out, in March 1916, a tiny plebiscite to ascertain the wishes of the parishioners of nineteen parishes which were situated partly within Wales and partly outside it. Ballot papers were sent to men in the services. Eighteen of the parishes voted to be united with the Church of England.[34] The Commissioners worked industriously—indeed there is something incongruous in the picture of the three Commissioners and their staff working quietly in London among all the activity of the greatest war in history. But when they came to write their fourth report, in 1919, it was plain that they could not finish their work in the time laid down by the Welsh Church Act, which limited the life of the Commission to 31 December 1919.[35] On this ground alone, therefore, it became necessary to amend the Welsh Church Act.

The prolonged delay of the date of disestablishment also had a number of effects which meant that the Welsh Church Act would not have the exact consequences intended when it was passed, and so made a case for its amendment. Firstly, the Welsh Church continued to have the full benefit of its endowments for longer than intended by the Act, which brought some financial advantage to the Church. Secondly, the date on which the Representative Body would receive the commutation capital was delayed, so that the Church lost the income it would have received from the interest on this capital. Thirdly, the delay diminished the total value of the existing life-interests of the Welsh clergy, and hence diminished

---

* The three Commissioners were Sir Henry Primrose (chairman), Sir John Herbert Roberts, and Sir William Plender. Sir Herbert Roberts resigned in 1915 when he became leader of the Welsh Liberals in the House of Commons. The number was not made up to three again until 1921, when C. L. Forestier-Walker was appointed. On the death of Sir Henry Primrose in 1923, Sir Arthur Griffith-Boscawen was appointed chairman. There were other changes, and the signatories of the final *Report* were Wynn P. Wheldon and Megan Lloyd George.

the commutation capital, because under the Welsh Church Act only incumbents holding office at the date of the passing of the Act were entitled to compensation. By 31 December 1918, over 140 life-interests had lapsed through incumbents dying, retiring, or leaving Wales. They had been replaced by others who were still temporarily receiving income from endowments, but were not entitled to a life-interest.

Fourthly, the position of the tithe rent-charge was transformed during the war. In 1914 the value of tithe stood at £77 per £100, but being tied to a septennial average of the price of cereals it rose rapidly during the war, and in 1919 stood at £124. This increased the income of the Church for as long as it continued to receive tithe rent-charge. The Tithe Act of 1918 changed the position further. The Act fixed the value of tithe at £109 for a period of seven years from 1 January 1919; then from 1926 onwards it was to be assessed on a fifteen-year average of cereal prices. The Welsh Commissioners were uncertain in 1919 whether, for purposes of compensation, the tithe would be calculated according to the Tithe Act of 1918, at £109, or according to the Welsh Church Act, at the septennial average under the old system, which, if the date of disestablishment fell in 1919, would be £124. In the latter case the Welsh county councils would certainly lose by the transaction instead of gaining. In order to pay the commutation capital to the Church Representative Body, the Welsh Commissioners would have to raise a large loan. The repayment of this loan, with interest, would be the first charge on the tithe rent-charge which the county councils would receive. The county councils would be receiving tithe rent-charge at the rate of £109 until 1926, but might be meeting the charges of compensation paid at the rate of £124. Even if compensation were calculated at £109, the county councils would face the difficulty that interest rates had risen sharply during the war, so that it was quite possible that the repayment of a loan even to meet the lower figure would absorb all the income from the tithe rent-charge.[36]

It followed from these consequences of the delay of the date of disestablishment that all the parties concerned in the disendowment of the Welsh Church wished to see the Act of 1914 amended. The Welsh Commissioners needed more time to complete their work, and clarification of the question of the tithe rent-charge.

The county councils needed the same clarification, and might well also need some amendment to save them from the ironical fate of losing money when they had expected to gain. The Church probably gained financially from the delay, because the rise in the value of tithe more than offset the lapse of vested interests, and there was also the prospect of being able to invest the commutation capital at the high rates of interest prevailing at the end of the war.[37] But it was commonly held at the time that the Church was losing through the delay, and in any case Churchmen, as has been seen, always hoped for a favourable amendment of the Act, or even for its repeal.

Politicians too by 1918 had an interest in amending the Act rather than letting it stand. The matter had become a nuisance. Lloyd George and Bonar Law wished to maintain their wartime coalition when the war ended, and difficulties over the Welsh Church, while they would not be important, might be irritating when added to other problems. What might happen was shown by a leading article in the *Daily Express** on 29 August 1918, declaring that people could not vote in the dark in a general election, and asking what Lloyd George's views were on tariffs, Ireland, and the Welsh Church. "Is the Welsh Church to be sacrificed simply because the party of spoilers just tottering to its fall over the Irish crisis of 1914 was saved for a moment by the outbreak of the great war?" Lloyd George wrote the same day to Bonar Law that the reference to the Welsh Church was deliberately introduced to make it impossible for him to arrange matters with the Unionist leaders.[38] The picture was surely overdrawn, both by the *Daily Express* and by the Prime Minister, but there was some truth in it. The Parliament at the end of the war was still that elected in 1910, and over 180 Unionist M.P.s signed a memorial to Bonar Law to show their uneasiness about the Welsh Church Act.[39]

The question was resolved by agreement. A letter from Lloyd George to Bonar Law, dated 2 November 1918, set out the terms on which they would co-operate at the coming general election, and contained the following reference to the Welsh Church:

Finally, there is the question of Welsh Disestablishment. I am certain that nobody wishes to reopen religious controversy at this time. The

* This was the London *Daily Express*, not the Dublin *Daily Express* cited in chapters 2–5.

Welsh Church Act is on the Statute-book, and I do not think that there is any desire, even on the part of the Welsh Church itself, that the Act should be repealed. But I recognize that the long continuance of the war has created financial problems which must be taken into account. I cannot make any definite proposals at the present moment, but I do not believe that once the question of principle no longer arises it will be found impossible to arrive at a solution of these financial difficulties.[40]

Bishop Edwards had seen Bonar Law on 22 October, and told him that Welsh Churchmen wanted amendment of the disendowment clauses, not repeal of the Act.[41] Edwards and Owen together had been informed of the text of this part of the letter in advance; it appears that Edwards was satisfied by its contents, while Owen was not.[42] The arrangement proved generally acceptable in the coalition, though Lord Robert Cecil resigned from the government rather than accept it.* Thus a policy of amending the Welsh Church Act was generally accepted. It remained to be seen what sort of amendment would come about.

The Amending Act, 1919

Bishop Edwards had interviews to discuss terms for amendments to the Welsh Church Act, with Bonar Law in January 1919, and with Lloyd George in February. It is not clear what he asked for—his own account is that it was a capital sum of about £1,500,000; Miss Eluned Owen writes that it was £2,500,000.[43] In April 1919 the Church Parliamentary Committee asked for a modification which would have cancelled the whole effect of disendowment: that the endowments should pass to the bodies to which they had been assigned, but that the Exchequer should repay the Church in full for the loss.[44] These sweeping proposals met no reply from

---

* Lord Robert Cecil did not regard disestablishment as being very serious, but disendowment was another matter. ". . . the taking away of endowments, much needed for the work of the Church, which had belonged to her for centuries, seemed to me, as it still seems, quite indefensible, and I decided to resign rather than make myself responsible for such a step" (Lord Robert Cecil, *All the Way* (London 1949), p. 146). Cecil's resignation at this point threatened to cut him off from his work to create a League of Nations, to which he was deeply committed. He was saved from this sacrifice by Lloyd George, who allowed him to go to Paris with the British delegation.

the government. The transition from war to peace, and the negotiations for a world settlement in Paris, occupied all energies, and
in the new Parliament elected in December 1918 there was no
great interest in the Welsh Church. So in fact nothing was done
to produce an amending Bill. On 6 June Edwards agreed with the
Home Secretary, Shortt, on 1 April 1920 as the new date for disestablishment; but that was all.[45]

Events began to move when Lloyd George came back from
Paris, at the end of June 1919. Edwards at once went to see him,
though at first no results were achieved.[46] There were further
delays, and then suddenly on 24 July Bonar Law told Edwards
that he must get a draft Bill ready to give the Prime Minister
on 26 July. Edwards called in Owen and Frank Morgan; they
found someone with experience in the drafting of legislation; and
after an all-night session on 24–25 July a draft Bill was taken to
the printer.[47] It was an extraordinary procedure thus to hand over
the details of drafting to a tiny group of Welsh Churchmen, even
though they operated within terms generally agreed with Lloyd
George, and did not insist on all their own demands.

The resulting Welsh Church Temporalities Bill, commonly
called the Amending Bill, went quickly, though not without some
difficulties, through both Houses. Most of the opposition came
from Conservative Churchmen, especially the Cecils—Lord Hugh,
Lord Robert, and the Marquess of Salisbury. On the second
reading in the Commons (6 August 1919), the Bill was carried by
182 votes to thirty-seven, with only three Welsh Liberals voting in
the minority, along with thirty-four Conservatives.[48] In the Lords,
amendments were carried in committee to return all graveyards
to the Church and to leave the withdrawal of the Welsh dioceses
from the Convocation of Canterbury to the choice of the Welsh
Church. But these amendments were rejected by the Commons,
the peers accepted the position, and the Bill received the Royal
Assent on 19 August 1919.[49]

The provisions of the Amending Act of 1919 were as follows.
The existence of the Welsh Commissioners was extended, and the
new date of disestablishment fixed at 31 March 1920. The Act laid
down that the life-interests whose capitalized value, under the
commutation scheme, was to be paid to the Representative Body,
should include all those existing at the time of the passing of the

Welsh Church Act—that is, they would include all those interests which otherwise lapsed since 1914.[50]

The Act also provided for a grant of £1,000,000 to be paid by the Exchequer to the Welsh Commissioners to help them to meet the payment of the commutation capital to the Representative Body. Commenting on this clause, the Welsh Commissioners wrote that without it the scheme of disendowment laid down in the Act of 1914 and amended in 1919 could not have been carried out in its entirety. The Commissioners had to raise a loan to pay the commutation capital to the Representative Body of the Church, and the value of the property alienated from the Church would have been insufficient to provide security for this loan. The Commissioners wrote that: "There would have been an end of disendowment in any effectual sense. The property of the Church would have been transformed both in character and in tenure, and would have been diminished by the cost of effecting the transformation. But no portion of it would have been available for appropriation to secular purposes."[51] The Exchequer grant meant in effect that the government gave the Commissioners £1,000,000 so that the Commissioners could pay the Church the commutation capital without depriving the county councils of all benefit from the process of disendowment. This amounted on the one hand to a government grant towards commutation—which was a sort of re-endowment—and on the other to a government grant to the county councils, made in a strangely roundabout and delayed manner. Delayed, because even under the Amending Act, given the size of the loan to be serviced and repaid, the county councils would not enjoy the revenue from the secularized Church property until 1950.

The clauses of the Amending Act which did much to make the Exchequer grant necessary were those which dealt with the question of the tithe rent-charge. These laid down first that the value of the tithe rent-charge for purposes of commutation was to be that of January 1920, using the method of the septennial average —that is, for this purpose the Tithe Act of 1918 was to be ignored. The value by this process proved to be over £140.* It was next provided that the value of the tithe for the purpose of calculating the annuities of the Welsh clergy was to be that fixed by the Tithe

* The exact figure was £140 12s. 7d.

Act of 1918, £109. As the Welsh Commissioners pointed out, the Amending Act thus prescribed that identical words in the Welsh Church Act of 1914 should be interpreted in one sense for commutation and in another sense for the payment of annuities to those who had commuted. The beneficiary, receiving the difference between the two methods of calculation, was the Representative Body of the Church in Wales, to which the commutation capital was paid. The Welsh Commissioners, in their dealings with the tithe rent-charge, were bound by the Tithe Act of 1918, setting the value at £109. They therefore received tithe rent-charge at this value, while paying commutation calculated at the higher value of £140. Without the Exchequer grant this would not have been possible.[52]

The financial effects of the Amending Act, and its final scheme of disendowment, on the Church in Wales are extremely difficult to assess. The man in the best position to do so, having helped to draft the Act and then seen the results of it as Secretary of the Representative Body of the Church, Frank Morgan, said in 1935 that the task was "almost impossible".[53] A calculation depended on the value of tithe rent-charge, of land and houses, and of investments; the last of these depended on interest rates as well as on the value of the securities involved. A difference of one per cent on the interest received on the commutation capital, for example, could make a difference of some £35,000 in the income of the Welsh Church. There was also the question of the subsequent history of the tithe rent-charge in England, which would have to be borne in mind in estimating the relative position of the Church in Wales as against what it would have been if it had kept its endowments.

In 1919, Bishop Owen estimated that the Amending Act deprived the Church in Wales of a revenue of £48,000 per annum from its ancient endowments, whereas the Welsh Church Act of 1914, if put into force in 1919, would have deprived it of at least £102,000. He reckoned that, of the difference, £30,000 came from the adoption of a double basis for the value of tithe rent-charge, and another £22,500 from the vested interests which would otherwise have lapsed.[54] This estimate was used for practical purposes at the time. At a meeting of the Governing Body in January 1920, Bishop Edwards launched an appeal to make good the losses of disendowment, giving the figure of £48,000 per annum and hoping to raise a sum of £1,000,000 to replace this revenue.[55] Bishop Owen was always careful in his calculations, and this one deserves respect, though in view of all the variables involved it appears rather too precise.

What can be stated with certainty from the reports of the Welsh Commissioners is that in 1921 the total commutation capital under the Amending Act of 1919 was provisionally set at £3,515,000. From this there was to be deducted the value of glebe lands which the Representative Body was free to buy back from the Welsh Commissioners if it chose.[56] There were minor changes in the figure, so that by the time the transaction was completed in 1931 the position stood thus:

Commutation capital paid to Representative Body:	£3,427,379
Value of glebe and other land transferred to Representative Body:	£ 133,757
TOTAL	£3,561,136[57]

The bulk of the commutation capital was paid over to the Representative Body in two instalments. In 1920 there was paid the £1,000,000 of the Exchequer grant.[58] Then in 1922 a further sum of £2,275,000 was paid over, after the Treasury had intervened to guarantee a loan of that amount by the National Debt Commissioners to the Welsh Commissioners.[59] The remainder of the commutation capital was paid over in smaller amounts between 1920 and 1931.

In 1921 it was possible for the Welsh Commissioners to ascertain the income from the secularized property which passed into its hands at the date of disestablishment in 1920. This was as follows:

	GROSS	OUTGOINGS (INCLUDING RATES, TAXES, COST OF COLLECTION)	NET
Tithe rent-charge	£213,350	£86,750	£126,600
Interest on tithe redemption moneys (less tax)	£400		£400
Rents of lands and houses	£36,250	£13,500	£22,750
TOTAL	£250,000	£100,250	£149,750[60]

In 1921 the revenue received was insufficient to pay the interest on the capital owed to the Representative Body.[61] This helps to show the confusion into which high interest rates, changes in the value of tithe rent-charge, and the anomalies of the Amending Act of 1919 had plunged the scheme of disendowment. In one sense, the revenue received by the Welsh Commissioners, just described, was the amount lost by the Church; but in real terms this loss was diminished by the high interest rates available for the investment of the commutation capital.

There was little opposition to the Amending Act. As has been said, the Cecils and a few other Conservatives spoke and voted against the Bill. Lord Hugh Cecil called it robbery; Lord Salisbury thought the Welsh bishops simple-minded to accept it.[62] After analysing the terms of the Act, especially the way in which the different valuations of the tithe rent-charge worked to the benefit of the Representative Body, these views are a little surprising. As Bishop Owen wrote at the time, "Lord Robert [Cecil] thinks we bishops have been gulled, which, to me, is a very good joke, but we shall have to play the part of silly lambs for a bit."[63] The remaining spokesmen of the old Welsh Nonconformist Liberalism had a better case for opposing the Act. Llewelyn Williams wrote: "Wales has been betrayed. The Church has won in the last lap of the race." He saw Lloyd George as the betrayer, and the settlement as "the crowning act of our lost leader's apostasy".[64] Wales had been sold, he said, and the Church re-endowed with £1,000,000 of public money.[65] As has been seen, there was much justification for this view, but only three Welsh Liberal M.P.s voted against the second reading. From the *South Wales News*, earlier a strong protagonist of disestablishment and disendowment, there was no editorial comment at all during the passage of the Act. In the *North Wales Observer and Express* there was only one comment: that Wales wanted to get the Church question disposed of once and for all to concentrate on other long-delayed social reforms.[66] *Welsh Outlook* wrote that everyone would welcome the end of a distracting issue at a time when organized religion was faced with the greatest crisis since the Reformation.[67]

Bishop Owen, after some thirty years of fighting disestablishment and resisting compromise, felt it necessary to explain in print why he accepted the Amending Act. He still claimed that this Act and that of 1914 were based on wrong principles—the confiscation of property without compensation, and the refusal by the State to recognize religion. He still held that the long fight had been necessary. But by 1919 there was no hope of reversing disendowment, and even an attempt at raising a controversy on the issue would have been damaging to the Church, which needed to know the terms of disendowment in order to arrange its own affairs.[68] It was an overwhelming case, especially considering how far disendowment had been circumvented, even if it had not been reversed.

General acquiescence in the Amending Act of 1919, however, scarcely meant that that Act and the Welsh Church Act together made a good settlement of the Welsh Church question. When compared with the coherence of the planning and passing of the Irish Church Act, the handling of the Welsh Church issue was uncertain, even bungling. Between 1909 and 1914 Asquith's government held to no visible principle on the questions of disendowment and compensation. The Bill of 1909 was swingeing; that of 1912, especially as amended, was moderate. At one point commutation was denied, as being undesirable and even impossible; at another it was granted. Then there was the series of muddles and contradictions on the question of postponement. Finally, under Lloyd George's government, the Act of 1919 was drafted in extraordinary circumstances and contained strange anomalies. Bishop Owen, writing privately, called it "a huge hanky-panky job after George's best style".[69] The *Church Times* said much the same at greater length. The Act, it wrote, was "typical of the present government. It has behind it no principle whatever, and the old principles alike of Churchmen and Liberationists are scrapped in its provisions." Churchmen had held that the property of the Church was sacrosanct; Liberationists that state money should not be used for religious purposes. Yet the Church was to lose its property, and the Treasury to give £1,000,000 towards the cost of disendowment.[70] It was all very strange, even comic.

One serious point emerged from the episode, as Sir Henry Lunn perceived. It was demonstrated that "the relation between Disestablishment and Disendowment is a purely arbitrary one".[71]

The extent of disendowment proposed for the Church in Wales varied enormously, according to the attitudes of ministers, Parliament, and public opinion, and also simply with circumstances and the pressure of events. Of connection in principle between disestablishment and disendowment nothing remained.

What did remain was the symbolic act of disestablishment itself. The *South Wales News* greeted the day of disestablishment (31 March 1920), with a touch of the old rhetoric, as "the end of a struggle for religious freedom and equality which lasted forty years". It even wrote once more of "the insulting dominance of an alien sect". By 1920 these were almost meaningless phrases. Religious freedom was never in question during the period of the struggle; the Church was no longer alien, even assuming that it once had been; only the matter of equality retained any significance. What took place on 31 March 1920 was the creation of a symbolic equality between Churches in Wales through the act of disestablishment. It may well be that in Wales this was a necessary step, with beneficial results for both Nonconformists and Churchmen. At any rate it was notable that the *South Wales News*, having worked off its old phrases, welcomed the new episcopal Church to the circle of free Churches, and shortly afterwards welcomed Edwards, an old enemy, as the first Archbishop of Wales, with a sympathetic account of the ceremony at which he was elected.[72]

The date of disestablishment was also that of disendowment, on which the secularized property of the Church in Wales passed into the control of the Welsh Commissioners. The first charge upon it was the servicing and repayment of the loans raised by the Welsh Commissioners to pay the commutation capital to the Representative Body of the Church in Wales. Only when this was met would the property or its proceeds pass to the county councils and the University of Wales. While the property was in the control of the Welsh Commissioners, there were two developments of particular interest.

One concerned the burial grounds. It will be recalled that under the Welsh Church Act those burial grounds which derived from private benefactions, and those which were closed, were to pass to the Representative Body of the Church; the others were to pass to various local authorities. It will be recalled also that this was a provision to which many Welsh Nonconformists had attached particular importance. The Act of 1914 had given no option in this matter, except to the Representative Body in the case of closed burial grounds; in other cases the different bodies concerned were simply to accept the burial grounds. The Act of 1919, however, laid down that local authorities need not accept the property if they did not wish, unless the Home Secretary so directed. When it came to the point, most local authorities took advantage of this provision and declined to take over the burial grounds. In 1934, out of the 919 burial grounds which passed into the hands of the Welsh Commissioners for transfer to local authorities, only 149 had been transferred, and the other 670 remained.[73] (One reason, perhaps, was that it was discovered that so many additions to burial grounds had been made by private benefactions that often the local authorities were only entitled to receive parts which were relatively little used.[74]) The Welsh Commissioners were reluctant to spend money on the upkeep of these burial grounds left in their hands, because they regarded themselves as trustees for the county councils and the University, but in fact they were forced to spend a certain amount on repairs. An attempt in 1927 to pass a Bill empowering the Commissioners to transfer to the Representative Body burial grounds which were refused by the local authorities failed. In 1935 the Commissioners recommended that the Home Secretary should either use his powers to direct the local authorities to accept the burial grounds, or introduce legislation to deal with the problem in some other way.[75] Finally, the Welsh Church (Burial Grounds) Act of 1945 dealt with the situation, and in 1946 the Commissioners transferred the burial grounds to the Representative Body.[76]

The second matter of interest was the fate of the tithe rent-charge. For a number of years, the Welsh Commissioners reported that all was going smoothly. They collected the rent-charge partly through agents and partly directly, without difficulty. But, with the onset of the depression, they found towards the end of 1931 concerted action to refuse payment, just as there was in England at the same time.[77] In 1932 the position worsened, and they reported that in the Vale of Clwyd and other parts of Denbighshire the main cause of default was not the agrarian depression but an agitation to force the Commissioners to remit or reduce the rent-charge itself.[78] In 1933 this resistance in Denbighshire continued, and spread to areas in Cardiganshire and Montgomeryshire. (It is notable that both Denbighshire and Cardiganshire were centres of active opposition to the tithe in the 1880s and 1890s.) There was even one incident reminiscent of the old tithe war, when a landowner and some other men prevented the auction of some of his cattle which had been distrained for the payment of the tithe rent-charge. The Commissioners refrained from using auction sales thereafter.[79] These difficulties were less severe and widespread than those in England, but it was none the less significant that a change in the purpose to which the tithe rent-charge was to be put did not prevent opposition to paying it when times were hard. Also, neither the lapse of time nor the fact that the tithe was paid by landlords instead of by tenants changed the areas which were most militant.

In Wales, the agitation against the tithe rent-charge died out during 1934 and 1935.[80] In England, the difficulties were more serious, and the question was eventually settled by legislation. The Tithe Act of 1936 extinguished the tithe rent-charge, and compensated the tithe-owners (including the Welsh Commissioners) by an issue of three per cent government stock, at a value lower than that of the previous tithe rent-charge. The Welsh Commissioners were to receive stock of a nominal value of approximately £4,081,000, yielding an income of about £122,500 per annum. Their average net income from tithe rent-charge between 1925 and 1936 was over £152,000 per annum.[81] The Welsh Commissioners were thus able, earlier than had been expected, to discharge their liabilities to the National Debt Commissioners and to proceed with the distribution of the secularized property to the county councils and the University, though the value of the property itself was diminished. The outstanding debt to the National Debt Commissioners was paid off in 1937. The market value of the stock had fallen since 1936, so that stock to the nominal amount of £1,841,236 was transferred to meet a debt of £1,620,288.[82]

The Welsh Commissioners hoped at this point that the transfer of property would come about quickly. In the event, it took place in a series of transactions between 1942 and 1947, in which the Commissioners handed over to the beneficiaries assets consisting of land, stock, tithe redemption annuities, and cash, to a total value of £3,455,813 10s. 8d. This was distributed as follows:

COUNTY COUNCILS

Anglesey	£221,983 4s. 11d.
Brecon	138,732 1s. 5d.
Caernarvon	164,263 9s. 1d.
Cardigan	85,770 16s. 0d.
Carmarthen	130,209 0s. 8d.
Denbigh	259,917 2s. 2d.
Flint	105,158 17s. 6d.
Glamorgan	291,149 10s. 1d.
Merioneth	38,199 12s. 5d.
Monmouth	340,630 18s. 4d.
Montgomery	198,290 12s. 11d.
Pembroke	229,576 5s. 3d.
Radnor	120,787 3s. 11d.

BOROUGH COUNCILS

Cardiff	10,719 4s. 0d.
Merthyr Tydfil	124,923 13s. 3d.
Newport	3,267 5s. 4d.
Swansea	3,038 2s. 11d.

UNIVERSITY OF WALES   989,196 10s. 6d.[83]

In accordance with the Welsh Church Act, the councils prepared schemes for the use of the funds. These are of a common type, and allow help to be given for educational purposes (help for poor scholars); libraries, museums, and art galleries; social and recreational purposes; the protection of historic buildings and records; medical and social research; help for persons on probation and discharged prisoners; the welfare of the blind and the old; the upkeep of burial grounds vested in the Representative Body; and finally contributions to voluntary charities.[84]

The Church in Wales after Disestablishment

Disestablishment and its aftermath in Wales had none of the drama and conflict which attended the same events in Ireland fifty years earlier. This was partly, no doubt, because in Wales the process of disestablishment was long drawn out, from 1914 to 1920, instead of a comparatively brief eighteen months. More important, the years of Welsh disestablishment were full of drama and convulsions of quite another kind, affecting everyone, and putting events in a different perspective from that of the quiet years of 1869–70. Also, there were not the same causes of conflict within the Church in Wales as in the Irish Church. There was no serious opposition, either to the bishops of that day or to episcopacy as such. There were differences of churchmanship within the Welsh Church, but neither the national atmosphere nor the historical circumstances which caused the movement for Prayer Book revision in Ireland.

The Church in Wales had first to accept its separation from the Convocation of Canterbury. It can scarcely be believed that any other decision was possible, though Bishop Edwards, as Chairman of the Governing Body, formally sought the advice of Archbishop Davidson as to whether the Welsh dioceses should try to retain their place in Convocation or not. Davidson advised acceptance of the Welsh Church Act and the formation of a new province. This undoubtedly coincided with the wishes of most Welsh Churchmen at the time. The Governing Body passed a resolution in favour of a new province at a meeting at Llandrindod Wells in June 1919, with only one dissentient vote. The Bishop of Bangor, who opposed the policy, and who also held that the meeting itself was unconstitutional because the proper notice had not been given, absented himself. At Rhyl on 6 January 1920 the Governing Body confirmed its decision. The Bishop of Bangor called for a vote by orders: the bishops voted three to one in favour; the clergy were unanimous; among the laity, there was only one dissentient, the Diocesan Registrar of Bangor. Davidson then took the formal steps of releasing the Welsh bishops from their oaths of obedience to himself as their Metropolitan, and declaring in Convocation on 10 February 1920 that the Welsh dioceses were free to form themselves into a Province.[85] A. G. Edwards was elected the first Archbishop of Wales by the Welsh bishops on 7 April 1920.

This separation carried with it obvious advantages, even though before 1914 it had been opposed. As the *Guardian* recognized, many Welshmen who were not Churchmen would be proud that the Welsh Church had its own individual existence and institutions.[86] There were other advantages in forming a compact body with its own organization; it is difficult to see how some sort of affiliation with the Church of England could have worked, administratively as well as in terms of sentiment. It will be remembered that opposition to separation from the Church of England had arisen in large part from fear of narrowness and exclusive nationalism in a Welsh Church. Archbishop Edwards in his autobiography described being cut off from England as the one great loss in disestablishment.[87] Frank Morgan, giving evidence to the English Archbishops' Commission on Church and State in 1931, thought that there was still some danger in nationalism, which he found much stronger in the Church than before disestablishment. He found particularly dangerous the tendency to demand that bishops should always be Welsh-speaking, which limited the range of choice.[88] An indication of the difficulty which could be caused was given in 1923, when the new diocese of Swansea and Brecon was carved out of St David's. An obvious candidate for the new bishopric was the Suffragan Bishop of Swansea, Bevan, who was Welsh by birth but spoke no Welsh. Archbishop Edwards, however, spoke in favour of having a Welsh-speaking bishop. Bevan was elected, but Edwards abstained from voting at the confirmation of his election by the Welsh bishops. This was in spite of the fact that it could be convincingly argued that the character of the new diocese was not such as to make Welsh a practical necessity for its bishop.[89]

The episode showed some of the difficulties which could be raised by nationalism, but it showed too that they could be overcome. The second Archbishop of Wales, C. A. H. Green (who was himself Welsh-speaking), discounted the dangers of isolation and narrowness. In view of the constant traffic, in persons, books, and ideas, across the border, he did not think that these dangers were serious.[90] It appears that one of the spectres conjured up during the campaign against disestablishment was less alarming when seen at close range.

In the constitution of the Church in Wales the bishops held a powerful position. It was on their authority and initiative that the whole constitution-making procedure was set in motion in 1914.[91] The election of the first archbishop by the bishops themselves was a symbol of their position. The constitution declared that the archbishop and diocesan (as distinct from suffragan) bishops formed in themselves the Provincial Synod of Wales, with the right to meet apart from the Governing Body.[92] They held, too, a special position within the Governing Body itself.

The Governing Body was created as the supreme authority in the Church in Wales, with power over constitutional and administrative matters, and also over questions of doctrine, forms of worship and ceremonial, and discipline. It was to consist of three orders: the order of bishops (i.e. diocesan bishops); the order of clergy; and the order of laity. In the orders of clergy and laity the majority of members were elected, the clergy by the clerical members of diocesan conferences, laymen by the lay members of diocesan conferences. There were to be a number of *ex-officio* members (deans and archdeacons), and a number of co-opted members, clerical and lay. Equality in elected representation for the dioceses was decided on in 1917, as was a proportion of two lay representatives to one clerical. It was a large body, having 492 members in 1924, and 506 by 1931.[93]

In the Governing Body an important distinction was drawn between legislative procedure, or Bill procedure, which was necessary when dealing with matters of faith, discipline, and ceremonial, and procedure for other matters. Bills had to be initiated by a majority of the order of bishops, and then passed by a two-thirds majority in each order voting separately. In the voting, the order of bishops was to vote last, and to have the right to withdraw for consultation before doing so. It will be seen that in matters to which this procedure applied, the bishops were given a position of very great power—indeed, since only they could initiate Bills, their power was in one sense absolute. In other matters, constitutional and administrative, voting was again by orders, but a simple majority of each order sufficed to carry a measure.[94]

It is interesting, in contrast with the framing of the constitution of the Irish Church, that the extremely powerful position of the bishops in the Governing Body met with very little opposition. At the Convention in Cardiff in October 1917, an amendment was moved to the standing orders of that body, which provided for voting by orders. It was defeated by 348 votes to fourteen.[95]

Besides the Governing Body, the other central organ in the constitution of the Welsh Church was the Representative Body.

Here the parallel with the Irish Church was close. The function of the Representative Body was to hold and administer the property of the Church in Wales, for which it was responsible to the Governing Body. It was to consist of the archbishop and diocesan bishops, *ex officio*; four clergy and eight laymen from each diocese, elected by the diocesan conferences; fifteen co-opted members, who might be clerical or lay; and a number of members nominated by the bishops or created life-members by the Governing Body. It was thus much smaller than the Governing Body, though still quite large for working purposes, with a total of 105 members (thirty-six clerical, sixty-nine lay) in 1931.[96]

Diocesan synods after the Irish model were not created in Wales, though according to Frank Morgan there was some wish to do so at the time of disestablishment.[97] Instead, the diocesan conferences already in existence before disestablishment were kept in being, and were given the responsibility of electing representatives, clerical and lay, on the Governing and Representative Bodies. They also had certain limited administrative functions. The diocesan conferences consisted of persons elected by ruridecanal conferences, themselves consisting of the clergy of a deanery and laymen elected by the parochial church councils. All lay members of the ruridecanal conference and bodies above it had to be communicants; for the electoral roll of the parishes, at the bottom of this intricate system of indirect elections, the qualifications were age (eighteen years), residence, confirmation, and the signing of a declaration accepting the constitution of the Church in Wales.[98]

The constitution of the Church in Wales thus concentrated much power in the Governing Body, and within the Governing Body gave great authority and initiative to the bishops. The system of appointing bishops, always important, was in these circumstances of particular significance. The method devised in 1919 was to place the election of a bishop in the hands of an electoral college representing the whole Church. (A resolution had been moved in the Governing Body in September 1918 that elections should be by the diocesan conference of the diocese concerned, but this was abandoned.[99]) By this means the danger of dividing a diocese through its electing its own bishop was avoided, and the principle was recognized that the appointment of bishops is something which concerns the whole Church. In these ways it was certainly better than the system adopted in Ireland at the time of disestablishment, and indeed the Church of Ireland adopted a similar method in 1959.

In Wales, the electoral college was to consist of the archbishop and diocesan bishops; six clerical and six lay electors from the vacant diocese; and three clerical and three lay electors from each of the other dioceses. Nominations were to be made when the college first met, when every member might make a written nomination. Election had to be by two-thirds majority, and, if this was not forthcoming, the college had to start again with a new set of nominations. If after three days of voting the college failed to elect, the appointment was to lapse to the Archbishop of Canterbury—one last link with the former primate of the Welsh dioceses. When the method was first introduced, there were four dioceses in the province, and the vacant diocese could therefore exercise a veto if all its electors voted together. With the existence of six dioceses after 1923, this was no longer the case. Frank Morgan claimed to have had considerable influence in devising the system, and to have modelled it on that used in papal elections —the same device of locking the cathedral while the college was in session was adopted, and there were strict provisions for secrecy. Morgan told the English Archbishops' Commission on Church and State in 1931 that there was "quite general satisfaction or even enthusiasm" over the method of election. He asserted in particular that it left no place for canvassing, because no one knew before the meeting who would be nominated. This may not be wholly true, since the number of eligible persons was bound to be fairly small; but it is clear that the dispersal of the electoral body over the whole country, coupled with some uncertainty about nominations, gave much less scope for canvassing than election by diocesan synods.[100]

Elections to the archbishopric of Wales (which, as distinct from Ireland, was not tied to any one see, but could be held by any diocesan bishop) were to be made by a special electoral college. This consisted of the diocesan bishops, and the first three clerical and the first three lay episcopal electors on the list of each diocese. Only those who were already diocesan bishops were to be eligible, and election had to be by two-thirds majority. If after three days of voting the college failed to elect, the appointment was to lapse to the Archbishop of Canterbury.[101]

In appointments to benefices, it was also provided that the Church as a whole should have some influence, though the major role was given to the diocese. In a cycle of seven successive appointments to a given parish, the diocesan board of patronage was to have four turns, the bishop of the diocese two turns, and the provincial patronage board one turn. The point of this last provision was to ensure movement between dioceses on occasion. According to Frank Morgan, the early years of the scheme's working saw a great increase in the influence of the bishops on appointments.[102]

Whenever the constitution and system of appointments of the Church in Wales may be compared with that devised at the time of disestablishment by the Church of Ireland, the impression is one of centralization in Wales as against wider dispersal of powers in Ireland. It is true that both formed a supreme legislative body, though they chose different names for it, and both had a Representative Body to administer property and finance. But in Ireland there were diocesan synods; in Wales only diocesan conferences. In Ireland, the diocesan synods elected the bishops; in Wales, bishops were elected by an electoral college representing the whole Church. In Ireland, the parish had considerable, sometimes perhaps excessive, influence on the appointment of incumbents; in Wales, the preponderant influence lay with the diocese. In Wales, great powers were given to the bishops (or, as Archbishop Green would certainly have put it, the authoritative position of bishops was duly recognized); in Ireland, they had smaller powers, hedged round with constitutional safeguards. The circumstances and traditions of the two Churches were different, and, given the position at the time of disestablishment, the Church of Ireland could scarcely have done other than it did. On the whole, it appears that the system of the Church in Wales worked more smoothly and produced fewer difficulties; on the other hand, the system of the Church of Ireland involved more of the laity all the way down the line in important decisions, which in Ireland in 1870 was of crucial importance.

In financial organization too the Church in Wales adopted a centralized system, as against the separate diocesan schemes which

prevailed in Ireland. In Wales, the Representative Body controlled the major part of the resources of the Church. It set up a
central fund, made up from the following elements: the post-1662
endowments; funds received from the Ecclesiastical Commissioners and Queen Anne's Bounty; the commutation capital; the
fund raised by the appeal launched in 1920; and the proceeds of a
provincial levy, an assessed contribution of £45,000 per annum,
collected by diocesan boards of finance from the parishes.[103] The
appeal of 1920 realized less than had been hoped—£722,522 at
the end of November 1934[104]—and there was disappointment in
Wales at the poor response from England, though it was recognized that the English Church too had its financial difficulties.[105]
However, considering that this fund was raised at the same time
as the regular provincial levy from the parishes, and that the
1920s were a time of frequent economic difficulties, and the early
1930s one of deep depression, this surely represented a financial
success.

Out of the central fund, the Representative Body paid the
annuities of the clergy entitled to compensation under the Welsh
Church Act, and stipends on a new scale to the clergy not so
entitled. For bishops, against former incomes of £4,200 per annum
(St David's £4,500), the new arrangements provided £1,600,
plus £800 for expenses, and an extra £400 for the three bishops
who had to keep up ancient palaces. For the clergy, whose previous stipends had ranged from over £1,000 per annum to about
£120, the new plan was to pay no one more than £600 and no
one less than £250, a minimum for incumbents accepted by the
Governing Body in January 1920. Thus there took place in Wales,
as there had in Ireland, the removal of gross disparities of income
which had arisen from historical accidents, and which bore no
necessary relation to responsibilities or work done.[106]

As was seen earlier, the final measure of disendowment of the
Church in Wales under the Acts of 1914 and 1919 was limited,
and it appears that its effects were successfully met by a combination of voluntary giving and good management by the Representative Body. In one aspect disendowment was in retrospect
welcomed both by the second Archbishop of Wales, Green, and
by the first Secretary of the Representative Body, Frank Morgan.
"To all our blessings", said Archbishop Green in 1935, "we have

one more to add, and it is not the least, as you will cordially agree—all our Tithes have gone."[107] His English audience doubtless took the point, for at the time the Church of England was in the midst of renewed difficulties over the collection of the tithe rent-charge, eventually to be settled by the Tithe Act of 1936 by an arrangement which meant a substantial loss to the Church.[108] Frank Morgan, speaking in 1931, took the same view—that the clergy were glad to receive their stipends quarterly on the appointed day, without the difficulties and uncertainties of the tithe rent-charge and rents under the old system.[109]

In Ireland, disestablishment was followed at once by revision of the Prayer Book, though the consequences of this revision proved to be much smaller than was at one time thought likely. In Wales, no such events followed. By the constitution any such change could only be made by a Bill, which meant that it must be initiated and supported by a majority of the diocesan bishops in the Governing Body. In 1926 a motion was carried by the clergy and laity in the Governing Body proposing that a committee be set up to consider the revised Book of Common Prayer then being produced in England; but the bishops declined to do so. Apart from this, there appears to have been little movement for change. Even the title page of the Prayer Book continued to bear the words "according to the use of the Church of England". It was only after the Second World War, in 1950, that the Governing Body decided to embark on a general revision of the Prayer Book, and a Commission was appointed which produced a number of revised services, including the Communion service which is at present (1969) being used for an experimental period of ten years.[110] At the time of Welsh disestablishment the controversy over ritualism and other matters which gave the impulse for revision in Ireland had burnt itself out. Without any similar impulse, and with plenty of other work to do, the Church in Wales did not embark on the venture in the early years of its separate existence.

In conclusion, it is interesting to note remarks by three Welsh bishops (who all became archbishops) which bear on the question of disestablishment. Edwards, who spent much of his life fighting against the process which eventually made him the first Archbishop of Wales, tried to draw a balance-sheet of the campaign and of disestablishment in his memoirs. He believed that the campaign itself had been worth while, and that it had achieved a measure of success. The crude demands of some disestablishers, for the secularizing of the cathedrals for example, or the pensioning off of the clergy, did not come about.[111] This point might be extended by emphasizing again that the final terms secured by the Church were much less damaging to it than those in the first three Disestablishment Bills. The point is difficult to judge, but it may be that they were also more equitable. The campaign, while certainly wasteful of much energy which might have been otherwise used, was from the Church's point of view not barren of results.[112]

Edwards described the forcible separation of the Welsh dioceses from the Church of England as an irreparable loss.[113] But he felt too that there had been positive gains, and placed first among them the weakening of sectarian bitterness. There were no longer any inequalities "by law established" to exacerbate other differences; the Church itself was no longer in perpetual alliance with one political party.[114] The mind of the Church had been changed for the better: "It was made clear to the most Erastian mind that establishment is not of the essence of the Church, and that in many cases it was doubtful whether it was for the well-being of the Church." He thought that laymen were taking a more active and interested part in the life of the Church, and that few would wish to return to the old conditions.[115]

From Edwards's comment about establishment not being of the essence of the Church, it is interesting to turn to the first visitation charge of the Bishop of Monmouth, Morris, in 1946. In this charge the Bishop told his clergy: "As incumbents you have a ministry to all the souls in your parishes. This includes Roman Catholics and Nonconformists as well as the unbaptized." This remark and others caused some stir, and in his second charge the Bishop substantiated his case from the wording of the Thirty-nine Articles, the Canons of 1603, the Book of Common Prayer (especially the ordinal), the forms of institution to cures of souls, and the constitution of the Church in Wales.[116] The point here is not the controversy which arose, but that by taking seriously the Church's own documents and its claim to be the Catholic Church in Wales, the Bishop could make a case which the fact of disestablishment did not affect. Disestablishment did not prevent the Bishop from claiming that the parish priests of the Church in Wales should minister to everyone in their parishes. Equally, even without these sweeping theoretical claims, it is hard to see how disestablishment could prevent a Welsh incumbent from serving anyone in his parish if they wished him to do so. Yet the importance of establishment as conferring a duty and opportunity to minister to all people in a country was an argument prominent in the campaign against disestablishment in Wales. It is still used on occasion about the position in England.*

Finally, Archbishop Green said to an English audience in 1935: "You ask me, 'Is all well?' I believe it is. . . . To Wales, Disestablishment has brought the end of a long and bitter controversy; if it be not revived, all Welshmen can henceforth be united in the service of their country. More cannot be expected, for Disestablishment is no panacea for schism."[117]

It was not only in Wales that a controversy had come to an end. The same was true for British politics in general, from which disestablishment disappeared as a live issue. The Liberation Society after the war had become not so much a shadow as a mere wraith of its former self. English Nonconformity had grave problems, in common with all Churches, and had ceased to gird at the symbolic inequalities of the establishment. The Liberal party, which had been the instrument of disestablishment in both Ireland and Wales, was by 1920 in fragments, broken by war, social change, and personal antagonisms. The Conservative party was far from broken, but it was changing both its character and its battle-fields. Lord Robert Cecil wrote in April 1922 that, before the war, British politics had been on a two-party basis, with the parties mainly divided by "their differences on certain great questions such as Ireland, the Franchise, the Church and the Land". All these issues had gone: the franchise question settled by the grant of near-universal suffrage; the Welsh Church

---

* For example, Max Warren, in *The English Church: A New Look*, ed. L. S. Hunter, p. 140: "The principle of establishment as understood in England has a definite territorial significance. The bishop, and by delegation the parish priest, has a distinct area of responsibility, and the responsibility is not confined to those of his own religious allegiance but in some sense embraces all those living in the area. . . . The 'established' Church is not a sect ministering exclusively to its own members. It has a concern for 'all sorts and conditions of men'."

question decided; the Irish question completely transformed; and little interest remaining in the land question. The issues in political thought and action had become quite different, and the Conservative party would have to reorient itself.[118]

Whether Lord Robert's view of the past was wholly correct or not, there can be no disputing his analysis with regard to the Church and establishment. What had been an important point of difference between the dominant political parties was so no longer. When next the question of disestablishment was asked, it was asked from within the Church of England, when the Prayer Book Measures of 1927 and 1928, to provide alternatives to parts of the 1662 Prayer Book, were both rejected by the House of Commons. The question was asked; a Commission (not the first, nor the last) on the relations between Church and State was set up; and in 1935 the Commission reported against disestablishment if other means could be devised of securing for the Church its "freedom of action in things spiritual".[119] The steps taken by the Church of England towards this freedom of action since the war of 1939–45 have been moderate, sensible, and almost unnoticed by the general public—a far cry from the great controversies of a hundred or even fifty years ago. A new *modus vivendi* has been worked out, and revised services with full legal authority behind them are in use.

None the less, the question of the establishment remains. The link between Church and State is valued by many as a symbol of an ideal relationship, or as an opportunity for the Church of England in society. Others see the establishment as still infringing the proper liberties of the Church, and as an obstacle in the path to union with other Christians. If and when the subject is again reopened for serious discussion, the experience of the disestablished Churches in Ireland and Wales should be remembered.

SELECT LIST OF SOURCES

The principal sources used for this study are listed below. Periodicals and newspapers are not listed, except for a few very important articles in periodicals. Detailed references to all sources appear in the notes.

MANUSCRIPT SOURCES

Personal papers

Asquith Papers (Bodleian Library, Oxford).
Gladstone Papers (British Museum, London).
Hughenden Papers: Disraeli Papers (Hughenden Manor, Buckinghamshire).
Spencer Papers: Papers of the fifth Earl Spencer (Althorp, Northampton).
Strachie Mss.: Papers of Chichester Fortescue, Lord Carlingford (Somerset Record Office, Taunton).
Tait Papers (Lambeth Palace Library).

Occasional reference is also made to the Balfour, Bright, Campbell-Bannerman, and Iddesleigh Papers (British Museum), and to the Burke Papers (papers of T. H. Burke, State Paper Office, Dublin).

Other papers

Home Office Papers, H.O. 45 (Public Record Office, London).
Chief Secretary's Office (C.S.O.), Registered Papers; Irish Privy Council, Minute Books and Letter Books (State Paper Office, Dublin).
Liberation Society Papers (Greater London Council Record Office).
Minutes of the Lambeth Conference, 1878 (Lambeth Palace Library).

PRINTED SOURCES
IRISH DISESTABLISHMENT

Royal Commission

Report of Her Majesty's Commissioners on the revenue and condition of the established Church in Ireland (H.C. 1867–8, xxiv).

The contemporary debate

ON DISESTABLISHMENT

Brady, W. Maziere, *Remarks on the Irish Church Temporalities*. Dublin 1865.
—— *The alleged conversion of the Irish Bishops to the reformed religion at the accession of Queen Elizabeth . . . disproved*. 5th edn. London 1867.

Brady, W. Maziere. *Facts or Fictions? Seven letters on the "Facts concerning the Irish Church", published by the Church Institution.* Dublin 1867.
—— *Essays on the English State Church in Ireland.* London 1869.
Daunt, W. J. O'Neill, *The Disendowment of the State-Church in Ireland.* London 1865.
De Vere, Aubrey, *The Church Settlement of Ireland, or Hibernia Pacanda.* London 1866.
—— *Ireland's Church Property, and the right use of it.* London 1867.
Dufferin and Ava, Marquess of, *Inaugural Address delivered before the Social Science Congress at Belfast in 1867.* Belfast 1867.
Ferrar, W. H., *The Title of the Irish Church to her Property, and the Consequences of her Disendowment.* Dublin 1868.
Fitzgerald, W., *Thoughts on the present circumstances of the Church of Ireland.* London 1860.
Foster, A. H., *The Irish Church Question.* Dublin 1868.
Freeman's Journal Church Commission, *The Church Establishment in Ireland.* Dublin 1868.
Gayer, A. E., *Fallacies and Fictions relating to the Irish Church Establishment.* Dublin 1868.
Gladstone, W. E., *A Chapter of Autobiography.* London 1868.
Godkin, J., *Ireland and her Churches.* London 1867.
Higginson, F., *The Beleaguered Church: not a Chapter of Autobiography.* London 1869.
Jones, Abraham, *Thoughts on the Established Church.* Dublin 1868.
Jones, W. Bence, *The Irish Church from the point of view of one of its laymen.* 2nd edn. London 1868.
Lee, A. T., *The Irish Church. Its present condition: its future prospects.* London 1866.
—— *Facts respecting the present state of the Church in Ireland.* 5th edn. London 1868.
Nugent, R., *The Church in Ireland and her assailants.* London 1868.
O'Brien, J. T., *The Church in Ireland: our duty in regard to its defence.* London 1866.
—— *The Case of the Established Church in Ireland.* 2nd edn. London 1867.
Russell, Lord John, *A Letter to the Right Hon. Chichester Fortescue on the State of Ireland.* London 1868.
—— *A second Letter . . .* London 1868.
—— *A third Letter . . .* London 1869.
Senior, Nassau, *Journals, Conversations and Essays relating to Ireland.* 2 vols. London 1868.
Skeats, H. S., *The Irish Church: an historical and statistical review.* London 1865.

Trench, F. F., *The Disestablishment and Disendowment of the Established Church in Ireland shown to be desirable under existing circumstances.* London & Dublin 1868.

Essays on the Irish Church, by Clergymen of the Established Church in Ireland (J. Byrne, A. W. Edwards, W. Anderson, A. T. Lee). Oxford & London 1866.

An Irishman's Glance at some anomalies in the Church Establishment in England. 2nd edn. Dublin 1866.

Church and State: with reference to the United Church of England and Ireland, by a Lay Churchman. London 1868.

Short Notes on the Irish Church Question, by a Layman. London n.d.

ON REORGANIZATION

Arthur, H., *Remarks on the new Sacramental Rubrics.* Dublin 1874.

Beresford-Hope, A. J. B., *The Irish Church and its Formularies.* London 1870.

Church of Ireland, General Convention, 1870, *The Statutes passed in the General Convention of the Church of Ireland, 1870.* Dublin 1870.

Church of Ireland, General Convention, 1870: Committee to consider measures to check the introduction and spread of novel doctrines. . . . *Report.* Dublin 1871.

Fitzgerald, W., *Remarks on the new proposed Baptismal Rubric.* Dublin 1873.

Foster, A. H., *What is the Church of Ireland?* Dublin 1870.

Gwynn, J., *The Church of Ireland and her Censors.* Dublin 1874.

Hannyngton, J. C., *Commutation. Remarks on the conditions of safety.* Dublin 1870.

Jones, W. Bence, *The Future of the Irish Church.* Dublin 1869.

—— *What has been done in the Irish Church since Disestablishment.* Dublin 1875.

Lee, A. T., *The Irish Church Act. A popular account.* London & Dublin 1869.

Lloyd, H., *On the Financial Results of Commutation.* Dublin 1870.

Maberley, L. F. S., ed., *Protestantism v. Ritualism. The Maberley Correspondence.* Dublin 1870.

—— *The Introduction and Spread of Ritualism in the Church of Ireland under His Grace Archbishop Trench.* Dublin 1881.

MacDonnell, J. C., *Shall we commute?* Dublin 1869.

Maturin, W., *The Declaration on Kneeling and the new Irish Rubric.* Dublin 1874.

Monck, W. H. S., *The Irish Church and the Order of Bishops.* Dublin 1869.

Napier, Sir Joseph, *The Change proposed in the Ordinal.* Dublin 1873.

Plunket, William Conyngham (Lord Plunket), *The Dangers of Silence.* Dublin 1869.

—— *Moderate Revision essential to Church Unity.* Dublin 1874.

Plunket, William Conyngham, *The Prospects of Revision*. Dublin 1876.

Reichel, C. P., "The Constitution of the disestablished Church of Ireland", *Contemporary Review*, vol. XV (September 1870).

—— *Shall we alter the Ordinal?* Dublin 1872.

Salmon, G., *The Irish Church Convention*. London 1870.

Sherlock, W., *Suggestions towards the organisation of the Church of Ireland, based on that of the reformed episcopal Churches abroad*. Dublin 1869.

Trench, T. C., *Reconstruction of the Church in Ireland, and the use of commutation*. 2nd edn. Dublin 1869.

Woodward, T., *Commutation, Cui Bono?* Dublin 1870.

Reasons for not Postponing: a letter addressed to those who desire a revision of the liturgy, by Notans. Dublin 1870.

Other works

Alexander, E., ed., *Primate Alexander, Archbishop of Armagh, a memoir*. London 1913.

Bromley, J., *The Man of Ten Talents. A portrait of Richard Chenevix Trench, 1807–86*. London 1959.

D'Arcy, C. F., *Adventures of a Bishop*. London 1934.

How, F. D., *William Conyngham Plunket, a memoir*. London 1900.

Killen, W. D., *The Ecclesiastical History of Ireland*. 2 vols., London 1875.

Luce, A. A., *Charles Frederick D'Arcy, 1859–1938* (reprinted from *Proceedings of the British Academy*, vol. XXIV).

MacDonnell, J. C., *The Life and Correspondence of William Connor Magee*. 2 vols. London 1896.

McDowell, R. B., *Public Opinion and Government Policy in Ireland, 1801–1846*. London 1952.

Micks, E. C., ed., *The Constitution of the Church of Ireland*. Dublin 1960.

Moore, C., *A Chapter of Irish Church History: being some personal recollections of life and service in the Church of Ireland*. Dublin 1907.

Murray, R. H., *Archbishop Bernard*. London 1931.

Norman, E. R., *The Catholic Church in Ireland in the Age of Rebellion, 1859–73*. London 1965.

Patton, H. E., *Fifty Years of Disestablishment*. Dublin 1922.

Phillips, W. A., ed., *History of the Church of Ireland*. Vol. III, London 1933.

Seaver, G., *John Allen Fitzgerald Gregg, Archbishop*. Dublin 1963.

Shearman, H., "Irish Church Finances after the Disestablishment", in Cronne, H. A., Moody, T. W., and Quinn, D. B., ed. *Essays in British and Irish History in honour of James Eadie Todd*. London 1949.

Thornley, D. A., *Isaac Butt and Home Rule*. London 1964.

Trench, Richard Chenevix, *Letters and Memorials*, ed. by the author of "Charles Lowder". 2 vols. London 1888.

Webster, C. A., *The Diocese of Cork*. Cork 1920.

PRINTED SOURCES
WELSH DISESTABLISHMENT

Royal Commission

Report, Evidence, Statistics and Indexes of the Royal Commission appointed to inquire into the Church of England and other religious bodies in Wales and Monmouthshire (H.C. 1910, xiv–xix).

The contemporary debate

Bradley, J. F., *Religious Liberty in England. A scheme for providing and securing religious liberty in England and Wales.* London 1908.

—— *The Case against Welsh Disendowment.* London 1911.

—— *Nonconformists and the Welsh Church Bill.* London 1912.

Caird, D., *Church and State in Wales. The Case for Disestablishment.* 2nd edn. London 1912.

Cecil, Lord Robert, and Clayton, H. J., *Our National Church.* London 1913.

Clayton, H. J., *The Indictment and Defence of the Church in Wales.* London 1911.

Downing, S. E., *The Church in Wales, Disestablishment and Disendowment.* London 1915.

Edwards, A. G., *A Handbook on Welsh Church Defence.* 3rd edn. London 1895.

—— *Landmarks in the History of the Welsh Church.* London 1912.

Gibbon, J. Morgan, *Weighed in the Balance: the case for Welsh Disestablishment.* London 1911.

Green, C. A. H., *Disestablishment.* Cardiff 1911.

—— *Disendowment.* Cardiff 1911.

Morgan, J. Vyrnwy, *A Study in Nationality.* London 1911.

—— *The Church in Wales in the Light of History.* London 1918.

Owen, John, *Welsh Disestablishment: our duty.* Carmarthen 1911.

—— *The Welsh Disestablishment Bill: what it means.* London 1911.

—— *Statement to St David's Diocese on the acceptance of the Welsh Church Temporalities Act, 1919.* Carmarthen n.d.

Owen, Owen, *Welsh Disestablishment. Some Phases of the Numerical Argument.* Wrexham 1895.

Rees, J. Tudor, *Welsh Disestablishment: objections answered.* London n.d.

Spinks, W. H., *A Modern Church Catechism.* London 1912.

Wilkinson, J. Frome, *Disestablishment (Welsh and English).* London 1894.

Wilson, P. W., *Welsh Disestablishment.* London n.d.

Other works

Davies, E. T., ed., *The Story of the Church in Glamorgan*. London 1962.
—— *Religion in the Industrial Revolution in South Wales*. Cardiff 1965.
Edwards, A. G., *Memories*. London 1927.
Green, C. A. H., *Disestablishment and Disendowment: the experience of the Church in Wales* (reprinted from the *North Wales Chronicle*, 11 October 1935).
—— *The Setting of the Constitution of the Church in Wales*. London 1937.
Hamer, F. E., ed., *The Personal Papers of Lord Rendel*. London 1933.
Jones, Ieuan Gwynnedd, "The Liberation Society in Welsh Politics, 1844–1868", *Welsh History Review*, vol. I.
Lerry, G., *Alfred George Edwards, Archbishop of Wales*. Oswestry 1940.
Lewis, E., *Prayer Book Revision in the Church in Wales*. Penarth 1958.
Lunn, Sir Henry S., *Chapters from my Life*. London 1918.
—— *Nearing Harbour*. London 1934.
Morgan, J. Vyrnwy, *Welsh Religious Leaders in the Victorian Era*. London 1905.
Morgan, K. O., *Wales in British Politics, 1868–1922*. Cardiff 1963.
—— *Freedom or Sacrilege? A history of the campaign for Welsh disestablishment*. Penarth 1966.
Morris, E., *The Church in Wales and Nonconformity*. Newport 1949.
Owen, Eluned E., *The Early Life of Bishop Owen*. Llandyssul 1958.
—— *The Later Life of Bishop Owen*. Llandyssul 1961.

PRINTED SOURCES
GENERAL

Bell, G. K. A., *Randall Davidson, Archbishop of Canterbury*. 2nd edn. London 1938.
Benson, A. C., *Life of Edward White Benson*. 2 vols. London 1899.
Best, G. F. A., *Temporal Pillars. Queen Anne's Bounty, the Ecclesiastical Commissioners, and the Church of England*. Cambridge 1964.
Blake, R., *Disraeli*. London 1966.
Birks, T. R., *Church and State; or, National Religion and Church Establishments considered with reference to present controversies*. London 1869.
Chadwick, Owen, *The Victorian Church*. Part I. London 1966.
Church Assembly, *Church and State. Report of the Archbishops' Commission on the relations between Church and State: Report; Evidence of Witnesses*. London 1936.
—— *Minutes of Evidence*, typescript, available in the British Museum.
Cowherd, R. G., *The Politics of English Dissent*. London 1959.
Davidson, R. T. and Benham, W., *Life of Archibald Campbell Tait, Archbishop of Canterbury*. 2 vols. London 1891.

Figgis, J. N., *Churches in the Modern State*. London 1913.

Garbett, C. F., *Church and State in England*. London 1950.

Hanham, H. J., *Elections and Party Management. Politics in the age of Gladstone and Disraeli*. London 1957.

Magnus, Sir Philip, *Gladstone*. London 1954.

McClelland, V. A., *Cardinal Manning: his public life and influence*. London 1962.

Miall, A., *Life of Edward Miall*. London 1884.

Miall, E., *Title-deeds of the Church of England to her parochial endowments*. London 1862.

—— *The Social Influences of the State Church*. London 1867.

Monypenny, W. F. and Buckle, G. E., *The Life of Benjamin Disraeli, Earl of Beaconsfield*. New edn, 2 vols., London 1929.

Morley, John, *The Life of William Ewart Gladstone*. 2 vols. London 1906.

Ramm, Agatha, ed., *The Political Correspondence of Mr Gladstone and Lord Granville, 1868–1876*. 2 vols., London 1952.

Stanley, A. P., *Essays, chiefly on questions of Church and State, 1850–1870*. London 1870.

Temple, William, *Life of Bishop Percival*. London 1921.

Welldon, J. E. C., *The Religious Aspects of Disestablishment and Disendowment*. London 1911.

Williams, W. E., *The Rise of Gladstone to the leadership of the Liberal Party, 1859–68*. Cambridge 1934.

Victoria, Queen, *Letters of Queen Victoria*, second series, ed. G. E. Buckle. London 1926–8.

Vidler, A. R., *The Orb and the Cross*. London 1954.

—— *F. D. Maurice and Company*. London 1966.

NOTES

CHAPTER 1

1. Sir Maurice Gwyer, in Church Assembly, *Church and State: Report of the Archbishops' Commission on the relations between Church and State, 1935* (London 1936), vol. II, *Evidence of Witnesses*, p. 170 (to be cited as: Archbishops' Commission on Church and State, *Report*, and *Evidence of Witnesses*. The *Minutes of Evidence*, in typescript, are available in the British Museum).
2. See the summary of the Church of Scotland's position in Archbishops' Commission on Church and State, *Report*, pp. 52–6.
3. There is a clear analysis of the principal statutes in Sir Maurice Gwyer's evidence in ibid., *Evidence of Witnesses*, pp. 172–8.
4. *Ecclesiastical Polity*, vol. VIII, i, 2.
5. Norman Sykes, *Church and State in England in the XVIIIth Century* (Cambridge 1934), p. 284.
6. Quoted in A. R. Vidler, *F. D. Maurice and Company* (London 1966), pp. 167–8.
7. Article by Maurice, *Daily News*, 9 September 1868.
8. Quoted in Vidler, *F. D. Maurice and Company*, pp. 172–3.
9. Cyril Garbett, *Church and State in England* (London 1950), p. 146.
10. For an exchange on this subject in the 1860s, see Edward Miall, *Title-deeds of the Church of England to her parochial endowments*. London 1862; John Pulman, *The Anti-State Church Association and the Anti-Church Rate League unmasked; an exposure of the fallacies and misrepresentations contained in Mr E. Miall's "Title Deeds of the Church of England to her parochial endowments"*. London 1864.
11. See the discussion in Edward Miall, *The Social Influences of the State Church* (London 1867), especially pp. 8–12.
12. Edward Bickersteth to Disraeli, 21 March 1862, Hughenden Papers, B/XXI/B/490.
13. A. O. J. Cockshut, *Anglican Attitudes* (London 1959), p. 107.
14. 10 August 1868.
15. 1, 22 January 1869.
16. *Annual Register* (1865), pp. 93–4; (1867) pp. 163–4.
17. Tait to Gladstone, 5 October 1869; Gladstone to Tait, 28 October, 3 November 1869; Tait to Gladstone, 5 November 1869; Baring to Tait, 5 November 1869: Tait Papers, Personal Letters, ff. 284–5; 307–8; 324–5; 326–7; 330–1.
18. A. P. Stanley, *The Connection of Church and State, an address delivered in the Hall of Sion College, 15 February 1868, reprinted in Essays, chiefly on questions of Church and State, 1850–1870* (London 1870), p. 344.
19. See R. G. Cowherd, *The Politics of English Dissent* (London 1959), especially chapter 12.
20. See Arthur Miall, *Life of Edward Miall*. London 1884.
21. Liberation Society (to be abbreviated to Lib. Soc.) Papers, Executive Com-

mittee Minute Book, 1853–61, minute no. 1206, 27 September 1861, for Miall's and Skeats' paper; ibid., minutes nos. 1208, 1213, 1215–17, 4 and 18 October 1861, for the discussion and decisions.

22. Ibid., 1862–7, pp. 14–20; the quotation is from p. 15.
23. Ibid., 1862–7, p. 443; 1868–72, p. 146. For comparison, the income of the National Liberal Federation for the year 1881–2 was £1,981; that of the National Union of Conservative Associations for the same year was £1,099. H. J. Hanham, *Elections and Party Management* (London 1957), pp. 417–18.
24. Lib. Soc. Papers, Executive Committee Minute Book, 1862–7, pp. 316–24.
25. Ibid., 1862–7, pp. 316–24, 456, 358–9, 410–12, 457–8; 1868–72, pp. 5–10.
26. Ibid., 1862–7, pp. 140–64, 228–9. Cf. *Liberator* (December 1863), pp. 188–189, 192–3.
27. Lib. Soc. Papers, Executive Committee Minute Book, 1862–7, pp. 272–3, 276–86 (report of Parliamentary and Electoral Committee, 21 July 1865).
28. Ibid., pp. 66–8, 19 September 1862.
29. Ibid., pp. 140–7, 150–1, 23 October 1863.
30. Ibid., pp. 292–5, 15 September 1865.
31. *The Times*, 4 September 1868.
32. E.g. Ewing to Tait, 6 April 1868, Tait Papers, Personal Letters, vol. 85, ff. 118–19.
33. Ewing to Tait, 11 March 1868, ibid., vol. 84, ff. 239–40.
34. Ewing to Tait, 15 April 1868, ibid., vol. 85, f. 137.
35. Alexander Ewing, *Some apology for Creeds, Church Establishments, and the Christian Ministry* (London 1868), especially pp. 6–8.
36. *Pall Mall Gazette*, 15 July 1868.
37. See 11 April, 18 April, 15 August 1868.
38. 20 July 1867.
39. 9 September 1868; 8 September 1869.
40. 10 August, 9 October 1868.
41. 22 September 1868.
42. *Westminster Review* (July 1868), pp. 151–2.
43. 29 August 1868.
44. 16 September 1868.
45. 4 September 1868.
46. *Blackwood's Magazine* (November 1868), pp. 577, 579.
47. 2 October 1868.
48. January 1869, p. 1.

CHAPTER 2

1. *Report of Her Majesty's Commissioners on the revenue and condition of the established Church in Ireland*, H.C. 1867–8, xxiv, Appendix, p. 249. (To be referred to as *I.C. Commission, Report.*)
2. W. Maziere Brady, *Essays on the English State Church in Ireland* (London 1869), p. 176 (an essay on the Irish Church Commissioners' Report reprinted from *Contemporary Review*, November 1868).
3. *Parl. Deb.*, third series, vol. 194, col. 451. *Note.* In this book, reference is made to the third, fourth, and fifth series of *Parliamentary Debates*. A stand-

ard form is used for all: *Parl. Deb.*, series number, volume number, column number. When, in the fifth series, Lords and Commons debates began to appear in separate volumes, these are noted.

4. A. T. Lee, *The Irish Church: its present condition and future prospects* (London 1866), pp. 68–70.

5. For example, James Godkin, *Ireland and her Churches* (London 1867), pp. 451–2, estimated that 17,000 acres of Church land in the diocese of Armagh, whose value was returned at £14,331 per annum, should have yielded about £30,000. He gave many such examples, as did the *Freeman's Journal* Commission on *The Church Establishment in Ireland* (Dublin 1868). Nothing could be done about such a situation, of course, until leases expired.

6. Hugh Shearman, "Irish Church Finances after the Disestablishment", in H. A. Cronne, T. W. Moody, and D. B. Quinn, ed., *Essays in British and Irish History in Honour of James Eadie Todd* (London 1949), p. 287.

7. See below, p. 136.

8. *I.C. Commission, Report*, p. xxx, Table XXI.

9. Ibid., p. viii. Cf. William Atkins, *The consideration of certain changes in the distribution and management of Church property, which would tend to render the Irish branch of the United Church more efficient . . .* (London 1866), pp. 18–19. Atkins, reading this paper at a conference of the clergy and laity of the diocese of Down, Connor, and Dromore in 1865, chose himself as an example of the oddity of the system: he was Dean of Ferns, without a cathedral and without duties.

10. *I.C. Commission, Report*, p. xxix, Table XIX. The remainder consisted of twenty-seven chapelries without a parish or district, and seven sinecure rectories.

11. Ibid., p. xxx, totals of Table XXII. These were subjected to detailed criticism by Brady in *Essays*, pp. 179–84. He found evidence of a few incomes of over £1,100, when the Report said there were none. All salaries paid by incumbents to curates were deducted to arrive at net revenues.

12. Ibid., p. xxx, Table XXI. The exempt jurisdiction of Newry and Mourne, not in any diocese, contained three benefices and 7,331 Church members.

13. Ibid., p. xxxi, Table XXIII.

14. R. B. McDowell, *Public Opinion and Government Policy in Ireland, 1801–1846* (London 1952), pp. 24–30, discusses the influence of Evangelicalism in Ireland—"the predominant force in Irish protestantism by the middle of the nineteenth century"—and the resulting missionary work.

15. W. A. Phillips, ed., *History of the Church of Ireland*, vol. III (London 1933), pp. 335–49; W. D. Killen, *The Ecclesiastical History of Ireland*, vol. II (London 1875), pp. 498–502, 504–5; Godkin, *Ireland and her Churches*, pp. 388–425. For a modern description of the Achill Mission, see T. W. Freeman, *Pre-Famine Ireland* (Manchester 1957), pp. 145–6.

16. Godkin, *Ireland and her Churches*, pp. 176–7, 207, 218–20; *Freeman's Journal* Church Commission, pp. 369–70. According to the *Freeman*, three-quarters of the Evangelical Anglicans in Dublin attended proprietary churches.

17. William Fitzgerald, *Thoughts on the present circumstances of the Church of Ireland* (London 1860), pp. 18–30.

18. *I.C. Commission, Report*, p. xxxii, Table XXV. A high proportion of Irish Church patronage was in ecclesiastical hands, the figures being: royal patronage, 146; lay, including trustees and Trinity College, Dublin, 309; ecclesiastical, 988; royal and ecclesiastical in turns, 47; royal and lay in turns, 5; royal, lay, and ecclesiastical in turns, 1; lay and ecclesiastical in turns, 20.

19. Henry Newland, *An Apology for the Established Church in Ireland* (Dublin 1829), pp. 25-7.

20. See *Dublin Evening Post*, 21 December 1861, 4 January 1862, 6 and 9 September 1862; *Daily Express*, 3 January 1862; *Irish Times*, 4 and 9 January 1862; *Dublin Evening Mail*, 25 August 1862. The appointments were those of Robert Gregg to Cork and Marcus Gervais Beresford to Armagh.

21. Net revenues of Irish sees, on the average of the three years ending 31 December 1831, were: *Archbishoprics*—Armagh £14,494; Dublin, £7,786; Cashel, £6,308; Tuam, £6,996. *Bishoprics*—Meath, £4,068; Clogher, £8,668; Down and Connor, £4,207; Derry, £12,159; Raphoe, £5,052; Kilmore, £6,225; Dromore, £4,216; Kildare, £6,061; Ossory, £3,322; Ferns and Leighlin, £5,730; Limerick, £4,973; Waterford and Lismore, £3,933; Cork and Ross, £3,901; Cloyne, £4,901; Killaloe and Kilfenora, £3,966; Elphin, £6,263; Clonfert and Kilmacduagh, £2,970; Killala and Achonry, £3,410 (*First Report of Commissioners on Ecclesiastical Revenue and Patronage, Ireland*, H.C. 1833, xxi, pp. 240-3).

22. Godkin, *Ireland and her Churches*, pp. 523-33. His claim that these bishops "were enabled by their incomes from the Irish Establishment to found families" was exaggerated—many became bishops *because* they came from wealthy families, though undoubtedly the revenues and patronage of their sees would still be useful.

23. The Minute Books of the Irish Privy Council record its ecclesiastical work along with all the rest. See the volume running from 7 January 1868 to 29 October 1875, pp. 5, 6, 20, 89, 118, 141-3 for examples of the functions mentioned above. For the Order in Council of 30 June 1868, p. 40. For an example of the correspondence which could build up over the approval of an episcopal order for the continuing of a union between parishes which had been united "from time immemorial", see Irish Privy Council Office, Registered Correspondence, 1868, no. 194. This involved letters from the Bishop of Tuam, two long minutes by the secretary to the Privy Council, and correspondence between the Privy Council and the Ecclesiastical Commissioners.

24. The correspondence is in H.O. 45 O.S. 7252/1-15. Cf. the arguments used in William Fitzgerald, *Thoughts on the present circumstances of the Church in Ireland*, pp. 14-18.

25. See the opinions by the Irish Law Officers, 5 November 1868 (Conservative) and 13 January 1869 (Liberal), that the Crown had power to issue writs to convene the Irish Convocation, and that there was nothing in the constitution of the Irish branch of the Church to make Convocation less legal there than in England—H.O. 45, O.S. 7252/17, 20.

26. G. Miller, *The present crisis of the Church of Ireland considered* (Dublin 1845), p. 4.

27. J. H. Whyte, *The Independent Irish Party 1850-9* (London 1958), p. 144.

28. Abraham Hume, *Results of the Irish Census of 1861*. London 1864. Figures substantially correct, but later amended, were available in 1861—see *The Times*, 17 July 1861. They were there given as follows: Roman Catholics, 4,490,583; Established Church, 678,661; Presbyterians, 598,992; other persuasions, 8,414. The last two figures differed considerably from the later returns.

29. E. R. Norman, *The Catholic Church and Ireland in the Age of Rebellion, 1859–73* (London 1965), chapter 4, "Birth of the National Association", describes in detail the Association's creation. This distinguished study has placed the whole period with which it deals in a new perspective.

30. Quoted, ibid., p. 150.

31. Ibid., pp. 177–81.

32. See, for example, *Liberator* (August 1861), p. 131; (September 1862), pp. 154–5; (December 1863), pp. 190–1; (June 1864), p. 81, quoting O'Neill Daunt urging Irish Catholics not to leave their cause to English voluntaries; (February 1865), pp. 25–6, welcoming the formation of the National Association as evidence that Irish apathy had been overcome.

33. Carvell Williams's report, 4 October 1867, Lib. Soc. Papers, Executive Committee Minute Book, 1862–7, pp. 479–81.

34. Ibid., pp. 460, 480, 485–7.

35. Ibid., 1868–72, pp. 2–4, 30–2.

36. *Parl. Deb.*, third series, vol. 182, cols. 973–1070; ibid., vol. 187, cols. 96–185.

37. *Liberator* (June 1867), p. 111.

38. 10 July 1868.

39. F. F. Trench (rector of Newton, Co. Meath), *The Disestablishment and Disendowment of the Established Church in Ireland shown to be desirable under existing circumstances* (London and Dublin 1868), p. 8.

40. *Freeman's Journal* Church Commission, pp. 43, 45, 50, 55–6, 58.

41. Ibid., p. 240.

42. Ibid., pp. 185–6.

43. Godkin, *Ireland and her Churches*, pp. xviii–xx.

44. Ibid., pp. 242–3.

45. *Freeman's Journal* Church Commission, pp. 159–61. "Profitable lands" were distinguished from the non-profitable, e.g. moorland or bog.

46. Ibid., pp. 206–7.

47. *I.C. Commission, Report*, p. 21.

48. *Parl. Deb.*, third series, vol. 194, cols. 1835–43.

49. *Freeman's Journal* Church Commission, pp. 12–13.

50. *Irish Ecclesiastical Record*, vol. IV (1868), p. 459.

51. *Freeman's Journal* Church Commission, pp. 7–9, and *passim*.

52. William Fitzgerald, *A charge....* (Dublin 1866), p. 10.

53. W. J. O'Neill Daunt, *Disendowment of the State Church in Ireland* (London 1865), p. 15.

54. *Freeman's Journal* Church Commission, pp. 11–13.

55. 27 June 1868.

56. 25 August 1868.

57. 24 September 1868.

58. 16 November 1868.
59. H. S. Skeats, *The Irish Church: a historical and statistical review*. London 1865.
60. A. E. Gayer, *Fallacies and Fictions relating to the Irish Church Establishment* (5th edn, Dublin 1868), pp. 3–4, 6–8, 9–13, 15, 17–19. Gayer, one of the Irish Ecclesiastical Commissioners, went very carefully through Skeats' figures, though often to little effect—he proved, for example, that two benefices which Skeats said had no Church members had in fact thirty-eight and thirty-seven respectively; their net revenues were £369 and £213.
61. A. T. Lee, "Some Account of the Property and Statistics of the Irish Church", in *Essays on the Irish Church*, by Clergymen of the Established Church in Ireland (Oxford and London 1866), p. 238; A. T. Lee, *Facts respecting the present state of the Church in Ireland* (5th edn, London 1868), p. 10.
62. A. T. Lee, in *Essays on the Irish Church*, p. 231 n. Cf. J. Byrne, "The Influences exerted on Ireland by the Irish Church Establishment", ibid., pp. 53–6; A. T. Lee, *Facts respecting the present state of the Church in Ireland*, p. 18; A. T. Lee, *Irish Church*, p. 62.
63. T. R. Birks, *Church and State: or, National Religion and Church Establishments considered with reference to present controversies* (London 1869), p. 416. For a good example of the defence of the Irish Church by extension, see ibid., pp. 327–48. Cf. *Church and State: with reference to the United Church of England and Ireland*, by a Lay Churchman (London 1868); A. T. Lee, *Church in Ireland*, pp. 5–6; *Quarterly Review* (April 1868), pp. 556–7; (July 1868), pp. 257–8.
64. A. T. Lee, *Church in Ireland*, p. 47; cf. ibid., p. 4; *Short notes on the Irish Church question*, by a Layman (London n.d.). This line of argument was made fun of by Trollope: "If we grant that St Patrick was a staunch Protestant, who hated the Bishop of Rome, abjured the mass, detested the five extra sacraments, had one wife and several children, and would have upheld the supremacy of Henry VIII if he had only heard of him in time, what then? What is that to us at the present day? We find the majority of the Irish people non-Protestants" (*St Paul's* (February 1868), p. 565).
65. F. D. Maurice, "The Irish Church Establishment", *Contemporary Review* (January 1868), pp. 54–65.
66. William Connor Magee, "The Irish Church Establishment: a reply to Professor Maurice", ibid. (March 1868), pp. 429–44.
67. A. T. Lee, *Church in Ireland*, pp. 68–70; the lower figure appeared in the early edition of his *Facts respecting the present state of the Church in Ireland*—he had the worst of a running fight with Maziere Brady. Cf. R. Nugent, *The Church in Ireland and her assailants* (London 1868), pp. 3–8.
68. J. T. O'Brien, *The Case of the Established Church in Ireland* (2nd edn, London 1867), pp. 4–9, 25–30, sets out both the arguments mentioned in this paragraph.
69. *Quarterly Review* (April 1868), pp. 552–6; W. H. Ferrar, *The title of the Irish Church to her property, and the consequences of her disendowment*. Dublin 1868; A. T. Lee, in *Essays on the Irish Church*, pp. 229–30; F. Higginson, *The beleaguered Church; not a chapter of autobiography*. London 1869; *Church*

and State, by a Lay Churchman; *Short notes on the Irish Church question*, by a Layman.

70. *Parl. Deb.*, third series, vol. 194, cols. 1668–9.
71. *Quarterly Review* (April 1868), p. 558.
72. Skeats, *The Irish Church*, p. 60; O'Neill Daunt, *The Disendowment of the State-Church in Ireland*, pp. 13–14.
73. Lowe to Gladstone, 3 February 1869, Gladstone Papers, 44301, ff. 37–8.
74. 28 March 1868.
75. 9 January 1869.
76. See Skeats, *The Irish Church*, p. 61.
77. J. T. O'Brien, *The Church in Ireland; our duty in regard to its defence* (London 1866), p. 7.
78. James Byrne, "On the general principles of the establishment and endowment of religious bodies by the State, with special reference to Ireland", in *Essays on the Irish Church*, p. 19.
79. Ibid., p. 3.
80. Ibid., p. 48.
81. James Byrne, "The influences exerted on Ireland by the Irish Church Establishment", in *Essays on the Irish Church*, p. 306.
82. Ibid., p. 309.
83. Godkin, *Ireland and her Churches*, pp. 498–507, 555–8.
84. Byrne, in *Essays on the Irish Church*, pp. 21–3, 35–6.
85. Ibid., pp. 53–6.
86. See p. 54, above.
87. J. T. O'Brien, *The Case of the Established Church in Ireland*, pp. 60–1.
88. Nassau Senior, *Journals, Conversations and Essays relating to Ireland* (London 1868), vol. II, p. 277: Whately in conversation with Senior, 16 November 1862.
89. Cf. Norman, *Catholic Church and Ireland*, pp. 185–6, 282.
90. A. T. Lee, in *Essays on the Irish Church*, p. 257, note (e); cf. A. T. Lee, *Facts respecting the present state of the Church in Ireland*, p. 12.
91. April 1868, p. 573; cf. p. 576.
92. November 1868, p. 639.
93. A. T. Lee, *Church in Ireland*, p. 59; Ferrar, *The Title of the Irish Church to her property; Church and State*, by a Lay Churchman; cf. Beresford (Archbishop of Armagh) to Gladstone, 23 November 1868, Gladstone Papers, 44416, ff. 224–8.
94. Fitzgerald, *Thoughts on the present circumstances of the Church of Ireland*, p. 22.
95. Cullen to Cardinal Barnabo, of the Propaganda in Rome, 5 April 1868, quoted in Norman, *Catholic Church and Ireland*, p. 341.
96. June 1868, p. 460.
97. April 1868, pp. 566–7; July 1868, pp. 262–7; October 1868, pp. 560–1.
98. Colonel Stuart Knox moved on 30 March 1868, before the debate on Gladstone's resolutions on the Irish Church, that Article V of the Act of Union be read to the House.
99. For example, *Quarterly Review* (April 1868), p. 564.
100. A. H. Foster, *The Irish Church Question. A letter to the Right Hon. William Ewart Gladstone, M.P.* (Dublin 1868), pp. 20–2. Ferrar, *The Title of the Irish Church to her property*.

101. Warburton to Gladstone, 24 March 1868, Gladstone Papers 44414, ff. 196–204.
102. *Quarterly Review* (January 1867), p. 262.
103. *Letters and Memorials of Richard Chenevix Trench*, edited by the author of *Charles Lowder* (London 1888), vol. II, pp. 59–60, quoting Trench's charge to his diocese, 1868.
104. See, for example, J. Bromley, *The Man of Ten Talents. A portrait of Richard Chenevix Trench, 1807–86* (London 1959), pp. 167–8, quoting Trench's charge of 1866; Abraham Jones, *Thoughts on the Established Church* (Dublin 1868), p. 13.
105. *An Irishman's glance at some anomalies in the Church established in England.* Dublin 1866.
106. A. T. Lee, *Church in Ireland*, pp. 5–6; *Church and State*, by a Lay Churchman; *Quarterly Review* (April 1868), pp. 566–7, (July 1868), pp. 257–8.
107. See generally Mary Paraclita Reilly, *Aubrey de Vere: Victorian Observer* (Lincoln, Nebraska 1953); W. Ward, *Aubrey de Vere, a memoir*. London 1904; Norman, *Catholic Church and Ireland*, pp. 305–11.
108. Aubrey de Vere, *The Church Settlement of Ireland, or Hibernia Pacanda* (London 1866), pp. 4, 25, 32–3.
109. Ibid., p. 30.
110. Aubrey de Vere, *Ireland's Church Property, and the right use of it* (London 1867), pp. 22–3.
111. De Vere, *Church Settlement of Ireland*, pp. xix–xx.
112. De Vere, *Church Settlement of Ireland*, Preface; *Ireland's Church Property*, *passim* and especially p. 26.
113. For Moriarty's views, see Norman, *Catholic Church and Ireland*, pp. 311–18.
114. De Vere, *Ireland's Church Property*, p. 49.
115. Ibid., pp. 2–3.
116. See W. Maziere Brady, *Facts or Fictions? Seven letters on the "Facts concerning the Irish Church", published by the Church Institution.* Dublin 1867; *The alleged conversion of the Irish Bishops to the reformed religion at the accession of Queen Elizabeth . . . disproved.* 5th edn. London 1867; "The Irish Church Commissioners' Report", in *Essays on the English State Church in Ireland.*
117. Brady, *Essays on the English State Church in Ireland*, p. 155. Brady himself sought an appointment in England from Gladstone in return for his role in the public debate on the Irish Church question; Gladstone was sympathetic but did nothing. Gladstone to Fortescue, 30 July 1869, and an enclosed letter, Brady to De Vere, 29 July 1869, Strachie Mss, 324, CP 1/55, 56.
118. Brady, *Essays on the English State Church in Ireland*, pp. 86–7.
119. W. Maziere Brady, *Remarks on the Irish Church Temporalities* (Dublin 1865), pp. 17–18.
120. Brady, *Essays on the English State Church in Ireland*, p. 84.
121. Brady, *Remarks on the Irish Church Temporalities*, pp. 4–5.
122. Brady, *Essays on the English State Church in Ireland*, p. 154.
123. Ibid., pp. 93–5.
124. Brady, *Remarks on the Irish Church Temporalities*, pp. 23–4.
125. Article in *Dictionary of National Biography*. Spencer to Gladstone, 28 December 1865, 3 June 1866, show Bence Jones being consulted and

quoted on agricultural matters: Gladstone Papers, 44306, ff. 1, 12–13. There is a small collection of Bence Jones's papers, mostly about the boycotting, in the present home of the family at Glenville, County Cork. I am very grateful to Colonel Bence Jones and his son, Mark Bence Jones, for allowing me to see these papers.

126. W. Bence Jones, *The Irish Church from the point of view of one of its laymen* (2nd edn, London 1868), pp. 10–12. Bence Jones's view of the Irish character has some affinity with that to be found in the works of Miss Honor Tracy, notably *Mind You, I've Said Nothing!* (London 1953).

127. Bence Jones, *The Irish Church*, pp. 14–16.

128. Ibid., p. 33.

129. W. Bence Jones, *The Future of the Irish Church* (Dublin 1869), pp. 26–7.

130. Bence Jones, *The Irish Church*, p. 45.

131. Ibid., p. 29.

132. Ibid., pp. 16–19, 30, 34–7.

133. Ibid., pp. 33–4.

134. *Parl. Deb.*, third series, vol. 182, cols. 372–82.

135. Grey to Tait, 18 March 1868, Tait Papers, Personal Letters, vol. 85, ff. 113–15.

136. Ibid., Grey to Bright, 27 March 1868, Bright Papers, 43389, ff. 169–70; Earl Grey, *Letter to John Bright, Esq., M.P., respecting the Irish Church* (London 1868).

137. Grey to Tait, 5 May 1868, Tait Papers, Personal Letters, vol. 85, ff. 162–7.

138. Lord Russell, *Letter to the Right Hon. Chichester Fortescue on the state of Ireland*. London 1868; *A second letter* . . . London 1868; *A third letter* . . . London 1869; R. T. Davidson and W. Benham, *Life of Archibald Campbell Tait, Archbishop of Canterbury* (London 1891), vol. II, pp. 32–4; Lord Dufferin, *Inaugural Address delivered before the Social Science Congress at Belfast in 1867* (Belfast 1867); J. M. Ludlow, "Between two Stools", *Contemporary Review*, December 1868.

139. Ludlow, in *Contemporary Review* (December 1868), pp. 572–3.

140. See below, pp. 149–53.

141. See Norman, *Catholic Church and Ireland*, pp. 157–87, chapters 5 and 6.

CHAPTER 3

1. *Pall Mall Gazette*, 1 January 1868; *Saturday Review*, 18 January 1868.

2. *Saturday Review*, 15 February 1868.

3. Granville to Russell, 3 January 1868, Clarendon to Granville, 4 February 1868, Lord E. Fitzmaurice, *The Life of Granville George Leveson Gower, second Earl of Granville, 1815–1891*, vol. I (London 1905), pp. 518–19.

4. Argyll to Gladstone, 13, 30 January 1868, Gladstone Papers, 44100, ff. 183–5, 192–9.

5. Gladstone to Argyll, 1 February 1868, ibid., f. 200.

6. P. Magnus, *Gladstone* (London 1954), pp. 188–9; R. Blake, *Disraeli* (London 1966), p. 475; *Globe*, 3 February 1868.

7. In a speech at Edinburgh, 1867, quoted Monypenny and Buckle, vol. II, p. 289.

8. *Saturday Review*, 29 February 1868.
9. *Freeman*, 27 February 1868.
10. Norman, *Catholic Church and Ireland*, p. 150; *Freeman*, 9–13 January 1868.
11. *Daily Express*, 20 January, 5, 6 February 1868.
12. "What shall we do for Ireland?", *Quarterly Review*, January 1868; *Pall Mall Gazette*, 24 January 1868.
13. Hughenden Papers, B/LX/A/1, "Legislation for Ireland. Memorandum", 1 March 1868.
14. Undated memorandum by Hamilton, endorsed by Corry "Spring of 1868", and on internal evidence probably prepared between 28 February and 2 March (Hughenden Papers, B/XX/H/101aa).
15. Disraeli to Derby, 4 March 1868, Monypenny and Buckle, vol. II, pp. 353–4.
16. Disraeli to the Queen, 4 March 1868, *Letters of Queen Victoria*, second series, vol. I, pp. 509–11.
17. See Cairns to Disraeli, 2 March 1868, Hughenden Papers, B/XX/Ca/17, and Mayo's speech in the Commons on 10 March, with its mention of levelling up, not down, as the best solution of the Irish Church question, below, p. 84.
18. Mayo to Disraeli, 11 February 1868, Hughenden Papers, B/XX/Bo/51.
19. Disraeli to the Queen, 4 March 1868, cited in n. 16 above.
20. *A Letter to the Rt. Hon. Chichester Fortescue on the State of Ireland.*
21. Gladstone to Bright, 10 December 1867, Bright Papers, 43385, ff. 20–1, printed in W. E. Williams, *The Rise of Gladstone to the Leadership of the Liberal Party, 1859–68* (Cambridge 1934), pp. 162–3.
22. *Parl. Deb.*, third series, vol. 190, col. 1764.
23. Ibid., vol. 191, col. 32.
24. Ibid., cols. 941–5. The odd discrepancy between the two votes arose because in the second division two Liberals voted by mistake in the wrong lobby (J. E. Denison (Viscount Ossington), *Notes from my Journal when Speaker of the House of Commons* (London 1899), p. 222).
25. *Parl. Deb.*, third series, vol. 191, cols. 1675–9.
26. Williams, *Rise of Gladstone*, p. 10.
27. See the Introduction. The book itself is dated 22 September 1868. The delay brings out the nature of Gladstone's act: he did not want to influence the election, as nearly any politician would, but simply to explain himself.
28. See A. R. Vidler, *The Orb and the Cross* (London 1945), pp. 41–4. Dr Vidler's keen analysis makes the argument clearer than Gladstone succeeded in doing.
29. *Chapter of Autobiography*, pp. 18–19, 20, 22, 25.
30. Ibid., pp. 14–15, 59–61; "Mr Gladstone's Apologia", *Quarterly Review* (January 1869), pp. 123–4.
31. *Chapter of Autobiography*, p. 62.
32. The best accounts are in Gladstone's own *Chapter of Autobiography*; Williams, *Rise of Gladstone*; and Norman, *Catholic Church and Ireland*.
33. *Chapter of Autobiography*, pp. 27–37; cf. Gladstone to Bright, 10 December 1867, Williams, pp. 162–3, which puts the same explanation more

briefly; Magnus, *Gladstone*, pp. 68–70, which includes the quotation from Peel.

34. *Chapter of Autobiography*, p. 31.
35. Gladstone to Bright, 10 December 1867, Williams, p. 162.
36. *Chapter of Autobiography*, pp. 32–5, 38–9.
37. Gladstone to Chichester Fortescue, 11 December 1867, Strachie Mss, 324, CP 1/10.
38. Gladstone to Townshend Mainwaring, 15 July 1864, Gladstone Papers, 44534, f. 100.
39. Gladstone to Phillimore, 13 February 1865, Gladstone Papers, 44277, ff. 245–6; John Morley, *The Life of William Ewart Gladstone* (2 vols. London 1905), vol. I, p. 686.
40. Fortescue to Gladstone, 29 March 1865, Gladstone Papers, 44121, ff. 10–11; *Morning Herald*, 30 March 1865; *Parl. Deb.*, third series, vol. 178, cols. 420–34.
41. Gladstone to Brady, 15 April 1865, Gladstone Papers, 44535, ff. 45–6.
42. Gladstone to Fortescue, 7 April 1866, Strachie Mss. 324, CP 1/7; see *Parl. Deb.*, third series, vol. 187, cols. 121–31.
43. *Daily Express*, 8 May 1867.
44. Gray to Gladstone, 2 September 1867, Gladstone Papers, 44413, ff. 121–5; resolutions prepared at a meeting of Irish bishops under Cardinal Cullen, 1–3 October 1867, Norman, *Catholic Church and Ireland*, pp. 332–4.
45. Gladstone to Gray, 6 September 1867, Gladstone Papers, 44413, ff. 134–5.
46. Gladstone to Fortescue, 1 December 1867, Strachie Mss. 324, CP 1/8a.
47. Gladstone to Bright, 10 December 1867, Williams, pp. 162–3.
48. Gladstone to Fortescue, 11 December 1867, Strachie Mss. 324, CP 1/10.
49. See Morley, I, p. 876; Williams, *Rise of Gladstone*, pp. 158–60—they argue for both Manchester and Clerkenwell; Norman, *Catholic Church and Ireland*, p. 340, thinks Manchester was probably decisive.
50. See Norman, *Catholic Church and Ireland*, chapter 6 generally, especially pp. 259, 265–6, 273. On p. 259, for example: ". . . he attempted to put an end to the Mayo university plan by proposing his famous Resolutions on the Church in its place."
51. Argyll to Gladstone, 21 December 1867, Gladstone Papers, 44100, ff. 178–81. D. A. Thornley, *Isaac Butt and Home Rule* (London 1964), pp. 32–3.
52. V. A. McClelland, *Cardinal Manning, His Public Life and Influence* (London 1962), chapter 6, especially pp. 162–3, 168.
53. Manning to Gladstone, 28 March 1868, to Anderson, 2 April 1868, ibid., p. 172.
54. Cullen to Manning, 8 April 1867, ibid., p. 164.
55. Moriarty to Monsell, 2 March 1868, copy marked for Gladstone by Monsell, Gladstone Papers, 44152, ff. 98–113.
56. MacColl to Gladstone, 15 September 1866, Gladstone Papers, 44242, ff. 368–71.
57. Norman, *Catholic Church and Ireland*, p. 336, and n. 6, where an analysis of the signatories is given; Fortescue to Gladstone, 14 December 1867, Gladstone Papers, 44121, ff. 60–3.
58. Gladstone's election address is printed in *Blackwood's Magazine* (November 1868), pp. 630–2.

59. *Parl. Deb.*, third series, vol. 190, col. 1391.
60. Monypenny and Buckle, vol. II, p. 355.
61. Ibid., pp. 59-62.
62. Disraeli to Corry, 16 October 1866, Hughenden Papers, B/XX/D/22.
63. Monypenny and Buckle, vol. II, p. 358.
64. Open letter to Lord Dartmouth, Monypenny and Buckle, vol. II, p. 360.
65. Disraeli to the Queen, 23 March 1868, the Queen to Disraeli, 24 March 1868, *Letters of Queen Victoria*, second series (London 1926-8), vol. I, pp. 516-19.
66. Derby to Disraeli, 25 March 1868, Hughenden Papers, B/XX/S/485. Derby added significantly: "I know my opinions are not those of the majority." Text of the amendment, *Parl. Deb.*, third series, vol. 191, col. 507.
67. Cairns to Hardy, 1 April 1868, A. E. Gathorne Hardy, ed., *Gathorne Hardy, a Memoir* (London 1910), vol. I, pp. 267-8; *Parl. Deb.*, third series, vol. 191, col. 503.
68. 12 March 1868.
69. Both 1 April 1868.
70. Hardy's speech, *Parl. Deb.*, third series, vol. 191, cols. 575-99; Knox (Dungannon), cols., 627-8; Schreiber (Cheltenham), cols. 634-7.
71. Tait Papers, Personal Letters, vol. 85, ff. 144-5.
72. Cranborne's speech, *Parl. Deb.*, third series, vol. 191, cols. 533-40; Peel's speech, ibid., cols. 721-8.
73. Denison, pp. 222-5.
74. Taylor to Disraeli, 19 April 1868, Hughenden Papers, B/XX/T/112.
75. *Parl. Deb.*, third series, vol. 191, col. 924.
76. Monypenny and Buckle, vol. II, p. 365.
77. Hardy to Disraeli, 7 April 1868, Hughenden Papers, B/XX/HA/26.
78. *Daily Express*, 15 April 1868. The *Record* (6 April 1868) commended Disraeli's speech, but lamented that his sincerity was not to be relied upon.
79. 4, 7, 11, 15, 25 April 1868.
80. 20 May 1868.
81. "The Political Prelude", *Fortnightly Review* (1 July 1868), pp. 103-14.
82. *Pall Mall Gazette*, *Globe*, 7 July 1868.
83. *Globe*, 27 October 1868.
84. *Quarterly Review* (April 1868), p. 556.
85. Ibid. (October 1868), pp. 566, 541.
86. *Blackwood's Magazine* (November 1868), p. 622.
87. Advertisement in *Saturday Review*, 15 August 1868.
88. *Globe*, *Pall Mall Gazette*, *The Times*, 18 August 1868.
89. Taylor to Disraeli, 9 April 1868, Hughenden Papers, B/XX/T/108 and 108a.
90. *The Times*, 18 June 1868.
91. Monypenny and Buckle, vol. II, p. 400.
92. *Daily Telegraph*, 31 July 1868.
93. Hughenden Papers, B/XX/D/105.
94. "... the great feature of national opinion is an utter repudiation by all classes of the High Church party." Disraeli to the Queen, 21 August 1868,

Blake, p. 508. Cf. Disraeli to Stanley, 21 August 1868, Monypenny and Buckle, vol. II, p. 400.

95. Disraeli to the Queen, 20 November 1868, *Letters of Queen Victoria*, second series, vol. I, p. 554; Blake, p. 509.

96. Disraeli to Stanley, 21 August 1868, Monypenny and Buckle, vol. II, p. 400.

97. Disraeli's address in *Blackwood's Magazine* (November 1868), pp. 625–7.

98. Stanley to Disraeli, 23 September 1868, Hughenden Papers, B/XX/S/817.

99. Stanley to Disraeli, 24 September 1868, ibid., B/XX/S/818.

100. Stanley to Disraeli, 29 September 1868, ibid., B/XX/S/824.

101. *Saturday Review*, 11 July 1868. The candidate in question was Shaw, standing for North Shields.

102. *The Times*, 15 July, 8 August 1868.

103. See *The Times'* summaries of election addresses published throughout July 1868.

104. Hanham, pp. 216–17.

105. I. Benson to Northcote, 21 September 1868, Iddesleigh Papers, 50037, ff. 181–2.

106. See the general account in Hanham, pp. 304–7; for details, the Home Office file on Murphy in the Public Record Office, H.O. 45, O.S. 7991.

107. *Pall Mall Gazette, Globe*, 13 May 1868, contain both accounts and comments. See also *Parl. Deb.*, third series, vol. 192, cols. 817–32, for a debate on these riots in the Commons.

108. *Manchester Guardian, Globe*, 26 May 1868.

109. *Manchester Guardian*, 5, 7, 8, 9 September 1868; *The Times*, 2, 4, 7, 8 September 1868; *Pall Mall Gazette*, 5, 8 September 1868; *Daily News*, 8, 9, 10 September 1868.

110. 12 September, 17 October 1868.

111. 6 January 1868.

112. 14 March 1868.

113. 3 October 1868.

114. 24 March 1868, Gladstone Papers, 44414, ff. 194–5.

115. Girdlestone to Tait, 13 April 1868, Tait Papers, Personal Letters, vol. 85, ff. 130–3.

116. 7 August 1868; ibid., ff. 177–8. Sir Walter Farquhar in 1869 was also thinking of James II and Macaulay, contrasting the behaviour of the English archbishops on the Irish Church Bill with Macaulay's description of the firmness of the Seven Bishops against the King (Farquhar to Tait, 7 June 1869; ibid., vol. 86, ff. 167–70).

117. Ewing to Gladstone, 11 April, 11 May 1868, Gladstone Papers, 44152, ff. 382–4, 385–6.

118. 9 March 1869, Tait Papers, Personal Letters, vol. 87, f. 87.

119. Stanley to Tait, undated, ibid., ff. 207–8.

120. *The Times*, 2, 3 July 1868.

121. *Pall Mall Gazette*, 3 July 1868; see their advertising, e.g. *Globe*, 4 August 1868.

122. *The Times*, 30 September 1868.

123. *The Times*, 12 October 1868.

124. T. Navin to Disraeli, 8 September 1868, Hughenden Papers, B/IX/G/15.

125. 25 November 1868, Gladstone Papers, 44095, ff. 317–18.
126. Memorandum by Grey, 4 December 1868, *Letters of Queen Victoria*, second series, vol. I, p. 563.
127. *Parl. Deb.*, third series, vol. 192, cols. 1917–18; cf. *Saturday Review*, 27 June 1868.
128. *The Times*, 6 November 1868.
129. J. Borough to Corry, 4 November 1868, Hughenden Papers, B/IX/G/55.
130. *The Rock*, 28, 29 September 1868. I am indebted to the Reverend Michael Hennell for this reference.
131. See Hardy to Disraeli, 18 August 1868, and the enclosed letter from James Bardsley, Hughenden Papers, B/XX/Ha/38; Hardy to Disraeli, 14 October 1868, ibid., B/XX/Ha/45; W. H. Cooke to Mowbray, 16 August 1868, and the enclosed letter from R. Gregory, ibid., B/IX/G/12b.
132. *The Times*, 3 September 1868.
133. *Parl. Deb.*, third series, vol. 192, cols. 789–92, 806–9. The *Pall Mall Gazette* described the House as astonished and incredulous as Disraeli made his statement—23 May 1868.
134. *Dublin Evening Mail*, 14 September 1868.
135. Hardy to Disraeli, 12 September 1868, Hughenden Papers, B/XX/Ha/40.
136. *Globe*, 21 September 1868.
137. Mayo to Disraeli, 4 October 1868, Hughenden Papers, B/XX/Bo/82.
138. Cairns to Disraeli, 20 October 1868, ibid., B/XX/Ca/55, 55a.
139. The *Saturday Review*, 28 August 1868, noted that while Gladstone was mentioned by name in nearly every election address, whether for praise or blame, Conservative election addresses seldom mentioned Disraeli. It argued that single-minded Conservatives did not feel that they were represented by Disraeli, and there may have been something in this.
140. *Daily Express*, 21, 22, 29 September 1868; *Belfast Newsletter*, 19 September 1868.
141. *Freeman*, 21, 23 November 1868.
142. Mayo to Disraeli, 10 September 1867: "This is an infernal country to manage. We have been forced to institute a few proceedings against some Orangemen for breaches of the Processions Act whereupon the North is 'up'. Impartiality is impossible—Statesmanship out of place. The only way to govern is the old plan (which I will never attempt) of taking up violently one faction or the other pitting them like fighting cocks and then backing one. I wish you would send me to India—Ireland is the grave of every reputation" (Hughenden Papers, B/XX/Bo/36). Mayo went to India, and was assassinated there.
143. Lanyon to Mayo, 29 January 1868, and enclosures; Mayo to Disraeli, 31 January 1868, Hughenden Papers, B/XX/Bo/49, 49a, b, c.
144. Disraeli to Stanley, 16 August 1868, Monypenny and Buckle, vol. II, p. 400.
145. Hanham, p. 198.
146. All these calculations were in the first leader of *The Times*, 2 November 1868.
147. Disraeli to Corry, 3 November 1868 (obviously, from its contents, after reading *The Times* leader of 2 November), Hughenden Papers, B/XX/D/111.

148. *Saturday Review*, 5 December 1868.
149. See J. Vincent, *The Formation of the Liberal Party, 1857–68* (London 1966), p. 27.
150. Grey to Tait, 5 May 1868, Tait Papers, Personal Letters, vol. 85, ff. 162–7.
151. See Norman, *Catholic Church and Ireland*, pp. 285–7.
152. Ibid. pp. 347–9; Thornley, *Isaac Butt*, pp. 37–45.
153. Hanham, pp. 316–17; Thornley, *Isaac Butt*, pp. 45–52; Bowyer to Disraeli, 25 November 1868, 7 December 1868, enclosing Moriarty to Disraeli, 4 December 1868, Hughenden Papers, B/XXI/B/717, 719, 719a.
154. Brand to Gladstone, 28 November 1868, quoted Hanham, p. 295.
155. Gibson to Gladstone, 19 November 1868, Gladstone Papers, 44416, ff. 206–7.
156. Report of Electoral Committee, 4 December 1868, Lib. Soc. Papers, Executive Committee Minute Book, 1868–72, pp. 102–10.
157. Ieuan Gwynedd Jones, "The Liberation Society in Welsh Politics, 1844 to 1868", *Welsh History Review*, vol. I, pp. 193–224.
158. J. G. Kellas, "The Liberal Party and the Scottish Church Disestablishment Crisis", *English Historical Review*, vol. LXXIX (1964), p. 32, n. 1.
159. Hanham, p. 212; *The Times*, 1, 3, 4, 11, 12, 14 August 1868, for reports and comment on the Wesleyan Conference. The membership of the Wesleyan connexion was nearly 350,000.
160. R. C. N. Hamilton to Col. Taylor, 20 October 1868, Hughenden Papers, B/XX/T/102.
161. Malmesbury to Disraeli, 24 November 1868, ibid., B/XX/Hs/157.
162. See *The Times*, 16 November 1868, for one of the last of their advertisements.
163. J. N. Graves to Disraeli, 1 November 1868, Hughenden Papers, B/X/B/105.

CHAPTER 4

1. Derby to Disraeli, 3 March 1868, Hughenden Papers, B/XX/S/483.
2. 20 November 1868; cf. 25 November 1868.
3. Argyll to Gladstone, 30 November 1868, Gladstone Papers, 44100, ff. 275–8.
4. Gladstone to Sullivan, 7 January 1869, ibid., 44418, f. 78.
5. Gladstone to Tait, 23 December 1868, ibid., 44417, f. 53.
6. 18, 21 December 1868.
7. Gladstone Papers, 44756, ff. 136–40.
8. Ibid., ff. 144–5; several papers headed "Queries on the Irish Church", ff. 183–94.
9. Ibid., ff. 147–55, 157–81.
10. Gladstone to Fortescue, 26 December 1868, Strachie Mss. 324, CP1/19; to Sullivan, 26 December 1868, Gladstone Papers, 44417, f. 261; to Granville, 29 December 1868, Strachie Mss. 324, CP1/54; Agatha Ramm, ed., *The Political Correspondence of Mr Gladstone and Lord Granville, 1868–1876* (London 1952), vol. I, p. 5, n. 5.

11. Granville to Gladstone, 31 December 1868, Ramm. vol. I, pp. 5-6.
12. Gladstone to Sullivan, 1 January 1869, Gladstone Papers, 44418, ff. 4-5.
13. Gladstone to Fortescue, 19 January 1869, Strachie Mss. 324, CP1/21.
14. Gladstone to Sullivan, 29 January 1869, Gladstone Papers, 44418, f. 231; to Bright, 3 February 1869, ibid., 44536, f. 109.
15. Copy in Gladstone's hand, ibid., 44757, ff. 108-12; further Ms. copy, ff. 113-19; printed copies, ff. 120-2, 123-5. Note on Cabinet meeting, ibid., 44637, f. 19.
16. Gladstone Papers, 44637, f. 21.
17. Copy in ibid., 44609, ff. 53-86—printed in Dublin, 15 February 1869.
18. Gladstone to Sullivan, 20 February 1869, ibid., 44419, f. 112.
19. Copy of 25 February, ibid., 44609, ff. 101-32; *A Bill to put an end to the Establishment of the Church of Ireland* . . . House of Commons, 1868-9, iii, 85-116.
20. Gladstone Papers, 44637, f. 28.
21. Phillimore to Gladstone, 17 April 1868, enclosing a letter from the Bishop of Montreal to Phillimore, 11 April 1868, Gladstone Papers, 44278, ff. 11-16; Bishop of Montreal to Gladstone, 28 August 1868, ibid., 44415, ff. 391-7. Sir Frederic Rogers to Gladstone, 22 January 1869, ibid., 44609, ff. 11-12, and enclosed paper, ff. 13-17.
22. Ibid., 44756, f. 145.
23. Ibid., f. 144.
24. Ibid., ff. 183-94.
25. Stopford to Gladstone, 22 December 1868, Gladstone Papers, 44417, ff. 233-4; Gladstone to Stopford, 24 December 1868, ibid., ff. 246-8; Stopford to Gladstone, 26 December 1868, ibid., ff. 257-9; Gladstone to Stopford, 3 January 1869, ibid., 44418, ff. 15-16. Cf. Gladstone to Fortescue, 24 December 1868, Strachie Mss. 324, CP 1/17, asking Fortescue's opinion of Stopford.
26. Undated paper by Atkins, enclosed in Lawson to Gladstone, 19 December 1868, Gladstone Papers, 44417, ff. 201-6; memorandum by MacDonnell, 29 January 1869, ibid., 44418, ff. 225-9; Woodward to Gladstone, 30 October, 6 November 1868, ibid., 44416, ff. 117-18, 149-51.
27. Miall to Gladstone, 23 January 1869, ibid., 44418, ff. 198-9; summary of the proposals, ff. 200-1; Gladstone to Miall, 27 January 1869, ibid., 44536, ff. 105-6; Lib. Soc. Papers, Executive Committee Minute Book, 1868-72, pp. 119-21, 124-5, 126, 128.
28. Norman, *Catholic Church and Ireland*, pp. 365-8. See *Dublin Evening Mail*, 13 January 1869, for extracts from these letters and editorial comments; 14 January 1869, noting the embarrassment of the *Freeman*; 19 January 1869, asserting that the prelates aimed at supremacy, not equality.
29. Memorandum by Gladstone, undated, probably December 1868, Gladstone Papers, 44756, ff. 134-5; Gladstone to Fortescue, 19 December 1868, Strachie Mss. 324, CP 1/16.
30. Summary of Liberation Society proposals, Gladstone Papers, 44418, ff. 198-9; Bright to Gladstone, 14 February 1869, ibid., 44112, ff. 83-6.
31. Woodward to Gladstone, 30 October, 6 November 1868, ibid., 44416, ff. 117-18, 149-51.
32. Gladstone to Woodward, 2 November 1868, ibid., ff. 121-2.

33. Memorandum by MacDonnell, 29 January 1869, ibid., 44418, ff. 225–9.
34. Suggestions by Stopford (undated), ibid., 44757, f. 41; Stopford to Gladstone, 6 February 1869, ibid., 44419, ff. 33–7; same to same, 27 February 1869, ibid., ff. 135–6.
35. Hartington to Gladstone, 12 February 1869, ibid., 44143, ff. 22–5.
36. Bright to Gladstone, 14 February 1869, ibid., 44112, ff. 83–6.
37. Gladstone to Bright, 15 February 1869, Bright Papers, 43385, ff. 28–9; to Hartington, 13 February 1869, Gladstone Papers, 44143, ff. 26–9.
38. Memorandum by Fortescue, 18 February 1869, ibid., 44121, ff. 116–17.
39. Gladstone Papers, 44756, ff. 136–40.
40. Ibid., f. 175.
41. Bright to Gladstone, 9 January 1869, Gladstone Papers, 44112, ff. 74–5.
42. Gray to Gladstone, 27 October, 5 November 1868, ibid., 44416, ff. 103–4, 130–7; 11 January 1869, ibid., 44418, ff. 116–19; Monsell to Fortescue, 23 January 1869, Strachie Mss. 322, CP 3/75 (on Cullen's attitude); see Norman, *Catholic Church and Ireland*, pp. 377–8.
43. Gladstone to Gray, 15 January 1869, Gladstone Papers, 44418, ff. 150–1.
44. Gladstone to Bright, 11 January 1869, Bright Papers, 43385, ff. 22–3.
45. Gladstone Papers, 44757, ff. 120–2.
46. Copy in ibid., 44609, ff. 53–86: see clauses 92, 96.
47. Argyll to Gladstone, 17 February 1869, ibid., 44101, ff. 21–2.
48. Paper by Stopford, 30 January 1869, ibid., 44419, ff. 6–7.
49. Two memoranda by Fortescue, 8 February 1869, ibid., 44121, ff. 97–103, 104–15.
50. Gladstone Papers, 44418, f. 127; *Parl. Deb.*, third series, vol. 194, col. 454.
51. Cather to Gladstone, 20 January 1869, Gladstone Papers, 44418, ff. 182–8.
52. Xavier Raymond, "L'Église d'état et l'Église libre en Irelande", *Revue des deux Mondes*, vol. 75 (15 May 1868), pp. 493–4; the whole article, pp. 465–503.
53. *The Times*, 24 August 1868.
54. Delane to Fortescue, 1 January 1869, Strachie Mss. 250, WW 22/5; Hinds to Gladstone, 14 December 1869, Gladstone Papers, 44417, ff. 122–3; Moriarty to Gladstone, 22 April 1868, ibid., 44414, ff. 280–3.
55. Memorandum by Gladstone, 21 January 1869, ibid., 44757, ff. 101–5.
56. Memorandum by Gladstone, 1 December 1868, ibid., 44756, ff. 57–8.
57. Power to Fortescue, 2 January 1869, Burke Papers; Gladstone to Fortescue, 5 February 1869, Gladstone Papers, 44536, f. 110; memorandum by Lambert, 8 February 1869, ibid., 44609, ff. 27–39.
58. These figures are amended ones from a memorandum by Lambert of 24 February 1869, Gladstone Papers, 44609, ff. 93–100. They are slightly higher than those in the memorandum of 8 February.
59. Petition from the Catholics of Cashel to Gladstone, 25 January 1869, Gladstone Papers, 44609, f. 20; Leahy (Catholic Archbishop of Cashel) to Gladstone, 30 January 1869, ibid., 44418, ff. 232–5.
60. Spencer to Fortescue, 11 February 1869, reporting on an interview with Cullen. The draft of 26 December and later drafts did provide that churches which the Irish Church did not claim were to be granted to the most numerous communion in the town or parish; this was dropped.

61. Gladstone Papers, 44417, ff. 138–42; printed in Trench, *Memorials*, vol. II, pp. 65–6.
62. Bruce to Gladstone, 31 December 1868, Gladstone Papers, 44086, ff. 10–11. See also above, pp. 36–7.
63. Gladstone to Bruce, 2 January 1869, Gladstone Papers, 44086, ff. 14–16.
64. Trench to Gladstone, 15 and 22 December 1868, ibid., 44417, ff. 153–4, 238–9.
65. Trench, *Memorials*, vol. II, pp. 72–3; cf. Bromley, *Trench*, pp. 180–1.
66. Trench, *Memorials*, vol. II, pp. 70–3, letters from Trench to T. C. Trench (4 January 1869) and Wilberforce (11 January 1869).
67. Gladstone to Trench, 14 January 1869, Gladstone Papers, 44418, f. 149; Trench, *Memorials*, vol. II, pp. 73–4.
68. Trench to Beresford, 15 January 1869, ibid., p. 74; Gladstone to Granville, 23 January 1869, Ramm, vol. I, p. 10.
69. C. S. Roundell (Lord Spencer's secretary), memorandum of conversation with Trench after dinner, 21 January 1869, Gladstone Papers, 44306, ff. 44–50; Gladstone to Spencer, 23 January 1869, ibid., ff. 51–3.
70. For Trench's repeated references to this point, see Trench to T. C. Trench, 4 January 1869, Trench, *Memorials*, vol. II, pp. 70–1; Roundell's memorandum, 21 January 1869, Gladstone Papers, 44306, ff. 44–50; Spencer to Gladstone, 26 February 1869, ibid., ff. 75–80. Trench and the Bishops of Limerick, Meath, and Derry all put this view at a meeting with English bishops at Lambeth, 9 February 1869: Tait Papers, Diaries, vol. 45, ff. 21–2; Tait's memorandum on the meeting, ibid., Miscellanea, Box 2; Magee to MacDonnell, 10 February 1869, MacDonnell, *Magee*, vol. I, pp. 215–17.
71. Resolutions by the Irish bishops, 3 February 1869, copy in Gladstone Papers, 44306, ff. 67–8; Knox's dissenting argument, f. 69.
72. The quotation is from Gladstone to Ellicott, 19 January 1869, Gladstone Papers, 44418, f. 171; cf. Gladstone to Childers, 18 January 1869, ibid., 44536, f. 100, and to Spencer, 28 January 1869, ibid., 44306, f. 62.
73. For the origins of this contact, which came about through Spencer, see Spencer to Gladstone, 17 and 22 January 1869, Gladstone Papers, 44306, ff. 38–9, 40–3; Magee to Spencer, 23 January 1869, ibid., ff. 55–8; Gladstone to Spencer, 27 January 1869, ibid., ff. 60–1.
74. Magee to MacDonnell, 10 February 1869, MacDonnell, *Magee*, vol. I, p. 215; memorandum by Magee for the Queen, 12 February 1869, copy in Gladstone Papers, 44419, ff. 53–62; Gladstone's notes on a memorandum by Magee, 13 February 1869, ibid., 44757, f. 129 (in which Magee's view of the vital nature of the post-Reformation endowments is recorded). Magee was willing to accept the corollary on the post-Reformation endowments, that pre-Reformation endowments should go to the Catholics. This was a form of levelling-up which the government could not accept; Granville to the Queen, 13 February 1869, Fitzmaurice, *Granville*, vol. II, pp. 7–8.
75. Confirmation of the vital nature of this condition is to be found in a memorandum drawn up by Sir Roundell Palmer in consultation with Archbishop Trench, 11 February 1869, which Palmer showed to Gladstone without revealing its origin. It set out certain terms, including the

retention of post-Reformation parochial (but not episcopal or capitular) endowments. Gladstone thought the suggestions crude. See Palmer, Part II, vol. I, pp. 116–18, Gladstone to Granville, 14 February 1869, Ramm, vol. I, pp. 12–13. Trench was uneasy that even so secret an approach should have been made, and hoped that Gladstone would make no reply.

76. W. Sherlock, *Suggestions towards the Organization of the Church of Ireland, based on that of the Reformed Episcopal Churches Abroad.* Dublin 1868.

77. William Conyngham Plunket, *The Dangers of Silence.* Dublin 1869.

78. See above, p. 126.

79. *Daily Express,* 17 March 1869.

80. Ibid., 5, 6, 7 January 1869.

81. *Dublin Evening Mail,* 3 February 1869; Sandford to Gladstone, 25 January 1869, enclosing a letter from Maziere Brady, 23 January 1869, Gladstone Papers, 44418, ff. 208–15.

82. *Belfast Newsletter,* 17 March 1869, registered cries of "Judas" during the bishop's speech; *Daily Express,* 17 March; *Freeman,* 18 March 1869.

83. *Daily Express,* 24, 26 March 1869.

84. *Belfast Newsletter,* 1, 2 April 1869, cf. 30 March 1869.

85. 18, 20 May 1869.

86. Irish bishops' resolutions 3 February 1869, Gladstone Papers, 44306, ff. 67–8; *Dublin Evening Mail,* 6 February 1869.

87. Lay and Clerical Association, circular to incumbents and church-wardens of all Irish parishes, 11 February 1869, copy in Gladstone Papers, 44609, ff. 51–2. The *Dublin Evening Mail,* 15 February 1869, supported the Association in this.

88. Gladstone to Spencer, 27 February 1869, Gladstone Papers, 44536, f. 120.

89. *Parl. Deb.,* third series, vol. 194, cols. 412–66. Gladstone gave this remarkable speech from notes which, apart from the figures and part of the peroration, consisted merely of headings: Gladstone Papers, 44660, ff. 170–206. The following analysis is based on this speech and the draft Bill —Irish Church Bill, H.C. 1868–9, iii, 85–116.

90. Clauses 3–9 dealt with the constitution and powers of the Commissioners, clause 41 with rights of appeal.

91. Clauses 10, 58.

92. Clause 22. See, for example, the comments of the *Saturday Review,* 6 March 1869.

93. Clauses 2, 13, 20, 21.

94. Clauses 14, 23.

95. Clause 15. Curates with an annuity were to be allowed to commute.

96. Clauses 16, 17, 18.

97. Clause 29.

98. Clause 26.

99. Clause 27.

100. Clause 28.

101. *Parl. Deb.,* third series, vol. 194, cols. 1753–4.

102. Clause 33. See on this provision Hugh Shearman, "State-aided land purchase under the disestablishment Act of 1869", *Irish Historical Studies,* vol. IV, 1944–5.

103. Clauses 36–40. Various other detailed provisions were made, for example, for the Presbyterian college at Belfast, and for cancelling the debt owed by Maynooth College to the Board of Public Works.

104. Gladstone's exposition of these figures, with the details of his estimates, is in *Parl. Deb.*, third series, vol. 194, cols. 451–4.

105. Above, p. 122; the intentions were set out in the preamble to the Bill and in clause 59.

106. Gladstone to Spencer, 15 March 1869, Gladstone Papers, 44536, f. 129.

107. *Parl. Deb.*, third series, vol. 195, col. 1386. For some of the complaints, see Spencer to Gladstone, 13 March 1869, Gladstone Papers 44306, ff. 90–3; *Report on the details of the Irish Church Bill, by a Committee of clergymen and laymen invited by the Archbishops of Armagh and Dublin to consider them.* Dublin 1869; *Quarterly Review* (April 1869), pp. 585–6.

108. Palmer, *Parl. Deb.*, third series, vol. 194, cols. 1921–2. J. T. Ball, one of the ablest of the Conservative Irish M.P.s, made similar points—ibid., cols. 1866–7.

109. See, for example, Disraeli, ibid., cols. 1684–5; *Report on the details of the Irish Church Bill*; *Quarterly Review* (April 1869), pp. 573–4.

110. Disraeli, *Parl. Deb.*, third series, vol. 194, cols. 1684–6; Shaw, ibid., cols, 1734–5.

111. Disraeli, ibid., cols. 1689–90.

112. Bence Jones to Northcote, 13 March 1869, Iddesleigh Papers, 50038, ff. 21–8.

113. Stopford to Gladstone, 8 March 1869, Gladstone Papers, 44419, ff. 184–5.

114. Spencer to Gladstone, 2 March 1869, ibid., 44306, ff. 85–8.

115. MacDonnell to Fortescue, 6 March 1869, Strachie Mss. 322, CP 3/79; to Spencer, 8 April 1869, Spencer Papers, Miscellaneous, 1869.

116. Clermont to Fortescue, 15 May 1869, Strachie Mss. 338, CP 3/173.

117. 2, 25 March 1869.

118. 10, 15, 25 March 1869.

119. Cullen to Gladstone, 11 March 1869, Gladstone Papers, 44419, ff. 198–9.

120. On Daunt's position, see Norman, *Catholic Church and Ireland*, pp. 343–4, 365–6.

121. Moriarty to Monsell, 2 April 1869, Strachie Mss. 322, CP 3/86.

122. April 1869, pp. 56–7.

123. July 1869, p. 203.

124. 2, 3 March 1869.

125. Tait Papers, Diaries, vol. 45, reverse of ff. 22–4, quoted with slight omissions in Davidson, vol. II, p. 18.

126. *Parl. Deb.*, third series, vol. 194, cols. 2128–32. This was a remarkably full vote: according to the Liberation Society's analysis, there were only seven pairs and six absentees, two Liberals and four Conservatives—a good reflection of the importance of the division (Lib. Soc. Papers, Executive Committee Minute Book, 1868–72, p. 138).

127. Disraeli to Tait, 24 March 1868, Tait Papers, Personal Letters, vol. 87, ff. 90–5, printed with minor omissions, Davidson, vol. II, pp. 18–19.

128. Memorandum by Tait, 10 April 1869, of his conversation with Disraeli that day, Tait Papers, Diaries, vol. 75, ff. 268–77; Gladstone to Fortescue, 13 April 1869, Gladstone Papers 44536, p. 143; cf. memorandum by

Hancock, 13 April 1869, ibid., 44610, ff. 1-9, and further note, 14 April 1869, ibid., ff. 10-11.

Some of the more important amendments proposed: to leave the Church all post-Reformation endowments; to increase the compensation paid to the clergy; and to sell the tithe rent-charge at eighteen years' purchase instead of twenty-two-and-a-half years'. Hancock calculated that this last proposal alone would diminish the sum at the Commissioners' disposal by nearly £2,250,000.

129. Gladstone to Manning, 3 June 1869, Gladstone Papers, 44536, f. 169.
130. *Parl. Deb.*, third series, vol. 195, cols. 1386-1403.
131. Irish Church Bill (as amended in committee and on consideration as amended, 13 May 1869), H.C. 1868-9, iii, 153-190.
132. Disraeli to Tait, 24 March 1869, Tait Papers, Personal Letters, vol. 87, ff. 90-5, printed with minor omissions in Davidson, vol. II, pp. 18-19.
133. Memorandum by Tait, undated, Tait Papers, Diaries, vol. 75, ff. 278-84; Tait to Disraeli, 8 May 1869, Hughenden Papers, B/XXI/T/8.
134. Cairns to Disraeli, 1 May 1869, Hughenden Papers, B/XX/Ca/68.
135. Cairns to Tait, dated "Hillary", 1869, Tait Papers, Personal Letters, vol. 87, ff. 40-3. Cf. Northcote to Disraeli, 14 May 1869, arguing that it would be best to amend the Bill in the Lords, unless its fervent opponents, who would in any case divide the House, would be so irritated as to let the party down later on. If so, it might be best to throw the Bill out (Iddesleigh Papers, 50016, ff. 74-5).
136. Tait's note on the meeting, Ascension Day, 1869, Tait Papers, Miscellanea Box 2; Magee to MacDonnell, 26 May 1869, MacDonnell, *Magee*, vol. I, pp. 225-6. Magee noted that Canterbury and York would speak against the Bill but not vote against it.
137. *The House of Lords and the Irish Church Bill. Proceedings of the deputations from Ireland to secure the rejection of the Bill on the second reading.* London 1869. Lord Enniskillen's copy is in the British Museum, with the threatening passages heavily marked. The bodies represented were: The Irish Church Conference, the Central Protestant Defence Association for Ireland, the Ulster Protestant Defence Association, the Irish branch of the Church Institution, the National Protestant Union, and the Constitutional Presbyterian Association.
138. *Daily Express*, 24 May 1869; cf. *Belfast Newsletter*, 21 May 1869.
139. *Daily Express*, 1-15 June 1869; see especially the leading article on 15 June. Cf. *Belfast Newsletter*, 24 May 1869, reporting a Protestant demonstration in Belfast, with a lyrical leading article on its importance—"yea, generations yet unborn will rise to bless the memories and cherish the words of the men who assembled . . ."
140. Tait Papers, Diaries, vol. 46, ff. 54-5.
141. Accounts of this meeting are in Ellicott (Bishop of Gloucester) to Tait, 5 June 1869, Tait Papers, Personal Letters, vol. 87, ff. 129-30; Cairns to Tait, 6 June 1869, ibid., ff. 131-2; Thomson (Archbishop of York) to Tait, 5 June 1869, ibid., ff. 146-7.
142. Denison, pp. 244-5.
143. Davidson, vol. II, pp. 20-2; Gladstone to Granville, 3 June 1869, Ramm, vol. I, p. 26.

144. General Grey to Tait, 4 June 1869, Davidson, vol. II, pp. 23-4.
145. Tait to Queen Victoria, 7 June 1869, Tait Papers, Personal Letters, vol. 87, f. 138; printed with omissions, Davidson, vol. II, pp. 27-8.
146. Queen Victoria to Derby, 7 June 1869, *Letters of Queen Victoria*, second series, vol. I, pp. 603-4.
147. Tait to Disraeli, 8 June 1869, Hughenden Papers, B/XXI/T/9, printed with omissions, Davidson, vol. II, pp. 27-8.
148. Memorandum by Granville, 4 August 1869, Ramm, vol. I, p. 40.
149. Derby to Queen Victoria, 9 June 1869, *Letters of Queen Victoria*, second series, vol. I, pp. 606-8.
150. *Parl. Deb.*, third series, vol. 196, cols. 1637-1740, 1794-1896; vol. 197, cols. 18-118, 162-304.
151. Lord George Hamilton, *Parliamentary Reminiscences and Reflections, 1868-1885* (London 1917), pp. 18-19.
152. *Parl. Deb.*, third series, vol. 196, col. 1662: "determined as we are earnestly to adhere to the principle and to the main provisions of the Bill—we are not only ready to gratefully welcome any alteration in the details which appeared to us likely to have a beneficial effect, but we should think it an absolute duty to carefully consider every alternative that may be proposed by your Lordships."
153. Ibid., cols. 1707-17.
154. *Parl. Deb.*, third series, vol. 197, cols. 81-96.
155. Ibid., cols. 267-301.
156. Granville to Queen Victoria, 17 June 1869. This letter and those of 14, 15, and 19 June give a sprightly account of the debate: *Letters of Queen Victoria*, second series, vol. I, pp. 609-11.
157. Vote and division lists, *Parl. Deb.*, third series, vol. 197, cols. 304-7.
158. Disraeli to Cairns, 27 June 1869, Hughenden Papers, B/IX/A/17h.
159. *Parl. Deb.*, third series, vol. 197, cols. 876-83. Granville did not call for a division on this occasion.
160. Ibid., cols. 1614-24.
161. Ibid., cols. 1025-81.
162. Ibid., cols. 1625-59. The *Scotsman's* analysis (14 July 1869) was: for Stanhope's amendment, the Duke of Cambridge, fifty Liberals and seventy Tories; against it, fifty-eight Liberals and fifty-six Tories.
163. Irish Church Bill (as amended by the Lords), 12 July 1869, H.C. 1868-9, iii, 191-232.
164. Ibid., 202. A similar proposition, made by Roundell Palmer, had been discussed in the House of Commons.
165. Ibid., 196.
166. Ibid., 204.
167. Ibid., 209.
168. Ibid., 211.
169. Ibid., 209.
170. Ibid., 191, 229-30.
171. Cairns to Disraeli, 27 June 1869, Hughenden Papers, B/XX/Ca/73.
172. Memorandum by Hancock, 12 July 1869, distinguished the following amounts: Bishop of Peterborough's amendment, £254,450; new arrangements for visitation fees, £20,000; Ulster glebes, £422,285; new arrange-

ments for private endowments, £212,957; new arrangements for compensation for curates, £519,150; fourteen years' purchase for commutation, £1,221,750; glebe-houses free of charge, £153,289. Total, £2,803,881. Gladstone Papers, 44610, ff. 151–6.

173. Ibid. The point about the interpretation of Stanhope's clause is more fully developed in a memorandum by Hancock, 13 July 1869, ibid., ff. 163–8.

174. Cabinet agenda and notes, 26 June 1869, Gladstone Papers, 44637, f. 74.

175. Cabinet agenda, 10 July 1869, ibid., f. 78; it refers to a memorandum on nine principal points of the Irish Church Bill, which is at f. 83, dated 17 July, which may be an error. (The date is in a different ink.)

176. Undated memorandum by Gladstone, ibid., f. 88.

177. *Irish Church Bill. Commons amendments to the Lords amendments,* 22 July 1869, H.C. 1868–9, iii, 237–44.

178. Lib. Soc. Papers, Executive Committee Minute Book, meeting of 18 June 1869, pp. 153–4, cf. p. 156; Parliamentary Committee Minute Book, 7 July 1869.

179. *Liberator* (September 1869), pp. 151–2.

180. J. H. Rigg to Gladstone, 30 June 1869, Gladstone Papers, 44421, ff. 73–7; Gladstone's note on this letter, f. 78.

181. Ibid., ff. 80–2, 90–2, 93–5, 113–14, 145–7, 148–9.

182. 14 July 1869.

183. 28 June, 14 July 1869.

184. Cullen to Manning, 13 July 1869, forwarded to Gladstone with Manning to Gladstone, 14 July 1869, Gladstone Papers, 44249, ff. 88–91; Cullen to Gladstone, 14 July 1869, enclosing resolutions passed by the Catholic prelates of Ireland in October 1867, ibid., 44421, ff. 150–4; Norman, *Catholic Church and Ireland,* pp. 379–81. Cullen argued to Manning that Stanhope's amendment would sow dissension within the Church, and make the voluntary system difficult while not giving enough endowment for even a tenth of the clergy.

185. Gladstone to Manning, 13 July 1869; Manning to Gladstone, same date, Gladstone Papers, 44249, ff. 81–3, 84–7. The M.P.s Gladstone was anxious about were Blake, Blannerhasset, and Moore.

186. *Irish Church Bill; Lords amendments to Commons amendments to Lords amendments,* 22 July 1869, H.C. 1868–9, iii, 233–6.

187. Cairns to Disraeli, 16 July 1869, Hughenden Papers, B/XX/Ca/76, reporting on a meeting between himself, Salisbury, Stanhope, Tait, and Lord Grey—Grey dissented from the others' conclusions. Memorandum by Disraeli, 18 July 1869, ibid., B/IX/A/17g.

188. Gladstone to Granville, 18 July 1869, Ramm, vol. I, pp. 35–6.

189. Fitzmaurice, *Granville,* vol. II, pp. 11–12, and p. 12, n. 1; Lord Malmesbury, *Memoirs of an ex-Minister* (London 1884), vol. II, p. 409.

190. Important accounts of these negotiations are in: a memorandum by Granville, 4 August 1869, Ramm, vol. I, pp. 40–2; a memorandum by Gladstone, 14 August 1869, Morley, vol. I, pp. 907–10; and Davidson, *Tait,* vol. II, pp. 40–2.

191. Gladstone to Granville, 18 July 1869, Ramm, vol. I, pp. 35–6. Cf. a memorandum of 19 July 1869, in Gladstone's hand, reckoning that

£900,000 to £1m., which the Lords were then asking, would be far too much; and an undated note, in which he thought £300,000 would be acceptable (Gladstone Papers, 44757, ff. 152-3).

192. Fortescue to Burke (the permanent head of the Chief Secretary's Office in Dublin), 23 July 1869, Burke Papers.

193. Spencer to Burke, 22 July 1869, ibid.

194. Bright to Gladstone, 30 July 1869, quoted in Williams, *Rise of Gladstone*, p. 175.

195. Gladstone to Tait, 24 July 1869, Tait Papers, Personal Letters, vol. 87, ff. 178-9.

196. Tait, Diary, 25 July 1869, Tait Papers, Diaries, vol. 46, ff. 40-7; printed Davidson, vol. II, p. 42.

197. August 1869, pp. 128-30.

198. 23, 27, 29 July 1869.

CHAPTER 5

1. Eleanor Alexander, ed., *Primate Alexander, Archbishop of Armagh, a memoir* (London 1913), p. 173.

2. Ibid., p. 183.

3. Trench to Tait, 9 August 1869, Tait Papers, Personal Letters, vol. 87, ff. 190-1.

4. Trench to T. C. Trench, 4 October 1869, Trench, *Memorials*, vol. II, pp. 106-7.

5. Trench's first Charge to his diocese after disestablishment, *Daily Express*, 20 October 1869.

6. Spencer to Burke, 30 August 1869, Burke Papers.

7. *Index to Irish Privy Councillors, 1711-1910* (Privy Council Office, Dublin Castle).

8. C.S.O. Registered Papers, 1870, 5570, 8614; C.S.O. Ecclesiastical Affairs Book (1860-71), p. 198.

9. Clause 66 (2).

10. Gladstone to Fortescue, 11 February 1870, Gladstone Papers, 44538, f. 68.

11. Spencer to Gladstone, 20, 24 February 1870, Gladstone Papers 44306, ff. 219-22, 227-30; Gladstone to Spencer, 21 February 1870, ibid., 44538, f. 83; Gladstone to Fortescue, 25 February 1870, ibid., f. 85; Gladstone to Beresford, 3, 9 March 1870, ibid., ff. 88-9, 96.

12. Spencer to Gladstone, 8 August 1870, enclosing Beresford to Spencer, 5 August 1870, Gladstone Papers, 44306, ff. 296-300, 301-4; note of the deputation's arguments, 8 August 1870, ff. 306-7; Spencer to Gladstone, 17 August 1870, ff. 308-9; Beresford to Spencer, no day given, August 1870, Spencer Papers, Miscellaneous, 1870 (boxed under H-K, where there is also a copy of the memorial presented by the deputation).

13. Lambeth Conference, 1878, Minutes, vol. II, ff. 81-4.

14. *Irish Ecclesiastical Gazette* (January 1869), pp. 5-6; cf. ibid., February 1869, pp. 33-4. (To be cited as *I.E.G.*)

15. *I.E.G.* (April 1869), p. 81.

16. *I.E.G.* (June 1869), pp. 126-7.

17. Above, p. 127.
18. Sherlock, *Suggestions towards the Organization of the Church of Ireland*.
19. Bence Jones, *The Future of the Irish Church*.
20. Dublin 1869.
21. *Daily Express*, 5 August 1869.
22. Ibid., 20 August 1869. Bishop Knox of Down had set a precedent by calling a diocesan conference in 1862—A. M. G. Stephenson, *The First Lambeth Conference, 1867* (London 1967), p. 28.
23. G. Salmon, *The Irish Church Convention* (London 1870), p. 7. C. P. Reichel, "The Constitution of the Disestablished Church of Ireland", *Contemporary Review* (September 1870), pp. 181-3.
24. C. P. Reichel, *Contemporary Review* (September 1870), p. 181.
25. *Daily Express*, 12, 13, 14, 15 October 1869; C. P. Reichel, *Contemporary Review* (September 1870), pp. 182-3; Salmon, *The Irish Church Convention*, p. 8; Bence Jones to Tait, 21 October 1869, Tait Papers, Personal Letters, vol. 87, ff. 201-2.
26. There is a list in *I.E.G.* (February 1870), pp. 36-7.
27. *Daily Express*, 5, 7, 28 January 1870; Reichel, *Contemporary Review* (September 1870), pp. 9-10; Bence Jones to Tait, 25 January 1870, Tait Papers, Personal Letters, vol. 87, ff. 221-2. Bence Jones's letter is decisive testimony to the amicable nature of the meetings, because he always joyously retailed episodes of strife to the Archbishop.
28. Salmon, *Irish Church Convention*, p. 9.
29. Reichel, *Contemporary Review* (September 1870), p. 193.
30. Stopford to Gladstone, 10 March 1870, Gladstone Papers, 44425, ff. 231-233.
31. Bence Jones to Tait, 6 November 1870, Tait Papers, Personal Letters, vol. 87, f. 279.
32. Spencer to Gladstone, 25 November 1870, Gladstone Papers, 44306, ff. 334-5.
33. The constitution may be found in Church of Ireland, General Convention, 1870, *The Statutes passed in the General Convention of the Church of Ireland, 1870* (Dublin 1870); or in the *Irish Church Directory*, 1872. Valuable commentaries are to be found in Salmon, *Irish Church Convention*, and in Reichel, *Contemporary Review*, September 1870.
34. Voting figures, *I.E.G.* (April 1870), p. 89.
35. Salmon, *Irish Church Convention*, p. 13.
36. See above, pp. 128-9. See also *Daily Express*, 21 August 1869, for a meeting of clergy and laity in the diocese of Down to discuss forming a Diocesan Synod; ibid., 30 August 1869, for similar meetings in the dioceses of Limerick and Tuam; Trench, *Memorials*, vol. II, pp. 113-14, for a meeting in Dublin, 30 November 1869; C. A. Webster, *The Diocese of Cork* (Cork 1920), pp. 357-9, for meetings in Cork.
37. C. F. D'Arcy, *Adventures of a Bishop* (London 1934), p. 133.
38. H. E. Patton, *Fifty Years of Disestablishment* (Dublin 1922), p. 108.
39. *I.E.G.* (1 December 1893), p. 958; cf. ibid. (24 November 1893), p. 940.
40. Phillips, vol. III, pp. 378-9.
41. *I.E.G.* (1 May 1891), p. 368.
42. *Irish Times*, 22 May 1920.

43. Gregg, in Archbishops' Commission on Church and State, *Minutes of Evidence*, vol. III, p. 529.

44. C. P. Reichel, *Contemporary Review* (September 1870), p. 189.

45. *Church of Ireland Gazette* (the new name of the *Irish Ecclesiastical Gazette*) (May 1920), p. 293.

46. F. J. Hackett (Rector of Killdollagh, Coleraine), "The Church Problem in Belfast", *Church of Ireland Gazette* (18, 25 February 1910), pp. 125-6, 145-7.

47. See letters from the Dean of Cashel (M. W. Day), ibid. (25 February 1910), p. 158; from "Kilmacduagh" and T. A. P. Hackett, ibid. (18 March 1910), pp. 218-19.

48. Ibid. (24 March 1910), p. 237.

49. *I.E.G.* (December 1878), pp. 351-2.

50. *Church of Ireland Gazette* (16 May 1919), p. 314; ibid. (23 May 1919), p. 332; ibid. (29 August 1919), pp. 550-1. In the last of these articles it was argued that the diocese of Meath, with fewer than seventy clergy and 10,000 Church-people, no longer made sufficient work for a bishop.

51. Ibid. (5 December 1919), pp. 778-9.

52. *Irish Churchman* (29 January 1920), pp. 8-10. The *Irish Churchman* paid much less attention to the crisis than did the *Gazette*, and wanted less drastic remedies.

53. For summaries of the report, see *Church of Ireland Gazette* (7 May 1920), pp. 292-4; *Irish Times*, 30 April 1920.

54. *Church of Ireland Gazette* (21 May 1920), p. 332; *Irish Times*, 20 May 1920.

55. *Church of Ireland Gazette* (22 October 1920), p. 654; ibid. (12 November 1920), pp. 689-90, 696; *Irish Times*, 10-14 November 1920; D'Arcy, *Adventures of a Bishop*, pp. 222-3; Patton, pp. 302-5.

56. *Church of Ireland Gazette* (12 November 1920), p. 696, and 19 November 1920, p. 710; *Irish Churchman* (25 November 1920), pp. 8-9.

57. R. H. Murray, *Archbishop Bernard* (London 1931), p. 128. Bernard eventually braved the hateful process, and ended as Archbishop of Dublin.

58. G. Seaver, *John Allen Fitzgerald Gregg, Archbishop* (Dublin 1963), p. 70. He gives an example of canvassing and ambition in an election for the see of Cork in 1912 (see pp. 70-1).

59. Webster, *Cork*, pp. 360-1; *Irish Church Advocate* (April 1875), pp. 250-1. Walsh was elected at Ossory in 1878, when Gregg moved back to Cork.

60. *Church of Ireland Gazette* (Supplement, 20 October 1911), p. 912.

61. C. I. Graham, "Methods of Episcopal Appointment", *Irish Church Quarterly*, vol. II (1909), pp. 280, 286; J. A. F. Gregg in Archbishops' Commission on Church and State, *Evidence of Witnesses*, p. 221.

62. *Church of Ireland Gazette* (23 May 1919), p. 328.

63. Ibid. (29 August 1919), pp. 552, 556.

64. Gregg in Archbishops' Commission on Church and State, *Evidence of Witnesses*, p. 221, and *Minutes of Evidence*, vol. III, p. 507.

65. E. C. Micks, ed., *The Constitution of the Church of Ireland* (Dublin 1960), pp. 84-94.

66. Alexander, pp. 290-1.

67. *I.E.G.* (June 1874), pp. 107-8; ibid. (August 1874), p. 150; ibid. (14 June

1889), pp. 487–8; ibid. (9 December 1910), pp. 1041–2; *Irish Church Advocate* (December 1878), pp. 644–5; Alexander, pp. 288–9.

68. *I.E.G.* (14 August 1891), pp. 674–5; ibid. (21 August 1891), pp. 688, 694; cf. ibid. (December 1879), pp. 740–1.

69. Alexander, pp. 288–90; *I.E.G.* (14 June 1889), pp. 487–8; *Church of Ireland Gazette* (9 December 1910), pp. 1041–2.

70. Ibid. (31 October 1919), pp. 694–5.

71. William Fitzgerald, *Remarks on the new proposed Baptismal Rubric* (Dublin 1873), pp. 9–10.

72. *I.E.G.* (September 1874), p. 161; ibid. (May 1875), pp. 98–9; ibid. (July 1876), p. 211; ibid. (May 1879), pp. 517–18; *Irish Church Advocate* (July 1875), pp. 304–5.

73. *I.E.G.* (July 1879), pp. 577–8; the *Church of Ireland Gazette* (9 December 1910), p. 1042, remarked that it was still a handicap to have anything more than a Pass degree.

74. *I.E.G.* (3 January 1880), p. 7.

75. December 1878, pp. 644–5.

76. Gregg in Archbishops' Commission on Church and State, *Evidence of Witnesses*, pp. 216–17; *Minutes of Evidence*, vol. III, p. 525.

77. John Bernard (at that time Bishop of Ossory), "Forty Years of Disestablishment", *National Review* (June 1914), pp. 650–1.

78. James Godkin, *Religious History of Ireland* (London 1873), p. 309.

79. Reichel, *Contemporary Review* (September 1870), p. 180.

80. Bence Jones to Tait, 6 November 1870, Tait Papers, Personal Letters, vol. 87, f. 280.

81. L. F. S. Maberley, ed. *Protestantism v. Ritualism: the Maberley Correspondence*. Dublin 1870; Trench, *Memorials*, vol. II, pp. 125–30; Bromley, *Trench*, pp. 196–200; *I.E.G.* (May 1870), pp. 117–20, 145–6; ibid. (July 1870), pp. 173–4.

82. L. F. S. Maberley, *The Introduction and Spread of Ritualism in the Church of Ireland under His Grace Archbishop Trench*. Dublin n.d.

83. A. H. Foster, *What is the Church of Ireland?* Dublin 1870.

84. Notans, *Reasons for not Postponing. A letter addressed to those who desire a revision of the liturgy*. Dublin 1870.

85. *Address of the Protestant Defence Association to the Members of the Church of Ireland* (Dublin 1873), signed by Lord James Butler and the secretary, T. H. Thompson.

86. Reverend Lord Plunket, *Moderate Revision Essential to Church Unity*. Dublin 1874; F. D. How, *William Conyngham Plunket: a memoir* (London 1900), pp. 104, 106–8. Plunket was in 1874 Precentor of St Patrick's Cathedral, Dublin; he later became successively Bishop of Meath and Archbishop of Dublin.

87. Trench, *Memorials*, vol. II, p. 130.

88. *I.E.G.* (May 1870), pp. 145–6.

89. For example, Bence Jones to Sandford (Tait's chaplain), 26 November 1870, Tait Papers, Personal Letters, vol. 87, ff. 294–6.

90. For example, letter by Maberley, *Church Record*, 1 May 1876. He wrote that attempts at revision were being thwarted by the unfair working of the two-thirds majority rule. He proposed an appeal to all those who

would not subscribe to the Church of Ireland as it stood to print "a thoroughly Scriptural Prayer Book", and start services in the Rotunda and other public halls. The *Church Record* endorsed these suggestions, and threatened that the laity would leave the clergy alone in the churches (pp. 189–90).

91. *I.E.G.* (September 1870), p. 404, reporting speech by Colonel Dennis. The extreme wing did not spare even the moderate revisionists. The *Church Record* (1 November 1876), pp. 338–9, denounced Plunket as an advocate of union with Rome.

92. *I.E.G.* (September 1870), pp. 229–30.

93. Salmon, *Irish Church Convention*, pp. 5–6.

94. D'Arcy (*Adventures of a Bishop*, pp. 42–4), actually described what happened as a schism, though small and without consequences. Among those who seceded were Archdeacon William Lee of Dublin, Maturin at All Saints, Grangegorman, and Lyster, rector of Killucan.

95. See the motion against the two-thirds rule, April 1874, *I.E.G.* (April 1874), p. 68; *Irish Church Advocate* (April 1875), pp. 254–5.

96. Bence Jones to Tait, 6 November 1870, Tait Papers, Personal Letters, vol. 87, f. 281.

97. Alexander to Disraeli, 11 May 1871, Hughenden Papers, B/XXI/A/139.

98. Lambeth Conference, 1878, Minutes, vol. II, ff. 91–5.

99. See W. Sherlock, "The Story of the Revision of the Irish Prayer Book", *Irish Church Quarterly*, vol. III (1910), pp. 12–32, 144–66.

100. *Report* of the Committee to consider Measures to check the Introduction and Spread of Novel Doctrines opposed to the Reformed Church. Appointed by the General Convention of the Church of Ireland, 31 October 1870. Dublin 1871.

101. *I.E.G.* (June 1873), pp. 402–3.

102. See Patton, pp. 42–50; *I.E.G.* (May 1874), pp. 90–2; ibid. (April 1875), pp. 73–4; ibid. (May 1875), p. 101; ibid. (May 1876), p. 145; Trench, *Memorials*, vol. II, pp. 174–5, 194–5.

103. Alexander, pp. 188–9; Phillips, vol. III, pp. 382–4.

104. See the Preface to the Irish Prayer Book of 1879; Alexander, pp. 185–7. On all the above matters, the reader may refer, among a large literature, to: (1) On the Ordination Service, C. P. Reichel, *Shall we alter the Ordinal?* Dublin 1872; Sir J. Napier, *The Change proposed in the Ordinal*. Dublin 1873; *I.E.G.* (June 1873), pp. 403–4; (2) On Baptism, W. Fitzgerald (Bishop of Killaloe), *Remarks on the new proposed Baptismal Rubric*. Dublin 1873; Lord Plunket, *The Prospects of Revision*. Dublin 1876; H. Arthur, *Remarks on the New Sacramental Rubrics*. Dublin 1874; (3) On the Communion Service, W. Maturin (*The Declaration on Kneeling and the New Irish Rubric*. Dublin 1874), gives a High Church view unusual in Ireland.

105. The canons may conveniently be found in the Irish Prayer Book of 1879.

106. Gregg in Archbishops' Commission on Church and State, *Evidence of Witnesses*, p. 219.

107. *I.E.G.* (May 1874), pp. 87–8.

108. *I.E.G.* (May 1877), pp. 145–6; Traill at Belfast Church Congress, 1910, *Church of Ireland Gazette* (Supplement, 14 October 1910), p. 855.

109. Lambeth Conference, 1878, Minutes, vol. III, f. 96.

110. Quoted in Patton, p. 61.
111. J. H. Bernard, *The Present Position of the Irish Church* (London 1904), pp. 20–2; this was a paper read to the Anglo-Irish Church Society at Westminster Abbey in December 1903.
112. Seaver, *Gregg*, pp. 141, 169, and generally chapter 10.
113. There is an excellent account of this subject in Hugh Shearman, "Irish Church Finances after the Disestablishment", in H. A. Cronne, T. W. Moody, and D. B. Quinn, ed. *Essays in British and Irish History in honour of James Eadie Todd* (London 1949), pp. 277–301. The detailed study on which this essay was based was Dr Shearman's Ph.D. thesis at Trinity College, Dublin, "The Economic Results of the Disestablishment of the Irish Church" (1944). This section is very largely based on Dr Shearman's work, which for clarity and comprehensiveness could not be improved upon. A short general account by one who was involved in the financial problems of disendowment is A. Traill, "Irish Church Finance since Disestablishment", *Irish Church Quarterly*, vol. I (1908), pp. 3–8, 112–22.
114. The first figure was that given by the Royal Commission on Irish Church Temporalities in 1868, the second what the Commissioners for Church Temporalities in Ireland made the property yield (Shearman, *Essays*, p. 281).
115. See below, p. 204.
116. See J. A. Galbraith (one of the secretaries of the Representative Church Body), *Observations on the commutation table prepared by Mr Alexander G. Finlaison . . . for the Church Temporalities Commissioners* (n.d., n.p.); W. Farr, *Report on the value of annuities and life interests under the Irish Church Act*. Dublin 1871. Galbraith argued that a table more favourable to the Irish clergy should be used; Farr, using much the same material, concluded that with the twelve per cent the fund would be adequate and could be expected to leave a surplus. I am very grateful to Mr Anthony Round, a member of a firm of actuaries, for elucidating and weighing the technical arguments.
117. See generally, Church of Ireland, Representative Body, *Report on Commutation*. Dublin 1870.
118. T. Woodward, *Commutation, Cui Bono?* Dublin, 1870.
119. J. C. MacDonnell, *Shall we Commute?* Dublin 1869.
120. For the Representative Church Body meeting, see *I.E.G.* (March 1871), pp. 53, 57–8. Among many pamphlets in favour of commutation, see, for example, J. C. Hannyngton, *Commutation, Remarks on the Conditions of Safety*. Dublin 1870; A. T. Lee, *The Irish Church Act*. Dublin 1869; H. Lloyd, *On the Financial Results of Commutation*. Dublin 1870; T. C. Trench, *Reconstruction of the Church in Ireland, and the Use of Commutation*. 2nd edn. Dublin 1869.
121. *Report* of the Commissioners of Church Temporalities in Ireland, H.C. 1876, xx, p. 16.
122. See the table in Shearman, *Essays*, p. 284. £7,570,401 was paid in commutation of clergy annuities (including the bonus), and a further £478,046 in commutation of the annuities of various officials.
123. Church of Ireland, Representative Body, *Report of the Committee on Compositions*, presented on 18 November 1874. Dublin 1874.
124. Shearman, *Essays*, p. 289.

125. See W. Bence Jones, *What has been done in the Irish Church since Disestablishment*. Dublin 1875; Bence Jones to Tait, 13 January 1876, 29 July 1876, Tait Papers, Personal Letters, vol. 96, ff. 7–9, 163–6; J. Gwynne, *The Church of Ireland and her Censors*. Dublin 1874. Bishop Alexander of Derry compounded on terms highly creditable to himself and advantageous to the Church. He accepted a large reduction in his income, and left in the hands of the Representative Church Body a composition balance which secured an income of £2,000 per annum for the see of Derry.

126. Church of Ireland, Representative Body, *Report* (1890), p. 141. These figures are only those for subscriptions; to arrive at the Church's income for a given year there must be added income from investments and other sources. In 1889 the income from investments was £291,872, and from other sources £33,060, giving a total, with subscriptions, of £495,657.

127. Bence Jones to Tait, 17 September 1870, Tait Papers, Personal Letters, vol. 87, f. 269.

128. C. Moore, *A Chapter of Irish Church History: being some personal recollections of life and service in the Church of Ireland* (Dublin 1907), p. 64.

129. See above, p. 178.

130. *Church of Ireland Gazette* (11 November 1910), p. 955; Traill, speaking in the Down Diocesan Synod.

131. Shearman, *Essays*, p. 285.

132. Ibid., p. 289.

133. Ibid., p. 287.

134. Traill, *Irish Church Quarterly* (1908), pp. 116–17.

135. Ibid.; *I.E.G.* (6 November 1880), pp. 810–11; Patton, pp. 87–90.

136. *Irish Church Directory* (1872), pp. 27–104, and ibid. (1873), pp. 39–116, give tables of the annuities being paid and of the proposed new parochial incomes. The figures are discussed in *I.E.G.* (22 October 1872), pp. 205–6; cf. Bernard, *National Review* (June 1914), pp. 652–3.

137. Shearman, *Essays*, pp. 291–4, is a masterly and conclusive exposition of this question; but cf. Bence Jones, *What has been done in the Irish Church since Disestablishment*, pp. 5–9. Bence Jones had no doubt that what he had personally witnessed was "a curate scramble"; he gave examples of unnecessary appointments, and sternly asserted that such things should not have happened if God's Church had any higher end than monetary gain.

138. Shearman, *Essays*, p. 295.

139. See D. Thornley, "The Irish Conservatives and Home Rule, 1869–73", *Irish Historical Studies*, vol. XI (1958–9), pp. 200–22.

140. *Daily Express*, 5 August 1869.

141. "The Church of Ireland", *Church Quarterly Review*, vol. 19 (January 1885), pp. 447–80.

142. Bence Jones to Tait, 7 July 1870, 17 September 1870, Tait Papers, Personal Letters, vol. 87, ff. 231–3, 268–71; cf. Nugent to Tait, 7 November 1870, ibid., ff. 284–5.

143. Archbishops of Canterbury and York to Archbishop of Armagh, 21 February 1870, Tait Papers, Personal Letters, vol. 87, ff. 223–4.

144. Thomson to Tait, 3 May 1870, ibid., ff. 225–6.

145. The replies of the bishops to Tait's circular, all sent during August 1870,

are in ibid., ff. 239–67; see Magee to Tait, 4 August 1870, 5, 11, 18 November 1870, ibid., ff. 251–4, 275–8, 286–9, 290–1.

146. *I.E.G.* (March 1871), pp. 53–5; ibid. (April 1871), p. 78, listing the contributions of the bishops. Sandford to Tait 23 February 1871, Tait Papers, Personal Letters, vol. 88, ff. 322–3; MacDonnell, *Magee*, vol. I, p. 265.

147. *I.E.G.* (February 1872), p. 297; ibid. (17 July 1880), pp. 540–1.

148. Phrase used, ibid. (October 1871), p. 206.

149. A. J. B. Beresford-Hope, *The Irish Church and its Formularies. A letter to the Lord Primate of All Ireland.* London 1870.

150. *Guardian*, 5 May 1875; *Daily Express*, 18 May 1875; *I.E.G.* (May 1875), p. 97; Liddon to Gladstone, 6 and 8 May 1875, Gladstone Papers, 44237, ff. 99–100, 103–5.

151. The *I.E.G.* was willing to except the *Record* from such a sweeping condemnation, on the strength of a frequent column on Irish Church matters, drawn largely from the *Gazette* itself—*I.E.G.* (17 December 1881), p. 885.

152. Butcher (Bishop of Meath) to Tait, 7 December 1872, Tait Papers, Personal Letters, vol. 90, ff. 225–6; Alexander to Tait, ibid., vol. 92, ff. 195–196; address by Dean and Chapter of Armagh, 30 August 1877, Tait Papers, Official Letters, Box 81.

153. Tait's memoranda on bishops' meetings, Tait Papers, Miscellanea, Box 2. The last attendance by Irish bishops recorded in these was by the Archbishop of Armagh and the Bishop of Limerick on 8 July 1871 to discuss the Athanasian Creed.

154. Lambeth Conference, 1878, Minutes, vol. II, ff. 89–97.

155. G. Salmon, "Some Experiences of a Disestablished Church", *Contemporary Review*, vol. 49 (March 1886), pp. 305–6.

156. Phillips, vol. III, p. 325, puts the argument for a revival in the first half of the century.

157. Gregg, in Archbishops' Commission on Church and State, *Evidence of Witnesses*, p. 215.

158. Gladstone, speaking on Miall's motion for the disestablishment of the Church of England, 16 May 1873, *Parl. Deb.*, third series, vol. 216, col. 39. Cf. *Church of Ireland Gazette* (25 August 1911), pp. 723–5, an article on the results of disestablishment.

159. Murray, *Bernard, passim*; the author throughout his book gives the strong impression that Bernard was afraid of isolation and sought always to broaden his Church's outlook. A. A. Luce, *Charles Frederick D'Arcy, 1859–1938*, reprinted from *Proceedings of the British Academy*, vol. XXIV, pp. 9–11.

160. Bernard, *National Review* (June 1914), pp. 647–9.

161. *I.E.G.* (7 December 1894), p. 968; *Church of Ireland Gazette* (25 August 1911), pp. 723–5; interview given by Archbishop Plunket to *Western Mail* (3 November 1892), quoted in How, *Plunket*, pp. 83–7.

162. Bernard, *National Review* (June 1914), p. 647. Cf. Gregg, in Archbishops' Commission on Church and State, *Evidence of Witnesses*, p. 215: "We all know where we are and what we may do. Discipline is certainly tight and the sense of law strong."

163. A. Peel, ed., *Letters to a Victorian Editor, Henry Allon, Editor of the British Quarterly Review* (London 1929), p. 12.
164. How, *Plunket*, p. 195; Patton, pp. 95, 134–5.
165. D'Arcy, *Adventures of a Bishop*, pp. 187–94; Patton, pp. 262–3. During this crisis the General Synod again passed resolutions against Home Rule.
166. *Church of Ireland Gazette* (1 August 1919), p. 492.
167. Archbishops' Commission on Church and State, *Evidence of Witnesses*, p. 212. Gregg went on to say that he was not to be taken as meaning that he liked disestablishment *per se*—the fact that the Irish Church had weathered the storm was no argument for administering the same discipline to others.

CHAPTER 6

1. Spencer to Gladstone, 26 March 1869, Strachie Mss., CP 1/43.
2. Gladstone to Spencer, 28 April 1869, Gladstone Papers, 44536, f. 152.
3. 30 September 1868: "When the Church question is settled, we shall agitate the land question, if indeed it be advisable to postpone it so long. One at a time, however, is a salutary maxim."
4. Spencer to Gladstone, 28 August 1869, Gladstone Papers, 44306, ff. 126–8.
5. 20 February 1869, quoted in Thornley, *Isaac Butt*, p. 65.
6. Ibid., pp. 53–6, 65–9, 71–3.
7. Thornley, *Isaac Butt*, p. 72.
8. Spencer to Sligo, 3 November 1869, Spencer Papers, Miscellaneous, 1869.
9. Fortescue to Gladstone, 12 October 1869, Gladstone Papers, 44121, ff. 190–201.
10. Ibid., 44306, ff. 191–2.
11. Spencer Papers, Miscellaneous, 1869.
12. Spencer to Gladstone, 9 March 1870, Gladstone Papers, 44306, ff. 233–44. The figures he gave for agrarian outrages were: 1866, 87; 1867, 123; 1868, 160; 1869, 767; the first two months of 1870, 694. There was in 1870 some change in the way the figures were drawn up, but not such as seriously to affect the comparison.
13. Thornley, *Isaac Butt*, p. 87.
14. D. Thornley, "The Irish Conservatives and Home Rule", *Irish Historical Studies*, vol. XI (1959), pp. 200–22.
15. Shearman, *Essays*, p. 284.
16. *Accounts of the Irish Land Commission in respect of Church Temporalities in Ireland*, H.C. 1924, xiii, 113, pp. 3–7 give details of all the expenditure of the Church Temporalities Commissioners under the Irish Church Act.
17. Stephen O'Sullivan to Gladstone, 17 July 1869, Burke Papers.
18. Maguire to Fortescue, 7 December 1870; Godley (Secretary to the Church Temporalities Commissioners) to Fortescue, 22 December 1870; Fortescue to Maguire, 23 December 1870: C.S.O., Registered Papers (1870), 22539.
19. *Parl. Deb.*, fourth series, vol. 23, cols. 1467–8.
20. *Accounts of the Irish Land Commission in Respect of Church Temporalities in Ireland*, H.C. 1924, xiii, 113, pp. 7–13. A number of these transactions involved the payment of large lump sums, which the Commissioners had to borrow.

21. Gladstone to Morley, 19 September 1892, Gladstone Papers, 44549, f. 11. Gladstone was wondering whether the fund might be raided yet again. It is, incidentally, at least doubtful whether Conservative governments made more use of the fund than Liberal ones.

22. See the leading articles between 8 October and 17 November 1869.

23. Letter in *Guardian*, 13 October 1869.

24. 27 October 1869. The *Church Times* too remained cool, questioning the significance of the outcry against Temple—15 October 1869.

25. The petition, dated October 1869, and comments are in Gladstone Papers, 44422, ff. 277-8.

26. Gladstone to Liddon, 26 February 1871, ibid., 44237, ff. 51-2.

27. 13 April 1871.

28. Magee to MacDonnell, 27 February 1871, quoted in MacDonnell, *Magee* vol. I, p. 266.

29. Magee to MacDonnell, 15 January 1870, 7 July 1871, ibid., pp. 243, 276.

30. Ellicott to Tait, 2 February 1871, Tait Papers, Personal Letters, vol. 89, ff. 135-8.

31. Ellicott to Tait, 10 October 1872, ibid., vol. 90, ff. 195-7.

32. Tait to Disraeli, 8 July 1874, ibid., vol. 93, ff. 226-7.

33. Memorandum by Salisbury, 2 March 1874, Hughenden Papers, B/XX/Ce/178.

34. Salisbury to Disraeli, 22 February 1874, ibid., B/XX/Ce/170.

35. Tait Papers, Personal Letters, vol. 95, ff. 9-14. Thomson was at the time a sick man, and it may be that his view was coloured by his illness.

36. *Liberator* (July 1865), p. 144.

37. *Liberator* (October 1869), pp. 157-8.

38. Lib. Soc. Papers, Executive Committee Minute Book, 1868-72, pp. 177-186: report of parliamentary committee on future policy, presented 1 October 1869.

39. K. O. Morgan, *Wales in British Politics, 1868-1922* (Cardiff 1963), pp. 30-35.

40. See Ieuan Gwynedd Jones, "The Liberation Society and Welsh Politics, 1844 to 1868", *Welsh History Review*, vol. I, pp. 193-224.

41. S. M. Ingham, "The Disestablishment Movement in England, 1868-74", *Journal of Religious History*, vol. 3 (1964), pp. 42-4, gives an interesting discussion of the education controversy in relation to disestablishment.

42. Norman, *Catholic Church and Ireland*, p. 364.

43. F. W. Hirst, *Early Life and Letters of John Morley* (London 1927), vol. II, pp. 1-10.

44. R. T. Shannon, *Gladstone and the Bulgarian Agitation, 1876* (London 1963), pp. 149-51, 168-9.

45. C. S. Miall, *Miall*, pp. 350-1.

46. Ingham, in *Journal of Religious History*, vol. 3 (1964), pp. 47-9, records an attempt in 1871-2 by the Liberation Society to recruit working class support. It failed within the year.

47. Chamberlain to Allon, 13 February 1874, Peel, *Letters of a Victorian Editor*, pp. 43-4.

CHAPTER 7

1. Morgan, *Wales in British Politics*, pp. 42–3, 46–53, 98–102. In all this section I am much indebted to this lucid and penetrating work.
2. Kenneth O. Morgan, "Liberals, Nationalists and Mr Gladstone", *Transactions of the Honourable Society of Cymmrodorion* (1960), p. 46.
3. Morgan, *Wales in British Politics*, pp. 5, 9–10.
4. E. T. Davies, *Religion in the Industrial Revolution in South Wales* (Cardiff 1965), chapter 1. Canon Davies argues for the truth of this assertion while accepting that the allegiance of very many workers to Nonconformity was tenuous, and that others lost contact with religious bodies altogether.
5. F. E. Hamer, ed., *Personal Papers of Lord Rendel* (London 1933), p. 306.
6. *The Times*, 4, 13 November 1885; A. C. Benson, *Life of Edward White Benson* (London 1899), vol. II, pp. 62–4.
7. See K. O. Morgan, *Freedom or Sacrilege? A History of the Campaign for Welsh Disestablishment* (Penarth 1966), p. 12. It is of some interest that Joseph Conrad, the novelist, living in England in 1885, predicted general calamity as the result of the general election of that year: "Disestablishment, Land Reform, Universal Brotherhood are but like milestones on the road to ruin" (Jocelyn Baines, *Joseph Conrad* (London 1960), p. 81).
8. Morgan, *Wales in British Politics*, pp. 67–8. There were complicating circumstances, so that not all the 229 votes were worth their face value, but the total was none the less impressive.
9. Ibid., pp. 76–93.
10. Benson's diary, 24 February 1893, Benson, vol. II, p. 518.
11. Gladstone to Spencer, 23 July 1892, and the attached list of measures in Spencer's hand, Spencer Papers, Gladstone, vol. 4.
12. *Personal Papers of Lord Rendel*, pp. 198–9; Morgan, *Wales in British Politics*, p. 138.
13. Ibid., pp. 139–41.
14. Salisbury to Balfour, 25 January 1892; Balfour to Salisbury, 24 July 1892, Balfour Papers.
15. *Report, Evidence, Statistics and Indexes* of the Royal Commission appointed to inquire into the Church of England and other religious bodies in Wales and Monmouthshire, H.C. 1910, vols. xiv–xix. Vol. I (Cd. 5432), *Report*; vols. II–IV (Cd. 5433–5), *Evidence*; vols. V–VIII (Cd. 5436–9), *Statistics and Indexes*. The controversies about the Commission and its report turned on other matters than the organization and property of the Church. See Morgan, *Wales in British Politics*, pp. 231–5, 261–2.
16. Royal Commission on the Church and other religious bodies in Wales, vol. I, *Report*, p. 6.
17. Ibid., p. 6.
18. Ibid., p. 7.
19. Ibid., p. 8.
20. Ibid., p. 9.
21. Ibid., p. 10. The discrepancy of four acres between the total area given and the sum of the separate areas for the Welsh and English dioceses arises out of the rounding of the figures of roods and poles.

22. Ibid., Appendix A, p. 4. It must be borne in mind that the value of tithe varied with the price of cereals.
23. Ibid., pp. 12–14. The revenue of the Ecclesiastical Commissioners from Welsh sources was actually £35,609; but regular annual payments to St David's College, Lampeter, and for the provision of Welsh services in London, took £1,850 of this.
24. Ibid., p. 13.
25. Ibid., p. 13.
26. Ibid., p. 14.
27. *Parl. Deb.*, fifth series, Commons, vol. 37, cols. 953–4.
28. Morgan, *Wales in British Politics*, p. 12.
29. E. T. Davies, "From the Restoration to Disestablishment", in E. T. Davies, ed., *The Story of the Church in Glamorgan* (London 1962), p. 81, discusses the figures for Monmouthshire. E. T. Davies, in *Religion in the Industrial Revolution in South Wales*, pp. 33–41, discusses some of the figures for South Wales in more detail.
30. E. T. Davies, in *Church in Glamorgan*, pp. 70–1, discusses the paucity of evidence available on eighteenth-century bishops of Llandaff, and shows that at least one of them, Barrington (1770–82) carried out ordinations and visitations regularly, and was aware of the need to appoint Welsh-speaking clergy in Welsh-speaking districts.
31. The Bishop of St David's, "The Eighteenth Century Background of Church Life in Wales", *Journal of the Historical Society of the Church in Wales*, vol. V (1955) pp. 67–82.
32. E. T. Davies, *Religion in the Industrial Revolution in South Wales*, pp. 22–6.
33. Lady Llanover to Gladstone, 14 November 1869, Gladstone Papers, 44423, ff. 118–27.
34. E. T. Davies, *Church in Glamorgan*, pp. 82–6; *Religion in the Industrial Revolution in South Wales*, pp. 118–27.
35. A. G. Edwards, *Landmarks in the History of the Welsh Church* (London 1912), pp. 220–2; cf. A. G. Edwards, *Memories* (London 1927), pp. 75–6.
36. J. Vyrnwy Morgan, *Welsh Religious Leaders in the Victorian Era* (London 1905), p. 25.
37. See Morgan, *Wales in British Politics*, pp. 32–3, for an account of Hughes's appointment, and Gladstone's view of its significance.
38. See Lady Llanover to Gladstone, 18 March 1870 (Gladstone papers, 44425, ff. 271–4), remarking that, if Gladstone had not appointed a good man, he had at least appointed a Welshman.
39. Morgan, *Wales in British Politics*, pp. 83–4; speech by J. T. D. Llewelyn at the Church Congress at Cardiff, *The Times*, 3 October 1889, for details of the progress claimed by the Church.
40. G. F. A. Best, *Temporal Pillars* (Cambridge 1964), pp. 470–1. See generally on this subject pp. 465–72. Dr Best describes the situation as "The church's worst financial crisis since the middle of the sixteenth century" (p. 471).
41. Archbishop Benson wrote to Gladstone that not even the Ecclesiastical Commissioners could go on spending on the collection of tithe rent-charge twice as much as the amount to be collected—15 July 1889, Gladstone Papers, 44109, ff. 173–4.

42. Morgan, *Wales in British Politics*, pp. 84–9.
43. Best, p. 475.
44. *North Wales Observer and Express*, 25 January 1889.
45. 8 February 1889.
46. 19, 23, 26 January 1889.
47. Cf. E. T. Davies, *Religion in the Industrial Revolution in South Wales*, pp. 134–5. In the area he was studying, "the situation as revealed in census Sunday of that year [1851] reflected the Church at the very nadir of its fortunes. . . ."
48. Morgan, *Freedom or Sacrilege?*
49. *Parl. Deb.*, third series, vol. 201, col. 1297.
50. See pp. 229–30 above, and Gladstone's speech in the House of Commons, 23 February 1893, *Parl. Deb.*, fourth series, vol. 9, col. 284. Also Gladstone to Carvell Williams, 25 January 1893, Gladstone Papers, 44549, ff. 58–9, published in the *South Wales Daily News*, 30 January 1893. Generally, see K. O. Morgan, "Gladstone and Wales", *Welsh History Review*, vol. I, pp. 65–82, and the article in the *Guardian*, 7 March 1894, on the occasion of Gladstone's retirement.
51. See Gladstone's comments on T. E. Ellis in his letter to Rendel, 3 September 1892, Gladstone Papers, 44549, f. 6; Gladstone to Spencer, 3 May 1895 (Spencer Papers, Gladstone, vol. IV): "There is some flavour in the Welsh Bill that is rather too sharp for my taste." P. Stansky, in *Ambitions and Strategies. The struggle for the leadership of the Liberal Party in the 1890s* (Oxford 1964), pp. 165–6, shows that Gladstone objected to the denial of the right to commute.
52. R. Jenkins, *Asquith* (London 1964), pp. 18–19; *Liberator* (May 1892), pp. 77–83.
53. Jenkins, pp. 84–5.
54. S. McKenna, *Reginald McKenna* (London 1948), chapter 2 and pp. 135–6, 283; Frank Owen, *Tempestuous Journey* (London 1954), pp. 165–6.
55. Quoted in Eluned E. Owen, *Later Life of Bishop Owen* (Llandyssul 1961), p. 251.
56. Morgan, *Freedom or Sacrilege?*, p. 32.
57. Memorandum by Archbishop Davidson of a conversation with the Bishop of St Asaph (Edwards) on 21 February 1906, quoted in G. K. A. Bell, *Randall Davidson* (London, second edn, 1938), p. 504. In order to get disestablishment through without contention, Lloyd George held out hopes of a settlement on disendowment which would be favourable to the Church. He made a similar attempt in 1910—Morgan, *Wales in British Politics*, p. 260.
58. Lloyd George to Campbell-Bannerman, 19 October 1907, Campbell-Bannerman Papers, 41240, ff. 105–8.
59. See his foreword to J. Morgan Gibbon, *Weighed in the Balance: the case for Welsh Disestablishment*. London 1911.
60. Sir Henry S. Lunn, *Chapters from my Life* (London 1918), pp. 294–304.
61. *British Weekly*, 23 May 1912.
62. *Western Mail*, 31 October 1912.
63. Ibid., 16 December 1912.

64. *First Report from the Select Committee of the House of Lords on matters affecting the Church in Wales* (4 August 1914), pp. 58–166; cf. the account in Eluned Owen, *Later Life of Bishop Owen*, pp. 214–19.
65. Quoted in Eluned Owen, *Later Life of Bishop Owen*, pp. 131–2.
66. Robert Blake, *The Unknown Prime Minister* (London 1955), p. 161n, quoting Bonar Law's notes on a conversation with Asquith, 15 October 1913.
67. For example, Gladstone, *Parl. Deb.*, fourth series, vol. 9, col. 206.
68. 24 February, 17 May 1893.
69. The Bills were these: Established Church (Wales) Bill, H.C. 1894, iv, 281–98; H.C. 1895, iii, 65–84; H.C. 1909, ii, 251–78; H.C. 1912–13, 39–72, 73–108 (as amended in committee), 109–152 (as amended in committee and on report).
70. Above, p. 204; Asquith, *Parl. Deb.*, fourth series, vol. 23, col. 1471.
71. The amendment on cathedrals was accepted on 18 June 1895, ibid., vol. 34, cols. 1420–31; that on closed burial grounds on 20 June, ibid., cols. 1439–41, 1569–72; that on 1662 on 17 June, ibid., cols. 1307–10.
72. McKenna, ibid., fifth series, Commons, vol. 37, col. 954.
73. Ibid.; also vol. 45, cols. 1555–1606.
74. McKenna, ibid., vol. 37, cols. 953–4.
75. McKenna, ibid., cols. 955–6.
76. Asquith, ibid., fourth series, vol. 23, cols. 1464–5.
77. T. E. Ellis to Asquith, 15 January 1895, Asquith Papers, Box 66, f. 15.
78. Asquith, *Parl. Deb.*, fourth series, vol. 23, col. 1467.
79. Undated note by Asquith, in file marked "Papers circulated to Cabinet, January 1895", Asquith Papers, Box 66, f. 24.
80. *Parl. Deb.*, fourth series, vol. 34, cols. 1598–1616.
81. Asquith, ibid., vol. 23, cols. 1475–6.
82. Ibid., cols. 1477–8; cf. above, pp. 203–4.
83. Debates of 10 January and 3 February 1913, *Parl. Deb.*, fifth series, Commons, vol. 46, cols. 1549–1608; vol. 47, cols. 1829–83.
84. William Temple, *Life of Bishop Percival* (London 1921), p. 247.
85. The Welsh Church Act, 4 & 5 George V, c. 91, received the Royal Assent on 18 September 1914. A discussion of its provisions may be found in S. E. Downing, *The Church in Wales, Disestablishment and Disendowment*. London 1915. Downing was Secretary to the Ecclesiastical Commissioners. Its disendowment provisions are analysed in the *First Report of the Commissioners of Church Temporalities in Wales, 1914–16*, Cd. 8166, xxxvii, 535, pp. 1–2.

CHAPTER 8

1. Benson, vol. II, p. 686.
2. Bell, *Davidson*, pp. 1351–2.
3. Benson, vol. II, pp. 520, 569, 573–7.
4. 24 February, 17 March 1893.
5. *Church Times*, 10 March 1893.
6. *Church Times*, 5 April 1895 (a leader discussing Bayfield Roberts's *History*

of the English Church Union); 7 February 1913, supplement, article on "The Church and the State"; 14 February 1913.

7. Temple, *Percival*, pp. 118–21. Percival felt his isolation. He wrote to Asquith (15 November 1908): "My 13 years in this Tory Backwater [Hereford], wh. began amidst the turmoil of yr. Welsh Disestablishment Bill, with all the clerical, political, episcopal and arch-episcopal cold-shouldering & isolation involved, have been very trying . . ." (Asquith Papers, vol. 22, pp. 5–6).

8. For example, memorandum on Welsh Church Bill by Russell, 28 March 1895, Asquith Papers, Box 67, ff. 57–62.

9. See Edwards, *Memories*; G. Lerry, *Alfred George Edwards, Archbishop of Wales*. Oswestry, 1940; Eluned E. Owen, *The Early Life of Bishop Owen*. Llandyssul, 1958; *The Later Life of Bishop Owen*.

10. Morgan, *Wales in British Politics*, p. 233; Eluned Owen, *Later Life of Bishop Owen*, pp. 146–8,

11. Eluned Owen, *Later Life of Bishop Owen*, pp. 148, 151.

12. Ibid., pp. 158–73.

13. Ibid., pp. 93–108.

14. Morgan, *Wales in British Politics*, p. 260.

15. Extracts from letters (Edwards to Owen, 18, 22, 28 February 1911; Owen to Edwards, 20, 26 February 1911, and one undated) quoted in Eluned Owen, *Later Life of Bishop Owen*, pp. 146–8.

16. Ibid., pp. 226–7.

17. *First Report from the Select Committee of the House of Lords on matters affecting the Church in Wales*, 4 August 1914.

18. Owen to Frank Morgan, quoted in Eluned Owen, *Later Life of Bishop Owen*, p. 230.

19. *Parl. Deb.* fifth series, Commons, vol. 44, col. 1576: "Does anyone doubt that if after you have carried that measure [the Welsh Church Bill] the election is against you . . . the first act of the new Parliament would be to reverse what you are doing now."

20. Eluned Owen, *Later Life of Bishop Owen*, p. 205.

21. 17 May 1912.

22. Edwards, *Landmarks*, pp. 255–9; Morgan, *Wales in British Politics*, pp. 272–3.

23. *Parl. Deb.*, fourth series, vol. 9, col. 284.

24. Quoted in *Church Times*, 16 March 1894.

25. *Parl. Deb.*, fifth series, Commons, vol. 3, col. 1532.

26. The case from the national demand of Wales and the right of Wales to be treated as a separate country is well put in: D. Caird, *Church and State in Wales. The Case for Disestablishment* (2nd edn, London 1912), chapter 1; P. W. Wilson, *Welsh Disestablishment* (London n.d.), chapter 2; W. H. Spinks, *A Modern Church Catechism* (London 1912), pp. 24–9. Caird was at the time secretary of the Liberation Society; his book is a full and able statement of the whole case for Welsh disestablishment.

27. *Parl. Deb.*, fourth series, vol. 23, col. 1491.

28. Cf. Bonar Law in the Commons, 28 November 1912: "I do not deny for a moment that the opinion of Wales should count in this matter, but I deny absolutely that the opinion of Wales should be decisive in this

matter. It has no right to be decisive, and still less has it a right to be decisive on a question which affects England as well as Wales" *(Parl. Deb.,* fifth series, Commons, vol. 44, cols. 1576-7).

29. *Western Mail,* 23 April 1912; *North Wales Observer,* 26 April 1912.
30. E.g. Griffith-Boscawen, 1893, *Parl. Deb.,* fourth series, vol. 9, cols. 241-2.
31. See Morgan, *Wales in British Politics,* pp. 180, 216, 249-51.
32. *The Times,* 20 October 1911.
33. *Western Mail,* 9 January 1914. Disestablishment in fact figured in only half a dozen Welsh Liberals' election addresses—Morgan, *Wales in British Politics,* p. 251.
34. 26 April 1894.
35. *Parl. Deb.,* fourth series, vol. 23, col. 1700.
36. Ibid., fifth series, vol. 37, col. 950.
37. See the case developed at length in Caird, *Church and State in Wales,* chapter 4 and pp. 45-6, 52-3.
38. Morgan Gibbon, *Weighed in the Balance,* p. 54.
39. J. Vyrnwy Morgan, *A Study in Nationality* (London 1911), p. 284.
40. *Parl. Deb.,* fourth series, vol. 23, col. 1505.
41. Memorandum by Archdeacon Owen Evans and Lord Hugh Cecil, Royal Commission on the Church and other religious bodies in Wales, vol. I, *Report,* p. 93; cf. ibid., pp. 30-6. The figures were 402,632 Welsh monoglot and bilingual, 127,778 English monoglot. These figures covered great variations between the denominations: of the Wesleyans, 44·8 per cent were English monoglot; of the Baptists, 39·5 per cent; of the Congregationalists, 15·9 per cent; and of the Calvinistic Methodists, 14·4 per cent.
42. See Edwards, *Landmarks,* pp. 1-90.
43. J. Vyrnwy Morgan, *The Church in Wales in the Light of History* (London 1918), pp. 66-7. The whole book argues the case that the Church made a considerable contribution to Welsh life and culture during the period from the sixteenth century to the nineteenth.
44. Memorandum by Evans and Cecil, Royal Commission on the Church and other religious bodies in Wales, vol. I, *Report,* p. 104, quoting *Evidence,* para. 48313.
45. H. J. Clayton, *The Indictment and Defence of the Church in Wales* (London 1911), p. 1.
46. Memorandum by Evans and Cecil, Royal Commission on the Church and other religious bodies in Wales, vol. I, *Report,* pp. 88-90.
47. Vyrnwy Morgan, *The Church in Wales in the light of History,* pp. xv, xviii.
48. Memorandum by Evans and Cecil, Royal Commission on the Church and other religious bodies in Wales, vol. I, *Report,* pp. 90-104. This memorandum pointed out that both the Nonconformist Churches and the established Church were conscious of the problem posed by increasing use of English by the young.
49. *Parl. Deb.,* fifth series, Lords, vol. 13, col. 1199.
50. For examples of how the question of numbers could take up the time of public men, see Asquith Papers, Box 67, ff. 122-33: correspondence between Asquith and Edwards, the Bishop of St Asaph, 18 April-6 May 1895, on numbers attending Nonconformist Sunday schools; and Eluned Owen, *Later Life of Bishop Owen,* pp. 93-108, showing the immense labour

Owen put into getting figures of communicants and other matters from the diocese of St David's for submission to the Royal Commission.

51. *Parl. Deb.*, fourth series, vol. 23, col. 1456.
52. Sir R. Webster, ibid., cols. 1537–8.
53. For good examples on each side, see A. G. Edwards, *A Handbook on Welsh Church Defence.* 3rd edn. London 1895; Owen Owen, *Welsh Disestablishment. Some Phases of the Numerical Argument.* Wrexham 1895.
54. Memorandum by Evans and Cecil, Royal Commission on the Church and other religious bodies in Wales, vol. I, Report, pp. 135–6.
55. J. Frome Wilkinson, *Disestablishment (Welsh and English)* (London 1894), p. 22.
56. Royal Commission on the Church and other religious bodies in Wales, vol. I, *Report*, p. 20.
57. Memorandum by J. Morgan Gibbon, ibid., pp. 181–2; memorandum prepared by Sir John Williams, and signed by Sir Francis Edwards, Sir David Brynmor Jones, and J. Morgan Gibbon, ibid., pp. 187–237; report by Sir John Williams, ibid., pp. 249–395.
58. Memorandum by J. H. Davies, ibid., pp. 159–66.
59. Memorandum by Evans and Cecil, ibid., pp. 137–58.
60. Memorandum by Evans and Cecil, ibid., p. 133.
61. Ibid., p. 54.
62. For use of the various figures and discussion of them by advocates of disestablishment, see Caird, *Church and State in Wales*, pp. 46–51; Gibbon, *Weighed in the Balance*, pp. 62–102; Wilson, *Welsh Disestablishment*, chapter 4.
63. Edwards, *Landmarks*, p. 258.
64. Clayton, p. 7.
65. 24 January 1913. The *Guardian* had adjusted the Nonconformist figures to allow for members of Welsh chapels in England, included in the Calvinistic Methodist and Congregationalist Yearbooks. Cf. the table in Morgan, *Wales in British Politics*, Appendix C, p. 314. It will be noted that the figure for Easter communicants for the Church in Wales in 1912 was a long way below the 193,000 communicants claimed in 1905 in returns to the Royal Commission.
66. John Owen, *The Welsh Disestablishment Bill: What it means* (London 1911), p. 17; Edwards, *Landmarks*, p. 258.
67. Edwards, *Landmarks*, pp. 242–6.
68. Lord Robert Cecil and H. J. Clayton, *Our National Church* (London 1913), p. 188.
69. See Garbett, *Church and State in England*, pp. 129–31; Leslie S. Hunter, ed., *The English Church: a new look* (London 1966), *passim.*
70. Garbett, *Church and State in England*, p. 129.
71. *Parl. Deb.*, fifth series, Lords, vol. 13, cols. 1201–2.
72. See K. S. Inglis, *Churches and the Working Classes in Victorian England* (London 1963), for an account of how several different bodies and individuals struggled with the problem of gaining contact with the urban masses, with little success. See A. Dansette, *Histoire religieuse de la France contemporaine* (Paris 1952), vol. II, pp. 614–37, for a discussion of the problems of the Roman Catholic Church in France in the twentieth century.

73. For this conception in Wales after disestablishment, see below, pp. 327–8.
74. *Church Times*, 18 May 1894.
75. 14 February 1913.
76. Vyrnwy Morgan, *A Study in Nationality*, pp. 293–4.
77. J. Fovargue Bradley, *Nonconformists and the Welsh Church Bill* (London 1912), p. 33.
78. Above, p. 261.
79. Letter to *The Times*, 4 December 1911. Cf. J. E. C. Welldon, *The Religious Aspects of Disestablishment and Disendowment* (London 1911), pp. 72–84, for the conditions in which he thought a national Church might reasonably be maintained. These were: (1) it should be stronger in numbers and influence than any other religious body; and (2) it should be in sympathy with the temper of the national religious life. He thought the Church of England met these two conditions, and that Wales was not a separate country.
80. John Owen, *Welsh Disestablishment: Our Duty* (Carmarthen 1911), pp. 3–4.
81. *Western Mail*, 27 January 1914; cf. Eluned Owen, *Later Life of Bishop Owen*, p. 211.
82. Caird, *Church and State in Wales*, preface, and pp. 20–7.
83. J. Fovargue Bradley, *Religious Liberty in England. A scheme for providing and securing religious liberty in England and Wales* (London 1908), pp. 3–4.
84. Ibid., p. 13.
85. Ibid., p. 6.
86. Ibid., p. 5.
87. See Benson, II, pp. 99–103, 526–7; cf. Benson to Balfour, 5 May, 22 June 1896, on the Benefices Bill, Balfour Papers.
88. *Parl. Deb.*, third series, vol. 201, col. 1297.
89. *Guardian*, 16 May 1894; *Church Times*, 23 April 1909; C. A. H. Green, *Disestablishment* (Cardiff 1911), p. 5.
90. Memorandum by Evans and Cecil, Royal Commission on the Church and other religious bodies in Wales, vol. I, *Report*, pp. 88–90.
91. Lunn, *Chapters from My Life*, p. 311.
92. Eluned Owen, *Later Life of Bishop Owen*, p. 139.
93. Evidence of Archbishop of Canterbury, 14 July 1914, *First Report from the Select Committee of the House of Lords on matters affecting the Church in Wales*, 4 August 1914, pp. 20–3.
94. Caird, *Church and State in Wales*, pp. 80–2; *South Wales Daily News*, 21 July 1914.
95 Lunn, *Chapters from My Life*, pp. 294–304 (a list of members of the committee appears on pp. 298–9; it included two bishops—Oxford and Lincoln—Scott Holland, Hensley Henson, D. C. Lathbury, Scott Lidgett, J. H. Shakespeare, Sir Edward Fry, and Fovargue Bradley). See also letters to *The Times* from Henson (14 October 1911), F. B. Meyer (16 October), Ellis Griffith (17 October), Lunn (5 December).
96. Morgan, *Wales in British Politics*, pp. 268–9; *Cardiff Times*, 4 January 1913.
97. The case is set out at length in Caird, *Church and State in Wales*, chapters 10 and 11, on which the following section is largely based.
98. Letter to *The Times* by Percival, 4 May 1894, stating that the funds of the Church were public property; the principle to be safeguarded was that

they should still be used for spiritual or philanthropic purposes. Speech by Gore in Convocation, *Church Times*, 3 May 1912: ancient endowments had been given when the Church was a national institution, fulfilling functions for the whole nation, which it could not fulfil after the division of the people into different religious bodies. Frome Wilkinson, *Disestablishment (Welsh and English)*, pp. 33–4: The Church holds its property as a national trust, but has ceased to be truly national.

99. Edwards, *Landmarks*, chapters 4 and 5.
100. Eluned Owen, *Later Life of Bishop Owen*, pp. 21–3.
101. Ibid., p. 262; Vyrnwy Morgan, *A Study in Nationality*, pp. 256–68; John Owen, *the Welsh Disestablishment Bill*, pp. 17–18; *Church Times*, 20 December 1912. One of Bishop Owen's regular points was that the four poorest dioceses of the whole Church were being singled out for disendowment.
102. *Parl. Deb.*, fourth series, vol. 23, col. 1519. The speaker was J. E. W. Addison.
103. J. Fovargue Bradley, *The Case against Welsh Disendowment* (London 1911), pp. 12–18, 59–64. One of the Welsh Nonconformists he quoted was Morgan Gibbon, *Weighed in the Balance*, pp. 133–6.
104. Bradley, *The Case against Welsh Disendowment*, pp. 72–3.
105. See above, p. 255.
106. John Owen, *Welsh Disestablishment*, pp. 10–12.
107. For the purposes to which the Church funds were eventually put, and are still being devoted, see below, p. 318.
108. Wilkinson, *Disestablishment (Welsh and English)*, pp. 39–40.
109. Temple, *Percival*, pp. 137–8, 244–5, 247. Cf. Lunn, *Chapters from My Life*, p. 300; Lunn writes that the Nonconformists he knew in 1911–12 rejected concurrent endowment. On a point of detail, it seems highly likely that a periodic review to redistribute endowments would merely have invited a round of competition and ill-feeling between Churches every ten years, or whatever length of time was fixed.
110. Letter from John Morgan (writing as a Conservative and Churchman, from Aberystwyth), *The Times*, 19 August 1910.
111. *Parl. Deb.*, fifth series, Commons, vol. 47, cols. 2075–2134.
112. Welldon, *The Religious Aspects of Disestablishment and Disendowment*, pp. 16–17.
113. 18 May 1894.
114. John Owen, *The Welsh Disestablishment Bill*, p. 14.
115. 14 February 1913.
116. *The Times*, 10 May 1911. Brynmor Jones was addressing the Congregational Union of England and Wales.
117. Asquith to King George V, 16 April 1912, Asquith Papers, vol. 6, ff. 131–2.
118. *Parl. Deb.*, fifth series, Commons, vol. 37, col. 956.
119. Caird, *Church and State in Wales*, pp. 90–3; cf. J. Tudor Rees, *Welsh Disestablishment: objections answered* (London n.d.), pp. 35–7, where a figure for the Church's income after disendowment of £436,000 is arrived at.
120. Eluned Owen, *Later Life of Bishop Owen*, p. 134; *Parl. Deb.*, fifth series, Commons, vol. 37, col. 954.

121. Edwards, *Landmarks*, pp. 247–8.
122. Caird, *Church and State in Wales*, chapter 12; Wilson, *Welsh Disestablishment*, chapter VI; Rees, *Welsh Disestablishment*; Spinks, *Modern Church Catechism*, pp. 16–19.
123. The interview is reprinted in How, *Plunket*, pp. 83–7.
124. Spinks, *Modern Church Catechism*, pp. 12–13; *South Wales Daily News*, 20, 24 January 1913; above, pp. 256–7.
125. Edwards, *Landmarks*, p. 260.
126. Ibid., pp. 251–2.
127. Edwards, *Handbook on Welsh Church Defence*, pp. 48–50.
128. *The Times*, 1 May 1912; cf. Clayton, *Indictment and Defence of the Church in Wales*, pp. 27–8.
129. See above, p. 261.
130. 15 July 1910, p. 562; 10 February 1911, p. 118.
131. *South Wales Daily News*, 7 March 1893; *Church Times*, 10, 17 March 1893; Eluned Owen, *Early Life of Bishop Owen*, pp. 144–5; Morgan, *Wales in British Politics*, p. 141, refers to a draft of August 1893.
132. *Parl. Deb.*, fourth series, vol. 23, cols. 1696–7.
133. *Parl. Deb.*, fourth series, vol. 23, col. 1771.
134. Memorandum by Carvell Williams (undated, but apparently December 1894), Asquith Papers, Box 66, ff. 16–22. Cf. *South Wales Daily News*, 25 February 1895.
135. Fovargue Bradley, *Case against Welsh Disendowment*, pp. 33–42, 72–3.
136. *Western Mail*, 15 September 1911.
137. C. A. H. Green, *Disendowment* (Cardiff 1911), pp. 5–6.
138. 3 May 1912.
139. *Church Times*, 10 January 1913; *Parl. Deb.*, fifth series, Commons, vol. 46, cols. 873–5.
140. Eluned Owen, *Early Life of Bishop Owen*, p. 124.
141. Eluned Owen, *Later Life of Bishop Owen*, p. 139; cf. John Owen, *Welsh Disestablishment*, p. 2, and Edwards, *Landmarks*, p. 263, where Edwards writes of the forces of materialism gathering strength in Wales.
142. Eluned Owen, *Later Life of Bishop Owen*, pp. 211–12.
143. Lunn, *Chapters from My Life*, *passim* for his career and work; pp. 294–8 for his reasons for intervening in the Welsh Church controversy, and for the rejection of his appeal by Welsh Nonconformists. Letters in *The Times*, 5 December 1911 (Lunn), 6 December 1911 (Owen), 7 December 1911 (Edwards).

CHAPTER 9

1. Davidson to Asquith, 6 and 10 August 1914; Owen to Asquith, 10 August 1914, Asquith Papers, vol. 13, ff. 191–2, 201–3, 204–5. Owen told the Prime Minister that to alienate Church property at such a time would be widely seen as an act of dangerous presumption, weakening men's hopes of receiving God's blessing in the war.
2. *Parl. Deb.*, fifth series, Commons, vol. 65, cols. 2297–8.
3. Ibid., vol. 66, col. 783.

4. Ibid., cols. 882–920. The debate was concerned mainly with Ireland.
5. Davidson to Asquith, 15 September 1914, Asquith Papers, vol. 13, ff. 212–15.
6. Davidson to Asquith, 15 September 1914, ibid., ff. 216–19. He added that he had had visits from two leading English Nonconformists, Scott Lidgett and Shakespeare, who, he wrote, "simply stand aghast" at the Bill. Cf. his speech in the House of Lords. *Parl. Deb.*, 5th series, Lords, vol. 17, cols. 661–7.
7. Davidson to Asquith, 15 September 1914, Asquith Papers, vol. 13, ff. 216–19.
8. Eluned Owen, *Later Life of Bishop Owen*, p. 241; Edwards, *Memories*, pp. 267–8. Bishop Owen took the same view.
9. Eluned Owen, *Later Life of Bishop Owen*, pp. 306–23, for various speculations about the length of the war. In July 1916, for example, Bishop Owen thought that it would be over before the next Christmas; Frank Morgan, the Bishop's close ally, thought a little later that it would end in August 1917—see p. 312.
10. Ibid., p. 309.
11. Ibid., pp. 307, 309.
12. Memorandum on the Postponement Bill by Lord Beauchamp, 8 March 1915, Balfour Papers, enclosed with Lord R. Cecil to Balfour, 12 March 1915.
13. Beauchamp to Lansdowne, 9 March 1915—if the Bill passed all its stages in the Lords that day, "the House of Commons could take it tomorrow before the adjournment" (ibid.).
14. Lunn, *Chapters from My Life*, pp. 305–7; *Western Mail*, 2 January, 12 February 1915.
15. 2 January 1915. Cf. the statement of the S.E. Carmarthenshire Free Church Council that the terms were already "too generous towards the anti-National Church"—*Western Mail*, 9 January 1915.
16. *Western Mail*, 11, 16 March 1915. The deputation consisted of the chairman of the Congregationalist Board, the secretary of the Presbyterian Board, and the chairman of the Baptist Board.
17. *Parl. Deb.*, fifth series, Commons, vol. 70, cols. 1782–1822.
18. Lord R. Cecil to Balfour, 12 March 1915, enclosing Asquith to Cecil, 9 March 1915; Balfour to Cecil, 13 March 1915, Balfour Papers; *Parl. Deb.*, fifth series, Lords, vol. 18 cols. 633–5.
19. Letter quoted in Lunn, *Chapters from My Life*, p. 307.
20. *The Times*, 15 September 1915.
21. *Parl. Deb.*, fifth series, Lords, vol. 25, cols. 82–118; ibid., Commons, vol. 93, cols. 1788–9.
22. Eluned Owen, *Later Life of Bishop Owen*, pp. 324–31; Owen to Balfour, 17 March 1917, enclosing Owen to Bonar Law, 13 March 1917, Balfour Papers.
23. Eluned Owen, *Later Life of Bishop Owen*, pp. 250–1, 254–6.
24. Ibid., pp. 259–65. Frank Morgan was also much involved in the work of the joint committee.
25. Ibid., pp. 265–7.
26. Ibid., pp. 317–21, 333–4.

27. *Western Mail*, 1 October 1917; Eluned Owen, *Later Life of Bishop Owen*, p. 334. See the *Official Report of the Proceedings of the Convention of the Church in Wales held at Cardiff, October 2–5 1917*. Cardiff n.d. I am very grateful to the Bishop of St Asaph for lending me his copy of this report.

28. *Official Report* of the Convention, pp. 11–26 (Sankey's opening speech), 50–69, 155–69, 219–26; *Western Mail*, 2–6 October 1917; Eluned Owen, *Later Life of Bishop Owen*, pp. 350–1.

29. Owen in *Western Mail*, 24 September, 6 October 1917. Owen and Edwards both denied that the Church had accepted the Act at a meeting of the Executive of the Church Defence Committee on 27 November 1917; the Executive was strongly of the opinion that the Act had been accepted —Eluned Owen, *Later Life of Bishop Owen*, pp. 348–9. An old opponent of the established Church, Llewelyn Williams, wrote (*Welsh Outlook* (October 1917), p. 358) that the Convention marked the acceptance of disestablishment.

30. *Western Mail*, 25 September 1918.

31. Ibid., 25–8 September 1918; Eluned Owen, *Later Life of Bishop Owen*, pp. 366–7.

32. Ibid., pp. 367–8.

33. *First Report of the Commissioners of Church Temporalities in Wales* (to be abbreviated to *CCTW*), 1914–16, Cd. 8166, xxxvii, 535, pp. 3–4, 6–7. This process involved sending complicated forms to all Welsh incumbents. There was some move to withhold the information, on the ground that this would make the operation of the Act impossible—this was not carried out, but still the forms came in very slowly.

34. *Second Report of CCTW* (1917–18), Cd. 8472, viii, 93, p. 4. The Welsh Church Act provided that the wishes of the parishioners were to be ascertained in parishes actually divided by the Welsh border. Parishes in England but in Welsh dioceses were to be transferred to the Church of England; those in Wales but in English dioceses were to be transferred to the Church in Wales.

35. *Fourth Report of CCTW* (1919), Cmd. 41, xi, 109, pp. 2–3.

36. This account of the effects of the delay of the date of disestablishment rests on ibid., pp. 4–5.

37. For an example of the dispute on this point at the time, see W. Llewelyn Williams, "Disendowment: the present position", *Welsh Outlook* (October 1917), pp. 358–60, arguing that the Church was not losing as a result of the war. Correspondence followed between Llewelyn Williams and Bishop Owen, ibid. (November 1917), pp. 399–401, and (December 1917), pp. 438–9. Even Owen, who held that the Church was losing, admitted that higher interest rates would make commutation more profitable.

38. Frank Owen, *Tempestuous Journey*, p. 492.

39. Eluned Owen, *Later Life of Bishop Owen*, pp. 369–70.

40. *The Times*, 18 November 1918.

41. Edwards, *Memories*, pp. 282–3.

42. Eluned Owen, *Later Life of Bishop Owen*, pp. 375–6.

43. Edwards, *Memories*. pp. 292–5; Eluned Owen, *Later Life of Bishop Owen*, pp. 385–7. Owen wanted nearly two-and-a-half million.

44. Edwards, *Memories*, pp. 290–2; *The Times*, 2, 10 April 1919.

45. Eluned Owen, *Later Life of Bishop Owen*, pp. 391–3.
46. Ibid., p. 394.
47. Ibid., pp. 399–403, including an account by Ram, the draftsman who was called in to help; cf. Edwards, *Memories*, pp. 301–4, an account which does not mention Owen.
48. *Parl. Deb.*, fifth series, Commons, vol. 119, cols. 459–510.
49. Ibid., Lords, vol. 36, cols. 951–73, 1045–6; ibid., Commons, vol. 119, cols. 1861–8, 2097–2109.
50. The government obtained an opinion from the Law Officers that there were no such things as vested interests lapsed since 1914 (*Parl. Deb.*, fifth series, vol. 119, col. 462). The Welsh Commissioners, however, had been clear that the Act of 1914 meant that these interests had lapsed— *Fourth Report of CCTW* (1919), Cmd. 41, xi, 109, p. 5.
51. *Fifth Report of CCTW* (1920), Cmd. 609, xiii, 73, p. 4.
52. Welsh Church Temporalities Act, 9 & 10 George V, c. 65; *Fifth Report of CCTW* (1920), Cmd. 609, xiii, 73, pp. 2–4, discusses the effects of the Act from the point of view of the Welsh Commissioners.
53. Archbishops' Commission on Church and State, *Evidence of Witnesses*, p. 141; cf. ibid., *Minutes of Evidence*, vol. II, p. 314, where he explained some of the difficulties.
54. John Owen, *A Statement to St David's Diocese on the Acceptance of the Welsh Church Temporalities Act, 1919* (Carmarthen n.d.), p. 20; cf. Eluned Owen, *Later Life of Bishop Owen*, p. 405; Bell, *Davidson*, p. 983.
55. *Western Mail*, 8 January 1920; Eluned Owen, *Later Life of Bishop Owen*, pp. 431–2.
56. *Seventh Report of CCTW* (1922), Cmd. 1656, vii, 207, p. 3. The Representative Body decided to buy back all the glebe land.
57. *Seventeenth Report of CCTW* (1931–2), Cmd. 4144, vi, 469, p. 5.
58. *Seventh Report of CCTW* (1922) Cmd. 1656, vii, 207, p. 3.
59. Ibid., p. 3 and footnote; *Eighth Report of CCTW* (1923), Cmd. 1835, x, 147, pp. 3, 5–6; Eluned Owen, *Later Life of Bishop Owen*, pp. 454–65. The Welsh Commissioners declined to borrow in 1920 or 1921 to pay over the commutation capital, on the ground that rates of interest were so high that it would be impossible to meet the wish of Parliament that the secularized property should be handed over to the county councils unencumbered in 1950. The action of the Treasury in guaranteeing a loan, which the Commissioners had to take up, surprised and embarrassed them. According to Miss Owen's account, the Treasury's intervention was brought about by Bishop Owen going to see Lloyd George on 3 February 1922.
60. *Seventh Report of CCTW* (1922), Cmd. 1656, vii, 207, pp. 5–6. The figures have been rounded.
61. Ibid., pp. 6–7.
62. *Parl. Deb.*, fifth series, Commons, vol. 119, cols. 467–73; ibid., Lords, vol. 36, col. 915.
63. Eluned Owen, *Later Life of Bishop Owen*, p. 420.
64. Llewelyn Williams, "The Great Betrayal", *Welsh Outlook* (September 1919), p. 227.

65. *South Wales News*, 25 August 1919, reporting a speech by Llewelyn Williams.
66. 1 August 1919.
67. September 1919, p. 222.
68. John Owen, *A Statement to St David's Diocese on the Acceptance of the Welsh Church Temporalities Act, 1919.*
69. Eluned Owen, *Later Life of Bishop Owen*, p. 420.
70. 8, 22 August 1919.
71. Sir Henry S. Lunn, *Nearing Harbour* (London 1934), p. 169.
72. 31 March, 8 April 1920.
73. *Eighteenth Report of CCTW* (1932–3), Cmd. 4404, x, 203, p. 9; *Nineteenth Report of CCTW* (1933–4), Cmd. 4672, ix, 643, p. 2; *Twentieth Report of CCTW* (1934–5), Cmd. 4962, vii, 277, pp. 11–14.
74. Ibid., p. 11.
75. For the reluctance of the Commissioners to spend money on the burial grounds, see *Thirteenth Report of CCTW* (1928), Cmd. 3124, vii, 443, p. 9. For the necessity of doing so when the condition of walls and trees became a public danger, see *Fourteenth Report of CCTW* (1929–30), Cmd. 3356, viii, 493, p. 11; cf. *Twentieth Report of CCTW* (1934–5), Cmd. 4962, vii, 277, p. 14. The recommendation to the Home Secretary, ibid., p. 15.
76. *Thirty-second and Final Report of CCTW* (1946–7), p. 7.
77. *Seventeenth Report of CCTW* (1931–2), Cmd. 4144, vi, 469, p. 4.
78. *Eighteenth Report of CCTW* (1932–3), Cmd. 4404, x, 203, pp. 4–6.
79. *Nineteenth Report of CCTW* (1933–4), Cmd. 4672, ix, 643, pp. 3–5.
80. *Twentieth Report of CCTW* (1934–5), Cmd. 4962, vii, 277, p. 5; *Twenty-first Report of CCTW* (1935–6), Cmd. 5248, vii, 865, p. 3.
81. *Twenty-second Report of CCTW* (1936–7), Cmd. 5534, ix, 449, pp. 2–4; cf. Best, *Temporal Pillars*, p. 479.
82. *Twenty-third Report of CCTW* (1937–8), Cmd. 5822, ix, 173, p. 3.
83. *Thirty-second and Final Report of CCTW* (1946–7), p. 5.
84. I am very grateful to the Clerks of the County Councils of Anglesey, Caernarvon, Cardigan, Denbigh, Flint, Merioneth, Monmouth, Montgomery, and Pembroke for giving me information about the schemes prepared and administered by these counties. I am particularly grateful to Mr W. E. Bufton, the Clerk of the County Council of Denbigh, for his help in correspondence.
85. Bell, *Davidson*, pp. 986–90; Eluned Owen, *Later Life of Bishop Owen*, pp. 426–31; *Western Mail*, 9, 12 June 1919, 7, 8 January 1920.
86. 19 June 1919.
87. Edwards, *Memories*, pp. 328–9.
88. Frank Morgan in Archbishops' Commission on Church and State, *Minutes of Evidence*, vol. II, pp. 305, 313, 333.
89. Eluned Owen, *Later Life of Bishop Owen*, pp. 485–95. Owen supported Bevan.
90. C. A. H. Green, *Disestablishment and Disendowment: the experience of the Church in Wales* (reprinted from the *North Wales Chronicle*, 11 October 1935).
91. See C. A. H. Green, *The Setting of the Constitution of the Church in Wales* (London 1937), pp. 13, 192–3.

92. Ibid., p. 187.
93. *Directory and Year Book of the Church in Wales* (1924); Frank Morgan in Archbishops' Commission on Church and State, *Evidence of Witnesses*, p. 139.
94. On the constitution and working of the Governing Body, see Green, *Constitution of the Church in Wales*, pp. 191–203.
95. *Official Report* of the Convention, pp. 36–46. C. A. H. Green, then Archdeacon of Monmouth, made a powerful defence of the position of bishops within the Church. Bishop Owen had a copy of the proceedings of the Irish Convention of 1870, and reminded his audience of the Irish debates on the issue.
96. Frank Morgan in Archbishops' Commission on Church and State, *Evidence of Witnesses*, p. 139.
97. Archbishops' Commission on Church and State, *Minutes of Evidence*, vol. II, p. 336.
98. Green, *Constitution of the Church in Wales*, pp. 130–7, 175–6.
99. *Western Mail*, 28 September 1918.
100. Green, *Constitution of the Church in Wales*, pp. 24–6; Archbishops' Commission on Church and State, *Evidence of Witnesses*, p. 139, *Minutes of Evidence*, vol. II, pp. 306–7.
101. Green, *Constitution of the Church in Wales*, pp. 213–16.
102. Archbishops' Commission on Church and State, *Evidence of Witnesses*, p. 144, *Minutes of Evidence*, vol. II, pp. 325–6. The diocesan patronage board included only two lay representatives from the parish concerned, out of a total of nine members, including the bishop of the diocese— *Constitution of the Church in Wales* (1921), chapter 7, section 9.
103. Green, *Disestablishment and Disendowment*. The provincial levy (or "quota") has grown with the years.
104. Ibid.
105. Eluned Owen, *Later Life of Bishop Owen*, pp. 447–9; Edwards, *Memories*, pp. 325–6.
106. Frank Morgan in Archbishops' Commission on Church and State, *Evidence of Witnesses*, pp. 142–3. In the course of time, many parishes have acquired new endowments to augment the stipends of their clergy.
107. Green, *Disestablishment and Disendowment*.
108. See above, pp. 316–17, and Best, *Temporal Pillars*, pp. 477–9.
109. Frank Morgan in Archbishops' Commission on Church and State, *Evidence of Witnesses*, p. 143.
110. Ewart Lewis, *Prayer Book Revision in the Church in Wales* (Penarth 1958), is a very clear account of the subject up to that date.
111. Edwards, *Memories*, p. 315.
112. Contrast Morgan, *Freedom or Sacrilege?*, p. 34: "In the event, it may be doubted how much either side gained from its acrimonious campaigns."
113. Edwards, *Memories*, pp. 328–9.
114. Ibid., p. 327.
115. Ibid., pp. 315–16.
116. The Bishop of Monmouth (Edwin Morris), *The Church in Wales and Nonconformity* (Newport 1949), especially pp. 1, 10, 18–19. His first charge was delivered on 13 May 1946, the second on 3 May 1949.

117. Green, *Disestablishment and Disendowment.*
118. Memorandum on the political situation, in the form of a letter to Colonel Heaton-Ellis, the chairman of the Hitchin Unionist Association, April 1922, Cecil Papers; printed in *The Times*, 22 April 1922.
119. Archbishops' Commission on Church and State, *Report*, pp. 48–51.

INDEX

Date Due